VIKINGS IN SCOTLAND

VIKINGS IN SCOTLAND

An Archaeological Survey

JAMES GRAHAM-CAMPBELL
and
COLLEEN E. BATEY

EDINBURGH
University Press

© James Graham-Campbell and Colleen E. Batey, 1998

Edinburgh University Press
22 George Square, Edinburgh

Typeset in Bulmer
by Pioneer Associates, Perthshire, and
printed and bound in Great Britain by
Cambridge University Press

Reprinted 2001

A CIP record for this book is available from the
British Library

ISBN 0 7486 0641 6 (paperback)
ISBN 0 7486 0863 X (hardback)

The right of James Graham-Campbell and Colleen E. Batey
to be identified as authors of this work has been asserted
in accordance with the Copyright, Designs and
Patents Act 1988.

CONTENTS

LIST OF ILLUSTRATIONS

ABBREVIATIONS

BAR	British Archaeological Reports
Brit./Int. Ser.	British/International Series
HMSO	Her/His Majesty's Stationery Office
NMRS	National Monuments Record of Scotland
NMS	National Museums of Scotland
Proc. Orkney Antiq. Society	Proceedings of the Orkney Antiquarian Society
Proc. Soc. Antiq. Scot.	Proceedings of the Society of Antiquaries of Scotland
RCAHMS	Royal Commission on the Ancient and Historical Monuments of Scotland
ROSC	Review of Scottish Culture
SUAT	Scottish Urban Archaeology Trust

ACKNOWLEDGEMENTS

This book has been long in the making, but even though the authors hope that the delay in its completion has been to its ultimate advantage, we feel it only appropriate to begin by recording our gratitude to Edinburgh University Press for the exceptional patience which they have displayed during its prolonged gestation. If the truth is to be told, the original version of this book was conceived as long ago as 1979, at a meeting between James Graham-Campbell and Archie Turnbull, the then Secretary to the Press. No progress was in fact made until 1988–90, when J. G.-C. was awarded a British Academy Research Readership in order to pursue the archaeological study of Scandinavian Scotland. However, the need then to fulfil several outstanding commitments meant that this project never reached publication stage in the time available.

Back in 1991, J. G.-C. had come to realise that his own concentration on the artefactual evidence from Scandinavian Scotland meant that the overall objective of completing a modern synthesis of the full range of the archaeological evidence would best be served by collaboration with someone who was directly engaged in Viking/Late Norse settlement and environmental archaeology. Colleen Batey accepted the challenge; tasks were assigned and a start made. Deadlines came and went, as we both struggled to find sufficient time to devote to writing this book amidst all our respective university and museum obligations. Texts were exchanged and rewritten so that we might jointly accept responsibility for our errors and omissions.

That we have managed to reach the end at all is obviously thanks to the help and support received from many different people, but most notably of course from our long-suffering partners. We are particularly grateful to those of our colleagues who have allowed us to refer to their work in progress and to those who have given permission to use their photographs and other illustrations, as listed below. J. G.-C. would like to add his particular thanks to Olwyn Owen for her previous assistance in his study of the silver hoards and to Caroline Paterson for her current work on the pagan Norse grave-goods which, on completion, will inevitably necessitate the re-evaluation of some of the material presented here. C. E. B. would particularly like to express her gratitude to Camilla Dickson and to the several generations of fieldwork teams who have shared the experience of excavating these challenging Norse sites, and especially to those who have processed tonnes of environmental samples recovered from them. Without their contribution, both excavators and specialists alike would have been less able to understand the role played by these sites in Scandinavian Scotland. Indeed, if this book had been completed in the early 1980s, as first envisaged, it would certainly have been very different in its scope. It is only since then that several of the major excavations outlined in this book have been undertaken and the results assimilated. The role of Historic Scotland in funding much of this work is a matter for general acknowledgement.

We are both most grateful to Susanne Atkin for having undertaken the important task of indexing this volume.

James Graham-Campbell   Colleen E. Batey
Institute of Archaeology   Art Gallery and Museum
University College London   Kelvingrove, Glasgow

October 1997

PHOTOGRAPHIC ACKNOWLEDGEMENTS

Caitlin Evans was responsible for realising the maps (Figures 1.1, 2.1, 4.1, 5.2, 5.7, 6.1, 6.3, 7.1, 7.8) and Chris Smith for re-working Figure 3.5. Permission to reproduce illustrative material was granted by a number of individuals and institutions: The Trustees of the National Museums of Scotland (Figures 1.3, 1.5, 3.4, 4.3, 4.4, 4.5, 5.3, 5.4, 5.6, 6.6, 7.5, 7.6, 7.11, 12.1, 12.2, 12.3, 12.4, 12.5, 12.6, 12.7, 13.9); RCAHMS (Crown Copyright: Royal Commission on the Ancient and Historical Monuments of Scotland: Figures 5.8, 7.3, 9.6, 9.9, 13.2, 13.3, 13.8); Historic Scotland (Crown Copyright: Figures 7.13, 8.1, 8.2, 9.1, 9.2, 9.5, 13.5); Society of Antiquaries of Scotland (Figures 5.5, 6.4, 7.2, 7.7, 9.3, 10.2, 13.1, 13.4).

Leslie and Elizabeth Alcock (Figure 6.4); James Barrett (Figure 11.3); Colleen E. Batey (Figures 1.6, 1.7, 3.6, 10.1, 10.10, 11.2, 13.6); Gerry Bigelow (Figure 10.3); Cassell Academic (Barbara Crawford: Figures 3.1, 3.2, 3.3); Trevor Cowie (Figure 5.1); Barbara Crawford (Figure 10.4); Stephen Dockrill (Figure 1.4); Norman Emery (Figure 10.9); Kate Gordon (Figures 7.4, 7.10, 8.3); James Graham-Campbell (Figure 9.8); Tom E. Gray (Figure 6.5); Highland Council Archaeology Service (Figure 4.6); Peter Hill (Figure 10.11); John R. Hunter (Figures 9.7, 10.5); Sigrid H. H. Kaland (Figure 7.12); Alan Lane (Figure 3.5); Frances Lincoln Publishers Ltd (Figures 2.3, 2.4); Lorraine McEwan (Figure 10.8); Gunni Moberg (Figure 4.2); Christopher D. Morris (Figures 10.6, 10.7, 11.1, 13.4, 13.7); David Munro: SUAT (Figure 6.7); Orkney Library, Photographic Archive (Figure 3.7); Anna Ritchie (Ian G. Scott: Figure 9.3); Ian G. Scott (Figure 1.2); Alan Small (Figure 10.2); Sotheby Parke Bernet & Co. (Figure 6.2); Universitetets Oldsaksamling, Oslo (Figure 2.2); William Vaughan (Figure 9.4); Trevor Woods (Figure 11.4).

INTRODUCTION

THE VIKING PERIOD

Icelandic historians of the twelfth and thirteenth centuries believed that Harald Finehair, who died about AD 930, was the first king to have ruled over the whole of Norway. They also believed that the Norse expansion overseas, to the West, was a result of the political unrest associated with the creation of his kingdom. Twentieth-century historians, however, believe that this represents a simplification of events, both in Norway and in the West. Even if a major role in building the Norwegian kingdom is to be attributed to Harald, it was a process that continued throughout the Viking period and beyond, with his family only retaining the kingship for a couple of generations. In the West, Norse settlement was already taking place before the mid-ninth century after a period of occasional contact. This was no doubt peaceful in origin, but ceased to be so when both Britain and Ireland became regular targets for Viking raids at the end of the eighth century.

The eighth century in Scandinavia was a period of rapid technological, economic and social development which not only paved the way for the Viking period itself, but also continued throughout the three centuries of its duration. The Viking period has traditionally been considered to begin with the first Scandinavian raids in the West, as recorded in contemporary written sources, given that the word *víking* is not a Scandinavian ethnic label, but is descriptive of what they did. The Vikings were pirates.

The first western raid to be well documented took place on the Northumbrian island monastery of Lindisfarne in AD 793, although there is some evidence for piratical activity beginning slightly earlier in the English Channel, no doubt attracted by the growth in maritime trade. The Viking period in Scandinavia is transitional between prehistoric and historic times – a period which witnessed the emergence of the three nation-states of Norway, Sweden and Denmark, and their conversion to Christianity. These major developments proceeded variously and thus do not present us with any obvious end-date for the period as a whole. In Scandinavia, the tradition is to place the close of the Viking period at about 1050 on the basis of the end of the Viking involvement with England, so as to mirror its beginning. The most obvious event in this connection is the Norwegian invasion of 1066 which ended with the defeat and death of King Harald Hardrada at the battle of Stamford Bridge, although as late as 1085 there was a failed Danish plan to invade England once again.

VIKING PERIOD AND LATE NORSE SCOTLAND

A lack of historical sources means that the date of the earliest Viking incursions into Scotland has gone unrecorded. Contacts across the North Sea between western Norway and the Northern Isles will have existed before the start of the Viking period proper, but their frequency and nature are unknown.

The historical record for Viking raiding anywhere in Scotland presumably opens in 794, when the *Annals of Ulster* record the 'Devastation of all the islands of Britain by the gentiles'. The monastery of Iona, off Mull, in the Western Isles was sacked in 795. However, given the inadequacy of the documentary evidence for this period over much of Scotland, these were not necessarily the first such events. In fact, there are virtually no contemporary records which even mention the Northern Isles of Orkney and Shetland, through which the Viking ships which reached the Western Isles must have passed. It has even been suggested that the 793 raid on Lindisfarne was the work of Norwegian Vikings who had missed their course to the north of Scotland.

The lack of written sources presents an even greater problem for dating the establishment of the first Norse settlements in Scotland. The prelude of Viking raiding on the West is known both from the historical record and from the booty carried back to Norway, but there is only archaeological evidence available to date the start of the second phase of the Viking period in Scotland – that of the establishment of a permanent Norse presence – seemingly towards the middle of the ninth century.

Before the ninth century was out, extensive Scandinavian land-taking had taken place in the north and west of Scotland and the most intensively settled territory had become formalised into the Earldom of Orkney, with the Orkney earls belonging to the family of the Earls of Møre in western Norway. In Scotland, as in Scandinavia, the Viking period marks the transition from prehistoric to historic times and there is a similar problem in selecting a suitable date to mark its end, and thus the beginning of what has become known as the Late Norse period – the centuries immediately following the Viking period during which political and cultural links between Norway and Scotland remained strong and for which a much increased body of documentary sources is available.

A date which has been favoured in this connection, because close to that taken as marking the end of the Viking period in other parts of Europe, is the death of Earl Thorfinn the Mighty (one of the most famous of the Orkney earls) in about 1065. If, however, we were to look for an end-date to mirror the onset of raiding from Norway which marks its beginning, then the westward expeditions of King Magnus Barelegs of Norway inevitably attract attention, the last of these ending with his death in Ireland in 1103. However, the choice between a date of c. 1050 or c. 1100 to mark the end of the Viking period in Scotland is of no great relevance in the present context, for this book is primarily concerned with the Norse archaeology of Scotland – and much of the archaeological material cannot be so precisely dated. It is necessary to deal instead with an overlapping chronology in which the 'Viking period' covers the ninth to eleventh centuries and the 'Late Norse period' is taken to begin about 1050.

The chronological scope of the present survey commences in the eighth century with the native background, that is with some account of the Pictish, Scottish and British peoples encountered by the Vikings. It concludes in the later twelfth century so as to embrace the important economic developments which are evident during the transition from the Viking period to the Late Norse period, thus also including the earldom of the crusader Earl Rognvald (d. 1158) who commissioned the Cathedral of St Magnus in Kirkwall, a magnificent Romanesque building which forms a potent symbol of Orkney's standing in medieval Europe.

The word 'Viking' will be used here of the true Vikings, those who took part in the Viking raids, instead of loosely, as is so often (and inaccurately) the case, of the Norse in general. A 'Viking base' is thus a base from which Vikings went raiding, but a 'Norse settlement' in Scotland is a settlement occupied by people of Scandinavian origin or descent, some of whom might of course, from time to time, have engaged in Viking activities. An occasional exception is made, however (as in our title!), for the conventional use of the term 'Viking' as a chronological and regional label where its usage has become well established and there is no scope for confusion – as in 'Viking art', for example, meaning the Viking period art of Scandinavia or, indeed, of Scandinavian Scotland.

'Scandinavian Scotland' is used here in the same manner as Dr Barbara Crawford in her inter-disciplinary book to which she gave this title (in 1987), using 'Scotland' in its modern meaning. Of this choice she wrote that the 'title has been used for lack of a better one to describe those maritime and insular parts of north Britain which were settled and influenced by peoples speaking a Scandinavian tongue . . . "Scandinavian Scotland" is intended to be an umbrella term, bringing within its scope all parts of Scotland influenced by Scandinavian peoples, whether Norwegian, Danish or Irish-Norse'. Ultimately, the use of the term 'Scandinavian Scotland' is justifiable because 'for a few centuries the northern and western coasts of Scotland were a part of the Scandinavian world' in the sense that they were to a greater or lesser extent under 'the parent political authority of Norway'. Crawford's spellings of the names of peoples, places and sources have also normally been followed here in order to avoid confusion.

The fact that the Viking period archaeology of the Isle of Man is remarkably rich in quality and quantity has meant that books concerning this period in both Scotland and England have often included some account of the Manx material. In fact, Man never formed part of the Danelaw in England, nor later of Cnut's Anglo-Danish empire, but it was intimately connected with Scandinavian Scotland. At their most powerful the earls of Orkney were capable of extending their control to Man which, in turn, became the seat of a line of kings who dominated the Hebrides. However, the establishment of the Kingdom of Man and the Isles was an achievement of Godred Crovan who conquered Man in 1079 and thus this episode belongs to the Late Norse period rather than to the Viking period proper. The Viking period archaeology of the Norse settlers in Man is thus only included here by way of general comparison and as evidence for contact between Scandinavian Scotland and the Irish Sea region. To have discussed the Manx material in detail would have unbalanced the content of this book, the purpose of which is to consider the full range of the Norse archaeological material from the modern territory of Scotland.

Chapter 1

SCOTLAND BEFORE THE VIKINGS

SCOTLAND'S TOPOGRAPHY AND THE NATURAL BACKGROUND

The varied topography of Scotland, ranging from high barren mountains to lowland areas of good fertility, may well have felt familiar to many of the incoming Vikings, and it has been pointed out that there would have been little need for the Norse settlers from such areas as Rogaland to modify their lifestyles in Scotland to any great extent. However, the lush greenery of Orkney, parts of northern Scotland and the machair of the west would have seemed attractive to incomers from other parts, who had left behind small farms with fragmented holdings.

Orkney, north-east Scotland and the Moray Firth area provided the Scandinavian incomers with low-lying fertile lands in coastal locations, commanding sea-routes, marine resources and farming potential. Created through the kindness of geology, rich soils developed on the Old Red Sandstones which were moulded by erosion into a low-lying undulating landscape – some of the islands of Orkney rising no more than twenty metres above sea-level. These rock types are also to be found in Kintyre, a west coast area equally blessed with fertile land, which was 'thought to be more valuable than the best of the Hebridean islands, though not as good as the Isle of Man', according to the late twelfth-century *Orkneyinga saga*.

These areas form a stark contrast to the often harsher environments of Shetland and much of the west of Scotland. In this case, the hard Lewisian Gneisses have produced a barren landscape lacking good soils. The thirteenth-century *Chronicle of Man* records, in relation to the gift by King Reginald of Man of the island of Lewis to his brother Olaf, that: 'Lewis . . . [is] but thinly peopled, because it is mountainous and rocky, and almost unfit for cultivation . . . Olaf took possession . . . and dwelt there; living, however, very scantily'.

Even today, less than 1 per cent of Harris is cultivable, the rest is largely given over to rock and peat. Of course, there are important exceptions to this picture: amongst the windblown shell sands of the western coasts of the Outer Hebrides, and on some of the Inner, more intensive settlement and productive arable cultivation has always been possible. Today these are some of the most beautiful places in Scotland, as they no doubt seemed to the Norwegians. Elsewhere in the west, the Tertiary Igneous rocks of Skye, Mull and Arran, have weathered to produce good fertile soils, in addition to those formed on limestone belts, as found on Mainland Shetland to the north.

Climatically, it was probably a little milder during the Viking period in Scotland than today, but whether, for example, it was sufficiently warm for the requisite length of time in the year to enable grain to dry naturally is difficult to judge. It is the case that there are apparently no early grain drying kilns, but there are Late Norse examples known in the North, as at Beachview, Birsay, in Orkney. The recovery of a large quantity of charred grain from a Viking period building identified as a smithy at the Udal, North Uist, may indicate that a specific type of building was not required at this date, and that other structures may have served a dual purpose. Lack of such evidence need not point to climatic variations, more to the selective nature of the surviving evidence. There can be no doubt, however, that the Scottish climate was milder in the winter than in much of Norway. This had the significant effect of enabling animals to be overwintered outside, so reducing the hay requirement and the need for autumn slaughter, and allowing the increased production of wool for cloth.

SCOTLAND ON THE EVE OF THE VIKINGS

Three distinct groups of Celtic peoples occupied the area we know today as Scotland on the eve of the Viking period (Figure 1.1). The Picts dominated much of Scotland, with major population concentrations between the Firth of Forth and the River Dee and in Sutherland, Caithness and Orkney. The Scots were to be found mainly in the west; and the British occupied the lowlands to the south, dividing them with the Angles of Northumbria.

THE PICTS

Intensive investigation in recent years into the Picts now enables a much clearer picture to be drawn for, even as late as the early 1960s, they were considered in archaeological terms to be 'a problem'! Writing in 1962, F. T. Wainwright considered the evidence available for the Picts in Orkney, and concluded that 'archaeological confirmation of the historical conclusion that there were Picts in Orkney and Shetland comes from the so-called "Pictish" symbols and symbol stones.' For the rest of his discussion he was forced to focus on written sources and place-names. One of the major breakthroughs in expanding knowledge of the Picts in Orkney came in the identification of a distinctive Pictish building style, excavated intially at Buckquoy in Birsay. Although this cellular type of building had been seen in varying forms elsewhere in Scotland, most specifically as broch extra-mural settlement in Caithness, such as at Yarrows, this excavation confirmed a Pictish context.

An anonymous twelfth-century Norwegian historian wrote: 'The Picts were little more than pygmies in stature. They worked marvels in the morning and evening building towns, but at midday they entirely lost their strength and lurked through fear in little underground houses.'

Combined with Roman comments concerning the tradition of body painting or tattoos, the Picts were remembered as barbarians in school history-books. The reality seems to have been somewhat different. It is true that one of the most distinctive hallmarks of Pictish culture, the symbol stone, found throughout areas of Pictish presence, still evokes mystery and controversy over the meaning of the stereotyped images carved on the stones, including fish, combs and mirrors. However, evidence of distinctive Pictish settlements is now available, as also of their forms of burial and types of jewellery.

1.1 Map of the Early Historic Kingdoms of Scotland: places mentioned in the text.

The Picts were a group of indigenous peoples in Scotland, named first in AD 297 by the Romans as the *Picti* or 'Painted Ones' (probably as a result of body painting or tattooing). They were recognised into the ninth century when the Kingdom of the Picts came to a gradual end under political pressure from both the Scots and the Vikings. During the intervening years, however, Pictland – comprising tribal confederacies centred in northern Pictland at Inverness, from Ross to Orkney, and in southern Pictland, in Fife, Perthshire and Angus – developed a distinctive cultural identity. Throughout both main regions, the place-name record can help locate Pictish presence: such elements as *pit-*, meaning a piece of land, as in Pittenweem or Pitlochry for example. In the case of the Pentland Firth, named by the Vikings as 'Firth of the Picts', the name has changed from *Péttlandsfjörður*, the Norse form of Pict being incorporated in this case.

Historical records of the Pictish kings do not survive before the sixth century, and by the end of that century Pictland had begun to be converted to Christianity. Conversion had a profound effect on Pictish art in its many forms, introducing elaborate crosses into the design repertoire of the sculpture which remains one of the main sources of evidence we have today.

The earliest carved symbol-stones (Class I) probably date to the period up to the late seventh century and include incised symbols – animals, objects and other designs – on stones which have barely (if at all) been shaped. These are the most numerous of the surviving Pictish stones, with concentrations in Sutherland, the Inverness area and, particularly, the Aberdeen region. Amongst the many good examples of this class of stone are Dunrobin with a fish, mirror, comb and tuning fork, and Aberlemno 1 incorporating comb, mirror, dumb-bell, serpent and V-rod.

Following these, with the advent of Christianity, the stones are shaped into slabs, and have a cross on one face with a wide range of symbols usually on the reverse; these are termed Class II stones. Less common numerically than Class I, they predominate in the area of southern Pictland: Perth, Angus and Fife. In this group, good examples include Glamis 2, with a finely executed Celtic cross on the main face, as well as two opposing male figures, a centaur, cauldron, deer head and a triple disc symbol. A particularly interesting example from Cossans, Angus, provides a rare illustration of a Pictish high-prowed boat with oarsmen and an accompanying seated figure facing forward in the prow (Figure 1.2).

Class III stones overlap chronologically with those of Class II; they are carefully shaped and prepared pieces of stone with elaborate cross designs as a dominant feature, some feature figural embossed scenes and date to the late eighth to ninth century. Distributed widely throughout Pictland, they do however predominate in southern Pictish areas with a small but significant scatter northwards.

These stones can appear in isolation, especially Class I types, and are suggested as representing boundary or burial markers, but there are also some collections of Class II stones at important church sites, as at Meigle and St Vigeans. Some examples include inscriptions in ogam, a linear script; these are often unintelligible, but where they can be read, a personal name is often included.

The stereotyped symbols, which include fish, crescents and V-rods, dumb-bells, serpents, mirrors and combs, are highly distinctive of the Picts. Examples of some of these motifs appear on metalwork, such as the crescent-shaped plaque from the Laws, Monifieth, on the Tay estuary.

The distinctive form of pre-Viking composite combs, short with a high back (and sometimes openwork decoration), is a hall-mark of examples from several Pictish sites. In fact, the form is so distinctive that it could never be confused with the longer Norse examples. There is currently debate about the origin of the raw materials in use for both Pictish and Viking combs, and this will be considered further below. Combs from Buckquoy and Saevar Howe, in Birsay, can be matched with ones from Burrian on South Ronaldsay, and the Udal on North Uist. The type is also portrayed on some symbol-stones, such as

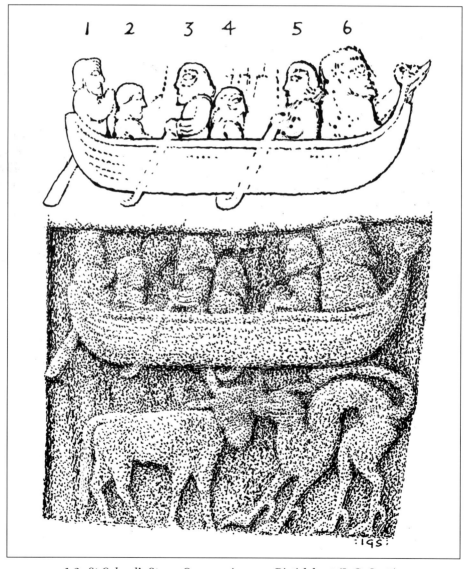

1.2 St Orland's Stone, Cossans, Angus: a Pictish boat (I. G. Scott).

1.3 Part of the St Ninian's Isle, Shetland, hoard of Pictish treasure (NMS).

Clyne Milton No. 2, and Golspie, both in Sutherland, and the Maiden Stone, at Pitcaple, Aberdeenshire.

Penannular brooches of a type found in the St Ninian's Isle treasure in Shetland (Figure 1.3), a large Pictish hoard deposited in the late Pictish period, are known to have been manufactured in Orkney, for example. Here the identification of these as Pictish rests on their form and context, rather than the presence of incised symbols.

Other types of artefacts with specifically Pictish origins include hipped bone pins, as found at Buckquoy, although there is a wide range of pin types which could be called Pictish, made in both bone and metal such as a fine bronze example from Machrihanish, Kintyre.

Recent archaeological advances in our understanding of the Picts have been consider-able, even if the view of Picts retiring to live in holes in the ground is hard to dispel, given that underground structures, souterrains, are common features in Pictland – still often locally termed 'Picts hooses'. It would be all too easy to see them as impractical refuges for endangered Picts, but the evidence suggests that these were underground stores for small surface buildings. Other buildings have been identified as Pictish houses; these are of a very distinctive cellular, almost amoebic form, built of stone with flagged floors. Although they have yet to be commonly found, examples have been excavated in Birsay, at Buckquoy (discussed below), in the final stages of activity at the Howe, Stromness, and at Scatness, Shetland (Figure 1.4); they are quite different in plan to the succeeding Norse buildings. Several other categories of settlement type may be Pictish; sub-rectangular structures have been identified, of the type found at Easter Kinnear in southern Pictland.

A small number of sites of Pictish date appear to be major power centres. The enig-matic site at Forteviot in Strathearn has a complex of structures (identified by crop-marks) which are compatible with its description as a palace; tradition has this site as a centre of the Late Pictish kings. The massive and unique stone arch from the site may have formed a chancel-arch or lintel to a royal church. A further group of sites which could be inter-preted as power-centres are the coastal promontory forts of northern Pictland – Burghead on the Moray coast is much the largest – which could have served as bases for a Pictish fleet. Although Burghead has been badly damaged by subsequent building development, the triple ramparts on the landward side of the promontory were remaining in the eighteenth century when planned by General Roy. The inner citadel may post-date the ramparts and

1.4 Pictish building at Scatness, Shetland (S. Dockrill).

has been dated to between the fourth and sixth century AD. About thirty stones with incised bull carvings are recorded from this site, although only six survive today. The significance of such a concentration is obscure, but suggestions have focused on a totemic function of the symbol, with its obvious implications for fertility. The use of timber-laced ramparts has also been noted at Dundurn, Perthshire, and may have been a feature of other contemporary defended sites.

One final area of progress in identifying and studying the material culture of the Picts is that of burial monuments. A distinctive class of Pictish burial monument is the cairn, found in several forms – circular, square and a combination of the two (dumb-bell), usually with a stone kerb. An extended inhumation, most commonly without grave-goods, was deposited in a long cist which was covered by sterile sand and the kerbed cairn built upon it. Early excavators failed in most cases to locate the burial beneath the sterile sand, due to the unusual practice of burial well below the cairn. This was certainly the case at Ackergill in Caithness. Several new sites have been identified with this type of burial peculiarity, including Sandwick in Shetland and Birsay in Orkney, as well as at Drumnadrochit and Garbeg on the mainland. In some cases, such as Watenan, Caithness, the cairn may have been surmounted by a symbol stone.

A separate tradition consists of inhumation burial in long-cist cemeteries, lacking grave-goods and usually also lacking surface markers; this remains the most commonly distinguished type, as at Hallow Hill near St Andrews. In recent years, large-scale aerial photographic programmes undertaken by the Royal Commission on Ancient Monuments for Scotland, amongst others, have distinguished groups of single graves surrounded by square ditches, and others with round ditches. These were discovered mainly in the area of southern Pictland – the Tay estuary and on the south side of the Moray Firth.

In the areas north of the southern Pictish area, cist cemeteries are less common, but smaller groups of a few cists have been distinguished at Saevar Howe and Oxtro broch in Birsay, for example, as well as at Dunrobin in Sutherland.

BIRSAY IN THE PICTISH PERIOD

There can be no doubt that Orkney was an important part of the Pictish kingdom and within that Birsay played a major role. The picture which is emerging is of an embryonic power base which was taken over by the Vikings. The nature of the Pictish evidence from Birsay and its hinterland is varied. Major discoveries include Pictish dwellings, both on the Brough of Birsay and on the Mainland (at Buckquoy and Red Craig); distinctive burial cairns; and extensive metalworking evidence on the Brough of Birsay. There has also been a re-assessment of the find circumstances of the 'three warriors' symbol stone from the Brough and its significance (Figure 1.5).

When all this evidence is combined, the status of Birsay in the Pictish period is revealed, and it does perhaps become easier to understand the nature of the take-over by the Vikings in this part of Orkney. If indeed Birsay was a major power-base in the pre-Viking period, it must surely have been taken by force by the Vikings. The precise nature of this take-over is of great interest and may affect our understanding of events elsewhere in Scotland.

The low, elongated settlement mound at Buckquoy was made up of the remains of farmstead(s) spanning the Pictish and Viking periods, but apparently lacking in conti-nuity between the two; in its upper part was a single male pagan Norse burial. The mound had been badly truncated by coastal erosion – as had Red Craig, a related settlement site nearby. The date range of the buildings at Buckquoy suggests that the Pictish phase spanned the seventh to eighth centuries, with possibly a brief hiatus before the arrival of the Vikings in the first half of the ninth century. A combination of distinctive building forms in conjunction with the artefact types (discussed below) secures these in the pre-Viking era.

The first phases to be identified were two successive cellular buildings, with small cells leading off a central area. Although much of one of these structures (House 6) had been lost through erosion, in the remaining part (a little less than half of the total area) was a central slab-lined hearth, with three rectilinear cells along one side of the main axis of the building. Part of this building had been destroyed by the building of subsequent struc-tures (Houses 5 and 4; see Figure 9.3).

House 5 was almost complete in plan; rather smaller in size, it had three cells sur-rounding a central hearth. The last phase of Pictish building comprised House 4 which was larger and of more sophisticated design, having a figure-of-eight-shaped plan. This consists of a large oval 'living-hall', with an elaborate central hearth and a circular paved cell opening off one end, and a smaller room, rectilinear in form, opening off the other, giving an overall length of some fourteen metres. The construction method for the walls of House 4 was essentially horizontally laid flagstones, but in parts, a basal course of upright slabs with horizontal courses was employed. One of the cells was partially dug into the ground, with the natural clay forming the equivalent of the lower courses of stone.

Only a few hundred metres away from Buckquoy, excavations at Red Craig revealed a figure-of-eight structure with an external ovoid plan, although its seaward edge was lost to coastal erosion. Two circular rooms, the larger some 4.5m in diameter, were examined. These were separated by a drystone pier, which may have acted as a fire back. In the larger room, a slab-lined hearth and conceivably an oven were located. The walls were built of horizontal slabs. Although internal post-holes were identified at Buckquoy, which give some idea of its roofing construction, no post-holes were noted at Red Craig, although post-pads could have formed part of the partially flagged floor. On the other hand, it has been suggested that the large amount of rubble found exclusively within the construction may have been the collapsed remains of a corbelled roof.

In addition to these structures, which must have been neighbouring farmsteads, there are several other mounds nearby which seem most likely candidates for contemporary structures. At the Point of Buckquoy, lying opposite the Brough of Birsay and a few hundred metres away from the site of Buckquoy itself, field-survey by Wainwright in the 1960s identified a number of low elongated mounds. At the time of his work, the most likely identification of these was as chambered tombs, but re-examination of the reports by Christopher Morris has strongly suggested that at least one of them may have shared the figure-of-eight ground plan.

Extensive excavation on the Brough of Birsay has been undertaken over several decades. Unfortunately, much of the earlier work which would provide a detailed context for the metalworking assemblages, discussed below, has never been published fully, although this is now in hand. That there were Pictish structures, underlying the Norse ones now visible on the site, is not doubted, but their precise form is unclear. The work undertaken by J. S. Richardson, and supervised by Mrs Cecil Curle, between 1936 and 1939 in the area east of the church, did reveal extensive Pictish material, but this was 'not related to any identifiable structures with the exception of one small well'. Work undertaken by John Hunter and Christopher Morris in the same area, Room 5 of Area II, suggested that a number of Pictish phases could be distinguished. Of these, Phase 1a predates the metalworking and is followed by a further three structural phases (1b, 2a and 2b). Of these, Phase 1a was a substantial stone structure, robbed and levelled in Phase 1b. A flagged floor provided a new surface for a structure there in Phase 2a and this collapsed in Phase 2b. A radiocarbon determination (uncalibrated) of 645±55ad is recorded for this final stage.

Work by Christopher Morris in the 1970s and 1980s in the area west of the churchyard (Area IV) revealed massive burnt timber posts from a building of pre-Viking date; although its form is generally squared, the nature of the superstructure is open to discussion. However, in the 1980s, work at the cliff edge by John Hunter revealed fragmentary structures of roughly cellular type, truncated by coastal erosion. One major structure (Structure 19) was defined by an inner wall-face of orthostatic slabs, with a suggested overall length of 18 metres. This dwelling had an elaborate central hearth and both it and its near neighbour were reused when they went out of domestic use, becoming areas of metalworking. These buildings were in use from the seventh to the early ninth century.

Precise parallels for these building forms are hard to find, but there are obvious similarities with post-broch structures, as at the Broch of Gurness in Orkney and less clearly at Jarlshof, Shetland. Recent excavations at Pool, Sanday, have revealed extensive structural remains including cellular buildings which were certainly extended in the Pictish period, if not originating then. At Skaill, Deerness in Orkney, Peter Gelling identified fragmentary rectilinear structures in the Pictish phase of occupation at the site which coincided with the presence of finer pottery. On North Uist, at the Udal, Iain Crawford has recorded cellular buildings in the period before the arrival of the Vikings.

Burials at Saevar Howe and Oxtro, both to the south of the modern Birsay village, can safely be classed as Pictish. This is particularly the case at Oxtro where they were associated – precisely how is not known – with a fine Pictish symbol-stone (with an incised eagle), unfortunately now lost. Beneath midden dumps from the Viking period, a series of circular kerbed cairns were examined on the Brough Road site, a few hundred metres only from the sites of both Red Craig and Buckquoy. Two cairns and a small number of cist graves were examined, in all some six burials in five graves spanning the Pictish and Viking periods. Of the surviving cairns, Number 2 was the best preserved, with an estimated diameter of about 2.4 metres. Although coastal erosion had already removed part of one edge, and Hurricane Flossie which hit Orkney in September 1978 removed a larger section, it was clear that there had been an extended inhumation beneath a sterile sand layer in a stone cist. Unfortunately, there were no associated symbol stones at this site, unlike that discovered at Watenan in Caithness (noted above), because it is clear that in some cases at least, the stones were acting as grave markers.

One of the greatest contributions to Pictish studies to result from the work in Birsay was the detailed analysis by Mrs Curle of the find assemblages recovered during excavations on the Brough in the 1930s. Although limited structural activity was distinguished in the areas east of the twelfth-century church (see Area II and House 5 above), a great concentration of bronze-working debris was located, much of it preserved by later Norse levelling up. The evidence consists of incomplete bar moulds, sheet bronze, and several hundred fragments of two-part clay moulds and shattered crucibles. The manufacture of penannular brooches is attested here, with decorative features similar to one of the brooches from the St Ninian's Isle hoard. There was also the casting of bronze pins in moulds formed from bone examples, some of which were found still in the moulds or nearby. A fine decorated lead disc may have been used as a former for a hanging-bowl escutcheon; its running spiral design suggests a date somewhere between the sixth and eighth century.

The fine Pictish symbol stone from the Brough of Birsay which portrays three warriors, with eagle, hippocamp, crescent and V-rod, and disc symbols, is of particular interest (Figure 1.5). It was initially suggested in print that it had stood at the head of a triple grave – presumed to be that of the three warriors depicted on the stone. However, in re-assessing the evidence, Mrs Curle showed that there had been confusion about its find-spot, which was either close to the west Graveyard wall or near the south Precinct wall, and that it had not headed a triple grave. The stone is, however, of exceptional quality and it might be suggested that it had marked a significant single grave at this political centre.

In addition to this symbol stone, there are ogam inscriptions from the Brough of Birsay, including one found in a stratified context during the most recent work there. Another such inscription was found on a stone built into the church wall, obviously reused. As with most such inscriptions, there is ambiguity in the reading, but a new study by Katherine Forsyth is eagerly awaited in print.

There is no doubt about the significance of Birsay at this period. Several sites in the immediate vicinity have produced evidence, in many cases complementary to each other, indicating a major concentration of activity which may have been centred on the Brough of Birsay. This concentration may, of course, be a function of the large amount of work undertaken there, but this need not necessarily be the case.

THE SCOTS

In archaeological terms, the Scots are elusive. In the late fifth century they crossed the short sea gap to Argyll in western Scotland from their homeland in Dalriada, the present area of County Antrim in Northern Ireland. It has been said that they 'came without luggage' and it is virtually impossible to distinguish elements of material culture which are unique to this group. They established forts in the areas they settled (such as Dunollie, overlooking Oban Bay), but archaeologically these are not so different from those of their Pictish neighbours. The major stronghold of Dunadd is considered to be the most significant of these Scottic defended places, with the shallow imprint of a foot on the hilltop being taken as part of the ritual surrounding the inauguration of kings or local chieftains. Recent excavations have produced much evidence of fine metalworking and a range of imported goods.

IONA

One site in particular which is known to have suffered at the hands of the Viking raiders is the island monastery of Iona, off Mull. The nature of the pre-Viking presence there has

1.5 Pictish symbol stone on the Brough of Birsay, Orkney (NMS).

been examined in some detail in recent years, and so it forms a suitable case for study here. Situated strategically in Scottish Dalriada, this 'cradle of Christianity' was a major meeting-place of cultural influences in the Early Christian period, being located close to both Pictland and Ireland, with Northumbria not that far away. Columba, who was born in Co. Donegal, founded Iona in 563 and he died there on 9 June 597. In 807 most of the monastic community fled to Kells in Ireland following the depredations of the Vikings. For nearly

200 years, during the period prior to the arrival of the Vikings in the 790s, it had been 'one of the most celebrated centres of Irish religious life'.

The Vikings would have encountered mainly timber buildings within earthwork enclosures and massive ditches. Through a combination of excavation, geophysical surveying and crop-mark analysis, the complex of enclosures on the island has been mapped. The main enclosure appears to have been largely rectilinear, but seemingly open on the seaward edge; at its greatest extent the enclosed area may have exceeded 8 ha (20 acres), thus making it comparable in size to Clonmacnoise in Co. Offaly, Ireland.

The earth and stone rampart, or vallum, with its ditch, and in some places a slight outer bank, is visible at the north and west of the site. Further study is, however, required to distinguish all elements of the Columban foundation on the island. For example, on the southern part of the site there are two successive and overlapping phases of activity represented, each a main enclosure with an annexe to the south-west. It remains unclear whether either relates to the Columban foundation and many of the other features located could be associated with later activity on the site. Excavation in the late 1970s, by John Barber, suggested that the focus of the Columban complex may have been the Reilig Odhrain area of the island, with the modern abbey being located in the area of the later expansion of the monastery (Figure 1.6). However, Ian Fisher and John Dunbar have pointed out more recently that its relationship to the Columban monastery remains uncertain; it may have originated as a burial ground for the secular aristocracy. The early monastic cemetery could have lain near the west end of the abbey church. Excavations in 1957 revealed the footings of a small squarish building on the narrow spine of rock named Tor an Abba, and to this spot has been tentatively ascribed the location of the original site

1.6 Iona: general view of the Abbey, with crosses (C. E. Batey).

of St Columba's cell. The precise overall area of the early monastic complex is thus still open to discussion.

Excavations by John Barber on a massive enclosure ditch produced unexpectedly rich deposits. The waterlogged fill of the ditch ensured the preservation of wooden turned vessels and leather shoe fragments, from a nearby leather-working shop, as well as evidence for the farming economy in which cattle predominated, with pollen indicating the growth of cereals nearby (see discussion below).

In the seventh century, Adomnan described the import of large timbers from the Scottish mainland for the construction and repair of major wooden buildings, as in Irish monasteries. Excavation supports this with the discovery of large post-holes and part of a building constructed with sill-beams or vertically set planking. The disposition of build-ings within the early enclosure seems to have been somewhat random, with working areas for fine metalworking and glass production interspersed with buildings. Adomnan described only one church building in the complex, possibly lying on or near the site of the medieval abbey. His description of the monastic complex is most illuminating: a church with attached chamber, a number of working or sleeping huts for the monks, a hut where Columba himself slept and another where he wrote, a house or houses for guest accommodation and a communal building with a kitchen and refectory. Some of these buildings stood round an open space, but other outlying buildings, including a barn and a shed, may have been outside the enclosing vallum. It was the communal building which Adomnan described as being repaired by oak timbers imported from the mainland, as well as referring to the use of wattles for the construction of a small building or hut. The location of specific events related to the life of Columba was marked by the erection of stone crosses. Today there are no surviving standing buildings earlier than the twelfth century, although 'St Columba's Shrine' is rebuilt on footings of Early Christian date.

The Iona group of carved stones is one of the largest in Britain or Ireland. It includes the remains of fourteen free-standing crosses and eight cross-bases, with other fragments which may have belonged to composite stone shrines as well as numerous funerary monuments. The quality of the workmanship is not thought to indicate the presence of a permanent school of stone craftsmen as is known from some other major monastic centres. The group of free-standing crosses may represent an early and experimental group of eighth-century date which does not derive from an established tradition at the site.

It would not be unexpected that the major ecclesiastical centre of the area would have close ties with significant contemporary local sites. Work by Ewan Campbell has shown that the movement of distinctive cross-inscribed quernstones within the area ties together Iona and Dunadd, as one of the major political centres of Dalriada. Indeed, it has been suggested that Dunadd may have acted as a redistribution centre of imported luxury goods, including ceramic vessels imported from France (E-ware) and glass, metalwork and orpiment (yellow colouring used in manuscript illumination, as in the *Book of Durrow*). This link is possibly referred to in Adomnan's *Life of Columba*, in which he refers to Columba visiting the '*caput regionis*' where he met Gallic merchants. Although controversy surrounds the identification of the site with Dunadd, the quantity of its imported goods, in particular of the Frankish pottery known as E-ware, could support the identification.

The Scottish entries preserved in the Irish annals were derived from an 'Iona Chronicle' which was a contemporary record made at Iona in the late seventh and eighth centuries. These entries include reference to both ecclesiastical and secular events and it is clear that Iona maintained close contact with mainland Argyll.

In addition, there may well have been other Dalriadic centres which had links with both Dunadd and Iona. The important crannog site at Loch Glashan, located just to the east of Dunadd, includes several sherds of E-ware in its assemblage (as well as one virtually complete vessel); items of leather and wood have been preserved by the wet conditions of the site. A leather jerkin and parts of shoes have been identified, in addition to wooden troughs and bowls; a seventh-century penannular brooch has also been recorded, of a type manufactured at Dunadd. This rich assemblage may conceivably suggest a status commensurate with, or at least complementary to, that at nearby Dunadd. More work needs to be undertaken to confirm such a proposal, but it is certainly a valid hypothesis that a network of high-status sites, possibly all serving slightly differing functions, existed in Dalriada during the period before Iona was attacked by the Vikings.

THE BRITONS AND NORTHUMBRIANS

The adjacent neighbours of the Picts and Scots were the Britons: at one time to the south-east in Gododdin, with *Dun Eidyn* (Edinburgh) at its heart, to the south and south-west in Strathclyde, with its principal stronghold on Dumbarton Rock in the Clyde, and Rheged further to the south, with Carlisle a major centre.

The political significance of *Alt Clut* or Clyde Rock at Dumbarton has been well-rehearsed in print, as the main centre of the British Kingdom of Strathclyde (Figure 1.7). It was excavated by the Alcocks in the early 1970s and initial expectations of an oval citadel suggested by the topography were not upheld. Large-scale clearance of the site must have taken place during later re-building phases, although traces of a timber and rubble rampart were identified on the vulnerable landward, eastern side of the rock. Due to severe disturbance of the stratigraphy on the rock, little or no detailed recovery of environmental material was feasible.

By the mid-sixth century, the Angles had established Bamburgh in Northumbria as their stronghold, spreading northwards into Lothian and fleetingly north of the Forth in the seventh century. In the south-west, Anglo-Saxon metalwork has been identified from sites such as Mote of Mark, Dundrennan and Luce Bay and it is presumed that the Anglian takeover was complete by the seventh or eighth century. In these areas, the Vikings encountered Anglo-Saxons as well as the Britons.

ASPECTS OF THE PRE-NORSE ECONOMY

Although widespread trading links can be identified in part through tracking the movement of certain types of artefacts, such as pottery, local exchanges and aspects of the economy are visible in more humble parts of the archaeological record. The early excavators of sites such as Dunadd or Birsay were little concerned with the recovery of animal bones, and no attempts were made to retrieve less obvious classes of material, such as carbonised grains and seeds. Evidence for cereal production was thus restricted to the presence of querns on a site, and the presence of pastoral farming in the economy was confined to the identification

1.7 Dumbarton Rock from the Clyde (C. E. Batey).

of cattle stalls within buildings, whereas line-sinkers (sometimes confused with loom-weights) attested fishing activity.

However, within the last twenty years of fieldwork, environmental archaeology has developed and become fully integrated into the research designs of most excavations. This is characterised by detailed on-site sampling procedures and, in many cases, on-site wet sieving and flotation, with the fineness of the meshes being reduced from centimetres to millimetres, and even microns as methods have progressed. This methodological revolution has increased awareness as information on the contemporary economy and environment has burgeoned. Although Pictish sites have not been particularly well-served in this respect, some aspects of the economy and local environment of Pictish sites can be understood to a certain degree. The information is, however, biased through differing sample sizes and approaches to recovery of material (for example, Buckquoy and Skaill, Deerness, were excavated before the common usage of sieving on site), but trends in the information can be brought together, most notably so far in the northern Pictish area settled by the Norse.

The available evidence for the Early Historic period elsewhere in Scotland is limited. There is some information for economic activities on Iona from written sources, although there is only a small amount of actual archaeological evidence. The extensive excavations at Whithorn which span this period did not, unfortunately, include a programme of detailed environmental work.

The northern areas under discussion here do not today support any significant tree growth. In the pre-Viking period, clearance of scrubby willow/aspen is suggested by the carbonised fragments recovered in the samples examined. Small fragments of hazel and birch could also have been from local trees, but larger timbers of pine, for example, could have been from driftwood, if not imported. A landscape of undulating green sward, with peat bogs (the main fuel source) and heather moorlands (supplying thatch, bedding and fodder), is not hard to imagine. Exploitation of the land, through pasture and arable cultivation, of the sea, for its many marine resources (fish, shells, seaweed, etc.) and of bird cliffs, are all supported by the available evidence.

PASTORAL FARMING

Animal bones survive well in many conditions, particularly the shell sands of northern and western Scotland and, despite fragmentation, are often identifiable to species and age. At Buckquoy the majority of the bones in the Pictish phases were of cattle, with fewer sheep and pig. This is echoed in the evidence from the Brough of Birsay sites excavated by Hunter. On the other hand, in Room 5 on the Brough of Birsay, T. J. Seller identified a predominance of sheep over cattle, with the rate of slaughter of young animals increasing from the Pictish into the Viking periods. The Buckquoy evidence has been interpreted as suggesting that the cattle were being bred for meat and hides – as suggested for Dundurn and Dunollie – whereas on the Brough, in the Room 5 assemblage, wool and milk products were of significance.

Although the deposits at Saevar Howe from the Pictish period were not fully investigated, the mammal bone assemblage reveals little change between the Pictish and Viking periods (seen also at Skaill), with a slight reduction in the number of sheep, which formed the largest part of the identified assemblage, with a slight increase in the smaller cattle bone assemblage.

The high degree of fragmentation of the assemblage from Room 5 on the Brough has been interpreted as the result of marrow extraction. However,the evidence was collected by use of a sieve with a 5mm mesh, whereas the lack of sieving at Buckquoy may well have militated against such material being recovered for comparison. Elsewhere, in some cases, bone fragmentation may be suggested as resulting from post-depositional factors – trampling or gnawing by dogs, for example, or perhaps even deliberate crushing for fertiliser. At Freswick in Caithness, where the majority of the environmental evidence which has been recovered relates to the Late Norse period, there is nevertheless a significant body of material which is probably related to Pictish activity (collected in this case on meshes of 1mm). On the basis of evidence from the infill of the broch at Freswick Sands, it is possible to suggest that sheep/goat were more common than cattle or pig, although the sample size is too small to be conclusive.

There is a wealth of recently published environmental information from the Howe, near Stromness in Orkney, a complex site which includes a substantial broch tower surrounded by cellular structures. The samples collected, many by means of flotation, provide much information about the economy and environment at several stages in the history of the site. Phase 8, the later Iron Age farmstead and settlement, is considered to date from the beginning of the fourth century AD, with its use extending into the eighth century. During this period agriculture was based on both arable and pastoral activities; cattle remained a feature of the economy throughout, but there was an overall increase in domestic animals in the bone assemblage (sheep and pig) because of a marked decline in the presence of red deer which had made up about 18 per cent of the Phase 7 assemblage. A greater percentage of the sheep population lived longer than in previous phases and it is suggested that the sheep flock was larger, possibly as a result of the decline in red deer grazing which would have provided competition for this limited resource.

In the west of Scotland, on Iona, the evidence for the economy and environment is more limited, but does indicate that cattle predominated and that red deer, sheep, pig, seal and various fish were also exploited. In fact, the monks of Iona had special rights to the hunting grounds of Mull. The eating of horse flesh is also suggested, presumably at the end of its useful life, and hides could be used for making vessels. The point has been made that this is not representative of the high degree of austerity recorded of Columba himself!

ARABLE FARMING

Evidence for arable farming is usually confined to carbonised seeds of the cultivated crops – bere barley and oats in particular. Room 5 on the Brough, Saevar Howe and Buckquoy have no carbonised seed recorded from their pre-Viking layers; however, this is likely to be a reflection on the samples taken rather than the true situation. The carbonised seeds of oats and grass from Hunter's sites on the Brough suggest that there was likely to have been cereal cultivation nearby.

At the Howe (Phase 8) there was extensive evidence of arable activity, with changes in the use of resources, such as wood, from the earlier phases; turves replaced the use of wood as a fuel. There was a concentration of naked barley, occasionally mixed with hulled barley, and an increase in the presence of oats, probably in the seventh century; it is suggested that this was being deliberately grown rather than a weed contaminent. Flax is also recorded for the first time at this site in Phase 8, as are edible fruits and nuts (such as crowberry and hazelnut) which had been deliberately collected. This diversification corresponds with that found on contemporary sites in Orkney, such as Pool on Sanday, and some of the Birsay sites. At Dundurn in southern Pictland, early phases of deposits produced over twenty wild cherry stones in human faeces.

Complementary evidence has, however, been recovered on the mainland of Scotland, at Freswick, Caithness. In the Pictish period, there are clear traces of cultivation marks in plots possibly manured by middens from the nearby settlement and/or by seaweed from the adjacent shoreline. It is feasible to suggest that large areas of Freswick Links and the surrounding area were under cultivation at this period, although sometimes only for brief spells. Crops of bere barley and oats are suggested, and it is significant that there are no major discernible differences in this part of the economy between the Pictish–Viking and the Late Norse assemblages. Small juxtaposed fields are indicated by differences in the direction of cultivation in areas which are both spatially and temporally close. The lack of chaff in the carbonised assemblage could suggest growth of cereals elsewhere (as supported by the pollen examination from nearby Hill of Harley), but this is not conclusive as cereal pollen does not travel far. This might suggest that other, unidentified plants were being cultivated in these small fields or plots, possibly legumes such as Celtic beans.

Adomnan's *Life of Columba* refers to both arable and pastoral farming being practised by the monks at Iona. The main area of cultivation would have been on the western machair, as it still is today. Recent pollen-analysis has, however, demonstrated that cereals were being cultivated in the area of the abbey itself throughout the Early Christian period. Adomnan also refers to a mill-stone, and quernstones with the distinctive cross motif, discussed above, represent further evidence for grinding cereals.

The interesting survival of holly-leaves in the archaeological record from Iona provides an addition to the species known to have been exploited by the monks. Holly may well have been deliberately grown in the local hedgerows for use in the manufacture of ink, an essential commodity for the monastic scribes.

MARINE EXPLOITATION

Pictish ships were mentioned above, and it is no surprise that they were used to exploit the marine resource-base. Although it is clear that marine resources were extensively exploited in the Norse period, most sites examined to date have produced some evidence of fishing in the Pictish period. House 5 on the Brough of Birsay provided evidence for small-scale exploitation of cod, although Hunter noted the poor conditions for the survival of fish bone in the deposits. On the Orkney Mainland, at Saevar Howe, there is evidence for a range of fish in the Pictish period, including ballan wrasse with butchery marks on the bones. The size of fish does not vary appreciably between the Pictish and Norse periods and Hedges noted that both populations 'opted for similar strategies to cope with these problems, given very similar opportunities for marine resource use'. Even so, fish did not play a major role in the diet of the Picts at Saevar Howe or elsewhere.

The lack of surviving middens at Buckquoy, combined with the absence of sieving, has certainly affected the quantity of evidence from this site, for fish bones are generally small and fragile and thus recovered most effectively through wet sieving. However, conger eel, saithe, pollack, ling, cod, hake and ballan wrasse are all noted. This evidence suggests, as at the other sites, that both inshore line fishing and deep-sea fishing, with lines, may have been carried out in the pre-Viking period.

At the Howe, the most significant fish remains are those from the cod family, and much of the fishing seems to have been opportunistic, taking place from the shore itself or close inshore, with only rare forays into deeper waters.

At Freswick, the fish-bone survival is not as good for the Pictish period as for later periods because many of the earlier middens have become conflated and have been subjected to post-depositional changes. It is, however, clear that fish was being exploited in the Pictish economy at Freswick. It is important to realise that, at this site at least, between the Pictish and Viking/Late Norse periods 'it is not possible to detect any major change in kinds of fishes [caught] (although there are variations, as between saithe and ling).'

SEASHORE AND CLIFF EXPLOITATION

The extensive recovery of marine shells on Pictish sites, including common limpet, winkle, mussel and common European oyster, suggests that some were collected for human consumption. However, the bulk of this assemblage consists most commonly of limpets and winkles and it is probable that these were being used for fish bait, rather than as 'starvation food'.

The recovery of bones indicates that seabirds were sometimes caught and it is reasonable to assume that the traditional methods of fowling, as used in Foula or St Kilda until the turn of this century, were being practised. The presence of the fulmar in pre-Norse contexts at Freswick is of particular interest because it was thought to have been restricted to St Kilda prior to about 1750. The presence of eggshell from both seabirds and domestic species of fowl at Freswick suggests a further source of food available to the Picts.

Excavation at the Howe has produced one of the largest bird-bone assemblages in northern Scotland, with a preponderance relating to the later phases, especially Phase 8, the Later Iron Age. Many are food species – gannet, cormorant, golden plover, great auk and red grouse – all becoming increasingly popular in Phase 8. It is assumed that the larger birds would have been killed at the cliffs and brought back to the site, whilst others may have been caught nearby.

By combining the evidence from contemporary sites on both sides of the Pentland Firth, it is clear that the Picts fully exploited their local environment in a manner that would have been entirely familiar to the incoming Vikings.

THE EARLIEST CONTACTS BETWEEN
THE PICTS AND THE NORSE

There can be no doubt that there were contacts between Britain and Scandinavia prior to the documented violent arrivals of the late eighth century. The nature and date of the contact have recently been brought to the fore by the detailed analysis of antler combs from Scottish contexts, of both Viking and pre-Viking types, which has been undertaken in Norway. The provisional suggestion is that the raw material for both sets of combs is reindeer antler, imported from Norway. This is entirely appropriate for combs of Viking types; indeed, there is little evidence in Scotland for the local manufacture of such items. The problem lies with the pre-Viking combs examined. The comb-types are clearly distinguishable from the Viking examples, but the raw material apparently is not. Is it possible, or indeed likely, that the Picts were importing antler from Norway to make their combs? If this could be proven, it would cast a new light on the pre-Viking relationships between Scotland and Norway in the period before the raids took place. It is inevitable that such a suggestion has not met with universal acceptance, and the results of further studies are eagerly awaited.

THE RAIDS BEGIN

Towards the end of the eighth century, Western Europe began to witness seasonal raids from Scandinavia: the dawn of the Viking Age. Ferocious attacks are recorded on the coastal margins of the Carolingian Empire and on the kingdoms of the Anglo-Saxons, Picts, Scots, Britons and Irish to the west. Frequent targets were monastic and religious centres, prime sources of wealth and portable loot.

Surviving documentary sources for the raids on Britain and Ireland were written in most cases at first hand by the people who lived in these centres; through their experiences the Vikings remain damned in the history books of today. There can be no doubt that the writings of Alcuin (a monk from York at the court of Charlemagne), as also the *Anglo-Saxon*

Chronicle, transmit the fear of the era. The raid on Lindisfarne, off the Northumbrian coast of England, in AD 793 is graphically recalled:

> In this year dire portents appeared over Northumbria and sorely frightened the people. They consisted of lightning, and fiery dragons were seen in the air. A great famine immediately followed those signs, and a little after that in the same year, on 8 June, the ravages of heathen men miserably destroyed God's church on Lindisfarne, with plunder and slaughter.

This quotation from Alcuin, writing to the king of Northumbria, one of the most commonly cited for the period, could well have been repeated – at least in sentiment – at several of the centres further north.

The earliest reference to an attack on a Scottish monastery, recorded in the *Annals of Ulster* for AD 617, is to 'the burning of Donnan of Eigg with 150 martyrs'; the same year there was an attack on the Donegal coast. Whether this was pre-Viking Norse activity, or more likely the work of seaborne Pictish raiders, cannot be determined. However, the silence of the *Annals* in this respect, until the end of the eighth century, suggests that such activity was not being witnessed at the major monastic centres. Iona was then to be repeatedly attacked, in 795, 802 and 806 (when sixty-eight members were killed), suffering so badly that part of the community was forced to retreat for safety to Kells in Ireland. Plundering in the Hebrides is noted in 798 and the period which followed, into the 830s, saw a series of seasonal raids in the west, most particularly targeting Irish monasteries, with the 840s seeing the establishment of fortified bases, or *longphorts*, such as Dublin on the River Liffey.

Not all the targets for the Vikings would have been ecclesiastical and, certainly for Scotland, there is some suggestion that secular settlements were attacked as well at this period, although no such references appear in the written record. There are, however, later references to attacks on Dunnottar and Dumbarton. The initial period of raiding, during the late eighth and early ninth centuries, was a preliminary to more lasting contacts. It is clear, however, that the activity was not all in one direction. *Orkneyinga saga* tells that: 'One summer Harald Finehair sailed west to punish the Vikings, as he had grown tired of their depredations, for they harried in Norway during the summer, but spent the winter in Shetland or the Orkneys.'

Indeed, it is quite feasible that some Vikings did establish bases in northern and western Scotland (as may have been the case, for example, on Barra) from which to raid, although such have not yet been identified in the archaeological record. It is, however, not possible to determine whether particular raids were undertaken direct from Norway rather than from nearer at hand.

Reconsideration of the raiding activity has recently taken place in the light of the evidence from those pagan graves in Norway which contain items of undoubted Insular origin (that is to say from Late Celtic Britain and Ireland). Most of these are conventionally considered to be loot from the earliest days of Viking raids on the British Isles.

Chapter 2

THE NORWEGIAN BACKGROUND

SOCIETY

Life in Viking period Norway focused on the family, with society being kin-based for the purposes of religion, justice and defence, apparently operating through both the male and female lines (or so it was in the earliest surviving medieval laws). At the same time it was a stratified system, as is evident in the archaeological record from the differing size of farms and from variations in the quantity and quality of the grave-goods deposited in pagan Norse burials. At the apex of society were the kings and earls, vying for control, at the base were the thralls, or slaves (both native and foreign), whose economic importance was that they carried out the heavy work, outdoors as well as in. Most important of all, however, was the 'yeoman' class of free farmers ranging in status in-between, whether they held their own inherited 'family' land or were tenants of the aristocracy. The term 'udal' survives in Scandinavian Scotland from the Old Norse *óðal* as a technical term for inherited land bound by complex rules.

Such an aristocratic system may be considered as an essential prerequisite for the emergence of the Vikings whose raids were dependent on their leaders possessing sufficient wealth to provide and equip the necessary ships. Indeed, there is evidence to indicate that the bulk of Viking expeditions, and of the subsequent settlers, came from areas of Norway with the best resources and thus the most competition. These were the areas in the west which were already densely settled before the beginning of the Viking period, although there is no evidence for over-population or even much population pressure. Place-name studies have suggested that the Viking period was one of internal colonisation within Norway, quite apart from the Norse settlement overseas not only in Britain and Ireland, but also the Faroes, Iceland, Greenland and even (briefly) North America (Figure 2.1).

ECONOMY

The economy was based on agriculture, augmented by hunting and fishing, although trade was growing in importance. The balance between cultivation and animal husbandry will have varied from region to region, as also the contribution made by fishing. Cattle were important, but other than in mild coastal areas had to be housed in the winter, requiring much hay-making and the collection of fodder to supply those that were to be kept alive for its duration. Sheep and goats, being hardier, might survive outside; pigs were also raised and domestic fowl kept. Horses were used for riding and for traction, as well as

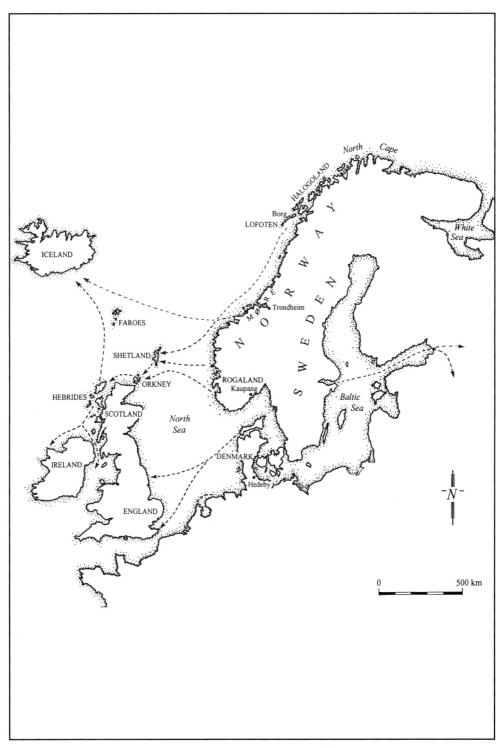

2.1 Map of Norway and Scotland in the Viking period.

being eaten, at least during the period before the widespread adoption of Christianity. Grain (oats and barley) was cultivated for bread and brewing; fruits and vegetables were gathered, although some such as leeks and cabbage seem to have been grown, as also was flax which was used for the production of both linseed oil and linen. In the mountainous interior of southern Norway, as also amongst the Lapps in the north, hunting and trapping for furs, skins and antlers (the latter traded for comb manufacture) would have provided the main livelihood for the inhabitants. Other specialised activities, in certain areas, would have been iron production and the quarrying of soapstone and of schist (for whetstones), all of which were widely traded commodities.

Norway's mountainous terrain and long coastline (Figure 2.1), interspersed with fjords and fringed with islands, imposed a pattern of dispersed settlement, of individual farms rather than villages. There were certainly no towns in existence at the beginning of the Viking period, although several had come into existence before its end. Chief amongst these was Trondheim, or Nidaros as it was then known, in Trøndelag in western Norway. This was the location of Norway's first permanent episcopal seat, during the reign of King Olaf III (1066–93), with a cathedral housing the relics of St Olaf – that is the bones of Olaf Haraldsson, the Norwegian king who was martyred in 1030. In 1152 or 1153 it became a metropolitan see, with its archbishop having authority over the bishops in the Norse settlements in the North Atlantic, from Orkney to Greenland, including the Isle of Man.

Trøndelag has good agricultural land and supported the wealthy earls of Lade, the most powerful family in the west of Norway. It was certainly one of the main regions involved in Viking expeditions overseas, as can be seen from its ninth-century graves containing Celtic metalwork from Scotland and Ireland, much of it ecclesiastical loot.

The best farming land in western Norway is in Rogaland, in the south-west, where a considerable quantity of Celtic metalwork has also been found. The other notable concentration of such souvenirs of the Viking raids is in the mid-western coastal region, directly opposite Orkney and Shetland, in the territory of the earls of Møre.

The largest of the most fertile regions of Norway is in the south-east of the country, around the Oslo Fjord, where the richest of all pagan Norse burials are known and where there flourished the ninth-century market-place of Kaupang in Vestfold. On geographical grounds alone it is not surprising that this region had fewer contacts with Scotland than western Norway, given that Bergen is closer by sea to Lerwick and Kirkwall than it is to Oslo. However, there is some Celtic metalwork from Kaupang and a brooch made from the boss of an enamelled cross was found in the Oseberg 'royal' ship-burial, as well as some other objects of Irish origin. Not all such material to have reached Norway had necessarily been looted, although this is clearly the case when church treasures have been cut up for conversion into jewellery. Western fashions for certain types of dress fastener, including Pictish brooches, were adopted in Norway and then copied (as also at Kaupang), with the copies occasionally finding their way westwards in return.

SETTLEMENT SITES

The actual Viking period farms of Norway have proved elusive with the result that few sites have been excavated, but these range in size from the small buildings at Ytre Moa, near the head of Sogne Fjord, in western Norway, to the massive longhouse at Borg, on the island of Vestvågøy, in Lofoten to the north. There is enough evidence to demonstrate that byres were not an integral part of Viking period houses, except in northern Norway, as had generally been the case at an earlier period. Some sites were in seasonal use, for particular purposes such as summer pasturing (*sætr* or shielings), fishing or hunting.

The six small rectangular buildings excavated at Ytre Moa, dating from the ninth/tenth centuries, were built of stone, lined with wood and with a wooden gable-end containing the entrance. They appear to have had different functions, including dwelling, byre and barn, although not all were in contemporary use.

The exceptional size of the building excavated at Borg, which is 83m long, implies that it was a chieftain's residence and farm, being a combined dwelling and byre; it was first built on this site in the period AD 600–800. In form it was a three-aisled linear structure, with side entrances, built of timber with an outer wall of turf. Its occupants possessed imported luxuries, gold and silver, with drinking glasses and pottery vessels of types found at Kaupang where they were brought from the Rhineland.

THE EVIDENCE OF OHTHERE

There exists a remarkable insight into the life of one of these wealthy chieftains of northern Norway, called Ohthere or Ottar, as a result of his having visited the court of King Alfred in about 890. The English king incorporated Ohthere's account of his life into his extended translation of Orosius' history of the world. Ohthere described how he lived in *Hálogaland* (perhaps meaning 'land of the aurora'), the farthest north of all Norwegians, for there were only Lapps living to the north of him. It is thought that his home may have been on the island of Bjarkøy, near modern Tromsø, where a chieftain is known to have resided at a later date. In which case there is archaeological evidence, including grave-finds, for some sparse Norse settlement to his north during the Viking period, but not sufficient to discredit his evidence.

Ohthere's wealth was derived from his personal status and from a mixed economy. Agriculture was of least importance to him, for he possessed only twenty cows, twenty sheep and twenty pigs, with horses for ploughing the little land that he cultivated. On the other hand he owned 600 reindeer, among which were six decoy-animals, which were highly prized by the Lapps for catching wild reindeer and such 'wild animals' were a major source of his wealth. Most important of all, however, was the tribute paid to Ohthere by the Lapps in furs (marten, otter and bear), reindeer hides, feathers (for bedding), ropes made of seal skin and whale hide, and whale bones (or walrus ivory), all of which he could use in trade.

Ohthere makes no mention of fishing, but he took to the sea for hunting both whales and walruses. He described a journey that he had made northwards to explore the coast (Figure 2.1), which he had then followed round until he came to what is now known as the White Sea. This was not a journey just taken out of curiosity, for he was after the walruses because of the 'very fine ivory in their tusks' and because 'their hide is very good for ship-ropes'.

The other voyage which Ohthere described to the king was one undertaken by him in the opposite direction, to the farthest south of Scandinavia – to Denmark – presumably for the purpose of trading his northern luxury goods for others, such as precious metals or Rhenish wine and the glass vessels to drink it from. His destination was Hedeby (known as Haithabu in German), which was Scandinavia's most important port and its largest town during the Viking period, although it was abandoned in the eleventh century for neighbouring Schleswig. Indeed, trade was presumably what had brought Ohthere to King Alfred's court in turn (and it is notable that Alfred's reign saw an influx of walrus ivory into England).

Ohthere's first destination on his trip to Hedeby lay in the south of Norway, a port called *Sciringes heal*, which is today identified with Kaupang (the latter place-name meaning simply a market). 'He said that one might sail thither in a month, if one anchored at night and each day had a favourable wind, and all the time should sail along the coast', after which it had taken him another five days of sailing to reach Hedeby.

Ohthere's route along the coast of Norway was that which gave the country its name, when travelled from the south: the 'North-way'. The multiplicity of islands which fringe most of the western coastline, with the notable exception of the exposed south-west corner, provides sheltered channels for easy communication, as did the fjords themselves, so that seemingly remote settlements were joined by the sea. Two days' sailing to Orkney or Shetland needed only a night at sea, with a direct crossing presenting no navigational problems; coastal sailing and island-hopping could then begin again so that the Western Isles or Hebrides were the 'South Islands' of Scandinavian Scotland – the *Suðreyjar* – when seen from the perspective of Norse mariners.

SHIPS

The earliest known sailing ship in Scandinavia is the ornate vessel from the Oseberg burial mound in Vestfold, south-east Norway, the construction of which has been tree-ring dated to c. 815/20. However, there are depictions of earlier sailing ships on stone monuments in the Baltic island of Gotland and rowing boats had clearly been adapted for the sail in Scandinavia well before the beginning of the Viking period. This development cannot therefore have been one of its causes, although it is self-evident that without sophisticated ships there could have been no Viking period. Different types of vessel were required for different purposes and there is evidence of an increasing variety during this period so that by the end of the Viking period, at any rate, there were specialised war-ships (the true 'long-ships') and broader cargo-ships for different purposes, for deep-sea voyages and for coastal traffic, with smaller boats being needed for river transport, for ferrying and for fishing.

There was, however, already variation in existence by the beginning of the Viking period, for the Oseberg ship is no ordinary Viking ship. Its shallow draft and somewhat weak construction, combined with its ornately carved prow and stern, suggest that it was a vessel for inshore waters only – a 'royal barge', as would have befitted the exceptionally wealthy woman who was buried in it. The ship found in the Gokstad burial mound, also in Vestfold, is more representative of those which will have been used by the original Viking raiders and the first generation of Norse settlers, as is demonstrated by the fact that replicas of it have crossed not only the North Sea, but the Atlantic Ocean as well! Its construction has been tree-ring dated to c. 895/900 and it is worth describing in some detail, as the basic principles are the same for all Scandinavian Viking period ships, whatever their particular functions.

The Gokstad ship is 23.3 m long and 5.25 m broad amidships where its hull is 1.95 m high (Figure 2.2). This is constructed from sixteen clinker-laid strakes on each side (over-lapping planks joined with iron rivets and caulked with animal hair), fastened to the keel and to the curved fore-stem and after-stem which formed the symmetrical bow and stern. The mast slotted into the keelson, a massive timber secured to the keel, which distributed its weight and transferred the power derived from the single square sail to the ship itself. It was steered by a side-rudder, attached near the stern on the right-hand or starboard side (so named from *stýra*, to steer). It was fully decked in the manner of war-ships, but unlike the cargo-ships which had central holds. War-ships, however, needed to be able to switch from sail to rowing power for manoeuvrability (so that their masts had to be lowerable), whereas cargo-ships were sailing ships with more firmly seated masts and only a few oar-ports on the half-decks for use on such occasions as docking in harbour. There are sixteen oar-ports on either side of the Gokstad ship, with wooden covers so that they could be closed when under sail, and there were thirty-two oars found along with other ship's equipment, including an anchor and a gangplank, but in this case there were no rowing benches, as in true war-ships, so that the oarsmen had presumably to sit on chests. The oars are made from pine, as is the decking, mast and yards, but the hull is built of oak, with the strakes split radially from logs and the keel formed from a single timber 18 m long.

The Gokstad ship-burial is also notable for the fact that it contained three small row-ing-boats of sizes similar to those more often found in pagan Norse graves than are large sailing-ships, even if all such are normally reduced to rows of iron rivets in the ground, as with those in Orkney, Colonsay and the Isle of Man. These boats are sufficiently narrow for each man to pull a pair of oars, so that a four-oared boat or *færing* would be rowed by two men, with a third at the steering-oar.

The shallow draught and light construction of many ships would have meant that they could sail up to any suitably shelving beach, to be readily hauled up and pushed out again when required. On the other hand, ports such as Kaupang and Hedeby had jetties to ease the unloading of cargo. Finally, it should be noted that it was usual for ships to be stored safely for the winter in a special type of building known as a *noust*, as it is still today in Orkney. For obvious reasons, these were constructed with an open end facing the shore and without internal roof-supports.

RELIGION

The importance of small boats in daily life throughout most of Norway during the Viking period is emphasised by their presence in the pagan Norse graves. This aspect of the burial rite is more likely to represent the status of the deceased rather than the provision of a means of water-transport to an after-life (and it is worth noting that the Oseberg ship was moored in its mound by means of a rope attached to a large boulder!). In fact, we do not know what the grave-goods signified to those who buried them or placed them on the pyre, for both inhumation and cremation were practised in Scandinavia during the Viking period. However, the provision of food in many cases does suggest that there was a belief in the need to supply the dead person for a journey of some kind (an idea for which there

2.2 *The Gokstad ship (Universitetets Oldsaksamling, Oslo).*

is also some support in the written sources), whereas the range of utilitarian possessions which furnish many graves, from weapons to sickles and spindles, could certainly be supposed to have been useful in an after-life, but in this respect the documentary evidence is all too vague and incomplete. Concern for the dead is also evident in the placing of graves close to farms, although others which are more isolated may be prominently sited and marked by mounds so as to be clearly visible to those passing by.

Our knowledge of the pre-Christian religious beliefs and practices of Scandinavia is altogether limited and partial, given that the fullest accounts were written by Christians several centuries after the conversion. There was a pantheon of gods, with assorted responsibilities, who were portrayed as human beings, even if in a supernatural world. Chief amongst them were Odin, Thor, Frey and Freyja, the latter two (brother and sister) being the god and goddess of fertility. Thor was worshipped all over the Viking world and his popularity came from his physical strength, utilized in his struggle against evil; his weapon was a mighty hammer, Mjöllnir, a divine symbol which was worn in pendant form by his adherents. Odin was the god of battle (although also of wisdom and poetry), who resided in Valhalla, the hall of slain warriors, whither they were brought from the battlefield by the supernatural women known as Valkyries. The cult of Odin seems to have been less popular in Norway than elsewhere in Scandinavia.

The pagan religion was a tolerant one and not organised in the manner of Christianity, with its hierarchical priesthood and buildings set aside exclusively for worship. Although place-name evidence indicates that there were numerous pagan cult-sites, at which the gods and other supernatural beings (such as spirits of place) would have been honoured, not much is known of the manner of worship, apart from ritual feasting. Chieftains and wealthy farmers appear to have had some priestly functions so that such a sacrificial feast (or *blót*) would have taken place on their own farms, in their own halls.

The vivid account of a pagan temple at Uppsala in Sweden, containing statues of the gods, and with a priesthood who carried out human and animal sacrifices, was written by the cleric Adam of Bremen who had never seen it for himself. His description dates from about 1075, by which time Christianity had taken considerable hold in Scandinavia, so that this temple complex at a royal centre may represent a late response by the old religion.

The first contacts many Norsemen will have had with Christianity would have been on raiding the monasteries of Britain and Ireland, but this Viking activity was not specifically anti-Christian in nature; rather, the monasteries provided easy targets as undefended 'honey-pots'. Christian slaves would have been brought back to Norway, as they were taken in due course by Norse settlers to Iceland. We know that in Ireland intermarriage began early and that monasteries continued to exist in proximity to Norse settlements, even if some others were utilised as Viking bases. There is no reason to suppose that the situation will have been very different in Scotland. There were doubtless many in the West, by the end of the ninth century, like Helgi the Lean, a prominent settler in Iceland who, believing in Christ, called his new farm Kristnes (that is 'Christ's point'), but who preferred to invoke Thor's protection when it came to voyages and other hard undertakings.

In such ways Christianity trickled into Norway, as also during the reign of its first Christian king, Hákon the Good (c. 935–60), who had been baptised in England; he brought over priests and built churches in western Norway, but did not set out to suppress paganism. Indeed, after he died in battle he was given a pagan-style burial and was considered to have gone to Valhalla. In contrast, both Olaf Tryggvason (from c. 995) and Olaf Haraldsson (from c. 1015) set about imposing Christianity by force where necessary. Olaf Tryggvason was credited with the official conversion of not only Norway, but also Orkney, the Faroes, Iceland and Greenland. After the latter King Olaf was killed at the battle of Stiklestad in 1030, although not a religious conflict, he was declared a martyr and his relics were honoured at Trondheim, as mentioned above.

THE *THING*

Justice in Scandinavia during the Viking period was administered at meetings of the *thing*, the public assembly of free men, which met regularly. These existed at both local and regional levels, presided over by chieftains, with also higher assemblies at provincial level. In Iceland, for instance, there came to be thirteen local *things*, organised within four Quarters, and a General Assembly or *Althing* (with a professional 'lawspeaker'). The *Althing* met annually for two weeks each summer, with those attending having to camp in temporary accommodation or booths. The place where the *Althing* met is called Thingvellir, meaning the 'Thing Plain', as does Tynwald in the Isle of Man, but similar *thing* placenames are to be found in Scandinavian Scotland as well, including Tingwall (in both Orkney and Shetland).

RUNES

Other aspects of Norse culture that were introduced into Scotland include runic writing and a series of distinctive art-styles. Runic script was designed for inscribing, consisting of vertical and diagonal strokes, and so was only suitable for short messages. The alphabet consisted of twenty-four characters and is known from its first six letters as the *futhark*; various forms of it were in use among the Germanic peoples. By the Viking period the *futhark* had been reduced to sixteen letters and there were two versions in use in Scandinavia (Figure 2.3), one traditionally called the Danish (or common) runes and the other, a more simplified and cursive version, the Swedo-Norwegian (or short-twig) runes. However, neither version was confined to the region from which it is named and some inscriptions are even mixed. There are numerous problems in reading runic inscriptions,

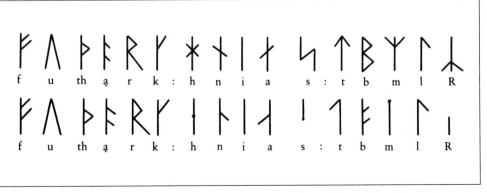

2.3 Viking period runes: two versions of the futhark, *without their variant forms. Above, the Common or Danish runes; below, the Swedo-Norwegian runes (after Frances Lincoln, 1980).*

even supposing that they survive complete, for spelling is always a problem given that there were not enough runes to cover all letters/sounds, various runes might be omitted in certain circumstances, and word division was not always indicated.

It is impossible today to determine just how literate the population of Norway during the Viking period would have been, given that the ideal medium for a runic inscription is a stick of wood which, even if not thrown on the fire after use, would be unlikely to have survived until the present day, other than in exceptional circumstances. Indeed, no such inscriptions on wood are known from Scotland. Despite all the difficulties, however, runic inscriptions are of the utmost importance as the only contemporary documents left to us by Viking period Norsemen.

VIKING ART

Scandinavian art was distinctively different from the styles current in pre-Viking Scotland so that objects, such as brooches, ornamented with Viking art are distinctive wherever they are found (most often, in fact, as grave-goods). The fact that not only the styles changed through time, but also the form of the objects which they embellish, provides a two-fold typological basis for dating the artefacts themselves and thus, by extrapolation, the contexts in which they are found.

Viking art is rarely representational, favouring animal motifs of a stylized nature to create its ornamental patterns, although ribbon-interlace was important for a while and plant motifs became fashionable in the tenth and eleventh centuries. The so-called Style III/E animals which were fashionable at the beginning of the Viking period, alongside other animal motifs borrowed from western Europe (notably a distinctive form of 'gripping beast'), are not represented on artefacts from Scotland, unlike the succeeding Oseberg style which continues the same motifs in a modified form throughout the first three-quarters of the ninth century. Inevitably, the different styles did not succeed each other in a neat chronological sequence and the Borre style, which seems to have developed about the mid-ninth century, continued in use until about the mid-tenth, thus overlapping for much of its life with the Jellinge style, which flourished during the first half of the tenth century.

The Borre style made use of the traditional motifs, although the form of the 'gripping beast' is re-modelled, but it also favoured tight interlace and knot patterns. It is the earliest style of Viking art known to have been copied in the Scandinavian settlements in the West, although there is little evidence (so far) for its reproduction in Scotland. The Jellinge style is based on an S-shaped animal motif (Figure 2.4), used to create open interlacing patterns, and from it developed the Mammen style, which is the first style of Viking art to incorporate plant motifs fully, although their first, tentative, appearance had taken place as part of the Borre-style repertoire.

The Mammen style marks the beginning of what is classified as Late Viking art and flourished during the second half of the tenth century. Its animal and plant motifs become elaborated as they are carried through into the Ringerike style, which was fashionable during the first half of the eleventh century, before being refined into the Urnes style, which represents the final phase of Viking art. The Urnes style was created towards the middle of the eleventh century and continued in use into the twelfth, as the pan-European style of Romanesque art entered Scandinavia through the Church; its motifs consist almost

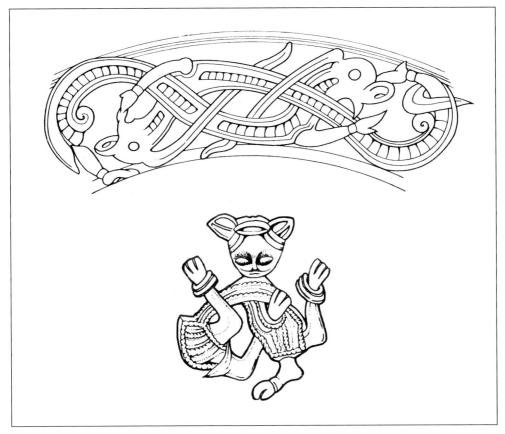

2.4 Two motifs from Viking art: above, a pair of S-shaped animals in the Jellinge style; below, a Borre-style 'gripping-beast' (after Frances Lincoln, 1980).

entirely of stylised animals, in marked contrast to the preceding Mammen and Ringerike styles.

DRESS AND WEAPONRY

During the Viking period in Norway, as in the rest of Scandinavia, there existed weaponry and ornaments, as well as tools and domestic artefacts (such as single-sided combs made of antler), which differed significantly in form from those in use during the pre-Viking period in Scotland. For instance, Norse weaponry was certainly superior in quality to that in use in eighth/ninth-century Ireland, as would have been the case generally in Scotland. However, this was not so with regard to the Anglo-Saxons, given that several ninth-century Anglo-Saxon swords have been found in pagan Norse graves. The acquisition of weapons by Vikings abroad is also illustrated in Scotland by the presence of native shield-bosses in a couple of male graves.

A man might be armed with just a spear or axe, but the complete weapon-kit of the wealthier warrior consisted of sword, spear, axe and arrows, with a shield for protection;

iron helmets and body armour are rarely found. Although single-edged swords are known from the beginning of the Viking period, the standard type was a double-edged weapon for slashing, with varying forms of hilt, although all were for single-handed use. Iron spear-heads varied in form depending on whether they were for throwing or thrusting. The circular wooden shield had a central rounded boss of iron to protect the hand which grasped a bar on the back. Depictions of Viking warriors show them wearing conical helmets, although the very few that survive are rounded, so that the others may have been leather caps (unless there was a belief that dead warriors did not require to be buried with their helmets).

Scandinavian women of standing during much of the Viking period, at least well into the tenth century, wore a form of folk-costume 'for best' which required an assemblage of brooches very different from that worn by the native women of any part of Britain and Ireland. Their graves are thus immediately recognisable, unless it is to be supposed that some of those who inter-married adopted this distinctive Scandinavian form of female dress. A pair of large oval brooches was used to fasten the shoulder straps of a dress of wool or linen, worn over a long shift. Beads might be strung between the oval brooches, or worn on a necklace, and sometimes small articles, like a needle-case or key, might be suspended from one of them. A cloak or shawl was fastened with a central brooch or pin of varying types, both native (such as trefoil and equal-armed brooches) and imported (including pieces of looted metalwork); a man's cloak was fastened on the right shoulder so as to leave his sword-arm free.

A common personal possession found in both male and female graves is a single-sided comb made from small plates of antler held together with iron rivets, for such were essential for the control of head-lice. In addition, a wide range of other belongings might also be selected for burial with the dead, whether tools, domestic utensils or even gaming pieces for amusement.

Chapter 3

SOURCES FOR SCANDINAVIAN SCOTLAND

A considerable variety of evidence is available for the study of Scandinavian Scotland, much of which is not archaeological in nature. It is proper for all such to be taken into consideration in any full account of the Viking and Late Norse periods in Scotland, but here the evidence of language and literature has deliberately been given a background role to that of archaeology. Nevertheless, these various other categories of evidence cannot simply be ignored and thus they will be reviewed briefly in this chapter (alongside the nature of the archaeological evidence itself) so as to reveal something of their potential, as well as of their limitations.

LANGUAGE

In the Northern Isles and Caithness the Norse language seems to have rapidly become dominant, replacing the native language or languages of the whole area; however long the latter may have survived this process, they were ultimately to be extinguished almost without trace. The dominant speech of the settlers was a form of western Norwegian, although whether predominantly north-western or south-western is disputed. The Norse dialects of Shetland, Orkney and Caithness – known as 'Norn' (a term first recorded in about 1485) – developed different characteristics, before they eventually succumbed to Scots, although Norn was a living language in Orkney and Shetland into the eighteenth century.

The situation in the West Highlands and Islands is one of far greater complexity than in the north, and there is little agreement about the length of time Norse persisted as a spoken language or the degree of Gaelic–Norse bilingualism which existed during the Viking period, as is demonstrated by the evidence of place-names.

Personal names reveal a similar pattern in that Gaelic names were taken into use amongst the Norse settlers in the Western Isles, whereas no Pictish names were adopted by those in the Northern Isles.

PLACE-NAMES

The most important body of linguistic evidence consists of Norse place-names, and this source material is of the greatest value for the study of Scandinavian Scotland, although not all areas have been subjected to the same degree of research and not all interpretations are universally agreed by the specialists in question.

At the most basic level, the distribution of Norse place-names informs us of the extent of Norse settlement and activity (Figure 3.1), but they are notoriously difficult to date. For instance, the sporadic distribution of Scandinavian names in parts of south-eastern Scotland, where there is no archaeological evidence for primary Scandinavian settlement,

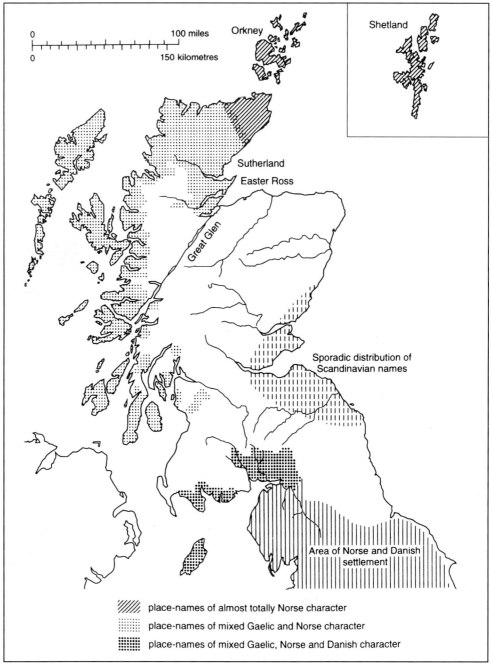

3.1 Areas of Scandinavian settlement in northern Britain (after B. Crawford, 1995).

may possibly date no earlier than the twelfth century and be attributable to English speakers moving northwards from the Danelaw. It is not surprising therefore that place-names by themselves are no longer considered to date the Norse settlement of Orkney and Shetland. Indeed, caution is now urged in any attempt even to try to use them for establishing a settlement sequence, even if some place-name elements do remain suggestive of infilling and may thus reflect a period of settlement expansion.

A major distinction that is customarily made in place-name studies is between habitative names (for settlements) and topographical names (those given to natural features, such as *dalr* meaning 'valley'). Among the most important types of habitative name introduced by the Norse settlers to Scotland are those incorporating such elements as *setr*, *bólstaðir*, *staðir*, *skáli* and *býr*, all of which may loosely be translated 'farm' (Figure 3.2), although this doubtless disguises a range of different meanings which would have been current at the time. *Skáli*, for instance (as represented to-day in the place-name Skaill), was used in Orkney at least of a high-status hall, although originally it signified a much more modest structure. On the other hand, it has also been demonstrated that some important early settlements in Orkney (as in Iceland) were named from prominent natural features, such as those ending in *-ness*, meaning 'headland' or 'point'. Some would argue therefore that areas which have many topographical Norse names, but hardly any habitative ones, may well have been more intensively settled than would appear at first sight.

This particular debate has centred mainly on the northern and western seaboards of mainland Scotland, for in the north-west habitative names are rare and in the west practically non-existent, as is illustrated, for example, by the distribution of *bólstaðir* names (Figure 3.2). The explanation offered for this in the past has been that these coastal regions were exploited primarily for their natural resources on a seasonal basis by the Norse settlers of the Western Isles: for summer grazing, for fishing and hunting, and for felling timber. There is, however, a growing body of archaeological evidence for Norse settlement during the Viking period along the north coast which is not matched in the west. The exploitation of the two areas may thus well have been different, but then the north coast forms an integral part of the sailing route linking the Northern Isles to the Norse settlements in the Hebrides – and thus Norway to the Viking kingdom of Dublin.

The Norse re-naming of the Scottish landscape was at its most extensive in Orkney and Shetland, a blanket coverage which can only be accounted for by the replacement of the native culture, but it does not follow that the native population was driven out or exterminated, particularly given the slave-keeping (and slave-trading) aspects of the Norse economy. Evidence is elusive for co-existence between native and Norse in the Northern Isles, except that the survival of certain Christian communities seems to be indicated by Norse place-names incorporating the word *papa* (or 'priest'), of which there are some sixteen in the Northern Isles and a couple in Caithness, with a further nine from the Northern Hebrides (Figure 3.3). Examples in Orkney include the islands of Papa Stronsay and Papa Westray – and, in Shetland, that of Papa Stour, as well as the site of Papil (or 'Priests' dwellings'), on West Burra, from which there is an important collection of Early Christian sculpture. A factor in favour of the survival interpretation, rather than the naming of abandoned sites from their previous occupants, is that no pagan Norse graves have so far been found on any of the 'Priests' islands', although there is always a danger in arguing from negative archaeological evidence.

The surviving Scandinavian place-names of Caithness suggest that Norse settlement was extensive, if less dense than in Orkney. However, the place-name evidence also shows that Norse settlement and control extended down the arable lands of the east coast through Sutherland to include Ross, with topographical names extending inland up the river valleys.

The Norse place-name pattern in the West Highlands and Islands is different from that in the Northern Isles, resulting not only from variation in settlement density and

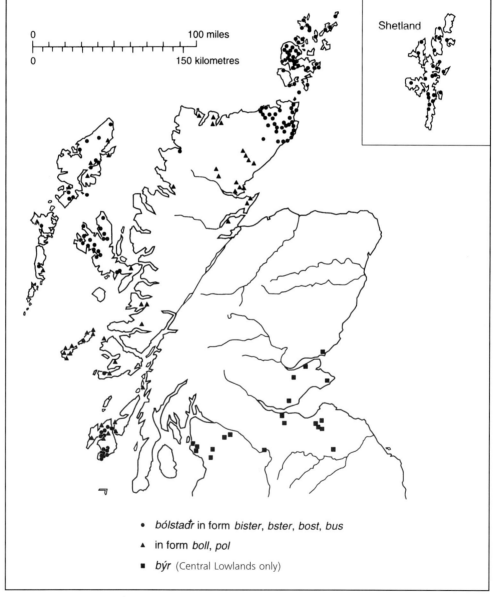

- • *bólstaðr* in form *bister, bster, bost, bus*
- ▲ in form *boll, pol*
- ■ *býr* (Central Lowlands only)

3.2 Bólstaðir *and* býr *names in central, north and west Scotland (after B. Crawford, 1995).*

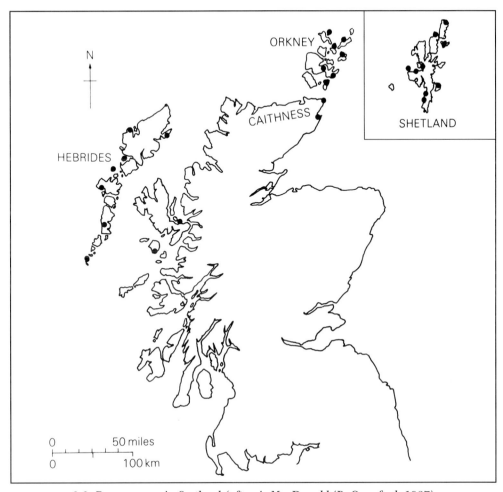

3.3 Papar *names in Scotland (after A. MacDonald/B. Crawford, 1987).*

consequent bilingualism, but also from being overlain by Gaelic. The overwhelmingly topographical nature of the mainland names has already been mentioned. In the Hebrides, it is clear that the greater part, if not all, of the Lewis landscape was renamed by the Norse, but the percentage of Norse to Gaelic names (in general terms) decreases from north to south and from the Outer to the Inner Hebrides, although there is a notable density of Norse names on the fertile islands of Coll and Tiree.

The Scandinavian place-names of south-west Scotland display connections with the Danelaw settlements of northern and eastern England and thus result from a separate phase of penetration, in the same way as the more scattered names of Scandinavian derivation in the south-east.

RUNIC INSCRIPTIONS

Another form of linguistic evidence is provided by inscriptions in Scandinavian runes, the only form of writing in use by the Norse settlers during the Viking period. However, most of the runic inscriptions from Scotland date to the Late Norse period, notably the massive collection at Maeshowe, in Orkney, and the eight scratched on the wall of St Molaise's Cave on Holy Island, by Lamlash Bay, on the east side of Arran. One of the latter states *Vígleikr stallari reist*, which is translated 'Vígleikr the [king's] marshall wrote'; this Vígleikr has been identified as one of King Hákon's commanders in his campaign of 1263, and it may well be that the others who left their names in the same cave also formed part of this expedition from Norway.

The largest group of runic inscriptions from Scotland (thirty-three in all) is that carved on stones which form part of the burial chamber in the great prehistoric mound at Maeshowe. These are, however, of twelfth-century date and tell us little of everyday life in Orkney, all or most of them having been carved by visitors, seemingly the Jerusalem-bound or home-coming crusaders who formed part of Earl Rognvald's expedition to the Holy Land in 1151–3. Indeed, the latest study of the Maeshowe texts, by Michael Barnes, concludes that 'most, if not all, are light-hearted medieval graffiti and that what they say is to be taken with a large pinch of salt'.

A recent listing of Scotland's runic inscriptions by Barnes (1992) has demonstrated Orkney's particular richness in this respect, even excluding Maeshowe, for a further fifteen have been recorded there as compared to only five in Shetland. Already, however, both totals have to be increased as a result of recent discoveries of fragmentary rune-stones: by two in the case of Orkney – one from Skaill, Sandwick (with two inscriptions on it), and the other from the island of Sanday – and one in Shetland, from the island of Noss. In addition, further inscriptions have been newly recognised on animal bones from Orphir in Orkney.

The runic inscriptions from Orkney and Shetland include the remains of several memorial stones, which are probably Christian, notably three fragments each from the Brough of Birsay, Orkney, and from Cunningsburgh in Shetland, although perhaps deriving from only two memorials in each case. There are runic graffiti on the prehistoric stones of the Ring of Brodgar (in the sort of 'twig-runes' used in Maeshowe), as well as some short inscriptions on portable artefacts. The latter are rarely informative: a seal's tooth pendant found at Birsay is inscribed *futhark*; a bone pin excavated at Westness, Rousay in Orkney, has only the a-rune repeated three times; and a steatite spindle-whorl from Orkney proclaims *Gautr reist rúnar*, that is 'Gautr wrote the runes'.

There are, in addition, several inscriptions now known from Orphir in Orkney. One of these is an incomplete stone which has generally been considered to be a graffito consisting of an impious reference to the round church there, but Barnes has recently suggested the more probable reading: 'No church is as pleasing to God as [this]'. The other published inscription from Orphir is on a piece of cattle rib from the Earl's Bu excavations; this seems to tell us, somewhat redundantly, that '. . . bone was in flesh . . .'! Another inscription has recently been identified on a cow's scapula and its reading is awaited.

On mainland Scotland there are now three rune-stones known from Caithness. The two published inscriptions are both from Thurso, one of which is on a cross found lying flat over an adult burial, stating that it had been made as an 'overlay' for a man called Ingolf (p. 69). A new (and as yet unread) find from Dunbeath is thus an important addition to this small corpus.

The only other mainland finds of genuine runic inscriptions are on two pieces of native metalwork, both of which are stray-finds. There is an unintelligible text on a lost crescent-shaped plaque, ornamented with Pictish symbols, from Laws, Monifieth, near Dundee, whereas the magnificent silver and gold, Irish-type, brooch found at Hunterston, Ayrshire, has inscribed on its reverse: *Melbrigda á stilk* (alongside some rune-like decoration). This means 'Melbrigda owns [this] brooch', but it must have been some two centuries old by the time it passed into his possession; interestingly, Melbrigda is a Celtic name even though he may be presumed to have been a Norse-speaker.

There are only three rune-stones from the west of Scotland, but each is of particular interest, not least because they are all specifically Christian memorials. The most complete is a cross-slab from the burial-ground of the ruined church of Kilbar, on the island of Barra in the Outer Hebrides (Figure 3.4). This was erected in memory of a woman called Thorgerd and, although its simple ornament is of somewhat degenerate character, it has similarities to the main Manx series. In contrast, a recumbent grave-slab on Iona copies another from the site (which in turn is most closely paralleled in Ireland), except for the addition of an inscription described as being 'purely Norwegian'; this states that 'Kali Olivsson laid this stone over [his] brother Fugl' (Figure 13.3). Finally, there is a small fragment of a cross-slab known from near the chapel on the small island of Inchmarnock, off the west coast of Bute; this displays the remains of a ringed cross carved in the same manner as those on the Manx monuments. The memorial formula on both the Kilbar and Inchmarnock stones includes the Celtic loan-word *kross*, as is the standard usage on Man, in place of the expected Norse word *steinn*, 'stone'.

These runic inscriptions constitute the only body of contemporary written sources left to us by the Norse settlers of Scandinavian Scotland, but their content tells us nothing of value of an historical nature – other than the simple fact that the knowledge of runes was one of the elements of Norse culture exported to the West. It is, however, notable that people in Scandinavian Scotland were using rune-stones as Christian memorials in two ways which were not common in Scandinavia at this period – by raising commemorative crosses and by laying a cross or slab over the dead. It would appear therefore that, as also on the Isle of Man, this represents a coming together of the Norse tradition for runic monuments with native traditions for Christian stone sculpture, but there are other stones dating to the Viking and Late Norse periods, without runic inscriptions, to be considered in Chapter 13.

DOCUMENTARY SOURCES

There are no Scandinavian documentary sources relevant to Scotland surviving from before the twelfth century. Indeed, there is little to be learnt from the documentary sources in general, whether the historical records (such as monastic annals) or the later saga literature, concerning the manner of the Norse land-taking and the nature of the settlement process. The Irish annals confine themselves to bald statements regarding raids on monasteries, such as that in the *Annals of Ulster* for 795: 'Devastation of Iona of Columcille, and of Inismurray and of Inisboffin'. From this must be conjured a picture of Vikings sailing down the west coast of Scotland *en route* to the west coast of Ireland, while some in that year are recorded as having raided both Skye and Rathlin Island, off the coast of Antrim.

3.4 Cross-slab from Kilbar, Barra, with a runic inscription on the back which reads: 'after Thorgerd, Steinar's daughter, this cross was raised' (NMS).

They were seemingly operating in the wake of the 'gentiles' who had the year before 'devastated all the islands of Britain'.

We are not told where these Vikings came from or whither they went with their booty. However, the finds of ecclesiastical loot already noted from Norway demonstrate that seasonal raiding parties were crossing the North Sea, but some scholars have assumed that 'raiding bases' were established in the Scottish islands as a prelude to permanent settlement.

For this there is no definite documentary or archaeological evidence, although such are known to have been established in Ireland during the 840s, and possibly as early as the 830s. It may as well be argued that it was the wealthy Norse settlers in the Northern and Western Isles, who were powerful enough to have wrested control over major settlements from the native population, who continued to participate in raids as they had done previously from their homelands.

The Irish annals have nothing to tell of Orkney, but there is one tantalising reference in the *Vita* or 'Life' of St Findan, an Irishman in the continental monastery at Rheinau, who in his youth, towards or about 840, had been carried off from Ireland by Vikings. He escaped from them in Orkney, being taken in by an abbot who had studied in Ireland and spoke his language. This is important evidence for the existence of a native monastery in Orkney at the time of the Norse incursions (but not the only evidence for the survival of Christianity). But did Findan escape from a Viking 'raiding base' or a 'permanent settlement'? The evidence of archaeology is such as to suggest that this event belongs to the period when actual settlement was taking place. It is also not far removed in time from an entry in the Frankish *Annals of St Bertin*, for 847, relating to the Western Isles: 'The Scotti, after being attacked by the Northmen for very many years, were rendered tributary and [the Northmen] took possession, without resistance, of the islands that lie all around and dwelt there.'

If we could trust the medieval Icelandic *Eyrbyggia saga*, then we could identify the conqueror of the Hebrides with Ketil Flatnose, who probably flourished around the mid-ninth century, despite saga-belief in his association with King Harald Finehair of Norway: 'After having landed in the west, Ketil fought a number of battles, and won them all. He conquered and took charge of the Hebrides, making peace and alliances with all the leading men there in the west.'

This suggestion of 'peace and alliances' contrasts with an interesting reference to the settlement of the Northern Isles contained in the late twelfth-century *Historia Norvegiæ* (in Anderson's translation):

> Certain pirates, of the family of the most vigorous prince Ronald, set out with a great fleet, and crossed the Solundic sea; and stripped these races (the Picts and the Papae) of their ancient settlements, destroyed them wholly, and subdued the islands to themselves.

It is, admittedly, hard to know how much credence to give to this traditional version of the total destruction which was supposed to have taken place some three centuries earlier, given that it was the same author who thought that the Picts 'were little more than pygmies in stature' and that they had to lurk underground at midday in order to conserve their strength! In general, however, it accounts for the fact that the earls of Orkney were of the family of Earl Rognvald of Møre (about 860) and, for various reasons, it is these days preferred to the saga traditions which attribute the imposition of Norse rule to King Harald Finehair at the end of the century.

The lack of contemporary documentary evidence relating directly to Orkney during the Viking and Late Norse periods is brought to an end with the writing of what is now known as *Orkneyinga saga* – an Icelandic history of the earls of Orkney, composed about 1200, incorporating a life of St Magnus, which is also known separately. It is of fundamental importance as a source for events in the earldom of Orkney during the twelfth century, but for the Viking period proper its contribution is debatable and needs careful historical interpretation, as do all the other references to the Norse in (or from) Scotland to be found elsewhere in the medieval saga literature. Such is beyond the scope of this archaeological study and, in any case, a detailed introduction to these sources is readily available in Barbara Crawford's book, *Scandinavian Scotland* (1987).

ORAL TRADITION

A remarkable body of Scottish Gaelic oral tradition has survived into the twentieth century, some part of which relates to the Vikings and other Norse themes. Its content cannot, however, be taken at face value as a straightforward form of historical source material. For instance, the heroic ballads and legends containing a 'Viking' element are set within a marvellous and magical world. Other legends are told as if factual, but are largely confined to accounts of raiding and plundering (or just possibly of punitive raids from Norway), for which there is no supporting evidence. As a result, D. A. MacDonald has stressed, 'it is, by and large, a thankless task to seek for much in the way of factual historical evidence in stories of this kind'.

One particular difficulty is that stories containing convincing local detail may well have been invented to explain the existence of particular topographical features (such as mounds) or of place-names. An unconvincing, but nevertheless entertaining, example of the latter has been provided by D. A. MacDonald, quoting an anecdote recorded on North Uist in 1971, concerning the name Cearsabhagh, which was probably once used for the whole of its port now known as Lochmaddy, even though it has since become confined to only one part of the bay. The story was that a number of Viking ships had got caught in a mist and been grounded, with the result that the crews had had to wade ashore, when one of the Vikings supposedly remarked: *Tha sinn cearr 'sa' bhàgh* (or 'We've got the wrong bay') – hence Cearsabhagh! A more scientific interpretation of this name has since been offered by Hermann Pálsson, who suggests that it derives from the Old Norse *Hjartavágr*, meaning 'Deer bay'.

For Orkney, the folklorist Bo Almqvist has accepted, as 'an old and genuine Norse tradition', a legend of contacts between the Picts and the Vikings, one version of which has been translated by him from an article by Jakob Jakobsen (1911), as follows:

> On Rousay it is told, according to Duncan Robertson, Kirkwa, that the first Vikings who came to the island did not dare to land, because of beings looking like elves or trolls who stood in front of them with shining spears.

This legend seems to reflect a tradition of initial conflict, but once again it would be a misuse of folklore to attempt to deduce specific facts from it. Indeed, as noted above, the idea that the Picts in Orkney had been 'little more than pygmies in stature' is to be found already in the late twelfth-century *Historia Norvegiæ*. In general, we should do well to be guided by Alan Bruford, who has concluded that

> If the distribution of local, and therefore locally prized, legends is any guide, Orkney and even Shetland are now less part of a Norse cultural province than of a Scottish one,

and there are indications that they fit best to a pattern involving movement, either way, along the Atlantic seaboard from Ireland to Iceland.

ARCHAEOLOGY

The archaeological material for Scandinavian Scotland can be broadly divided into three categories of artefactual, structural and environmental evidence. Many of the older finds are poorly recorded and much recent research is only gradually making its way into print, while chance-finds inevitably continue to be made (largely as a result of coastal erosion).

The artefactual evidence derives from various contexts, from pagan Norse graves, from treasure hoards, from settlement sites and from stray-finds of single objects. Acceptable references to the discovery of Viking period burials and hoards in Scotland extend back to the seventeenth century, but all too few have been recovered in the twentieth century with the aid of modern archaeological techniques. Our surveys of this material have therefore to make much use of antiquarian sources to provide the fullest possible picture of these categories of evidence for the origins, nature and extent of Norse settlement and for the wealth which the settlers acquired, as measured in silver and gold.

The first systematic survey of the Norse artefactual evidence from Scotland was undertaken during the second half of the nineteenth century by Joseph Anderson, who was Keeper of the National Museum of Antiquities of Scotland from 1869–1913. More recently, the majority of the known artefactual evidence was surveyed in 1925, during a two-month period, by the distinguished Norwegian archaeologist, Sigurd Grieg. Grieg's catalogue, entitled *Viking Antiquities in Scotland*, was published in 1940 (in Oslo), as Volume II of *Viking Antiquities in Great Britain and Ireland*, edited by Professor Haakon Shetelig. Although this major work has remained the starting-point for all subsequent discussion of the material from Scotland, it has long been recognised that it contains numerous misprints, duplications and other errors. There is now, in any case, a further seventy years of discoveries which need to be taken into account – most particularly in the realm of settlement archaeology.

The work of recataloguing the silver and gold hoards and single-finds has recently been completed by James Graham-Campbell (1995). Some few of the latter consist of personal ornaments buried as pagan Norse grave-goods, but there are, in all, about thirty-six (or more) actual hoards known from Scotland, which were deposited during the period c. 850–1200. No precise total can be given because of the uncertain nature of some of the early records and the fact that various old finds ended up in the melting-pot. Most of these hoards, although not all, are to be attributed to Norse activity so that their nature and contents are discussed separately below (in Chapter 12).

A new study of the pagan Norse graves is in progress which means that the summary of the burial material presented here is inevitably provisional, just as the future publication of recent excavations will modify, and thus supersede, our account of the archaeology of some of the Norse settlement-sites. A recent notional estimate puts the overall figure at about 130 pagan Norse graves from Scotland, from about half as many sites, for some are family cemeteries. This number does not seem very large (there being over 300 known from Iceland, for instance), but it seems probable that pagan burial practices were abandoned after only a generation or two in some areas and had completely ceased well before the 'official' conversion of the Earldom of Orkney attributed to Olaf Tryggvason at the end of the tenth century.

There are only a small number of cremations known from Scandinavian Scotland and thus the great majority of these Norse burials consists of clothed inhumations, with or without the additional accompaniment of grave-goods. Unfortunately, most of these are old finds which were poorly recorded, and the only cemetery to have been excavated in its entirety in modern times has yet to be published in full. Nevertheless, the burials and their contents provide an outstanding source of archaeological data of primary importance for the study of the settlement period and, as such, they form the basis for the regional archaeological surveys in Chapters 4–6. Some of the most interesting and better documented of the individual graves and cemeteries have been selected for fuller discussion in Chapter 7, with their interpretation considered in Chapter 8.

An additional category of artefactual evidence, which did not form part of Grieg's remit, is that of stone sculpture – in the form of memorial stones (as already touched upon above, under 'Runic inscriptions'). Indeed, there still exists no overall synthesis of this material for Scandinavian Scotland during our period, although there are some regional studies. On the other hand, the series of impressive hogback tombstones, which originated in the Danelaw territory of northern England during the tenth century, has been fully catalogued by James Lang.

The first excavations of Viking/Late Norse period settlements did not take place until the 1930s, apart from some eighteenth- and nineteenth-century fossicking at Earl's Bu, Orphir, in Orkney. The first Viking period farmstead to be discovered in Scotland was in 1934, at Sumburgh in Shetland, on the site for which Sir Walter Scott had invented the name 'Jarlshof'. Since then only a couple of other Norse sites have been excavated in Shetland, although new research is in progress. The majority of Norse settlements so far known from Scandinavian Scotland have been found in Orkney, but no more than about a dozen sites in all, which have seen varying degrees of excavation and publication. Only one site with structural evidence has yet been excavated on mainland Scotland, that overlooking Freswick Bay in Caithness, and some five or six in the Western Isles (poorly excavated or, as yet, unpublished), all of which are located in the Outer Hebrides. In consequence, we have no uniform picture of the nature and development of Norse settlement-sites in Scotland, for there exists neither a full geographical coverage in the distribution of excavated sites nor an even chronological spread of the evidence.

However, the excavation of settlement sites, and their associated middens, has greatly increased the archaeological database in recent years. Apart from the fundamental importance of the new environmental evidence for the economy of Scandinavian Scotland, during the Viking and Late Norse periods, our knowledge of the nature and variety of the Norse artefactual material has also increased dramatically (as, for example, concerning the manufacture and use of pottery: cf. Figure 3.5).

Overall, therefore, the archaeological evidence for Scandinavian Scotland is variable in its quantity and suffers from sundry limitations as to its quality. However, the above categories of material, together with the environmental data introduced below, are those which necessarily form the main basis for this survey, with the addition of a brief account (in Chapter 13) of the few standing buildings which survive today from the Late Norse period.

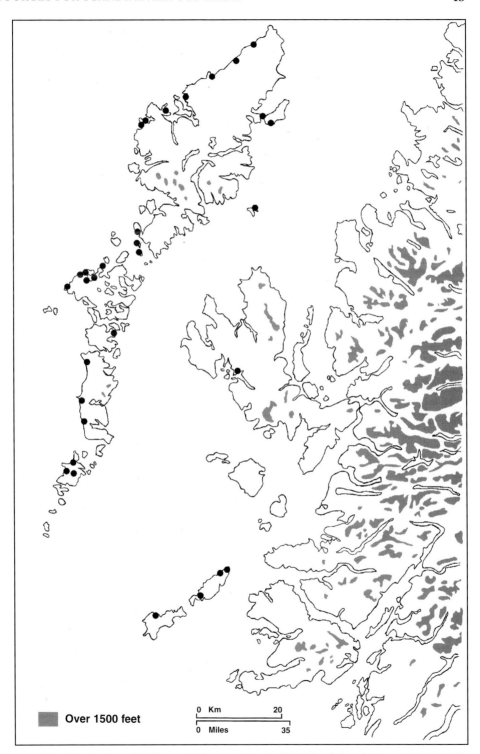

3.5 The distribution of Viking period pottery in the Hebrides (after A. Lane, 1983/1990).

ENVIRONMENTAL

The study of the Norse exploitation of the natural resources of Scandinavian Scotland has undergone rapid development during the last twenty-five years of settlement excavation. Earlier excavators of settlement-sites naturally collected animal bones, but were more concerned with establishing and dating structural sequences than with studying the contents of middens. For instance, barely more than a page is devoted to all the Viking/Late Norse period bones in the original (1954) report on the excavations at Jarlshof. To-day the excavation of middens is an established aspect of archaeology in itself, with fine-sieving and flotation techniques being used routinely for the recovery of even the smallest bones of such as rodents and fishes, as well as of carbonised grain (barley and oats) and other plant seeds (Figure 3.6). Research is now also undertaken into invertebrate fauna, for fossil insect remains (such as lice) can reveal much about the living conditions of humans and their domestic animals. Column samples are taken for the botanical study of pollen, establishing sequences revealing episodes of land clearance and crop cultivation.

Animals and plants were introduced to Scotland from Scandinavia during the Viking period, if not perhaps on the scale that was necessary in Iceland, but one major new crop seems to have been flax. Not all such introductions were necessarily deliberate, however, as is suggested by the modern distribution of different races of field mice of which there are distinct forms on eleven Hebridean islands, as well as St Kilda, and on three of the Shetland group. All these field mice are more like those of Norway than of mainland Britain, suggesting that they arrived as accidental passengers amongst the supplies on board Viking ships.

THE PEOPLE

Few well-preserved Viking/Late Norse period human skeletons have been excavated and there is no published synthesis of the little evidence which does exist. A cemetery at Newark Bay, Deerness, Orkney, containing about 250 individuals, is the only extensive one to have been excavated to which a Late Viking/Late Norse period date has been attributed, but only some preliminary statistics have been published to date. Adult life expectancy (at 20) was 40.4 years for males and 38.1 for females, but infant mortality was exceptionally high, with an estimated 260 deaths per 1000 at 0–1 year. These figures bring to mind both the wealthy woman buried in the cemetery on Cnip headland, Isle of Lewis, who is thought to have been aged between 35 and 40 years at death, and the woman buried in the Viking period cemetery at Westness, Rousay, Orkney, with a full-term infant, who had presumably died at childbirth. At the same time, they emphasise the exceptional longevity of the woman in the boat-grave at Scar, Sanday, Orkney, who died possibly in her seventies, when she was buried with a man probably in his thirties and a child of about ten. The other six burials to have been excavated at Cnip consist of two adult males and one female (all over thirty) and three children (one aged about six years, one of six–nine months and the other new-born), but the extent of this cemetery is not known. At Newark Bay, Deerness, the mean male height was 171.1 cm (5 ft 7¼ in) which, although short by modern standards, is comparable to that of pre-World War II Norwegians at 171.9 cm (5 ft 7½ in); the Cnip adults have been described as being of 'small

3.6 Environmental archaeologists sieving midden material for the recovery of small bones and carbonised seeds (C. E. Batey).

stature', the wealthy woman measuring only 160 cm (5 ft 3 in). On the other hand, St Magnus is estimated to have been an impressive 176.5 cm (5 ft 9½ in) and the man in the Scar boat-burial an exceptional 181 cm (5 ft 11 in), with the man buried in the mid-tenth century at Buckquoy, in Orkney, seemingly measuring between the two of them (5 ft 9 in to 5 ft 11 in). The bones identified as those of St Magnus were found in the south pier of the choir of St Magnus's Cathedral, Kirkwall, in 1919; the skull is damaged in a manner consistent with the saga account of his death, when Magnus requested that he be struck on the head rather than beheaded 'like a thief' (Figure 3.7).

There is much more to be deduced from skeletal remains than simply the sex, age and height of the deceased. As an example, it has been written (by Brothwell, Tills and Muir) about the Norse population at Newark Bay that they:

> had relatively good oral health, but joint (rheumatic) disease was clearly a problem and was advanced in various larger joints in some individuals . . . Of special note in the Deerness Norse is the fact that leprosy had probably arrived on the islands via Scandinavia by the 10th century (on the evidence of one skull). Large parasites, in the form of tapeworm, were probably affecting 2.0% of the early Newark people, a figure based on the occurrence of calcified echinococcus cysts in two individuals.

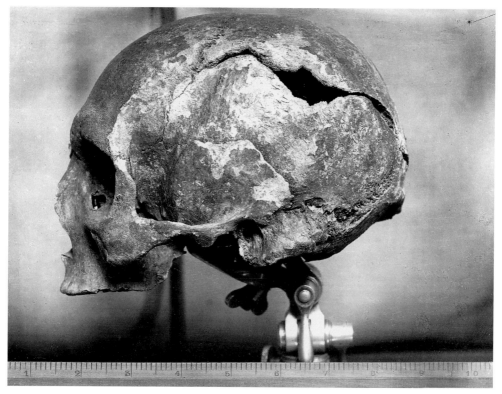

3.7 Side-view of the presumed skull of St Magnus, displaying damage consistent with the saga account of his death (Orkney Library, Photographic Archive).

Just as the study of modern mice can reveal the Norse ancestry of some, so also can that of the modern human population of what was Scandinavian Scotland. However, this is a complex area of investigation and the study of biological characteristics, such as pigmentation and blood groups, 'suggests some affinities between Orcadian and Scandinavian, but interesting differences'. The main problem of interpretation is not knowing to what extent such differences are attributable to the survival of pre-Norse genes in the community rather than to the intrusion of more recent Scottish ones. On the other hand, the gene frequencies of modern Norwegians will also have undergone modification since the Viking period, further complicating any such comparisons between the two countries.

Chapter 4

REGIONAL SURVEY PART I:
NORTHERN SCOTLAND

Doubt has been cast above on the idea that the Vikings who raided Ireland during the first thirty years of the ninth century were operating from 'pirate settlements' which they had established primarily for this purpose in the Northern and Western Isles of Scotland. Conversely, it has recently been suggested that the first permanent Scandinavian presence in the Northern Isles was not the result of any such form of forcible land-taking, but came about instead through peaceful penetration. Such is considered to have resulted in a period of integration or co-existence between Picts and Norse, with the settlers adopting initially a Pictish life-style. Only later, with the imposition of Norse rule, is it supposed that they chose to express their Scandinavian ethnic identity through such things as costume and burial practices. This hypothesis has found no more general acceptance than the former, in the light of our present archaeological knowledge. Indeed, Alfred Smyth has commented, in relation to the Irish annals, that 'these records of the earliest attacks strongly suggest that the Norwegians did not gradually infiltrate the Northern Isles as farmers and fisherman and then suddenly turn nasty against their neighbours'.

It is the case, however, that no one pattern of events accounts for the nature and extent of the Scandinavian presence in Scotland. The purpose of Chapters 4–6 is to review the archaeological evidence on a regional basis, concentrating for the most part on the events of the ninth and tenth centuries, beginning with northern Scotland – that is Orkney and Shetland, taken together with Caithness and Sutherland (Figure 4.1).

ORKNEY

The archaeological and place-name evidence for the overwhelming nature of the Scandinavian impact on Orkney and Shetland during the Viking period – as well as the historical evidence for the creation of the Norse Earldom of Orkney – has already been introduced. In fact, its quantity and quality is such that it constitutes the greater part of what is known about the Viking period archaeology of Scotland, with the result that it provides the main content of the later thematic chapters on burials, settlements and silver hoards. In this survey, it is not therefore necessary to do more than outline its range and nature; this will, however, serve to emphasise the prominent position enjoyed by Orkney, in particular, in the political and economic affairs of Scandinavian Scotland.

The fertile Orkney archipelago boasts the largest concentration of pagan Norse graves from any region of Scandinavian Scotland, including several cemeteries which are more

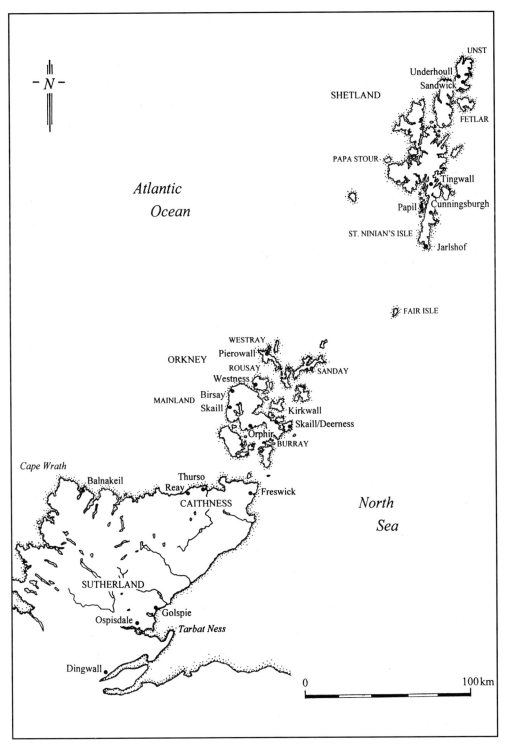

4.1 Map of the Northern Isles, Caithness and Sutherland: places mentioned in the text.

fully described in Chapter 7. The most notable of these is situated beside the Bay of Pierowall, at the northern end of Westray, which is the best harbour in the north of Orkney, lying on the route to and from Shetland – and other points north. Pierowall is to be identified with the appropriately named *Hofn* or 'Haven', mentioned in *Orkneyinga saga*, where there was said to be a *thorp* in the twelfth century, a settlement presumed to be akin to a village (Figure 7.8).

Evidence for a second pagan Norse cemetery on Westray is contained in the *New Statistical Account* (1841), which refers to 'the number of graves found in two extensive fields, one in the north and the other in the south of Westray', both of which had produced 'swords' and 'articles of dress'. Some other circumstantial evidence suggests that this southern cemetery may have been on the Links of Tuquoy and thus not far distant from an eroding Late Norse and medieval farm/church site, with some indications of earlier features, which has been partially investigated by Olwyn Owen.

The pagan Norse cemetery at Westness, on Rousay (pp. 135–8), shows continuity of use from its Pictish predecessor and includes two ninth-century boat-burials of well-equipped Vikings, as well as the richest grave of a Norse woman yet excavated in Scotland (Figure 7.11). This cemetery is situated on the headland of Moaness, beside the Bay of Swandro, where Sigrid Kaland has excavated a Late Norse farmstead, with a noust (boat-house) situated on the opposite side of the headland to the cemetery. A fine sword is also known from one or more graves which were found in the nineteenth century, in a field beside the Knowe of Swandro, near the excavated farm buildings, so that there is ample burial evidence for there also having been a primary Norse settlement in the immediate vicinity. Westness features in *Orkneyinga saga* because Earl Paul was staying with Sigurd of Westness when he was kidnapped in 1136, while out otter-hunting.

Several pagan Norse burials are known from the fertile island of Sanday, but with one exception these are old and poorly-recorded finds. The recent discovery, in 1991, was through coastal erosion at Scar; this is a high-status burial in the form of a boat-grave which contained three bodies, those of an elderly woman, a man and a child (see pp. 138–40). Another boat-grave may have been found at South Mires, in the 1790s, containing a sword, spear and shield, but the weapons are lost and the find is known only from a single reference.

A recent reassessment by Raymond Lamb has suggested the possible existence of a Viking period cemetery on the Ness of Brough, a small promontory on the north coast of Sanday, although some further information has since come to light and the Ness has recently been investigated by the BBC's 'Time Team'. On its southern tip, at a place known as the Styes of Brough, are four widely-spaced mounds some of which may have covered burials, but they have clearly been disturbed. It can, however, be confirmed that a poorly preserved sword (in the Hunterian Museum, Glasgow) was found in the nineteenth century, beside a skeleton, in a 'mound called Styes'. On the other hand, the Styes provenance given to a lost 'cauldron' is best considered unreliable; this object, which may well have been a shield-boss, was originally described as a helmet because it was said to have had a skull lying in it. Finally, a lost axe which has also been attributed to Styes in the past is now known to have been found elsewhere in Sanday, in 1866, as part of the contents of a grave which eroded out on the shore at Newark.

Amongst other burials recorded from Sanday are two found at or near the 'Broch of

Lamaness', which is identified with the headland of Lamba Ness across a small bay from the Norse settlement at Pool, excavated by John Hunter, where the incoming Vikings established themselves on the site of a Pictish farmstead (pp. 171–3). The first Lamba Ness burial was found in 1878 and is male, with sword, spear and axe; the apparent absence of a shield from this weapon-kit may be explained by one report, which seems to be referring to the same grave, that there was 'the remnant of a helmet' which 'crumbled into dust'. The other burial is of particular interest in that it is unusual for Scotland in being a cremation. A 'deposit of burnt bones was found about the centre of a mound', together with a pair of oval brooches, a bronze ringed-pin, a lignite arm-ring and an amber bead. The chance discovery of a ninth-century oval brooch and three beads at Braeswick, a short distance to the south, suggests the location of a further female burial in this same vicinity.

In general, there is a lack of primary Norse burials associated with settlement-sites which would help to illuminate the initial stage of Scandinavian land-taking. Such, for instance, is a disappointing gap in our knowledge of the Birsay Bay area, on mainland Orkney, despite all the archaeological activity which has taken place there since the 1930s. Pictish, Viking and Late Norse structures, middens and burials are strung out around the Bay of Birsay, focusing on a small tidal island off its north-west tip, known as the Brough of Birsay (Figure 4.2), which historical evidence implies was an earldom seat (as described in Chapters 9 and 10). The first bishop's seat on Orkney was established at Birsay by Earl Thorfinn.

There are no pagan Norse graves known from the Brough of Birsay itself and thus no apparent continuity of burial there from the Pictish period. There is, however, a single late inhumation at the site of Buckquoy, from the top of a settlement-mound, and it has been suggested that a small number of other mounds in the vicinity, on the Point of Buckquoy, may also cover Viking period burials. Some further burials have been excavated by Christopher Morris immediately to the south in the Red Craig area (Brough Road site). Finally, in the village of Birsay, a cist-grave containing just a bronze ringed-pin eroded out on the shore, by the church, in the nineteenth century; the pin belongs to a popular and long-lived Hiberno-Norse type, dating anywhere from the tenth to the mid-eleventh century, suggesting that this is most probably to be considered as a Christian burial.

At Buckquoy, the grave was dug into the mound created by a build-up of settlement from the Pictish to Viking periods, the latter consisting of a two-phase Norse farmstead (pp. 160–4). This plough-damaged burial was that of a man, aged 'in excess of 40 years' and 5ft 9in to 5ft 11in in height, who had been placed on his right side in a crouched position. He was accompanied by a spear, knife and whetstone, a bronze ringed-pin of the same Hiberno-Norse type as that from the Birsay Village grave, an iron buckle and a fragmentary bone mount with iron rivets, together with a cut silver halfpenny of the Anglo-Saxon king, Eadmund (939–46). Other graves found at Buckquoy consist of an undated cist-burial, lacking grave-goods, and a disarticulated neonatal from under the floor of the later of the two Norse farmsteads (a possible foundation ritual?), although the excavator, Anna Ritchie, noted that 'individual bones of babies were found elsewhere on the site, perhaps betraying a hardline philosophy towards infant mortality'.

The simple cist-grave found on Area 1 of the Brough Road site, during the excavation of Viking period middens and associated settlement remains, was that of a male, aged 50–60

4.2 *Aerial view of the Bay of Birsay, overlooking the village (Beachview, the parish church and sixteenth-century Earl's Palace), towards the line of the Brough Road (with Buckquoy) which leads to the Brough of Birsay in the background (G. Moberg).*

years, who suffered from a severe mouth infection and osteoarthritis of the spine. He was accompanied by a distinctive antler comb, dating to the ninth or tenth century. A fragmentary female burial was recovered nearby, from Area 2; she was in her fifties at her death which was caused by a blow to the base of her skull, although she too was suffering generally from poor health. Other isolated bone fragments were recovered in the immediate vicinity which must represent additional burials, but the actual number is unknown. The discovery of burials in a developing midden is perhaps somewhat unexpected, as it suggests a degree of disregard for the dead. It is, however, not without parallel elsewhere; for example, parts of the skull of 'a young person, probably female' were found in a midden of the Norse settlement at Jarlshof, Shetland. This Viking period burial practice may simply be a variant on the well-documented usage of existing mounds for this purpose in Scandinavian Scotland.

The Brough of Birsay carries a palimpsest of structures, both secular and ecclesiastical, not all of which have been excavated. Their number, variety and sequence together make the Brough a site of exceptional importance, however atypical, for our understanding of Orkney's standing in Scandinavian Scotland. There are rich and varied finds, including imports which reveal contacts with Scandinavia, the Irish Sea Vikings and Anglo-Saxon England, but manufacturing evidence was notably slight for such a high-status site, although not all of it has been excavated and part has already been lost to the sea.

The other major bay on the west coast of mainland Orkney is the Bay of Skaill, in the parish of Sandwick, where a handful of ill-recorded Norse graves is known, as well as a couple of fragmentary runestones. One of the better documented burials found in the nineteenth century was that of a man in a cist-grave, which was covered with slabs and a heap of water-worn boulders, forming a simple cairn. Such primary cairns are not commonly associated with pagan Norse burials in Scandinavian Scotland, but may well have been overlooked in the past given that so many investigated sites had first been denuded through erosion – or may just not have been recorded when the grave was an accidental discovery. In this case, the inhumation was accompanied by a spear, knife and whetstone, with a fine comb in a case, a possible arrow-head and an iron rivet. The leg-bone of a horse, some bones of small animals and birds, and the jaw-bone of a fish were also recovered, but these do not necessarily represent offerings to the dead man, for the construction of the grave may have taken place in a midden, as on the Brough Road site at Birsay. Indeed, it has been independently suggested that the location of the cist-grave was the top of a prominent settlement mound which is now eroding into the sea.

Two further long-cist burials near the shore of Skaill Bay were encountered by Gordon Childe during his excavation of the nearby prehistoric settlement of Skara Brae; both were described by him as 'intrusive'. Neither burial contained any grave-goods, but Childe argued that the north–south orientation of the one intact skeleton was 'in favour of a pre-Christian date' and observed that it agreed 'with that prevailing in Viking graves both in this country and in Norway'. However, an apparently isolated long-cist burial, oriented NNW–SSE, which was exposed in 1977 through coastal erosion at Sandside, Graemsay, has been radiocarbon dated to the calibrated range of AD 960–1300. In addition, it is no longer considered safe to suppose that any 'prevailing' orientation can be established among the pagan Norse graves of Scotland, given that the many poor records mean that it is impossible to generalise on this matter with any degree of confidence.

No farmstead has yet been discovered at Skaill to match its primary Norse settlement name, although had it been situated by the shore it might well, by now, have been removed by coastal erosion in the manner of the settlement mound mentioned above which contains structural elements. Skaill is, however, the find-place of the largest silver hoard known from the Viking period in Scotland, containing over 8kg of brooches, rings, coins and hack-silver (Figure 12.3).

One further pagan Norse grave from Sandwick parish worth mentioning is a poorly recorded nineteenth-century find from a mound at Lyking. This is of particular interest in being a cremation, but the only grave-goods recovered with the burnt bones were a spear-head, a comb and an iron buckle (Figure 4.3).

A further possible cremation is represented by a curious find from the Knowe of Moan, Harray, where a small cist – only 18in square – was associated with an Hiberno-Saxon mount and sixty-four beads (fifty-five glass, eight amber and one cornelian). A cist opened at Greenigoe, Orphir, in about 1889, was found to contain two beads (one amber and one glass), together with some fragments of woollen cloth, although no traces of bones were visible. The cloth includes one highly distinctive piece in the form of a fine worsted

4.3 Grave-goods from a pagan Norse burial at Lyking, Sandwick, Orkney (NMS).

diamond twill; this type is abundant in Viking period graves in Norway, where it was probably being made, but it is known from only one other grave in Scotland, a wealthy female burial at Cnip on Lewis.

On the east coast the site of another Skaill, in the parish of Deerness, has been partially excavated, where it was found that the Norse farmstead had displaced a native Pictish settlement (pp. 168–71). Another site on mainland Orkney that had been in native occupation for many centuries by the period of Scandinavian settlement is that of the Brough of Gurness, at Aikerness in Evie. Here a number of pagan Norse graves must have been located in and around the settlement mound, although with one exception, that of a woman wearing oval brooches and an amuletic neck-ring (Figure 8.2), these had been badly disturbed (pp. 127–9); the remains of the farmstead itself are vestigial. Near to Gurness is Tingwall, one of Orkney's *thing* places.

Other broch mounds which were used for Norse burial on mainland Orkney may include that of Howe, near Stromness, which produced a glass linen smoother in the nineteenth century, although no further artefacts which might be indicative of Viking period burials have been recognised from this site, despite extensive excavation in the late 1970s–80s. On the other hand, the suggestion that the prehistoric chambered tomb of

Maeshowe was entered and reused for the burial of a Viking warrior lacks conviction, although burnt material from turf within a rebuild of its encircling bank has been radio-carbon dated to the Viking period. The reason for this rebuild is unknown (as is its actual date), but it is possible that the great mound was chosen as a pagan cult-place – or it might well have been the site of an unrecorded *thing*, given its central location. Its Old Norse name of *Orkahaugr* does not help much in this respect because it seems to mean 'the howe (or mound) of the Orcs', with the latter being the tribal name preserved in the name of Orkney itself.

One further pagan Norse grave from Orkney Mainland is represented by the nine-teenth-century find of what must have been a male burial near the manse in the parish of Rendall. The contents of this grave are known only from a sketch of an Insular drinking-horn terminal, dated 1861, when it was noted as having been found with an 'iron cup' (presumably a shield-boss), as well as 'other fragments of iron'. Finally, there are two Viking period burials to be noted from individual mounds, at Stenness and Sandwick, both of which contained only a ringed-pin. If not actually Christian, these graves should at least be attributed to the period during which the use of grave-goods was in decline.

None of the pagan Norse graves in Orkney looks as if it is to be dated any earlier than the mid-ninth century and amongst the latest such graves must be the male burial at Buckquoy, on the Bay of Birsay, which contained a cut halfpenny of Eadmund (939–46). Pagan burial, with grave-goods, would therefore appear to have lasted at most for a period of about a hundred years, but the practice was doubtless variously abandoned by families and communities in different parts of the islands. Indeed, it was suggested above that a tradition of Christianity continued unbroken in Orkney, even if in an attenuated way, despite the paganism of the Norse ruling elite which lasted until the conversion of Earl Sigurd in 995.

Christian Norse burials are as difficult to recognise in Orkney as elsewhere, given the lack of grave-goods. At the site of Saevar Howe, on the Bay of Birsay, there is a Christian long-cist cemetery thought to date to the later Viking period, as the graves are superim-posed on some Viking period dwellings. Some broch-sites were also used for unaccom-panied burials including Oxtro, Birsay, where an unstratified ringed-pin has been found; also in the nineteenth century, a couple of secondary burials were excavated from the Broch of Burgar, Evie – the hiding-place of a remarkable (lost) Pictish treasure of silver vessels, ornaments and amber beads. Burials at Colli Ness, on Sanday, a possible broch-site occupied by a later chapel, included one with a gold ring (now lost), which might well have been of Late Norse date. However, the most important group of Norse Christian burials yet to have been excavated consists of the cemetery at Newark Bay, Deerness, which was mentioned above (pp. 50 and 52).

Further evidence for Christian burial takes the form of runestone memorials from the Brough of Birsay and Tuquoy, as well as such grave-markers as the eleventh/twelfth-century hogback stones (described below, p. 100) of which four are known from Orkney Mainland: Kirkwall (2), Skaill in Deerness parish, and a lost stone from the parish of Rendall (likened to that from Skaill). A twelfth-century hogback descendant, or 'kindred monument', is preserved in the graveyard of the church of St Boniface on Papa Westray.

The splendid tenth-century treasure from Skaill Bay has already been mentioned as the largest on record from Viking period Scotland, but Orkney also boasts the second heaviest such silver hoard, that from the island of Burray. This contained about 2 kg of silver, which was buried c. 997–1010, part in an alderwood vessel. The Burray hoard consists chiefly of plain penannular arm-rings and fragments of the standardised type known as 'ring-money' (pp. 238–9). Such material forms the normal contents, with or without coins, of the later tenth- and eleventh-century hoards from Scandinavian Scotland, including two other Orkney treasures: the oldest such find on record, dug up before 1688 and long since lost, which consisted of nine rings from a mound beside the Ring of Brodgar; and that found at Caldale in 1774 which was deposited c. 1032–40 (Figure 4.4).

Other Viking period finds of precious metal from Orkney include four gold finger-rings from Stenness (Figure 12.5) and a couple of (lost) gold arm-rings from the Broch of Burgar. Amongst the rich and varied material recovered during the excavations on the Brough of Birsay are four coins and three pieces of hack-silver, together with a fragment of gold; another such fragment is reported from the farmstead at Westness, in Rousay, as well as a silver finger-ring.

The six Orkney hoards, together with the single-finds of coins (nine in all) and other pieces of silver and gold, represent by far the largest concentration of such wealth in any part of Scandinavian Scotland. It is scarcely surprising therefore to find that the earldom had the resources in the Late Norse period to invest in stone architecture. Major secular and ecclesiastical buildings were both being erected in the twelfth century, but the most notable is the great Romanesque Cathedral which was begun by Earl Rognvald in 1137, to house the relics of St Magnus and to provide a new seat for the Orkney bishopric, in the developing market-centre of Kirkwall (Chapter 13).

Important Late Norse secular structures have been investigated on Orkney Mainland, not just at Birsay (both on the Brough and around the Bay at 'Beachview'), but also at Earl's Bu, Orphir, including a horizontal water-mill, and at Skaill in Deerness. These are described in Chapter 10, together with the excavated sites of Tuquoy, on Westray, and Westness, on Rousay.

The quantity of archaeological evidence for the Viking and Late Norse periods in Orkney, including that of the runic inscriptions for the latter, dominates the totality of this aspect of our knowledge of Scandinavian Scotland. Yet, even so, it is lacking in numerous respects. For instance, it is clear that Orkney Mainland is under-represented in the archaeological record in terms of pagan Norse burials. This may well be partly the result of inadequate recording in the past, for some graves are likely to have been disturbed by the extensive ploughing activity on the islands – and others will certainly have been lost through coastal erosion. At any rate, this situation would not appear to be due to a lack of modern fieldwork, for Orkney has benefited greatly during the last twenty-five years from a concentration of fieldwork resources, as demanded by its wealth of archaeological remains.

Other problems to be encountered in the interpretation of the Orkney evidence include the unrepresentative nature of the majority of excavated sites, which are mostly of high status, as well as the lack of any overall geographical coverage. In consequence, it must be emphasised that we are hardly yet in a position to present other than a generalised picture of this formative and dynamic period in Orkney's history, when its strategic position on the northern sea-routes, combined with its natural resources, enabled it to develop into a centre of considerable political and economic standing. That such limitations exist even

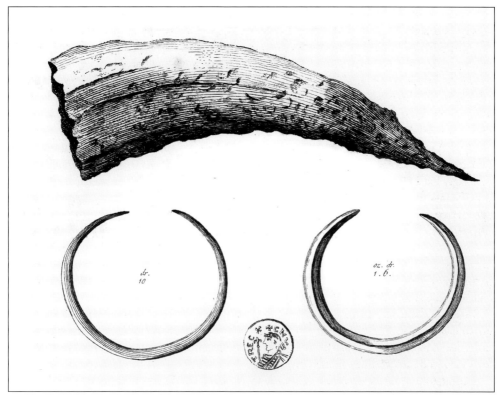

4.4 'Ring-money' and a coin of Cnut from the Caldale hoard, Orkney, with one of its two cattle horn containers (after R. Gough, 1778).

for Orkney means that we can do little more than sketch in an outline of the Viking period archaeology for the rest of Scandinavian Scotland.

SHETLAND

In comparison to Orkney, Shetland offered more restricted scope for Viking period settlement because environmental factors restricted the land suitable for use by Norse farmers, even when their mixed agricultural economy was supplemented with some fishing. In the absence of timber, peat was available for use as fuel, but Shetland possessed one important raw material in the form of steatite (also known as soapstone), which does not occur in Orkney. Steatite can be quarried easily with iron tools and its common occurrence in Norway had lead to its widespread employment by the Viking period for a variety of purposes; in particular, it took the place of pottery for bowls and other vessels used for both cooking and storage. The best studied of the Shetland quarries – that at Cunningsburgh, towards the southern end of the Mainland – is discussed in more detail below; however, other important sites being worked in the Viking/Late Norse period appear to have included Hesta Ness, on Fetlar, and Clibberswick, on Unst. Output seems to have been prolific and Shetland's steatite products would have been widely traded to north and south. Other evidence also suggests that the eleventh and twelfth centuries were a period during which Shetland's domestic economy developed from one that was pre-dominantly self-sufficient to one with a greater element of exchange/trade, based particularly on the export of dried fish.

Clibberswick is the location of the best-documented Viking period grave in Shetland, even though it was dug up as long ago as 1863. This is a ninth-century burial of a woman who was wearing a pair of early (Berdal-type) oval brooches in combination with a Borre-style trefoil brooch (Figure 8.3), as well as a couple of glass beads, and a plain silver arm-ring on her left wrist; however, both the beads and the ring are now lost. Another nineteenth-century find of a pair of oval brooches, together with a small bronze bowl which would originally have formed part of a container for a set of scales, is only recorded as being from 'a grave in Unst'. One other oval brooch is known from Shetland which was found 'in the face of Wart Hill while digging trenches or gun emplacements' during World War II, for the protection of Sumburgh Airport, but nothing else is recorded of what might have been another female burial. On the other hand, when the site for the Airport Control Tower was bulldozed, a male grave was disturbed which contained an iron sword and 'a small cooking pot'; these artefacts have been lost, but doubtless the small 'pot' was in reality a shield-boss.

There is only one other definite weapon-burial known from Shetland, in the form of an axe from a slab-lined grave in St Ola's churchyard, White Ness, Mainland. A possible male burial is, however, known from a once prominent mound at Clivocast, Unst, which was opened in 1875, when it was said to have contained 'human remains, armour, etc.'.

Among other finds of potentially pagan Norse graves from mainland Shetland is a possible secondary burial in the prehistoric mound of Housegord, Weisdale, known as the 'Fairy Knowe'. This is represented by a small whetstone pendant and a blue glass bead (the same whetstone/bead combination being known from a child's burial at Cnip, Lewis). A Viking period boat-burial seems to be suggested by the 'several dozen' iron rivets found in a disturbed oval mound, known as the 'Giant's Grave', above the beach at Wick of Aith, on Fetlar. According to local tradition, in the nineteenth century, a giant had been buried here with his boat inverted over him and his money under his head! A chance-find of ten glass beads from a peat-moss at Hillswick has sometimes been considered to represent another grave, but this is obviously uncertain.

The recent discovery of a Norse antler comb, with a stone spindle-whorl, by workmen landscaping an extension to the graveyard at Mail, on the Cunningsburgh coast, leaves one wondering as to their original context, as also that of a decorated bone strap-end which was found while excavating for its car-park. Whether these artefacts were redeposited from disturbed graves, or whether they represent midden material, there was certainly an important burial-place hereabouts. As well as Pictish ogam-stones and a unique carving of a cult-figure – a wolf-headed (or masked) man carrying an axe and a club – there are also the three Norse rune-stone fragments known from on or near this site, which were mentioned above (p. 42). The meaning of the name Cunningsburgh, from Old Norse, is 'king's fort' (or stronghold) and this combination of evidence suggests that the place had been a Pictish royal centre. As such, it would have been an obvious target for Viking annexation – and subsequent exploitation for its steatite.

Overall, however, the sum of the pagan Norse burial evidence from Shetland is slight in comparison with Orkney, although fieldwork has indicated the possible locations of further grave-sites, such as a boat-shaped setting of slabs at Breckon, on Yell. It may be, however, that pagan burial practices were abandoned earlier in Shetland than in Orkney under the influence of native Christianity. Robert Stevenson, in particular, has suggested 'that there is acceptable evidence for the continuation of Christian sculpture and Pictish writing in Shetland in the period 800–1050.'

A cross-slab from the island of Bressay, in the style of an earlier stone at Papil, in West Burra, is thought to date from the ninth or tenth century. It depicts hooded clerics, a horseman and beasts, with the addition of a late Pictish ogam inscription on the sides (Figure 4.5). Confusingly, of the three words that can be recognised, two are from the Gaelic for 'cross' and 'son of' whereas the third seems to be the Norse word for 'daughter'. The remaining words are presumed to be Pictish personal names and the inscription has been tentatively translated as reading: 'The cross of Nachtud the daughter of An Benise the son of Droan'. Another feature of the inscription which has provoked discussion is its use of two dots (:) as punctuation between the words, in the manner of many runic inscriptions, but not those in ogam. A fragmentary slab, with some ogam letters, from the White Ness cemetery in mainland Shetland (that containing the axe-burial noted above) has been attributed a tenth-century date by Stevenson, on the basis of stylistic parallels in the northern English Danelaw for its knot design and small bosses.

In addition to the Cunningsburgh Norse inscriptions, there are fragmentary runestones from Papil, Eshaness and Noss. Otherwise, the only other distinctive Norse sculpture consists of a solitary steatite hogback from St Ninian's Isle. This is devoid of any ornament and has been attributed an eleventh-century date on the basis of its form.

Turning to treasure, there are two fine gold rings, an arm-ring from Oxna and a finger-ring from Whalsay, which are both single-finds, as is a once magnificent silver 'thistle-brooch', of the tenth-century type which is otherwise known only in Scotland from the Skaill hoard; this was found in the hill above Gulberwick Bay, on the Mainland. Amongst the rich and varied material from the multi-period settlement site of Jarlshof, by Sumburgh Head, there are three single-finds of silver dating from the tenth to eleventh centuries: a stray Anglo-Saxon coin of Æthelred II (979–85), a large stick-pin (with Hiberno-Norse parallels), found in the ruined broch, and a piece of 'ring-money' which appears to have been hidden in a drain belonging to House I.

Something of the wealth of the native Shetlanders on the arrival of the Vikings is reflected in the hoard of Pictish brooches and other silverware that was hidden on St Ninian's Isle, as mentioned above. On the other hand, there are no ninth- or tenth-century Viking-type silver hoards from Shetland, with the single late exception of that from Quendale, Mainland, which was deposited c. 991–1000. All of its contents, other than half-a-dozen coins, are now lost, but it seems mainly to have consisted of 'ring-money' and hack-silver. A second hoard, of late eleventh-century date, has also been postulated from the same parish of Dunrossness, but there is little enough now to demonstrate its former existence, other than a coin of King Harald Hardrada of Norway, which is now in Copenhagen.

Such, then, is the totality of the gold and silver finds from Shetland and, as with the pagan Norse graves, this body of archaeological evidence is slight in comparison with Orkney. It is sufficient, however, to demonstrate that the Norse population of Shetland did

4.5 The Bressay cross-slab, Shetland, depicting hooded papar, *holding staffs, as the Vikings would have encountered them; the Late Pictish ogam inscription on its sides may show Norse influence (NMS).*

share in the growing wealth of the Orkney earldom, even if not to the extent of being able to finance major stone architecture comparable to that of Orkney in the Late Norse period. There are, however, some minor stone buildings, as well as some possible monastic establishments on remote sites, such as Strandibrough, Fetlar.

It is unfortunate that we know nothing of the graves of the original Vikings who took Jarlshof for their settlement. Such would have helped to establish the date at which the earliest Norse land-taking took place in Shetland, given that Sumburgh is a prime settlement location which had been in continuous occupation for many centuries. It is probable that they have been taken by the sea, during the coastal erosion which has removed part of this multi-period site. Indeed, two fragments of a sculptured grave-slab, thought to be of tenth/eleventh-century date, have been found on the eroded beach.

The artefactual evidence from the settlement itself is not such as to permit its first Norse phase to be dated any more precisely than to the ninth century, so that it is necessary to treat Hamilton's claim that the 'Viking colonists arrived about A.D. 800' with the utmost caution. In any case, as explained below (pp. 155–6), much of the Viking period archaeology of Jarlshof is confused, in part because of disturbance resulting from the settlement's continuity and expansion.

The little that is known of the Early Viking period settlement archaeology of Shetland is so far derived from this one site, for the supposed early farmstead which was excavated at Underhoull, Unst, is now attributed a later date, although a midden eroding nearby indicates that other Norse buildings must have existed there and thus the full sequence of its occupation is unknown. Current research on Unst is, however, beginning to fill this gap, for a well-preserved Viking period long-house with byre has been discovered at Hamar, with others located from field-survey. For the time being, at any rate, it is the Late Norse period that is the better understood – and not only at Jarlshof, but also at Sandwick, Unst, and at the Biggings, Papa Stour, sites excavated more recently which are considered below in Chapter 10.

Overall, many of the limitations in our archaeological knowledge of the nature and extent of Norse settlement in Shetland, as also in other parts of Scandinavian Scotland, may be attributed to the fact that the Vikings occupied the most environmentally favoured areas, the same as those which have continued in use until the present day.

In Shetland, as in Orkney, we can glimpse something of the Norse *thing*-system in, for instance, the naming of the Loch of Tingwall in the central belt of mainland Shetland. A stone-built causeway leads out into this loch to Law Ting Holm with its stone enclosure; the Shetland Lawthing is recorded as having met there in 1307 – and subsequently into the sixteenth century.

The journey between Orkney and Shetland can be treacherous, but a navigational mark and a safe haven *en route* is offered by Fair Isle. Its name is generally supposed to derive from the Old Norse for 'peaceful isle', but a more plausible interpretation would be that it means 'sheep island', as with the Faroe Islands. Fair Isle has yet to reveal any archaeological evidence for Norse settlement, despite a recent intensive field-survey, but such there must have been even before the period of the *Orkneyinga saga* in which it makes several appearances – most significantly as the location of a beacon to be lit to warn Orkney of an impending attack from Shetland.

CAITHNESS AND SUTHERLAND – TO THE MORAY FIRTH

The overlordship of the Orkney earls extended across the Pentland Firth and there is no reason to suppose that Scandinavian settlement of the north-east mainland of Scotland took place much later than in Orkney and Shetland, but there is no firm evidence. Norse farm-names are prominent in the landscape of Caithness, but less numerous than in comparable territory in the Northern Isles, suggesting less intensive settlement. In fact, the domination of the Orkney earldom extended south to the Moray Firth, apparently through force of arms, with which the burial and non-recovery of a Late Pictish treasure at Rogart, in Sutherland, might possibly have been connected. Norse farm-names thin out towards the Moray Firth, but there is a cluster on the good arable lands of Cromarty and Easter Ross. Dingwall, at the head of Cromarty Firth, is another *thing*-name and thus indicative of the imposition of a Norse administrative structure. The Scandinavian settlers must therefore have enjoyed political superiority in this area, even if it is probable that they were never in the majority. No Norse place-names have been recognised in northern Scotland to the south of Beauly.

In the context of the Orkney earldom, Sutherland was indeed the 'southern land'. Its interior valleys contain a scatter of Norse place-names which suggests that there were some inland links between the fertile and populous east coast and the north-west, although contact would ordinarily have been maintained by sea. Those who were *en route* from Norway to the Western Isles – and the Viking Kingdom of Dublin beyond – would inevitably have had to proceed around Cape Wrath, as and when the weather permitted.

Saga tradition attributes the conquest of Caithness, Sutherland, Moray and Ross to Sigurd the Mighty, Earl of Orkney, and Thorstein the Red, from the Hebrides. Sigurd died at the end of the ninth century (as legend has it, from being poisoned by a tooth in the severed head of a Scottish earl which was hanging from his saddle) and is said to have been buried on the banks of the Oykell; this suggests that he was campaigning at the time on the southern frontier of his earldom. The name *Syvardhoch*, meaning 'Sigurd's mound', is recorded in the thirteenth century for Sidera on the north side of the Dornoch Firth, which is the estuary of the River Oykell.

In fact, the most southerly find of a Scandinavian oval brooch is from nearby Ospisdale. This suggests a woman's grave, although there is no actual evidence for one having been found at the time (about 1830), any more than there is evidence to substantiate the well-established belief that the brooch was directly associated with part of a steatite vessel; this might as well be midden material. However, a pair of oval brooches is known from a definite burial on the coast near Dunrobin Castle, Golspie, whilst a few other Viking period arte-facts, which were found nearby, are also most likely to have been grave-goods from other graves, but these nineteenth-century discoveries went more-or-less unrecorded. This small concentration of pagan Norse burials is in an area known also to have been a centre of Pictish activity.

The most recent survey of the Viking period burials of Caithness documents five sites, with three more 'possibles', all of which are in the north-east. Most of these finds are poorly recorded, including a potential boat-grave at Huna, but one notable discovery was that (in 1786) of a grave in the top of a broch mound in Castletown, on the north coast; this contained a pair of tenth-century oval brooches, with a lignite arm-ring and a bone bod-kin. In contrast, a pair of oval brooches found (in 1840/41) in a stone cist, in the top of a gravel mound at Westerseat, has been placed in the 'possible' category because no further remains were noted, not even a skeleton. The largest known concentration of pagan Norse burials in Caithness is undoubtedly that at Reay, on the north coast to the west of Thurso, a site of known significance in pre-Viking times; this small cemetery complex is described in detail below (pp. 125–7).

Single-finds of note from Caithness include an oval brooch, which was recovered from a disturbed area of the shoreline on the eastern side of Thurso Bay, and a Scandinavian penannular brooch, discovered near Harrow on the north coast. Either or both of these ornaments might have been associated with a grave, but any direct evidence is lacking.

Further to the west, at Balnakeil Bay on the north coast of Sutherland (Figure 4.6), the burial of a boy was discovered in 1991; he was equipped with a full-sized weapon-kit and other grave-goods (see below, pp. 140–2). Then, at the nearby site of Keoldale, Durness, Tom Lethbridge mentioned, in 1950, 'a rifled barrow, which appears to have been that of a woman provided with tortoise brooches and padlocked chests', but this seems to be a reference back to the opening of a mound there in 1832. An account of this event, published in 1867, states that: 'a few miles from Durness . . . there are two cairns. One of them was opened many years ago, and I was told that the bottom of a brass candlestick was found in it; this was, no doubt, an elliptical Scandinavian brooch.'

Evidence of Late Norse Christian burials also continues to come to light in Caithness, in the form of cist graves without grave-goods, but such are as difficult to date in this area as elsewhere. However, a grave found in 1896 beside the ruins of St Peter's Church, in Thurso, was covered by a twelfth-century rune-inscribed cross; this is part damaged, but the text on what remains of its shaft reads '[made] this overlay in memory of Ingolf his [or her] father'. In 1989, part of a second rune-stone was spotted built into a wall of St Peter's Church – the remains of a memorial to a wife named Gunnhild.

There are only two Viking period silver hoards known from this mainland area of Scandinavian settlement, both of which contain 'ring-money'. In March 1889 the grave-digger

4.6 The fine sandy beach of Balnakeil, Sutherland, location of a pagan Norse burial, would have been an attractive haven for settlers (Highland Council Archaeology Service).

working in the churchyard at Tarbat, Easter Ross, found some coins and two rings. Then in April, 'after a decent interval', an opening was made to investigate further with the result that four more coins were recovered. Finally, in November 1891, the digging of another grave produced two rings and an additional coin, bringing the total contents of the hoard up to four rings and fourteen coins. However, the circumstances of its discovery could well mean that it was not retrieved in its entirety. Eleven of the coins were French, comprising two successive issues of the mint at the port of Quentovic, which date the deposition of this hoard to the very end of the tenth century or c. 1000. Two of the remaining Tarbat coins were illegible and the other was a late issue of Eadgar (d. 975), which had been minted in Chester. Tarbat Church, nearby to Portmahomack at the entrance to Dornoch Firth, was the site of an important Pictish monastery; this is currently undergoing excavation and more Viking period finds can be expected.

The other 'ring-money' hoard is coinless, consisting of eight rings which display such a close relationship in their form and finish that they give every appearance of being the work of a single silversmith; in addition, there is considerable similarity in their weights (51± 3 g). These were found in 1872 beside the ruins of a chapel of unknown date, known as 'Kirk o' Banks', which stands above the beach of Canisbay, on the north coast of Caithness. As with other such coinless finds of 'ring-money', its deposition cannot be dated more precisely than to the tenth or eleventh century, if most probably within the bracket c. 950–1050.

Despite this range of historical, place-name and archaeological evidence for Scandinavian settlement on the northern mainland of Scotland, few traces have so far been located of the settlement-sites themselves – and nothing at all of those of Viking period date. There is a gap for this period in the occupation sequence at Freswick Links, on the east coast of Caithness, but this hiatus is likely to be more illusory than real. Either the location of the Viking period settlement remains to be discovered or, more probably, given the intensive fieldwork which has taken place in this prime location, it has already been lost to coastal erosion. The important Late Norse structural and economic evidence from Freswick is described below, together with an outline of the results of more recent work at Robert's Haven, on the north coast of Caithness (in Chapter 10). Some traces of Late Norse activity have also been noted at Huna, the location of the possible boat-grave already mentioned, whereas another site with material of potential Viking/Late Norse period date is that of Cnoc Stanger, near Reay – itself important for its pagan Norse burials and other archaeological remains (pp. 125–7).

Chapter 5

REGIONAL SURVEY PART II:
THE WEST HIGHLANDS AND ISLANDS

There is a 300-mile sea-passage through the Hebrides between Cape Wrath and the Mull of Kintyre and this region, as a whole, is one so large as to present considerable environmental variation. This diversity is inevitably reflected in the nature and extent of the Scandinavian impact, but other factors have played their part. A brief description of the physical location of the Hebrides is quoted here from W. H. Murray's *The Islands of Western Scotland* (1973):

> The main body of the Hebrides takes clear shape as two archipelagos lying parallel to the coast, the outer overlapping the inner for sixty miles. The Outer Hebrides, thirty-five to fifty miles from the mainland, form a compact link 130 miles long. The Inner Hebrides, bigger and more scattered in a double rank 142 miles long, lie close in to the coast. Together they shield the west coast against the full assault of the Atlantic seas. Skye and the Small Isles, at the north end of the Inner Hebrides, receive a like benefit, but south of this overlap, Tiree, Coll, Iona, the Ross of Mull, Colonsay, and Islay, are every bit as exposed as the outer isles, and like them are lined to the west by sandy beaches. Shell-sand is a natural resource of great importance to island agriculture and Skye pays for its protection by the lack of it.

This shell-sand 'resource' takes the form of a *machair* plain (Figure 5.1), 'whose high relative fertility made it a heartland for west coast settlements at all periods', as Iain Crawford has observed. Nowhere more so than the narrow strip, 160km long, which forms the western littoral of the Outer Hebrides, creating a lime-rich 'lowland' area in the West Highland region.

It was noted above that the annals record the presence of Viking raiders in the Hebrides from the 790s, but it is the nature and distribution of Norse place-names which provide the most important clues as to the varying degrees of long-term Scandinavian influence, both between the islands and the mainland and within the islands themselves.

It is no surprise that the Norsemen knew the Hebrides as the 'Southern Isles', *Suðreyar*, or that the Gaels came to call them *Innse Gall*, 'Isles of the Foreigners', after they had passed under Viking control. That this took place towards the mid-ninth century is suggested by an entry, under the year 847, in the Frankish *Annals of St Bertin*: 'The Scotti, after being attacked by the Northmen for very many years, were rendered tributary and [the Northmen] took possession, without resistance, of the islands that lie all around and dwelt there'.

5.1 General view of Hebridean machair on Ensay (T. Cowie).

Norse place-names containing settlement elements occur most densely in the north, in Lewis and Skye; for Lewis, it has been calculated that 79 per cent of the village-names are purely Norse and a further 9 per cent are partly Norse, whereas in north-east Skye about 66 per cent of the settlement names are purely Norse. The pattern then changes between the Outer and Inner Hebrides, with the Outer Hebrides as a whole having a majority of Scandinavian settlement names, whereas the frequency decreases gradually from north to south in the Inner Hebrides. By contrast, the west coast of Scotland is generally lacking in Norse settlement names (Figure 3.2), the few exceptions including Ullapool in Wester Ross, but that does not mean that the Scandinavians confined their activities to the islands. Names containing the Scandinavian element *dalr*, meaning 'a valley, a glen', have a widespread distribution and this Norse naming of landscape features indicates the use of these mainland areas for the seasonal exploitation of their natural resources – for fishing, hunting, grazing and timber – although it is difficult to understand how the new valley names would have taken such firm root without the permanent settlement of some of the new Norse elite, as discussed in Chapter 3.

Iain Crawford has drawn attention to the possibility of using Norse personal names to help distinguish regions of greater and lesser Norse influence (or persistence):

> In the Mac Leod (Lod's son) territories or sub-kingdoms of the Siol Thorcuill and the Siol Thormaid (the descendants of Torquil and of Tormod), covering Lewis, Harris, Skye and the adjacent mainland, the other indigenous patronymics were, and are: Mac Aulay (Olafsson), Mac Askill (Asgeirsson), Mac Railt (Haraldsson), Mac Nicol (Nicolson) and Mac Sween or Suain (Sweynsson). And this is in complete contrast to the adjoining lands to the south, of Uist and Garmoran, where Mac Donald predominates and Norse names such as Mac Codrum (Gudrumsson) are rare, although a sub-stratum of Norse Christian names does persist.

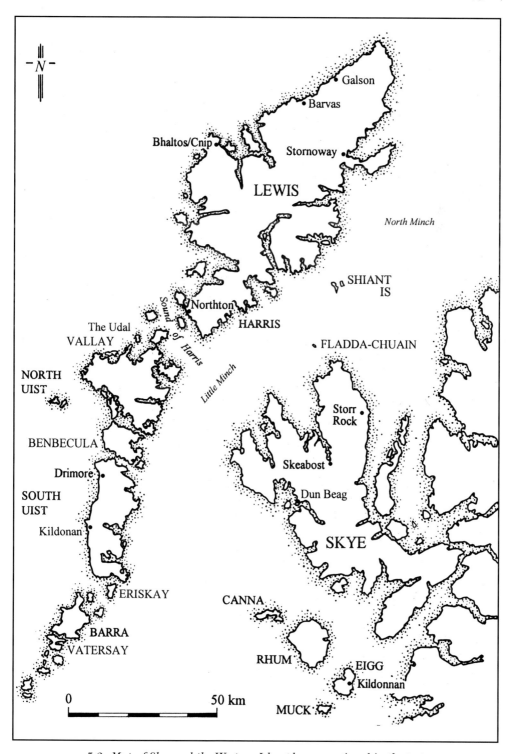

5.2　Map of Skye and the Western Isles: places mentioned in the text.

Crawford continues by stating that 'there are strong grounds here for arguing a precise boundary in distribution coinciding exactly with the line of a political frontier of at least 12th-century origin . . . and this is further emphasised by the distribution of Norse loan words into Gaelic', although these are few and present 'nothing like so drastic a picture as the place-name one'.

On combining all these aspects of the complex linguistic evidence, Crawford has proposed a broad division into three regions. The northernmost (Lewis, Harris, etc.) was completely overwhelmed during the ninth century and then 'remained Norse in overtone until the later mediaeval period, with the provisos that Gaelic may never have completely died out and did become the hierarchical language again, and that Norse may have persisted here in some level of society until the 15th century'. The central region (Uist, etc.) was 'at first overwhelmed by Norse intrusion' but subsequently 'experienced a re-assertion of Gaelic language and population from the south', whereas 'the region south of Ardnamurchan remained the basis for a persisting Gaelic Scot political unit, albeit with close Norse contact'.

THE NORTHERN REGION

Within the northern region, the area in which the place-name evidence has received the most detailed analysis is the Isle of Lewis where, according to Ian Fraser, there is a 'complete lack of identifiable pre-Norse place-names'. In this respect, therefore, the situation is similar to that encountered in Orkney and Shetland. All too little is known of the Norse archaeology of this northern region, despite its having been the area of densest Norse settlement and most persistent Scandinavian influence in western Scotland; however, our knowledge has begun to increase in recent years with the partial excavation of a settlement site and the discovery of pagan Norse burials, a silver hoard and some other chance-finds.

This evidence is particularly strong for the townships of Bhaltos (formerly spelt Valtos) and Cnip (Kneep) in the parish of Uig, with the best beaches on the west coast of Lewis. There is a particularly dense cluster of Norse place-names in this area and the eroding machair has revealed both burials and midden material. Some part of an extensive pagan Norse cemetery has been excavated on Cnip headland, including (in 1979) the grave of a wealthy woman, who had been buried in full Scandinavian costume, wearing oval brooches and a string of forty-four beads, together with various of her other belongings, including a Norse comb and an Irish ringed-pin, as well as a sickle laid upon her chest (Figure 5.3). Further excavations, close by (in 1992 and 1994), resulted in the discovery of a group of five burials, consisting of three adults, an infant and a new-born baby; a further child burial had been found some distance away in 1991. There are only a few grave-goods, such as amber beads and a couple of bone pins, but radiocarbon dating indicates that this cemetery was in use at least during the latter part of the ninth century. Although a date in the later tenth century was originally proposed for the well-equipped female grave, recent reappraisal of the grave-goods has resulted in the suggestion that this burial could be considered to date somewhat earlier.

A further well-dressed female burial was found some sixty years earlier, near Bhaltos School, but in this case the dead woman was equipped with what was most probably a weaving-sword in place of a sickle. A fragment of another oval brooch was amongst

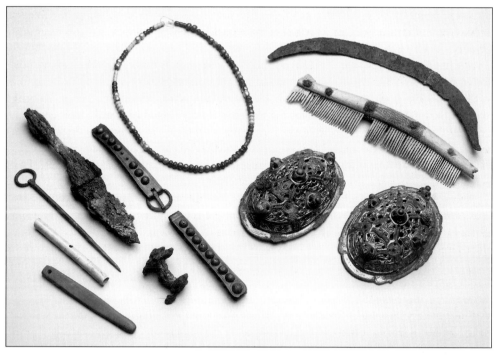

5.3 Grave-goods from the female Norse burial found at Cnip, Lewis, in 1979 (NMS).

midden material, including Norse pottery, which has been found eroding out at Mangersta, to the south of Uig Bay, and there is further Norse pottery from midden deposits near the shore at Cnip itself, as well as occasional past finds of bone and bronze pins without precise location. Finally, mention must be made here of the famous twelfth-century hoard of walrus-ivory chessmen, plain counters and a buckle which was discovered in 1831 in a sandhill at Ardroil on the southern shore of Uig Bay (Figure 13.9).

Despite this concentration of place-name and archaeological evidence for Norse settlement in this particular area of Lewis, the farmsteads of the new Norse elite remain unlocated. At least some degree of settlement-shift is evident, however, from the recent excavation of three pre-Norse sites on the Bhaltos peninsula, none of which revealed any evidence for continuity of occupation or for use during the Viking period.

Further up the west coast, eroding middens on the machair at Galson and at Barvas have produced Norse pottery – and from the former there is also a small but important assemblage of Viking period metalwork, including bronze pins, an enamelled mount and a coin of Eadgar (959–73). The discovery of the Norse pottery at Barvas led to small-scale excavation by Trevor Cowie, who located stratified midden deposits and the remains of at least two domestic structures of sub-rectangular form, with much additional pottery but no other diagnostic artefacts. Cowie's suggestion is that this represents a single-period Norse farmstead of tenth/eleventh-century date.

Other pottery of probable or possible Viking period date has been recognised by Alan Lane at five other sites in Lewis, including Aignish, near Stornoway – a sand-dune erosion site on the narrow neck of the Eye Peninsula. This has structural remains, with a hearth and floor from which also came a fragment of a single-sided antler comb, an iron rivet and bloomery cinder; these ruins were sealed by a midden which was said to have contained pottery similar to that from the floor-level below.

Stornoway is the find-place of one of only two Viking period silver hoards to have been found in Lewis. This was discovered as a result of metal-detecting activity in the grounds of Lews Castle. It consists of forty-two pieces of hack-silver, mostly fragments of 'ring-money', which had been wrapped up in cloth, together with two late tenth/early eleventh-century deniers from Normandy, and buried in a cattle horn. The other hoard is also small, but in contrast contains five complete objects – three pieces of 'ring-money' and two plain finger-rings; it was found during peat-cutting in Dibadale moss, at South Dell, Barvas.

No such hoards, or even single-finds of rings, have been made on Harris, which is like-wise lacking in any pagan Norse graves. In fact, there is only one Scandinavian artefact on record to date and that is a small fragment from one of the woman's equal-armed brooches of the type only known elsewhere in Scotland from the Scar boat-burial in Orkney. This was a chance-find made in the sand-dunes on the south-east of Chaipaval, Northton, which is within a mile of a multi-period settlement-site on the southern shore of Toe Head where Lane has recognised Viking period pottery amongst the erosion material.

Such pottery has also been found eroding out of middens on the neighbouring islands of Ensay and Killegray in the Sound of Harris. At the beginning of the eighteenth century, a grave was found at the west end of Ensay which was said by Martin Martin (1716) to have contained 'a pair of Scales made of Brass, and a little Hammer', both of which are now lost. This may well be a report of a Viking period grave, although there can be no certainty; a later reference (1900) to what must surely be the same burial, containing 'a small hammer, and a pair of small scales', transfers it to Killegray. A definite female Norse grave from an island in the Sound of Harris was, however, put on record in the eighteenth century when the Lord Bishop of Ossory exhibited an oval brooch to the Society of Antiquaries of London of which an engraving was published in 1763. This had been found 'together with a long Brass Pin and a Brass Needle, one on each side of a Skeleton, in the Isle of *Sangay*, between the Isles of *Uril* and *Harris*'. When 'Uist' can get trans-formed into 'Uril', it is scarcely surprising to discover that there is no such island as 'Sangay' in the Sound! Both Langay and Lingay have been proposed as alternatives, but these are small and barren (Lingay meaning simply 'heather island') and Ensay suggests itself as the more probable location.

Berneray, although the largest of these islands and with good machair, is known in recent years to have produced only one Viking period artefact of Scandinavian type – part of a carved whalebone plaque found at the base of eroding sand-dunes at Ruisgarry. There are, however, several ringed pins and a Borre-style strap-end, as well as other Norse material, now in the Royal Museum of Scotland (the Mackenzie collection), some of which were picked up in Berneray between the 1880s and the 1930s. Finally, there is part of a carved stone slab from a chapel dedicated to St Asaph (Cill Aiseam) with simple ornament which would appear to be of tenth-century date.

As discussed above (p. 39), the island of Pabbay – the second largest in this group – may well have been one of those left to its monks. From smaller Boreray there are two complete examples of so-called 'kidney-ringed' pins, with the shaft of a third, but nothing is recorded as to their find-circumstances. This type of ringed-pin is commonest in eleventh-century levels in Dublin, although its origins there lay in the tenth century, with its period of use having seemingly extended into the twelfth. It is not widespread outside Ireland, although four or five others are known from the Outer Isles, with a further example from the settlement at Tuquoy on Westray, Orkney, completing the corpus for Scandinavian Scotland.

Forty miles to the west lie the so-called 'St Kilda' group of islands, but this is, as Arnold Taylor has written, but 'a late name for *Hirt*, being an error made in a set of sailing directions prepared by L. J. Waghenaer through faulty copying from a chart of Nicolas de Nicolay published in 1583.' According to Taylor, the Gaelic name *Hirt* (anglicised to Hirta) is derived from the Norse *hirtir*, meaning 'stags', which he considered to be 'a very suitable name for a seaman, on approaching the islands, to give to their jagged outlines'. An alternative suggestion is, however, that the name means 'shield', after the distinctive shape.

A number of Norse place-names, including a few of the field-names on the largest island of Hirta, establish a Scandinavian presence and the naming of Oiseval, 'Eastern Hill', to the east of the present village indicates a similar location for their settlement, which has yet to be discovered. Excavations in Village Bay have, however, yielded pieces of steatite thought to have been carried downslope from a Norse settlement focus, by stream or water run-off.

What must have been a male Viking period burial was discovered by the Revd Neil Mackenzie (the minister from 1829 to 1843) while clearing the glebe, when he 'removed a mound in a little field'. The (lost) grave-goods consisted of a sword, spear and whetstone, as well as 'various other pieces of iron, mostly of irregular shape, and the use of which is not obvious'. A pair of oval brooches was recorded in the mid-nineteenth century, as part of the Anderson College Collection in Glasgow, but nothing is known of their find-circumstance. They too are now lost, but an old engraving shows them to have been of the commonest double-shelled type of late ninth/tenth-century date. Finally, there is a tantalising reference in *The Scots Magazine*, for June 1767, to news being received in Edinburgh 'from Glasgow, that some fishermen lately dug up on the island of St Kilda, two antique urns, containing a quantity of Danish silver coin, which by the inscription appears to have lain there upwards of 1800 years.' This last one can only suppose to be a printer's error for '800', but nothing is known of what became of these coins and thus of their true date and actual significance.

The broad channel between Lewis and the mainland is called the North Minch, becoming the Little Minch where it narrows between Harris and the Uists in the west and Skye to the east. In the North Minch, a few miles off the south-east coast of Lewis, lie the Shiant Islands where a probable Viking period date has been suggested by Alan Lane for a couple of sherds amongst pottery collected on Eilean Mhuire, the second largest of the group, but nothing is known of their discovery. Due south across the Minch is the small island of Fladda-chùain, off the northern tip of Skye, where a splendid gold finger-ring of eight plaited rods was found 'in a peat-moss' in the mid-nineteenth century (Figure 5.4).

The Isle of Skye consists of six peninsulas with a high and hilly interior which restricts the potential areas of settlement; its east coast is so close to the mainland that it has now been linked by a bridge. The main concentrations of Norse settlement-names are on the

5.4 Gold finger-ring, formed from eight plaited rods, found on the island of Fladda-chùain, off Skye (NMS).

northern peninsula of Trotternish and those of Vaternish and Duirinish to the north-west, but there are also clusters on the west coast beside Loch Bracadale and Loch Slapin. However, the wider distribution of Norse topographical names demonstrates detailed knowledge of the whole island which must have been taken under Viking control, even if there is no evidence of actual Scandinavian settlement in those eastern areas which have good agricultural potential, most notably the shores of Sleat peninsula.

There is little archaeological evidence for this Norse presence in Skye – nor is it known what the Vikings 'pillaged and devastated' in 795. Only one pagan grave has as yet been discovered, as a result of the investigation of a prehistoric cairn on the foreshore at Tote, Skeabost – an area with a concentration of Norse farm-names, where the River Snizort enters the sea, at the base of the Trotternish peninsula. The mound contained a secondary male Norse burial, seemingly a cremation, with the principal grave-goods comprising an axe, a bronze pin and an ivory bead, together with some variously identified iron fragments. To the north, a possible Viking period 'house and harbour' has recently been reported at Ard nan Eireachd, on Loch Snizort.

Among the great assortment of finds from the Iron Age broch of Dun Beag, which was dug out between 1914 and 1920, is a gold finger-ring in the form of a plain band to which a date in the Viking/Late Norse period has been attributed. This site is prominently located on the hillside near Struan, facing the mouth of Loch Bracadale. Amongst other evidence for the re-use of this broch during the Late Norse period, in some manner or other, is a coin of Henry II (1154–89), some bronze stick-pins and an ornamented belt-buckle. In addition, Lane has identified the only fully reconstructible pot to have been recovered during these 'excavations' as dating from the Viking period.

A chance-find of another gold finger-ring, of four twisted rods, is known from an unrecorded site in Skye, as well as three coinless silver hoards of which two contained complete or fragmentary pieces of standard tenth/eleventh-century 'ring-money', although one piece has stamped ornament on its terminals. However, the third unprovenanced hoard (now lost) appears to have been of late ninth- or early tenth-century date, in that its nineteenth-century description suggests that its linked rings were of an earlier type of Irish 'ring-money' (or 'penannular ingots').

In addition, there is one major Skye silver hoard which will be discussed in detail below (Chapter 12). This was found over the New Year of 1891/2 on the shore below the Storr Rock, an inhospitable location on the east coast of the Trotternish peninsula. It consisted of 111 coins and twenty-three fragments of hack-silver which had been deposited c. 935–40 (Figure 12.7).

No archaeological traces have yet been found of those Norsemen who were active on the north-west mainland despite the place-name evidence mentioned above. However, as previously noted, this is mostly topographical in nature and so more suggestive of seasonal exploitation rather than widespread permanent settlement. There are, however, a few exceptions (from *ból* or *bólstaðir*): notably Unapool, on the west side of the mouth of Loch Glencoul, on the coast of Sutherland; Ullapool, on the east shore of Loch Broom, in Wester Ross; and Erbusaig, opposite Skye, to the north of Kyle of Lochalsh.

THE CENTRAL REGION

The Sound of Harris is the most decisive strait to divide the Outer Hebrides, or the Long Isle as it is also known; in so doing it separates Lewis/Harris from the southern isles which provide the main Norse settlement area of the central region (Figure 5.2). This island chain consists of the Uists (North Uist, Benbecula, South Uist and Eriskay, with the offshore islands of Vallay, Kirkibost, Baleshare and the Monachs) and extends southwards to the Sound of Barra, with an almost continuous west coast machair. Barra itself has a cluster of small islands to its south.

The Uists have so far provided three excavated Norse settlements, with a fourth under recent investigation, but the evidence of pagan Norse graves from this part of the region is frustratingly fragmentary. One of the better, but nevertheless unproven, reports of Viking period burials relates to the northern end of North Uist, opposite Berneray. The *Inventory* account (from 1914) states that:

> On the brow of the hill rising some 30 feet above Rudh' a Charnain Mhoir, the north-west corner of the Otternish peninsula, facing the island of Berneray, about 7/8 mile north-east of Port nan Long, are several mounds of tumbled stones. Iron rivets of Viking type were noted.
>
> About 100 yards to the south on the summit of the hill is a small cairn of stones, Carnan Beag, in which Viking rivets have also been found.
>
> Both these sites have been rifled, and besides the rivets already noted, a number of glass beads and a hair comb of Viking type were recovered. A skeleton was also found in the first-mentioned burial.

Unfortunately, no further evidence is known for these presumed pagan Norse burials – even the artefacts now seem to be lost. However, fieldwork suggests that other Viking period burials may well lie beside the shore at the base of Suenish, the adjacent headland to the Otternish peninsula.

Turning westwards down the Atlantic coastline of North Uist, the next site with a potential pagan Norse burial is that reported on the tidal island of Vallay, where a spear-head was 'found beside some skeletal remains north of the cattlefold'. On the other hand, the most that can be said of a kidney-ringed pin (as above, p. 77), found in a 'burying ground in the Island of Heisker, adjoining North Uist', is that it might well have been used as a shroud pin in a Late Norse burial.

Other chance-finds of Viking period artefacts from North Uist are either from unknown locations, including a considerable number of bronze pins and other personal ornaments, or consist of eroding midden material. Amongst the latter is pottery from Cul na Muice, on the north side of Vallay, and from Eilean Maleit, a tidal islet near the south-west edge of Vallay Strand, where there are the remains of a complex, multi-period, stone structure.

A multi-period site at Garry Iochdrach on the south-west shore of Vallay Strand, which was excavated by Erskine Beveridge in 1912/13, has produced some neglected evidence for what would appear to have been a Viking/Late Norse period settlement. Beneath a modern sheep-fold, beside the remains of a wheelhouse, Beveridge discovered one com-plete end of a sub-rectangular domestic building 'about 7 feet in width by 18 feet in length', with its opposite end extending 'half-way under the south wall of the fold'; the interior was paved, including a centrally placed hearth '4 feet from its north wall' (Figure 5.5). Finds from this sheep-fold site include not only some possible Viking period pottery, but also a broken ringed-pin (probably of kidney-ringed type) and a block of worked steatite which are both likely to date to the Viking/Late Norse period.

In the late eighteenth century, 'a considerable number of Saxon coins were found in the Island of North Uist', but there is only one of Æthelred II on record, which does no more than suggest that this hoard was deposited sometime during the late tenth or early eleventh century. A similar date of deposition seems probable for a coinless gold hoard, which included five complete finger-rings (see p. 236); this was described, in 1865, as having been discovered 'in the Western Islands of Scotland', but there is later evidence to indi-cate that it was in fact found in North Uist, on the largest of its islands named Oronsay. This location, for the largest gold hoard of its kind to be known from Scandinavian Scotland, provides a further link in the chain of evidence for an extensive Norse presence across the machair plain of north-west North Uist, from Vallay to Otternish, with Aird a' Bhorrain at its centre where Coileagan an Udail (the Udal sand bunkers) are located – the site of a multi-period settlement with important Viking/Late Norse horizons.

As noted above (p. 25), 'udal' is the modern form of the Old Norse *óðal*, a name applied to inherited family land, and an *óðal*-man was the highest ranking amongst freeholders, enjoying the fullest rights and thus, if sufficiently wealthy and powerful, sometimes hard to distinguish from the true Norse aristocracy.

The nature of the Viking and Late Norse period occupation of the Udal, as revealed by Iain Crawford's excavations, is outlined below (in Chapters 9 and 10), but some of his discoveries are of particular relevance here for the origins of Scandinavian settlement in North Uist. Rectangular Norse structures were found superimposed on the cellular buildings of the native population, with an accompanying change in material culture, and the construction of a small sub-rectangular fortification, although its use was short lived. These combined circumstances suggest strongly that the Viking incursion into North Uist was violent in nature, with the existence of the fort further suggesting that the incomers

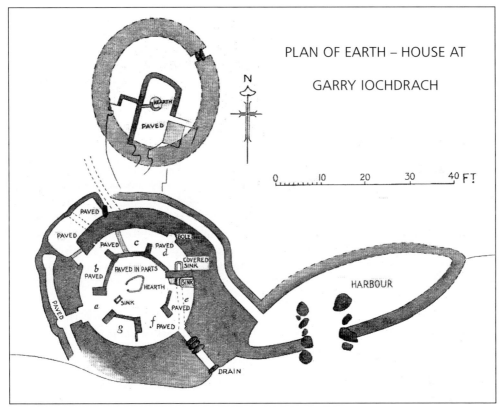

5.5 Plan of a sub-rectangular Norse structure to the north of an Iron Age 'earth-house' at Garry Iochdrach, North Uist; it is overlain by an oval sheep-fold (after E. Beveridge and J. G. Callander, 1932).

felt initially somewhat insecure. When this take-over happened cannot be established precisely on archaeological grounds, but a mid-ninth-century date is most probable on the basis of the artefactual evidence from the stratified site sequence. It is, however, unfortunate that we do not know where the Norse population of the Udal was buried so that we lack the chronological and other evidence which the grave-goods of the first generation of settlers might have provided.

Amongst the changes in the material culture at this period at the Udal was the introduction of a new style of pottery which differs in both form and construction from that which had been in use there until then. Given that some of this new-style Viking period pottery has possible analogies with the so-called 'Souterrain Ware' of north-east Ireland, it could be that these Viking incomers had been dislodged from the Irish coast, where ninth-century activity is recorded both historically and archaeologically – or at least that they had shared in such ventures.

There are no definite pagan Norse burials known as yet from Benbecula and South Uist, although the fragmentary remains of a classic Scandinavian type of single-sided antler comb were discovered during the nineteenth century 'in cleaning out a stone cist in a sandy hillock in South Uist'. The fact that a flint arrow-head was also found has been taken to suggest that this may have been a Viking period secondary burial in a prehistoric mound, as has been encountered elsewhere. However, given that a medieval ring-brooch and buckle were also recovered on this occasion, it may well be that the Norse comb itself derives from occupation debris on this unknown site.

A sand-dune area on the north-east coast of Benbecula, at Rosinish, which has suffered severe erosion, has revealed extensive evidence of multi-period settlement, with Viking period pottery from amongst the midden material. Further finds of such pottery have been made in South Uist from eroding middens in sand-hills to the west of Daliburgh, and on Kildonan machair, from what appears to have been another multi-period settlement, situated some 500 metres north-west of a suggested Late Norse ecclesiastical site (Cille Donnain), considered below in Chapter 13. The Kildonan machair has also produced a small fragment of a Scandinavian oval brooch from the same area as the pottery, and a plain-ringed, polyhedral-headed ringed-pin was found some 500 metres further to the north-west. In addition, from South Uist, there is an old find of another such ringed-pin from Loch Bornish, where a Viking period settlement has recently been excavated by the University of Sheffield.

The only Viking period site to have been published to date in South Uist was excavated at Drimore, in 1956, in advance of the Uist rocket-range programme. This settlement is considered in more detail below in Chapter 9, but here it is worth noting that the excavations were limited in extent to a single building (Figure 9.9), with the result that the overall conclusions which can be drawn from them are inevitably limited. The few diagnostic stratified finds, which include a fine hog-backed comb, can be broadly dated to the ninth/tenth centuries, although there is some other evidence to suggest multi-period use of the site. Given that no middens were excavated, few comparisons (other than structural) can thus be made between Drimore and the Udal. However, on the available evidence there is a notable contrast in the scarcity of pottery at Drimore (five sherds), with a relative abundance of steatite, used for vessels and spindle-whorls.

Finally, it should be noted that the Uists possess far fewer examples of the classic forms of Norse settlement-names than Harris and Lewis. Nicolaisen plots only one name in *staðir* from North Uist, with D. K. Olson adding one from South Uist, and two each in *bólstaðir* from both North and South Uist. Olson has also added a couple from Benbecula, which are no longer in use, as also one from North Uist. The rarity of names in *sætr* is, however, compensated for by the widespread use of *ærgi* (from the Gaelic word for 'shieling'), matched by its spread southwards in the Inner Hebrides and adjacent mainland, from southern Skye to Kintyre and Arran.

The southern end of the Uists terminates in a twenty-five-mile tail of smaller islands, first Eriskay and then across the Sound of Barra to a mostly uninhabited group of twenty islands, on either side of Barra itself which is the largest, at eight miles long by four wide. There is, from Eriskay, what would appear to be a typical tenth-century male grave assemblage – of sword, spear and whetstone – although the only information concerning their discovery is that they were 'dug up' on the island!

Barra, on the other hand, has produced a wealthy female grave, with ninth-century oval brooches, a ringed-pin and a comb, as also other grave-goods, most notably a range of textile-related equipment: an iron weaving-sword, pair of heckles and shears, as well as a bronze needle-case. The original account of this (1862) discovery at 'Ardvonrig', as a result of excavating a mound with a standing stone upon it, has given rise to some long-standing confusion as to the number and sex(es) of the burials at this site, largely because the weaving-sword was initially interpreted as an actual sword and the heckles as a shield-boss 'composed of thin iron rods, possibly inserted in a wooden frame'. Re-examination of the surviving artefacts in the British Museum, together with the original documentary sources, has enabled Kate Gordon to establish that these do, indeed, represent the inhumation of a single, high-status, female of late ninth/tenth-century date. However, the precise location of this grave remains somewhat problematical, in that 'Ardvonrig' is taken to be a variation of Ardvoray (or Ardvouray) – the name given to the peninsula of land between the west side of the main road at Borve and Borve Point. Several objects of varying medieval dates were given to the British Museum with the grave-goods, all of which were reported to have been found in the area around the mound. The existence of a possible Anglo-Saxon sword amongst this material may well be indicative of a second burial, although none of the rest of the material is indicative of a pagan Norse grave assemblage. An otherwise unrecorded pagan Norse grave is seemingly represented by a fine comb 'found in a stone cist on the island of Barra'.

A late tenth/early eleventh-century Christian burial is represented by a cross-slab, found in 1865 in the disused burial ground of the ruined church of Kilbar (Cille Bharra), the church of St Barr (or Finnbarr) from whom the island of Barra derives its Norse name. This cross-slab has parallels in its form and ornament amongst the Viking period sculpture on the Isle of Man and the Norse runic inscription on its reverse may be translated: 'After Thorgerd, Steinar's daughter, this cross was raised' (Figure 3.4).

On the basis of his re-appraisal of the pottery from the excavated wheelhouse site at Allasdale, Alan Lane has proposed that it was a multi-period settlement, with occupation during the Viking period, even if the bulk of the diagnostic finds are of Iron Age date. The distribution of some of the more indicative sherds has suggested to him that a sub-rectangular structure, published simply as an Iron Age 'working-area', might well have been a Viking period house, given the presence of a drain and hearth, which had subsequently suffered severe robbing for building stone. Indeed, the poor excavation records and limited finds mean that one should question whether or not any of the (sub)-rectangular structures do in fact date any earlier than the Viking period. Alison Young, who published the account of the Allasdale excavations, drew parallels for some of the pottery from the 'working-place' with sherds from another settlement-site on Barra, that of Dun Cuier, for which likewise no Viking period occupation was suggested. The finds from this site cannot readily be sorted, but Lane suggests that some Viking period activity is, indeed, indicated on the basis of the ceramic evidence.

The largest island to the south of Barra is Vatersay, for which there is a nineteenth-century report of a presumably pagan Norse warrior burial, with a horse. Amongst the southernmost of this group of islands, to the south of another named Pabbay, is the now deserted island of Mingulay. Mingulay remains well known amongst ornithologists for its bird-cliffs, but there is no archaeological evidence for a Scandinavian Viking period presence. However, Olson has added its place-name of 'Swansibost' or 'Sunisibost' to the list of Norse settlement-names derived from *bólstaðir*, although its location is unknown.

The islands of the Inner Hebrides, which form part of this Central Region, are those known collectively as the Small Isles: Eigg, Muck, Rum and Canna. All except Rum are fertile islands, but it is only Eigg which has so far revealed any definite archaeological evidence for Scandinavian settlement. A number of unexcavated stone settings on Canna, and the small island of Sanday, to which it is joined, have appeared as pagan Norse graves in various accounts (and thus on several maps), but they are now thought to represent the remains of shieling-huts and kelp-dykes. The whereabouts of a ringed-pin from the site of the memorial church on Canna, recorded in the *Inventory* as being 'in private possession', is no longer known.

A magnificent Viking sword was found on Eigg when a mound was levelled in about 1830, near to the chapel of Kildonnan, together with parts of a bronze-mounted bucket and a (lost) whetstone, as well as what appears to be a medieval bronze pot-leg – and thus intrusive. The sword-blade no longer survives, but the hilt (Figure 5.6) is a splendid piece of ninth-century craftsmanship. Recent analysis has shown that its cast components are basically brass and so would have had a golden appearance, but they are further decorated with silver wires and plates, the latter having stamped ornament inlaid with niello; the whole was assembled over a cement core.

Two adjacent mounds were subsequently opened, in 1875, some five or six hundred yards to the south of Kildonnan chapel, both of which had evidently also contained male burials of probable tenth-century date. The grave-goods in the larger of the two mounds consisted of a sword, spear, axe and whetstone, together with three beads, a Carolingian-style buckle and a plain 'ball-type' penannular brooch, both made of bronze. The latter was most probably made in Norway, where numerous such bronze brooches have been found in male graves dating from the first half of the tenth century. They are often coated with white metal, as is the case with the Eigg example, the better to imitate the large silver brooches of Insular manufacture which constitute their prototype. The burial in the adjacent mound in Eigg was less well equipped with grave-goods, but they were similar in that they consisted of a sword and whetstone, with two beads, together with an Insular buckle and a simple penannular brooch, both also made of bronze.

There is also a fine Viking period ringed-pin, of the polyhedral-headed type, from Eigg, although its find-circumstances are unknown. Finally, an unusual discovery is that of two stem-posts, each shaped from a single block of oak and stepped to take the side-planks of a boat. These were found in 1878, when a peat bog was being drained on the west side of the island. They have been supposed to date from the Viking period, but their forthcoming radiocarbon dates are awaited with interest.

THE SOUTHERN REGION

The southernmost region (Figure 5.7) corresponds to that of the Scottish kingdom of Dalriada. Its islands display clear evidence for Scandinavian settlement, in the form of Norse farm-names and pagan graves, but not its mainland heart in Lorn and Mid-Argyll. There the only supposed Viking period graves have rightly been dismissed, although one might continue to speculate about the significance of the (lost) find of a spear-head, which was described as 'composed of a mixture of brass and iron', in one of the prehistoric cairns at Kilmartin. As Leslie Alcock has commented: 'it is evident that Norse settlers were

5.6 Early Viking period sword-hilt from a pagan Norse grave on the island of Eigg (NMS).

effectively repulsed from the heartland of Dal Riata; and it is a reasonable speculation that a major role in the defence was played by the two strongholds of Dunadd and Dunollie'.

The chance-finds of Viking period artefacts from the mainland area of this region are also few in number, although their presence accords with the more-or-less continuous distribution of Norse topographic names, such as those containing *dalr*, with their evidence for Scandinavian activity and influence. The most notable such discovery is from its northern extremity, beside Loch Leven, in the form of a tenth-century bronze 'thistle-brooch', which was picked up beside a burn, between Kinlochleven and the mouth of Glencoe. Although it is clearly modelled on such as the large silver 'thistle-brooches' in the Skaill hoard (Figure 12.3), it should rather be compared to the smaller plain example from one of the Eigg graves, mentioned above.

A silver hoard is recorded from one of the Kilmartin cairns, consisting of 'a few coins'; these included one of Æthelred, so that it will have been deposited during the late tenth

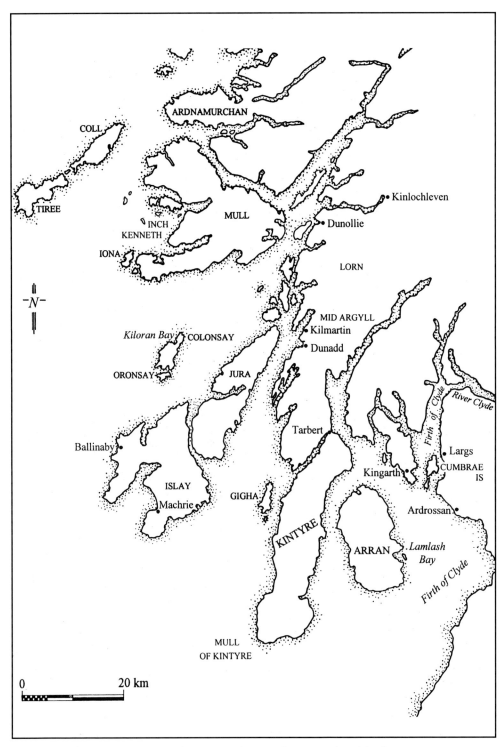

5.7 Map of Argyll, Arran and Bute: places mentioned in the text.

or early eleventh century. A supposed Viking/Late Norse period gold ring from Inverary Park has disappeared without trace. Finally, a folding balance-beam which has been said to be 'of Viking type', from St Columba's Cave near Ellary, on the north side of Loch Caolisport, is better described as being 'of Norse or medieval date' and need not have had anything to do with Scandinavian activity.

The northernmost of the Inner Hebrides in this Southern Region, are the small sister islands of Coll and Tiree, only two miles apart. They are both low-lying machair islands of equal size, although Tiree is the more fertile, with Coll having rather much moorland, but both share in the distribution of classic Norse settlement names.

Tiree may have produced two coin-hoards of similar date (the 970s) in the eighteenth century, but it has also been suggested that there was only one find which then became divided into two. There are, however, differing descriptions of the discovery; one account refers to the container as being a cloth bag, whereas the other describes it as 'an urn'. There may of course be some confusion between these two accounts – or both could be true of the one hoard if it had been in a bag which was buried in a pot! The use of a pot for this purpose is certainly feasible, given that Coll and Tiree mark the southern extent of the distribution of Viking period pottery in the Hebrides.

An oval brooch and a pin, from an unknown site on Tiree, are said to have been found in a grave, the pair to the brooch now being lost. Objects found during the eighteenth century in a stack-yard at Cornaigbeg are also lost, but the description of their discovery in the *Statistical Account* (1794) suggests the location of an important pagan Norse cemetery:

> In digging pits in sandy ground to secure potatoes during winter and spring, there were found at different times human skeletons, and nigh them the skeletons of horses. They seemed to have been compleatly armed, according to the times. Two handed swords were found diminished with rust; silver work preserved the handles; there were also shields and helmets with a brass spear. Nigh this was discovered another skeleton, holding the skeleton of an infant in its arms.

As noted previously, iron shield-bosses are often wrongly described as 'helmets' in such early antiquarian accounts of Viking period grave-goods.

Coll has produced only one possible pagan Norse grave, at Grishipoll Bay, where an inhumation burial in the sand-hills was apparently associated with an iron spear-head, although not of a diagnostic type. Two erosion sites at Cornaig, on the north coast of Coll, distinguished as Cornaig Lodge and Cornaigmore, have both produced examples of Viking period pottery, as has Feall Bay, in the south-west. Norse pins have also been found on Coll, as at Crossapol.

The mountainous nature of Mull means that settlement is largely confined to its coastal fringe where there is well-drained fertile soil. As yet, however, there exists no firm archaeological evidence for a Scandinavian presence, although such can be established from the distribution of Norse place-names, also extending to the mainland, as with Resipol on Loch Sunart, opposite the northern end of Mull. There is a nineteenth-century report of 'one or more' oval brooches (now lost) having been found on Mull, which is often taken as evidence for a female Norse burial, but nothing further is known about this find or its location. Alan Lane has recognised a possible Viking period sherd amongst those collected from a small oval fort at Mingary, in the north-west of Mull, which might therefore indicate some Viking activity in this fort.

The west coast of Mull consists of a large bay, twelve miles wide at its mouth, dotted with islands, including that of Inch Kenneth where a Viking period silver hoard was found in the nineteenth century. It contained some 100 coins, which show that it was deposited about 1000, but also 'three large silver rings or armillæ, resembling oriental bangles', which are lost, and a piece of fine silver chain (now in the British Museum).

The small island of Iona lies just off the south-west tip of Mull. As described in Chapter 1, the wealth of its prestigious monastery provided a magnet for some of the earliest Viking raiders, being sacked four times between 795 and 826. For greater safety, the relics of St Columba were divided and dispersed, and the headquarters of the Columban monastic federation transferred to Kells in Ireland, but Iona does not appear to have been abandoned by the monks and burial continued in the cemetery. When some of the earliest Norse settlers who had been subjected to Christianity in the Hebrides moved on to Iceland, they were reputed to have built churches dedicated to Columba.

In 980, Olaf Sihtricsson or Cuarán, the Norse king of Dublin, and formerly of York, retired to Iona 'in penitence and pilgrimage' after his defeat at the battle of Tara. His stay there, until his death, may well account for the presence of a hoard, found in 1950, consisting of over 360 coins, with a standard silver ingot (bent into a U-shaped loop), a small fragment of gold rod and the bezel of a silver finger-ring which is ornamented with gold filigree around a green glass setting; this latter is most probably of Anglo-Saxon workmanship. Most of the coins are also Anglo-Saxon (345 out of the 363 surviving), with the remainder consisting of the Viking kings of York, including Olaf himself, and three Normandy deniers, minted in Rouen. The total number of coins is greater than that in any other Viking period hoard from Scotland, with the possible exception of one of those from Tiree (variously estimated as containing from 200 to 500 coins). Its deposition date can thus be calculated sufficiently precisely as to suggest that its non-recovery was connected with a known Viking raid in 986. Then, according to the *Annals of Ulster*: 'Iona of Columcille was plundered on Christmas night; and they killed the abbot, and fifteen elders of the church'.

Amongst the tenth- and early eleventh-century stone sculpture on Iona is a grave-slab with a Norse runic inscription, a cross-head similar to some of those on the Isle of Man – and possibly even brought from there – as well as a cross-shaft with interlace ornament and a ship-scene for which Anglo-Scandinavian parallels have been suggested. These important monuments are discussed in greater detail in Chapter 13 (Figures 13.2–3).

Historically, little is known of Iona during the eleventh century, other than the names of abbots and occasional pilgrims, but it was an obvious place of importance for King Magnus Barelegs to visit during his expedition to the west in 1098, when he is said to have paid his respects to the 'small church of Columcille'. There is, however, at least a suggestion that Iona had become more than just a major Christian centre for the Hebridean Norsemen, for the thirteenth-century Icelandic source *Fargskrinna* refers to the *kaupstad* of Iona – that is a market-town or market-place – on the occasion of the visit by King Magnus. This indication of an economic role for Iona recalls the archaeological evidence for Norse commercial activity at this period at the major ecclesiastical centre of Whithorn in south-west Scotland (pp. 202–5).

THE SOUTHERN INNER HEBRIDES

To the south of Mull, and to the north-west of Kintyre, lies the group of islands sometimes known as the southern Inner Hebrides (Figure 5.7). The largest of these is Islay which, together with Colonsay and Oronsay, has an Atlantic machair coastline (reminiscent of the Outer Hebrides) with good agricultural potential, although exposure to westerly gales has inevitably had a restrictive effect on settlement patterns. Jura, on the other hand, is physically a hilly extension of the West Highlands, and its Old Norse name, meaning 'deer island', reflects its different role in the economy of the Scandinavian settlers – an island suited more to hunting expeditions than to permanent occupation.

Colonsay, Oronsay and Islay are relatively rich in pagan Norse burials, with a total of eleven reasonably well-documented examples and a further ten or more possible graves on record. Some of these are of sufficient interest and importance to merit detailed description and discussion in Chapter 7: notably, those from Càrn a' Bharraich, on Oronsay (Figure 7.2); a boat-burial at Kiloran Bay, on Colonsay (Figures 7.3–4); and a group of graves at Ballinaby, on Islay (Figures 7.5–6).

A (lost) female burial is also known from Islay, with a pair of oval brooches and an amber bead, which was found in 1845 on the side of the valley near Newton distillery. Another female burial eroded out of the sand-dunes at Cruach Mhór in the late 1950s, in an area which has also produced multi-period midden material and drystone walling. As all the artefacts from this site are unstratified surface-finds, their original associations are unknown, but there are several items characteristic of female Norse grave-goods. In addition to the remains of a pair of oval brooches and six beads (three jet or lignite, two glass and one amber), there is a group of textile equipment, including an iron weaving-sword, heckle(s) and a steatite spindle-whorl. Other possible grave-goods include a fragmentary sickle, one or two knives and a hone. A small bronze buckle, with simple Borre-style decoration, was also found on this site in 1978, but there is inevitably no way of knowing whether or not it derived from this same ninth/tenth-century grave.

A standing stone at Carragh Bhàn is supposed, in local tradition, to mark the grave of Godred Crovan, King of Man and the Isles (who died in 1095), but there is in fact a definite eleventh-century Norse grave-slab known from Islay. However, no burials were reported when it was discovered, about 1838, during field clearance at Dóid Mhàiri. This cross-slab (Figure 5.8) is unique in Scandinavian Scotland in its use of foliage ornament derived from the Ringerike style of Viking art, flanking a ring-headed cross of the Irish tradition.

Islay has the greatest concentration of Old Norse settlement-names in the Southern Hebrides, but no structures attributable to Scandinavian settlers have yet been recognised. It remains only to note the one Viking period coin-hoard which is on record from the island. This was found in 1850 on the farm of Machrie, at the southern end of Laggan Bay. It had been deposited in the 970s and is known to have consisted of over 120 coins, with some (lost) ingots and hack-silver, but the 1854 report states that 'only a small part was recovered from the finders by the Scottish Exchequer'.

The neighbouring island of Jura has produced no Viking period graves, hoards or artefacts indicative of Scandinavian settlement, although a diver in the Sound of Jura, in 1981, recovered a splendid gold arm-ring from the seabed, near Ruadh Sgeir. In contrast, Colonsay and Oronsay possess an abundance of evidence for Scandinavian settlement in

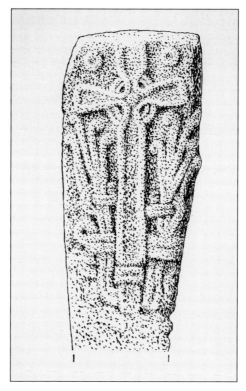

5.8 Eleventh-century cross-slab from Dóid Mhàiri on the island of Islay; the foliate motifs on either side of the cross-shaft are based upon the Ringerike style of Viking art (Crown copyright: RCAHMS).

the form of Viking period burials, although lacking Norse habitation names.

The most important of these pagan Norse graves is a boat-burial at Kiloran Bay in Colonsay, which was excavated in 1882/3 (discussed below, pp. 118–22), but a second boat-burial was excavated by Sir John M'Neill, in 1891, from an oval mound in the sand-dunes to the west of Machrins. This mound, which was made up of sand containing occasional slabs of schist, was described by M'Neill as having 'been disturbed, either by treasure seekers in former times, or, perhaps, more probably, by the burrowing of many generations of rabbits'. He recorded that it was about thirty feet long, which provides our only clue as to the probable size of the boat. As at Kiloran Bay, this contained a horse, weapons and 'an iron pot with handle entire'. The weapons consisted of a sword, axe and spear, with 'portions of shield bosses'. Other grave-goods included a plain horse-bit, and 'one amber bead, a penannular brooch of bronze, and a bronze pin were also found in sifting the sand'. The brooch is of native Pictish type, dating from the late eighth or early ninth century, but a later date for its burial is suggested by the fact that its original pin would appear to have been replaced by another of simpler form and longer length.

Another piece of native metalwork, reduced to a decorative plaque, was recovered in 1978 when a simple long-cist, containing a flexed inhumation (probably female), was excavated on the Machrins machair. The other surviving grave-goods consist of a plain ringed-pin, which appears from its position to have been used as a shroud-pin, an iron knife and a single nail, with a small dog, similar in size to a modern Welsh corgi; the upper part of the body did not survive as a result of a previous disturbance, which could well have resulted in the removal of any brooches. The radiocarbon date from the long bones, as initially published, was ad 780±70, but this has since been calibrated to the calendar date range of AD 709–1020, with a central date of 886, thus indicating that this is most probably a Viking period burial. It may perhaps have been associated with a group of four small houses, situated some fourteen metres away, but their single-roomed plans and slight nature suggest that they belong to a native building tradition.

A Hiberno-Norse stick-pin of the 'non-functional kidney-ringed' type, of eleventh/ twelfth-century date, was found close to a long rectangular hearth in the sand-dunes at the head of Tràigh nam Bàrc, near Garvard, where an old find of a burial in a 'stone coffin' is reported, with 'a sword, rusty and almost mouldered away . . . lying near the bones'.

Other possible pagan Norse graves in Colonsay have been suggested for the sand-dunes at Cnoc nan Gall, where rivets, a human tooth and a horse's tooth eroded out of a mound in 1902, and at Ardskenish where a plain ringed-pin and an Insular buckle of Viking period date were found in unknown circumstances in 1891. These finds could all have derived from eroding occupation levels or middens, rather than from burials, although the former is at least suggestive of a third Colonsay boat-burial, also containing a horse.

The smaller island of Oronsay is only separated from Colonsay at high tide – its Norse name, meaning simply 'tidal island', is one commonly encountered (as above in North Uist). A group of three or four graves at Càrn a' Bharraich is discussed in detail below (pp. 113–18), but it includes one of the earliest female burials known from Scandinavian Scotland, dating to the ninth century, as well as that of another woman whose brooches were made from looted shrine mounts, together with a male burial and a possible boat-grave (Figure 7.2). A further possible Viking period grave was excavated at Druim Arstail, in 1912, from an eroding – and probably disturbed – mound containing stones which seemed to form a circular setting. No skeletal remains were recorded, but the objects recovered consisted of a (lost) ringed-pin, half a (lost) blue glass bead and a fragment of a jet or lignite arm-ring, with also a couple of bronze nails and other fragments of bronze, as well as an iron nail.

There are no silver hoards known from either Colonsay or Oronsay, although it should be noted that there was a silver stick-pin amongst the grave-goods in the Kiloran Bay boat-burial.

KINTYRE

Kintyre is the peninsula which projects from the mainland of Argyll in such a manner as to separate the Atlantic Ocean from the waters of the Clyde (Figure 5.7). Its northern end is an isthmus between West and East Loch Tarbert, with the characteristic Gaelic place-name *Tairbeart*, meaning a 'portage'. *Orkneyinga saga* comments that this isthmus 'is so narrow that ships are regularly hauled across' and recounts how King Magnus Barelegs was drawn across in a boat, with himself at the helm, in order to lay claim to this 'island' for Norway. Also according to the saga, 'Kintyre is thought to be more valuable than the best of the Hebridean islands, though not as good as the Isle of Man'. The farms are strung out along both coasts, for the hinterland is hilly, but archaeological evidence for Scandinavian settlement is lacking. Indeed, the only known objects to be related to Norse activity in this area are the balance and weights which were found in 1849 on the adjacent island of Gigha. These have often been interpreted as grave-goods from a cist-burial; however, the description of their discovery, 'a few yards from the beach, at the south end of the east bay at Tarbert', in a 'square "box" of stone', beneath a large boulder, makes no mention of any other objects nor even of any skeletal remains. It seems more probable therefore that this valuable item, which can only be compared in Scandinavian Scotland (as a set) with the balance and weights in the Kiloran Bay boat-grave, had been concealed for safe-keeping beside the Gigha portage, protected by the stone 'box', with its location marked by the 'boulder' – never to be recovered by its owner.

Chapter 6

REGIONAL SURVEY PART III:
SOUTH-WEST, CENTRAL, EASTERN AND SOUTHERN SCOTLAND

The Mull of Kintyre, which forms the south-west corner of this part of Scotland, is no more than 22km from the nearest part of Ireland, but even Islay lies within sight of the northern coast of Ulster. Thus Rathlin Island, 8km off the coast of Co. Antrim, would presumably have appeared to the first Norse raiders and settlers as the southernmost of the Hebrides (Figure 6.1). Northern Donegal, and the Inishowen peninsula in particular, would also have provided an obvious landfall for those Viking ships which succeeded in penetrating the Minch. In consequence, the archaeological and other evidence for a short-lived Norse presence along the northern coast of Ireland requires some consideration here.

THE NORTH OF IRELAND

Rathlin, the site of a monastery established in 635 by the Abbot of Iona, is most probably to be identified with 'Rechru', the first place in Ireland known to have been raided by the Vikings. In 795, the *Annals of Ulster* record: 'The burning of Rechru by the gentiles; and Skye was pillaged and devastated'.

Archaeological evidence for a Scandinavian presence on Rathlin in the ninth century exists in the form of a number of poorly recorded, pagan Norse graves from Church Bay, but these are sufficient to suggest the existence of a cemetery – and thus actual settlement – rather than just a chance location for burial. In contrast, temporary expediency might be the explanation for the single grave of a Norse warrior whose grave, near Larne (also in Co. Antrim) was at a distance of only '70 yards from the sea, 5 ft. above high-water mark' – as also for that of the Norse woman who had been buried on the raised beach at Ballyholme, Co. Down.

In one of the Rathlin graves, together with some beads, was found a splendid silver brooch. Its form and decoration demonstrate that it was made by a Scandinavian craftsman in imitation of a native Irish brooch-type (the so-called 'bossed penannular brooch') which was in fashion during the second half of the ninth century. A second grave is known to have contained a sword, with a bronze bowl from a third.

The Larne Viking, who was found during railway construction in 1841, had been buried with his sword and spear, a fine comb and a ringed-pin to fasten his cloak. The Ballyholme woman was identified by her pair of Scandinavian oval brooches, but a fragmentary bronze

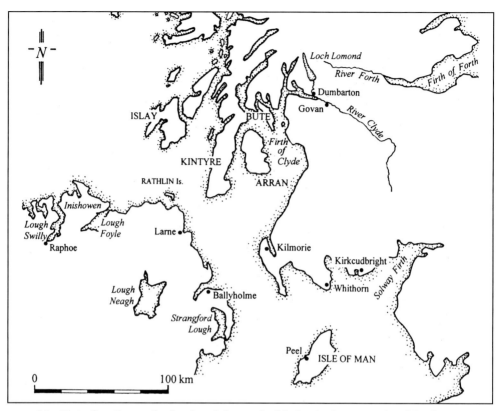

6.1 Map of south-west Scotland and the north of Ireland: places mentioned in the text.

bowl is also reported as having 'had a fine piece of chain attached [and] a quantity of wool inside it'. The identification of the other pagan Norse burials which have been suggested for the north of Ireland is far from probable, including a lost find of a sword, hammer and whetstone at Cah, near Banagher, in Co. Derry. A Viking period boat-burial has been postulated from a former bog at Ballywillin, Co. Antrim, where an oak boat (without iron rivets) was found in 1813, about a mile from the sea, 'in a mound about 40 feet in diameter, composed of stones and clay, but chiefly moss . . . Several bones have been found in it, to what species of animal they belong cannot be ascertained; the air speedily dissolves them. Some silver coins have been found in it, the letters cannot be distinctly discerned.' This contemporary description is taken from a newspaper account written by a local antiquary, but another source (also dated August 1813) identifies the coins as being of Edward III. It is of course possible that a medieval coin-hoard was concealed in a pagan Norse burial mound, but the fact remains that there is no surviving evidence by which the boat can be dated.

Finally, a possible Viking period cemetery has been suggested for the shore at Kinnegar Strand, on the west side of Lough Swilly (Co. Donegal), but the only known artefact of relevant date is a plain ringed-pin found on the beach amongst fallen stones, in the same area as the earlier discovery of a cist-burial containing a cremation which was thought to be of Bronze Age date.

Even if all these graves are taken into account, the pagan Norse burial evidence from the northern mainland of Ireland is insufficient to demonstrate that there was anything in the way of lasting Scandinavian settlement, as does likewise the general absence of Norse place-names. However, an important exception is provided by *Ulfrecksfiord*, an early name for Larne Harbour, in which the element 'fjord' has been compounded with the man's name 'Ulfrekr', suggesting that for some time it will have formed his base – in which context, it is worth recalling the Viking burial from near Larne, noted above. Two such Norse topographical names have survived in use for the sea loughs of Strangford (Co. Down) and Carlingford (Co. Louth), both of which open off the Irish Sea and were a focus of Viking activity in the 920s; the former means 'rough or rapid fjord', from the tidal currents in its narrow entry, and the latter is 'fjord of the hags', from the three mountain-tops (known as the Three Nuns), which form the main landmark for boats entering the lough. It was not far south of Carlingford, across Dundalk Bay, that in 841 the Vikings established, at Annagassan, one of their earliest winter-bases in Ireland.

The Irish historical sources provide clear evidence that as a direct result of successful Irish resistance the Vikings never succeeded in establishing permanent settlements along the northern coasts of Ireland. In 866, we are told that the king of the Northern Uí Néill rooted out 'all the nests of pirates' from Donegal to Antrim, although later Vikings were notably active in and around Inishowen during the 920s and 930s. This ninth-century eviction might well have led to a new phase of land-taking in western Scotland, which could have included some Norse by then familiar with the 'Souterrain Ware' of north-eastern Ireland, as suggested for the Udal, North Uist (p. 81).

In 921, a Viking leader by name of Alcob, with thirty-two ships, was terrorising Lough Foyle from an island base off Inishowen, until driven off by King Fergal of Ailech, who broke up one of the Viking ships after seizing its cargo. At the same time another Viking fleet, of twenty ships, was operating not far to the west on Mulroy Lough. Then later, in 939, after an Irish confederation had attacked Dublin and other Norse strongholds, Ailech was stormed by a Viking force which captured Muirchertach, the then king of the Northern Uí Néill, carrying him off to their fleet, but as 'God redeemed him from them', he was presumably released after payment of a ransom.

This period of Norse activity provides the most probable context for the deposition of four Viking period silver hoards, which consist mostly of arm-rings, in the northern part of Co. Donegal. Three of these coinless hoards are known from the Inishowen peninsula and the fourth was found near Raphoe, to the south-west (Figure 6.2). Given that there is no other archaeological material, nor any historical evidence, to demonstrate the presence of any tenth-century Scandinavian settlers in this area, it seems probable that this quantity of Hiberno-Norse wealth was the result of the short-lived presence in this area of Viking raiders. Indeed, there is no reason why some, at least, may not have formed part of the very cargo seized by King Fergal!

THE FIRTH OF CLYDE

Some of the earliest Viking raiders to have operated off the west coast of Scotland will have turned about the Mull of Kintyre into the Firth of Clyde, for one of their dead was buried, or at least commemorated, on the island of Arran, at Millhill – a site overlooking Lamlash

6.2 Silver hoard from near Raphoe, Co. Donegal, consisting of six arm-rings, four ingots and a piece of hack-silver; the arm-rings in the upper row are of the so-called 'Hiberno-Viking' type (Sotheby Parke Bernet and Co.).

Bay (Figure 5.7). A single-edged sword and a shield seem to have been placed together on top of a presumed burial, although there is no mention of a body having been found (in 1896), because the type of mineralised fly puparia within the boss are only consistent with its exposure for a considerable time, at least while the shield-board rotted and corrosion took place (personal communication, Andrew Whittington). These weapons may thus mark the site of a ninth-century cenotaph, although it is possible that cremated remains went unnoticed during the removal of the small gravel mound which contained them.

There is, however, a definite ninth-century Norse burial on the opposite side of Lamlash Bay, in a prominent position on King's Cross Point. This appears to have been the grave of a high-status woman whose cremated remains had been placed within a stone setting, under a mound. An iron lock-plate and clasp indicate the presence of a wooden chest in the burial, which may also account for the discovery of four rivets and an iron nail. More significant are the burnt remains of a whalebone plaque and a Northumbrian copper styca of Archbishop Wigmund of York (837–54), indicating a mid- to late ninth-century date for the actual burial.

However, caution needs to be exercised in interpreting this burial evidence as necessarily representing any significant Scandinavian land-taking, given the lack of any other archaeological evidence for a permanent Norse presence on Arran. Indeed, it has been argued from the evidence of the island's place-names that such never took place. In Nicolaisen's opinion:

> The majority of names speaks to us of an island that was thoroughly Gaelic for well over twelve hundred years, with a Norse adstratum in which references to permanent settlement, indeed any kind of settlement, are absent and in which hints at seasonal occupation and exploitation dominate.

This conclusion is based on the fact that the Scandinavian nomenclature of the island 'experiences the island from the sea, not only visually but also while exploring and utilising it. It is a sailor's toponymic vocabulary and that of the fisherman and the hunter and the herdsman involved in transhumance.' In other words, it is likely that Arran – as also Bute and Cumbrae – never experienced much in the way of permanent Scandinavian settlement, but were exploited instead by the Hebridean Norsemen in the same manner as the west coast of the Scottish mainland.

No pagan Norse grave is known in Bute with any certainty, given that the find circumstances of a Viking sword-hilt on Drumachloy Farm went unrecorded at the beginning of the century, although from a later period there survives a fragment of a Norse rune-inscribed cross from the island of Inchmarnock, off the west coast (p. 43). On Arran, a Norse carving comprising an interlace pattern has recently been identified at the mouth of

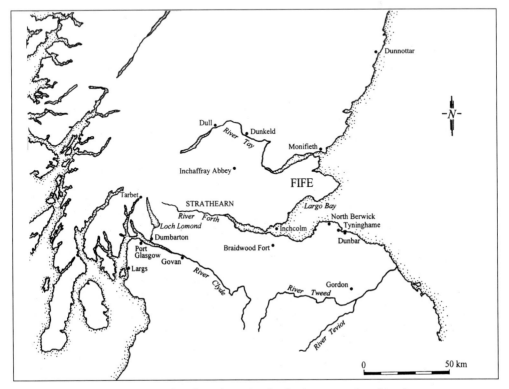

6.3 Map of central and southern Scotland: places mentioned in the text.

the southernmost of the King's Caves, at Blackwaterfoot. It has been suggested that ogam inscriptions and a large cross carved into the King's Caves may attest to a tradition that these natural sea caves had been used by early Christian hermits. From Millport, on Great Cumbrae, there is a sculptured stone, possibly part of a lintel, which is decorated with what has been described as 'a highly irregular interlace type with potential Viking characteristics.'

Only one other metal artefact of definite Norse type and Viking period date has been discovered in Bute, although there is a Late Norse gold finger-ring from a twelfth-century hoard found near St Blane's monastery, Kingarth. This is a bronze-capped lead weight related to those in the Kiloran Bay ship-burial on Colonsay (Figure 7.4), for use with a portable balance. It was amongst the objects recovered from a partially excavated settlement on the coast at Little Dunagoil, also near St Blane's monastery. The Norse character of the Dunagoil weight is particularly distinctive because its ornamental mount consists of an openwork boss from a Scandinavian oval brooch of late ninth/tenth-century date.

On the mainland opposite, there is a small group of Norse place-names around Largs in Ayrshire, but there are no reasons to suppose any early settlement in this area. A seasonal beach-market of interest to Viking raiders and/or traders may be suggested for Stevenston Sands, near Ardrossan, where eighth/ninth-century objects have been found, as well as an Arabic silver dirham of early tenth-century date. The only other archaeological evidence for Norse contact with this coastline is the great silver brooch, with gold filigree and amber settings, which was found on the hillside at Hunterston, opposite the Cumbrae Islands. This has an Old Norse inscription in Scandinavian runes on the reverse (p. 43), naming a Celt as the owner: 'Melbrigda owns [this] brooch'. The brooch, which is of Irish type, was already an heirloom when it came into the possession of the Norse-speaking Melbrigda, as it was made in the late seventh or early eighth century, whereas a tenth-century date has been suggested for the runic inscription.

On entering the Clyde, Viking raiders would have been confronted by the principal fortress of the Strathclyde Britons at Dumbarton Castle, anciently known as *Alt Clut* or Clyde Rock (Figure 1.7). The Rock stands at the junction of the maritime Clyde with the navigable rivers Clyde and Leven, controlling access to their two fertile valleys and ultimately to the North Sea beyond, for the Leven issues from Loch Lomond which would have led, by short portages, to rivers flowing east. It was thus perfectly possible for a Viking fleet desirous of crossing from the west coast to the east to have done so without sailing the northern route. There is evidence enough to indicate that this route was indeed travelled on occasion, but not that it came into regular use for communication between the Viking kingdoms of Dublin and York, as is sometimes suggested (Figure 6.3).

In 870, the *Annals of Ulster* record that Olaf and Ivar, 'two kings of the Northmen', sacked Clyde Rock after a siege of four months' duration, following which the name is heard of no more, so that we may share Leslie Alcock's belief 'that the destruction was complete'. Alcock's excavations on the Rock showed that the eastern (mainland) side of the summit was defended by a rampart of earth, rubble and timber, which had been destroyed by fire – an event attributable to the activities of Olaf and Ivar. In the area of this rampart were found two objects of distinctive Norse character and Viking period date: one is part of a sword-hilt, with ribbed ornament, and the other a lead weight incorporating a piece of an Irish glass bangle, although a second lead weight from the site, which is plain, might well also date from the Viking period (Figure 6.4). Alcock cautions properly against too readily assuming that the presence of these objects on Clyde Rock is likewise to be attributed to the activities of Olaf and Ivar, rather than to some earlier episode, either warlike or peaceful.

Olaf and Ivar's expedition was far from over with the successful plundering of the citadel, for in the following year it is recorded that the victorious kings went from northern Britain (*Alba*) to Dublin with 200 ships and a great booty of slaves from the Angles, the Britons and the Picts. The likelihood that they had embarked on their slave-raiding by way of the Leven and Loch Lomond is highlighted by a Viking warrior burial (or cenotaph), which could well be of this date, on the west side of the loch, at the outfall of Glen Fruin.

The evidence for this burial consists of a bent sword, a dented shield-boss and a spear-head, which were found together in 1851 in the top of a mound called Boiden, near the lower Bridge of Fruin, but which are now known only from nineteenth-century water-colours. There is no mention of a skeleton, but such may have decayed away more or less

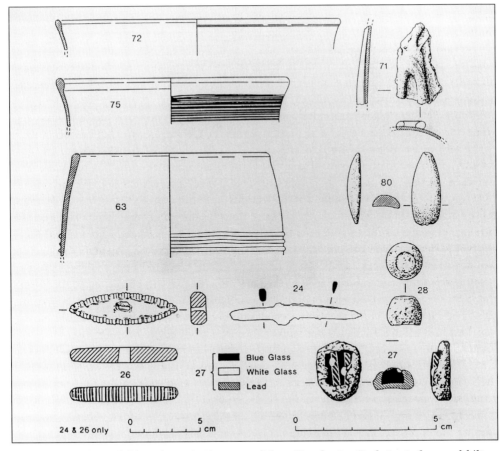

6.4 Viking period objects (nos 26–8) excavated from Dumbarton Rock: part of a sword-hilt and a lead weight set with a fragment of Irish glass bangle, together with a plain lead weight (after L. Alcock and E. A. Alcock, 1990).

completely, although the body might have been cremated for, in the Scandinavian homelands, this ritual could involve the deliberate destruction of weapons before burial, such
as the bending of sword-blades.

The fact that Olaf and Ivar were prepared to devote four months to the siege of Clyde
Rock suggests that it was a prize worth taking and that its subsequent destruction might
have been intended to open up the East Midlands to raiding from the west. It is worth
remembering, however, that Loch Lomond did not have to be approached by way of the
Leven, for it was also accessible by portage from Loch Long (at Tarbet), the overland route
said to have been taken in 1263 by the Norwegian invasion fleet.

THE CENTRAL LOWLANDS

Scattered across the Central Lowlands, amongst the English and Gaelic place-names, are
a small number of Norse names. These notably do not include any settlement-names
containing such generics as *staðir* and *bólstaðir* that were so typical of the northern and
western areas of Norse settlement. Instead, there are place-names with *býr* endings (Figure
3.2), which are normally assumed to reflect Danish influence, but there is a problem of
dating. As the place-name specialist Gillian Fellows-Jensen has commented, 'some may
derive from the Viking Age proper and others not have been coined until the eleventh or
even the twelfth century'. It would be unwise therefore to suppose that they, or those
around Largs, can be taken as evidence of much in the way of permanent Scandinavian
settlement in the Forth and Clyde estuaries at this period.

Alongside these place-names are sometimes mapped the 'hogback' stone monuments
which have a somewhat similar distribution across the Central Lowlands, but with outliers
to the south-east and in the far north (Figure 13.1). Hogbacks are named after their most
distinctive feature, being 'house-shaped recumbent monuments of the Viking Age with a
definitive curve to the roof ridge', in the words of James Lang who undertook their definitive study. They originated in the Viking Kingdom of York where they were a short-lived,
tenth-century fashion. The hogback has thus, in its origins at any rate, been classified as a
'Viking colonial monument', but even if all the Scottish hogbacks dated from the mid-tenth
century (when the type appears to have been first introduced from northern England), it
would be unwise to suppose that beneath every one of them must have lain someone of
Scandinavian descent. Innovations in grave monuments can spread and be adopted, and
then adapted, outside their area of origin in exactly the same way as fashions for anything
else. It is important to note that only a small number of the Scottish hogbacks are closely
matched in northern England, but amongst them is that on the Isle of Inchcolm in the
Firth of Forth, one from Tyninghame in East Lothian, and the earliest of a group of five at
Govan on the south bank of the Clyde (Figure 6.5). Indeed, Lang has even speculated that
the latter stone might have been imported by sea from Cumbria where it finds its closest
parallels.

Tempting though it has been for some to see the distribution of hogbacks as demon-
strating the presence of 'Scandinavian enclaves' in areas lacking much else in the way of
evidence for Scandinavian settlement, it is important to remember that this type of grave
memorial continued in Scotland to enjoy an occasional use down to the twelfth century
when they can certainly not be considered to represent more than a distant reflex of a

6.5 *The earliest of a group of five hogback stone monuments at Govan on the Clyde (T. E. Gray).*

much earlier Scandinavian influence. At the same time, it is reasonable to suppose that some Danelaw settlers will have taken refuge from the English in the north, before or at the time of the fall of York and the death of Eric Bloodaxe in 954. Some such refugees may well, for example, account for the naming of the farm of Humbie in East Lothian and, at the same time, for the introduction into the Central Lowlands of a fashion for hogbacks.

The most magnificent Scandinavian gold ring known from Scotland was found, at the end of the eighteenth century, in Braidwood Fort, a prehistoric hill-fort at Penicuik, Midlothian. Unfortunately, this massive neck-ring of twisted rods, described originally as 'a Roman girdle', met with the usual fate of such objects of precious metal at this date, being sold to a jeweller for its weight in gold. This late ninth/tenth-century ring has only a few parallels in Norway and Denmark for its great size and it must have been the property of a high-status Viking. However, the events that brought it to the Forth (and caused its concealment and non-recovery) are inevitably unknown, although Braidwood Fort might conceivably have served as a temporary base for a marauding force, during (say) Ivar's plunderings of the Central Lowlands in 903–4.

Another chance-find from Midlothian is a bronze, Baltic-style, penannular brooch found nearer the Forth, in 1811, in a gravel-pit at Gogar Burn. The find-circumstances are such that there is no way of knowing whether it formed part of a grave deposit.

The contents of a Viking period silver hoard found near Port Glasgow, at the end of the seventeenth century, are too poorly documented for the date of its concealment to be much more than guessed at. It comprises a couple of arm-rings and an unknown number of uncertain coins so that the proposed deposition date of 'c. 970' needs the addition of a question mark. Caution must therefore be exercised in its interpretation, for although it may well be, as Barbara Crawford has suggested, that the Port Glasgow hoard is 'a sign of Scandinavian activity (and some disturbance) in the region at the time when the Govan hogbacks were being commissioned', it could be that it only arrived in the Clyde estuary a generation later.

THE EAST MIDLANDS

The nature and extent of the Scandinavian presence in the east of Scotland has received little attention because there is no evidence of large-scale settlement. However, the wealthy East Midlands experienced repeated incursions from Viking raiders, at least two of which are known to have involved prolonged stays. Three main periods of Scandinavian activity can be recognised, when the evidence of the *Old Scottish Chronicle* is combined with that of the Irish annals. The first began in 839 and carried on into the reign of Kenneth mac Alpin (d. 858), the king of Dalriada who conquered or annexed southern Pictland, when 'the Danes wasted Pictland to Clunie and Dunkeld'. Next, during the reign of his son Constantine (862–76/7), there was a period of particular devastation when his kingdom was invaded three or four times by Hiberno-Norse and Scottish Vikings, with hostage-taking and the exaction of tribute, and 'the Northmen spent a whole year in Pictland'. The third phase started at the end of the ninth century, during the reign of Constantine's son Donald (889–900), who on one occasion defeated the Vikings – but they returned and took Dunnottar. Hiberno-Norse Vikings were back again at the beginning of the tenth century, after the succession of Donald's cousin Constantine II, when Ivar and his kins-men, expelled from Dublin in 902, went 'plundering Dunkeld and all *Alba*', before being defeated in Strathearn the following year. Later, however, Constantine (who gave up the throne in 943) allied himself with the Hiberno-Norse against the English, and it was other Vikings who killed his son, Indulf, in 962. During a reign of over forty years Constantine had been a powerful king, who had extended his authority south of the Forth.

It has been suggested that some of the few Scandinavian place-names in Fife and Lothian, as well as a couple in Angus, are to be attributed to this mid-tenth-century period of activity, with land being given in return for mercenary service (Figure 3.2). Simon Taylor has recognised at least six *býr* names in Fife, all of which belong to isolated farms, on marginal land, which may have been 'cleared and settled by those who named them'. In support of an early date for these names, Taylor points to there being 'a particular cluster of -*bý(r)* names in the vicinity of Inchcolm, with its important early hogback'. In fact, this 'cluster' consists of only three such names and it is doubtful whether this tenth-century hogback, from an important ecclesiastical site, should be used thus in support of their dating. It cannot be ruled out that they might instead belong to a later period, that of the twelfth-century 'influx into Lowland Scotland north of the Forth from Lothian and northern England of speakers of a northern Anglian dialect with Scandinavian features, many of whom had Scandinavian names' (cf. the discussion of similar names in the sections on the Central Lowlands and South-west Scotland).

On the other hand, Taylor also draws attention to a second group of place-names as evidence for tenth-century Scandinavian settlement in Fife and Kinross. This consists of at least six place-names which contain the Gaelic element *gall*, meaning 'foreigner, stranger', as applied to the Norse. Interestingly, these are all inland settlements and there may well be a good case for interpreting them as the farmsteads of Hiberno-Norse mercenaries in retirement.

The archaeological legacy of all this Viking period activity in the East Midlands is slight. Two Pictish silver brooches of late eighth/ninth-century type which were found together at Clunie near Dunkeld, in Perthshire, may well have been buried by, or because of, one of the Norse raiding parties; but this is mere speculation. Equally uncertain are the reasons for the deposition at Crieff, in Strathearn, of some fine decorative mounts of similar date, perhaps from a book-shrine. Amongst the silver from the largest known hoard of Pictish treasure, which was found in (or about) 1819 at Norrie's Law in Fife, is a fragment of a silver arm-ring of Hiberno-Viking type, dating to the late ninth or early tenth century, but none of the other surviving silver need be later in date than the seventh century. It has been suggested therefore that this piece of Hiberno-Viking hack-silver must represent a separate find made on the Largo estate, whether or not at Norrie's Law itself, which became amalgamated with the Pictish hoard before the remaining silver was donated to the National Museum (the greater part of it having been melted down on discovery). Whatever the story behind this stray-find, there is no doubt that Largo Bay would have made a fine haven for a Viking fleet on the Firth of Forth.

There are no tenth-century silver hoards from this region, although two or three are known of eleventh-century date from Fife and Perthshire. A mixed hoard found at Parkhill near Lindores Abbey, Fife, in 1814 is now lost, but there were said to have been 'some gold chains and bracelets', buried together 'with a considerable quantity of ancient silver coins' in a lidded stone vessel. It contained coins of Cnut indicating that it was not deposited much before about 1030. This suggests that its loss may well have taken place during the period when, according to *Orkneyinga saga*, Earl Thorfinn the Mighty spent some time laying waste to Fife (although Cnut himself led an army into Scotland in 1031).

A group of ten Hiberno-Norse coins is recorded only as having been found 'in Fifeshire in 1832' and it has been suggested that they might in fact be a parcel from the 1814 Parkhill find. No doubt, however, surrounds the more recent (1989) discovery of a small hoard of Hiberno-Norse pennies in a field at Dull in Perthshire (deposited c. 1025). Dull was a monastic site and this may explain the Irish connection indicated by these coins from Dublin, which is certainly the case with another recent Perthshire find, the openwork crest of an eleventh-century bell-shrine, from Inchaffray Abbey (Figure 6.6). This fine object, which is cast in copper alloy, but inlaid with silver and niello, is decorated with animal-head terminals and foliate interlace in the Irish version of the Ringerike style.

No pagan Norse burial has yet been found in the east of Scotland to represent the dead of the Viking raiders, armies or settlers, although there are single-finds of a ninth-century Anglo-Saxon sword from near Dollar, in Clackmannanshire, and of a possible Viking sword in Perth. In this connection it is important to note that the oft-quoted existence of

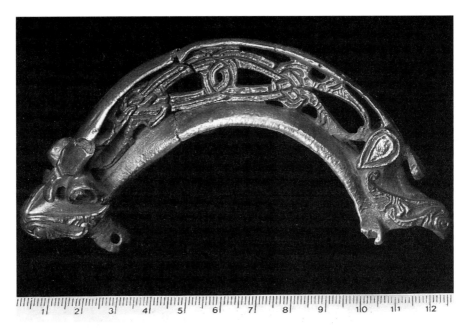

6.6 Mutilated crest from an eleventh-century bell-shrine, found at Inchaffray Abbey in Perthshire; it is decorated in the Irish version of the Ringerike style of Viking art (NMS).

a female burial with oval brooches at Errol, near Perth, has no factual basis. This supposed grave-find came into being in the 1950s as a result of confusion over some unreliable information concerning the unknown provenance of a fine pair of such brooches in Perth Museum, which were first recorded in the eighteenth century in a private collection. It is most probable that the single Scandinavian brooch from the Bridge of Earn, also near Perth, which takes the form of a stylised animal-head, is likewise a collector's item. This is a late Viking period example of a type that is specifically characteristic of the Baltic island of Gotland, where well-dressed women wore such brooches in pairs in place of the otherwise ubiquitous oval brooches. It stands out as being the only one of its kind said to have been found in Britain or Ireland.

Finally, from north of the Tay, there is one even more enigmatic find to be noted – a unique artefact in the form of a bronze crescent, with Pictish symbols on both sides, to which has been added a short inscription in Scandinavian runes. This was found in 1796 at the Laws, Monifieth, near Dundee, but it is now lost and so known only from a nineteenth-century illustration which 'does not give any basis for reconstructing the text', according to the Norwegian runologist Aslak Liestøl.

NORTH-EASTERN SCOTLAND

Further to the north-east, it is once again possible that the ninth-century Pictish silver hoard from Croy, near Inverness, was deposited and not recovered as a result of Viking activity. It has likewise been suggested that a Viking intervention may explain the presence of a splendid silver horn-mount, of ninth-century English workmanship, in the Pictish promontory fort of Burghead, on the north coast of Morayshire. Radiocarbon dating has demonstrated that Burghead was attacked sometime in the late ninth or early tenth century, but on this evidence alone the nationality of the attackers cannot be determined and there is nothing of Scandinavian character amongst the surviving material found in the fort.

It is worth noting, however, that *Orkneyinga saga* recounts how Earl Sigurd seized Moray at the end of the ninth century and built a fort there (see p. 258). Some such episode will doubtless account for the chance-find of a Viking sword at Gortons in Strathspey. As for pagan Norse graves, considerable uncertainty surrounds the discovery in 1829, at nearby Ballindalloch, of a man and a horse, given that the fragments of the horse's bit and a possible shield are now lost. On the other hand, a putative runic inscription on a stone from Knockando, also in Morayshire, has been shown by Aslak Liestøl to date from the eighteenth century!

SOUTH-EASTERN SCOTLAND

A group of late hogback stones in the Tweed and Teviot valleys has suggested to Barbara Crawford 'a long-established [Scandinavian] community which must have spread inland from the coast'. However, in the absence of any other archaeological evidence for 'long-established' Scandinavian settlements in the south-east, whether inland or on the coast, the hogbacks alone are not sufficient to demonstrate this unequivocally. The half-dozen monuments in question have mostly been attributed by James Lang to the late eleventh and early twelfth century, by which time hogbacks had been out of fashion in northern England for at least a century and so their use at this period suggests some links with the Central Lowlands. In addition, the distribution of Scandinavian place-names in Berwickshire is sparse and, as in the Central Lowlands, difficult to date. There is certainly nothing to indicate large-scale land-taking, and the evidence that we do have seems once again to be more suggestive of refugees and their descendants.

An earlier phase of Scandinavian activity must account for the presence of the one distinctive Viking period hoard from south-east Scotland. This coinless treasure was found in about 1838 during the clearance of a cairn at Gordon in Berwickshire. Once again it has been lost, although much detail is preserved in the fine engraving which was published in 1885 (Figure 12.4). The hoard consisted of only five pieces, including a gold finger-ring and a fragment of the same type of Hiberno-Viking arm-ring as that found at Largo in Fife. This latter points to an Irish Sea connection and suggests a date for its concealment in the late ninth or early tenth century. An obvious occasion for its deposition in this area is thus provided by the activities of Ragnall, a member of the Scandinavian dynasty of Dublin, who raided and fought in the Lowlands on several occasions, during the second decade of the tenth century, before he took the throne in York. Such events may also provide the explanation for the arrival of fine ninth/tenth-century antler combs, of classic Scandinavian type, at both the coastal sites of North Berwick and Dunbar (Figure 6.7), although one might well speculate as to the possible development of a northern trade in these essential toiletry requisites. Those made of antler were certainly the most durable – and both these examples have every appearance of being the products of specialised comb-makers.

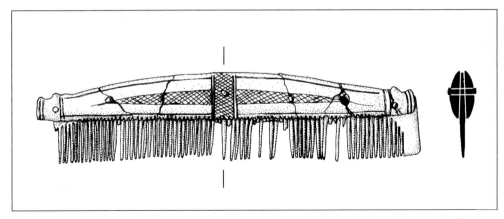

6.7 Viking period comb of classic Scandinavian type excavated at Dunbar, East Lothian (D. Monro: SUAT).

There are another two silver hoards from the south-east, which are to be dated to the tenth and eleventh centuries, but neither of them need have any 'Viking' connections. A hoard of Anglo-Saxon coins (deposited c. 930–50) was found near the ruins of St Helen's church at Cockburnspath, Berwickshire, in about 1831, together with what was described as 'an ancient rosary', but all are lost. The later hoard (c. 1000–25) found at Jedburgh, Roxburghshire, in 1827 is also lost; this is said to have contained 'a ring formed of silver wire, twined'.

SOUTH-WEST SCOTLAND

The nature and extent of the Scandinavian impact on Galloway and Dumfriesshire has often been exaggerated. Indeed, this part of the south-west mainland was more involved with Hiberno-Norse activity and Anglo-Scandinavian expansion from the northern Danelaw than it was with the rest of Scandinavian Scotland. Given the slightness of both the historical and archaeological record, the place-name evidence will be considered first.

The Scandinavian place-names of Galloway and Dumfriesshire differ markedly from those in northern and western Scotland, being linked most closely with those of north-west England. There are concentrations of Scandinavian place-names in eastern Dumfriesshire, with a fairly large area to the west and north of Kirkcudbright and a smaller area in the region of Whithorn (Figure 3.1). These would seem to be the result of a land-ward expansion of settlement by way of Cumbria, across the Carlisle plain, with a trickle extending along the coast to Galloway. This immigration from the northern Danelaw is most evident in the distribution of settlement-names with *býr* endings. According to Gillian Fellows-Jensen:

> The settlers in Dumfriesshire took over old-established settlements from their Anglian predecessors and would also seem to have split up some old estates into small inde-pendent units that were given names in -*by* . . . [they] would also seem to have cleared woodland in order to establish new settlements on virgin land – the *thveits*.

Thveit means 'clearing', but despite there being nineteen such place-names in Dumfriesshire (and it is particularly common in Cumbria), there is not a single example in Galloway. Gillian Fellows-Jensen has suggested that

> The settlers around Kirkcudbright may well have come by land from Dumfriesshire but it is also possible that they had crossed the Solway Firth from Cumberland. The sea-route is perhaps the more likely one to have been taken by the settlers around Whithorn. Richard Bailey has pointed to evidence for artistic contact in the Viking period between this area and the coastal plain of Cumberland, a contact which by-passes the Carlisle plain, Dumfriesshire and Kirkcudbrightshire.

However, this notion of a Gaelic-Norse sculptural province spanning the Solway has been criticised by Derek Craig in that only one element from the 'decorative package' in use in Cumbria – the so-called 'stopped plait' type of interlace – occurs on the Galloway stones. He comments:

> In this region too it is just one ingredient in a very distinctive local style, and like the disc-heads also found on these 'Whithorn School' stones it seems to be a feature more indicative of the relative date of such sculpture and the type of stone used, than of a Gaelic-Norse Solway province.

One Norse name of particular interest in Dumfriesshire is Tinwald. This is a *thing* name, as encountered in the Tingwalls of both Orkney and Shetland, and Dingwall on the Cromarty Firth (as also Tynwald in the Isle of Man). This is evidence therefore for the existence of a Scandinavian administrative centre, but as Fellows-Jensen observes, its location 'in an area where Scandinavian place-names are comparatively rare is rather strange. It must be significant that Tinwald is not far from the county town of Dumfries.' She continues:

> The settlers in Galloway cannot have been anywhere near as numerous as those in Dumfriesshire. There is no place-name evidence for fragmentation of large estates into *bys*, or for the clearing of woodland to establish *thveits*. There is, however, evidence that many of the settlements with Scandinavian names were among the more important settlements in the region.

There were, however, settlers of Norwegian origin who reached both south-west Scotland and north-west England by way of the west of Scotland, even though there are no examples of the familiar place-names in *staðir, setr* or *bólstaðir*. From a combination of sources, David Dumville has recently deduced 'that around 900 Galloway or some part of it fell under the control of vikings from the Western Isles', suggesting that the 'Gaelic-Scandinavian settlement in Galloway, Mann, and Cumbria was part of a progressive extension of viking-activity around the northwestern coast of Britain'.

Sculptural evidence has been much used in the past to argue for extensive Scandinavian settlement in Galloway, but this hypothesis has been thoroughly scrutinised – and rejected – by Derek Craig, as part of his wider study of the pre-Norman sculpture of Galloway and Dumfriesshire. In reaching this conclusion, he points to the absence from this material of Scandinavian runic inscriptions, of Scandinavian art-styles, of the circle-headed crosses and 'ring-chain' ornament, as found in the Isle of Man and Cumbria, and of scenes related to Norse mythology, with one possible exception from Kilmorie (Figure 6.8), to be discussed further below (p. 251). He also notes that 'there are no hog-backs, although like the Isle of Man, twenty miles to the south, this may also have to do with unsuitable geology'.

The evidence of pagan Norse burials is likewise slight for this region, there being only a couple of probable graves on record. A sword, plain ringed-pin and a bead were found, under unknown circumstances (before 1925), in St Cuthbert's churchyard in Kirkcudbright. Such Viking burials are also known from churchyards elsewhere in Britain and Ireland, including the Isle of Man, but this practice is one that is open to varied interpretation. More problematic is the following eighteenth-century account of a further Kirkcudbright-shire find, on its donation to the Society of Antiquaries of Scotland:

> A parcel of burnt human bones, among which are several teeth, found in the heart of a cairn, in the lands of Blackerne, and parish of Crossmichael, when the stones were taken to inclose a plantation in the year 1756. In the middle of the bottom of this cairn was found a coffin, composed of flat whin stones.

Part of a silver arm-ring and an amber bead were 'also found in the above mentioned cairn' and there is no doubt that the former is of Viking period type, as most probably also the

6.8 Cross-slab from Kilmorie, Wigtownshire, with a possible scene from the Sigurd legend; below the Crucifixion, there is depicted a figure between two birds and a pair of tongs, with a possible anvil (after J. Stuart, 1867).

bead. But is this a primary Norse burial; or a secondary Norse burial in a prehistoric cairn; or simply some precious objects hidden for safety in a prominent landmark?

A ninth-century Anglo-Saxon sword from near Ecclefechan, Dumfriesshire, was a single-find without any evidence of an interment. It is likewise difficult to make much of the chance-finds of a magnificent gold finger-ring from Tundergarth, also in Dumfriesshire, a plain silver arm-ring which was dropped in the Solway Firth, near Gretna, presumably during a crossing of the sands, a glass linen smoother from Kirkcudbright and another from Dalvadie in Galloway (previously thought to have been found in Islay).

This lack of archaeological evidence is matched by an absence of historical sources, although a couple of entries in the *Chronicle of Man* suggest that the rulers of nearby Man may have had control over estates in Galloway. When Magnus Barelegs conquered Man in 1098, the Manx chronicle relates that 'he subdued the people of Galloway to such an extent that he compelled them to cut timber and take it to the shore for the construction of his defensive positions' (that is to say, for the building of fortifications in Man rather than in Galloway itself).

It was presumably a variety of such economic resources which would have first attracted the Vikings to Galloway, as both raiders and traders. A mixed hoard found at Talnotrie, as a result of peat-cutting in May and June 1912, is difficult to interpret, although it is perhaps best explained as the property of a native metalworker. Only some of the objects and coins were spotted in the actual peat-moss; others were found as cut peats were being broken to put on the fire. At least a couple of pieces were retrieved from the ashes, whereas one of the pins was picked up in the garden by the finder's daughter! It is most unlikely therefore that the full contents of the Talnotrie hoard are now known. What survives consists of three Anglo-Saxon silver ornaments (two pins and a strap-end), a gold finger-ring, a globular pin-head of bronze and some scrap metal, together with a lead weight (capped with a decorative bronze mount), a cake of wax, a rough agate, a perforated disc of jet or lignite and three claystone spindle-whorls. In addition, there are the remains of fourteen coins, which date its deposition to the early or mid-870s. The majority of these are Anglo-Saxon, but amongst them are fragments of a denier of Louis the Pious and two Arabic dirhams. These foreign coins (as also the characteristic lead weight) suggest some form of contact with Norse traders in the region.

There is no record of the wealthy ecclesiastical centre at Whithorn having been raided, but then nothing is known historically of Whithorn between c. 833/6 and c. 1128. However, the evidence from excavation and of stone sculpture demonstrates its continued survival as a regional centre, even if it seems to have undergone a material decline in the ninth century. In fact, the recent excavations at Whithorn have thrown entirely new light on the vexed question of the nature and extent of the Norse presence in Galloway. By the eleventh century, as described below (pp. 202–5), the road approaching Whithorn was lined with the dwellings and workshops of seemingly Hiberno-Norse artisans, processing local raw materials into products for the Irish Sea trade.

THE IRISH SEA AND THE ISLE OF MAN

The presence of a Hiberno-Norse community at Whithorn in the eleventh century, with Dublin and wider Irish Sea connections, is highlighted by the discovery there of a

Hiberno-Norse coin of Dublin (another such is also known, as an old find) and of a Chester-minted coin of Cnut. But the Norsemen did not stop at modern borders! For some, the Northern and Western Isles of Scotland provided a convenient sailing-route from Norway and the North Atlantic islands – the Faroes and Iceland – into the Irish Sea and beyond for trade and exchange in luxury goods, such as the walrus ivory found in Dublin.

The story of Scandinavian settlement around the Irish Sea needs a book of its own, but the economic links between Scandinavian Scotland and this region during the Viking period, followed by the creation of the Kingdom of Man and the Isles in the Late Norse period, mean that its origins and something of its development need to be outlined here.

The earliest recorded presence of Vikings on the waters of the Irish Sea is for the year 798 when there was a raid on *Inis Pátraic*, identified with Holmpatrick, off the Dublin coast. Raiding continued on a sporadic basis for a generation, intensifying in the 830s, leading to the establishment of the first winter-bases, including both Dublin and Annagassan, as noted above (p. 95). Dublin survived to become a permanent settlement and a royal seat, although the Irish did succeed in temporarily driving out the Vikings in 902.

The most important collection of ninth-century Viking grave-goods in existence from Britain and Ireland was formed as the result of nineteenth-century railway construction in Dublin, being gathered up from pagan Norse burials at Kilmainham and Islandbridge. Kilmainham was the site of a monastery beside the River Liffey, some way up-river from the centre of the medieval and modern city, and it seems probable that it was seized to serve as the winter-base, or *longphort*, in 841. Later, when the Norsemen succeeded in re-establishing themselves at Dublin, some fifteen years after their expulsion, they chose a new and more convenient site nearer the river mouth. This was at the confluence between the Liffey and the Poddle, where the 'Black Pool' was located which is the meaning of the name 'Dublin'. There at any rate, the excavations of Breandán Ó Ríordáin, Patrick Wallace and their successors have revealed the extensive remains of a flourishing tenth-century and later settlement. This was fully urban in character and, in about 997, Sihtric III became the first of its kings to strike a Hiberno-Norse coinage.

There is no documentary evidence concerning the Scandinavian settlement of either the Isle of Man or north-west England, except that one of the Viking leaders, Ingimund, who was expelled from Dublin in 902, is known to have gone first to Anglesey, before being driven on to England where he and his followers were allowed to settle near Chester. This crisis may well have precipitated Scandinavian land-taking in Lancashire and Cumbria, although it has been suggested that those who moved eastwards from Ireland did so to join earlier Norse settlers. Place-name evidence in Cumbria suggests the presence of settlers from the Western Isles; others, as we have seen, moved westwards from the Danelaw. In fact, none of the pagan Norse burials from north-west England, nor any of the other archaeological evidence, need date from before about 900. The pagan graves are not themselves numerous and soon gave way to a wealth of Christian sculpture, some of which was to influence its development in Scandinavian Scotland. Finally, a dramatic reminder of the wealth of the Viking Dubliners is provided by a number of silver hoards, chief amongst them being the massive treasure found at Cuerdale, beside the River Ribble (near Preston) in Lancashire, which had been deposited c. 905. Much of the silver bullion in this 40kg hoard appears to be of Hiberno-Norse origin, although many of its coins were newly minted in Viking York.

The Isle of Man is rich in Viking period archaeology, with a quantity of finds which is all the more remarkable for its small size, but then the place-name evidence makes it clear that Scandinavian settlement was widespread. The first generation of Norse settlers received high-status burials under prominent mounds, but curiously none of them is female, leading to the suggestion that this land-taking was military in nature, with the Vikings taking Christian Manx women for their wives. Amongst the numerous tenth-century crosses and grave-slabs, for which Man is justly renowned, there are some with Norse runic inscriptions which record people with Celtic names.

The male grave-goods encompass the full range of weaponry and related equipment, including boat-burial at Balladoole and Knock y Doonee, and human sacrifice at Ballateare. The material has been conventionally dated within the bracket AD 850–950, but it may be suggested that the most lavishly equipped pagan graves in the best locations, to be identified with those of the primary settlers, are not likely to date much earlier than about 900.

The central location of Man, at the heart of the Irish Sea, has no doubt much to do with the growing prosperity of its inhabitants during the tenth and eleventh centuries. This wealth is represented by the contents of twenty silver hoards, but silver brooches and rings were not the only form of visible display, as is witnessed by the investment in decorated stone monuments and commemorative runic inscriptions.

Man is still noted for its annual open-air assembly held at Tynwald, on old Midsummer Day. This retains elements of the Norse *thing* in what is probably an unbroken tradition, with Viking period origins. The members of the Manx government, and other dignitaries, assemble on Tynwald Hill, a four-tiered artificial mound, after attending service in St John's Church and having processed down a ceremonial way strewn with rushes. All new laws are then publicly proclaimed, in both Manx and English, to the assembled populace – who have also gathered to enjoy a fair.

A major centre of Norse power in Man was situated on St Patrick's Isle at Peel, controlling the location of the only sheltered harbour on its west coast. This tidal islet is covered today by the remains of Peel Castle and the roofless Cathedral of St German. When the Vikings arrived, St Patrick's Isle was a religious centre with a cemetery which they utilised for the burial of their own dead. This was partly excavated by David Freke during the 1980s when half-a-dozen clothed burials were discovered, dating from the mid-tenth century, together with one more obviously pagan grave of a wealthy female. This 'Pagan Lady' had no brooches – and thus was presumably not buried in Scandinavian dress – but wore a fine necklace of seventy-one glass, amber and jet beads. A pair of shears, together with a comb, may have hung from her tablet-woven belt which was ornamented with a couple of amber beads and an ammonite fossil. Beside her had been placed her sewing-kit, but more impressively an iron cooking-spit, with a bunch of herbs and the wing of a goose. She also possessed a fine knife, with silver inlaid hilt, of Anglo-Scandinavian type. Indeed, it is quite possible that she was herself of Danelaw origin, as also maybe the rest of the group, given that Gillian Fellows-Jensen has argued from place-name evidence for some tenth-century immigration to Man from northern England.

During the later tenth/eleventh centuries there appears to have been a religious community on St Patrick's Isle, for this is the probable period for the construction of the earliest known ecclesiastical structures on the site – St Patrick's Church and the Irish-style round-tower. This was also the period of the construction of a small chapel in the cemetery in which was found a hoard of Hiberno-Norse coins, concealed there in the 1040s.

The excavations also revealed the existence of a Late Norse rampart, in the form of a stone-faced stony bank, which had probably carried a timber stockade. It was most likely constructed during the period when Magnus Barelegs ruled over the kingdom of Man and the Isles, from 1098 to 1103. As mentioned above (p. 109), he is recorded as having built fortresses on Man with timber from Galloway. A sophisticated Late Norse building, of timber-framed construction, was also discovered, dating from the late eleventh to the mid-twelfth century. In its first phase it had a suspended wood floor, reminiscent of that at the Biggings, Papa Stour, Shetland (p. 185); this was later replaced with stone flags which were, in turn, covered over with clay and a mortar surface. The date range for this high-status building encompasses the rule of Magnus, although it is not known whether he had royal apartments on the island. Later Norse kings certainly had accommodation there, Godred II dying on the island in 1187, as also Olaf II in 1237. The last Norse king, Magnus II, gave St Patrick's Isle to the Church, probably in 1257, and it became the seat of the Bishop of Sodor (*episcopus Sodorensis*), his title preserving to this day the Norse name for the Hebrides – the *Suðreyjar*, or Southern Isles.

Chapter 7

PAGAN NORSE GRAVES PART I: CASE STUDIES

In this chapter a closer look will be taken at selected pagan Norse cemeteries and burials in order to demonstrate more fully the archaeological potential of these graves, and their grave-goods, for an understanding of Scandinavian Scotland during the ninth and tenth centuries (Figure 7.1). The examples presented here provide a mixture of old finds reassessed and more recent finds which, in some instances, are still undergoing study at the time of writing. These case studies are followed, in Chapter 8, by a review of the burial rites and other aspects of this important part of the archaeological evidence for Scotland during the Viking period.

A good example of the problems encountered by modern archaeologists in attempting to make use of old 'excavation' records of pagan Norse graves is provided by the various accounts of the burials removed from a mound on Oronsay (by Colonsay) in 1891 and 1913, together with miscellaneous artefacts recovered from its vicinity on a number of other occasions.

CÀRN A' BHARRAICH, ORONSAY

The low mound of Càrn a' Bharraich (that is, the 'Cairn of the men of Barra') is in an area of sand-dunes on the east coast of Oronsay, but its shape and size were not recorded when it was first explored in April 1891, by Sir John M'Neill, although it was already suffering from rabbit-burrowing and erosion. It is uncertain whether the mound was entirely artificial in its Viking period construction, for there is some evidence to suggest that it was built up on the site of a Mesolithic shell-midden. Malcolm M'Neill's account of the excavation, published later that year, explains how the work began at the western edge of the mound, where one or two iron rivets were found, and then:

> Continuing the investigation, two narrow stones (4ft. and 4ft. 6in. respectively) were discovered in such a position as to suggest that they had originally stood erect on the summit of the mound whence they had fallen when their support failed on their western side; slabs of schist were observed in various positions in the exposed section, and, on probing the undisturbed portions, the entire mound was found to contain this material, here and there in large masses.

A few days later M'Neill opened two trenches on what seemed to him to have been the original ground-level. The first contained only sand mixed with shells, but the second produced two skeletons at the centre of the mound, about four feet below the top. These were in the extended position, with their feet pointing south-south-east. His description is as follows:

> the skeleton which lay furthest to the east had, near the head, *two beads*, one apparently of serpentine, the other of red amber; and adhering to the left collarbone, a *bronze brooch*, ornamented with gilt, with sockets (now empty), in which perhaps plates of amber may have been set. There was also found, near the head, a small *ivory object* in good preservation. Nothing else was found near the eastern skeleton except two portions of a *bronze ring* much corroded; the body was believed to be female, owing to the small size of the bones and teeth (the latter indicating considerable age), and to the presence of the ornaments.

Next to the woman's skeleton lay the second, identified as male on the basis of its larger stature (also with worn teeth). There was an iron knife on his right thigh and a ring of limpet shell.

The following day a third trench was dug through the centre of the mound:

> this excavation passed through a considerable bed of charcoal containing *boat rivets* and the *pieces of bronze produced*, but added nothing capable of identification except a *stone sinker* with a well-drilled hole for suspension and some curious groovings on the side and lower end.

A second brooch (the pair to the woman's) was found in the mound, although its find-spot was not recorded, as was also the case with the remains of a Celtic brooch-pin.

M'Neill's findings in his third trench would seem to suggest that the primary Norse activity on this site, represented by the 'considerable bed of charcoal containing rivets', involved the burning of what was presumably a boat (or, at least, part of one), perhaps in connection with a cremation burial. However, without any stratigraphical records, we cannot tell whether it was then or later that the pair of inhumation burials was placed in the main body of the mound.

The mound also contained a third inhumation, which was first noticed twenty-two years later when a skull appeared as a result of further erosion, for the excavated central area of the mound had been left exposed. A rudimentary investigation was undertaken by Neil M'Neill, the farmer on Oronsay at the time, who uncovered a pair of oval brooches, a ringed-pin and a bone needle-case. The skull, which was partly exposed in the sand,

> was reclining with its frontal aspect towards the east and its crown towards the south, the upper portion of the left side being exposed. Mr. M'Neill began prodding the sand with his walking stick, and immediately brought to the surface the two brooches and the pin, and the bone object with a hole through it . . .

The site was re-examined a few days later by M'Neill, together with Symington Grieve, when it was determined that the skeleton had originally lain with its head to the south and feet to the north; on this occasion a pair of iron shears was recovered. Grieve also estimated that, in relation to the other two inhumations, this new grave was positioned on the edge of their mound which had been some 35–40 feet in diameter. This location

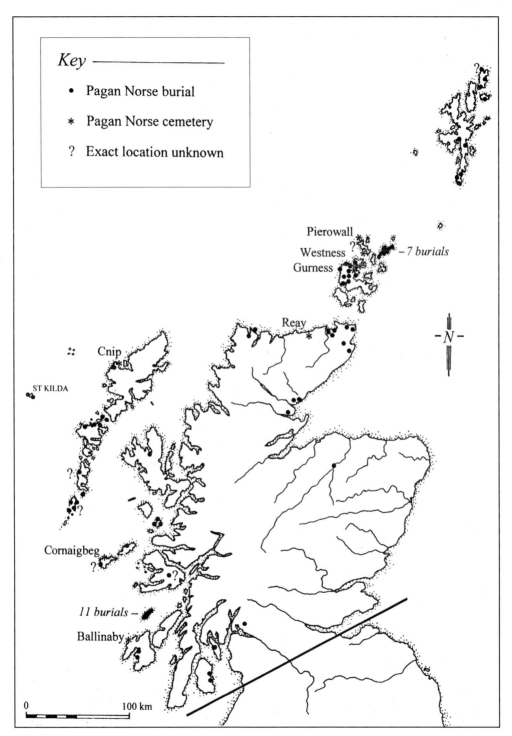

Key ————————

- • Pagan Norse burial
- * Pagan Norse cemetery
- ? Exact location unknown

Pierowall
Westness
Gurness
— 7 burials

Reay

Cnip

ST KILDA

Cornaigbeg

11 burials —

Ballinaby

– N –

0   100 km

7.1 Distribution of pagan Norse burials in northern and western Scotland, including some uncertain examples.

suggests that the burial discovered in 1913 was not contemporary with those discovered in 1891. It is not, however, clear whether it was secondary, with the missing lower limbs being the result of the 1891 excavation, or earlier and thus itself disturbed by the double inhumation.

An Early Viking period date for this female burial is indicated by the style of her oval brooches and of her ringed-pin which would have fastened her cloak. The brooches belong to the so-called 'Berdal type' (Figure 7.2), which is known to have begun production in the eighth century in southern Scandinavia. In contrast, the 'knobbed' ringed-pin is of a native Irish type (Figure 7.2). No such knobbed ringed-pins were found in the tenth-century levels of the Dublin excavations, although there is one from the ninth-century pagan Norse burials at Islandbridge. The shears and needle-case are well-known finds in female burials, both relating to textile work (cf. the Scar boat-burial, below), and are likely to have been worn suspended from a belt or brooch (Figure 7.2).

The pair of inhumations at the centre of the mound appear also to have been buried fully clothed, without additional grave-goods. Indeed, the man was carrying only his knife (now lost), for there are no real reasons for supposing that the perforated limpet shell, found near him by M'Neill, was in fact a Viking period artefact. However, as there are a couple of unstratified bronze pins from the mound (see below), it is probable that one of them will have served to fasten his cloak.

The woman's dress had been fastened not with the traditional Scandinavian oval brooches, but with a pair of brooches fashioned from clasps stripped from a Celtic 'house-shaped' reliquary and converted into brooches by the addition of iron pins in an act of Viking vandalism (Figure 7.2). These clasps would originally have held a carrying-strap, mounted on either end of some such Christian treasure as the well-known Monymusk reliquary, an eighth-century Pictish version of this Irish type of shrine. However, the Oronsay examples are more likely to be of ninth-century date, given the nature of their cast gilt ornament and amber settings, in the manner of the Derrynaflan chalice, Co. Kilkenny, and of contemporary Irish brooches.

The woman's two beads have already been mentioned, the serpentine and amber presumably having been chosen for their contrasting qualities – and maybe for amuletic reasons (particularly in the case of amber). These might have been worn either on a necklace or on a string between her brooches. The 'small ivory object' remains an enigma (being lost), but M'Neill regarded it as intrusive. He described it as 'a small finial of turned bone resembling the finials on the whale-bone ribs of an old umbrella', which makes it sound like the broken head of a dress- or hair-pin.

The 'two portions of a bronze ring much corroded' are presumably to be identified with what is now a single fragment of the ring from a ringed-pin which seems to belong to a separate pin which was picked up on the site in 1957. Both ring and pin are distinctive in having a white metal coating. In addition, there are the remains of the once grander brooch-pin, with its ring-shaped hoop, although it has now lost the settings of glass or amber which would have filled its circular terminals (Figure 7.2). However, it is not known which cloak-pin should be attributed to which of these two individuals – or even whether one might have belonged to the putative burnt burial, which is otherwise associated only with the (lost) stone line-sinker and some small bronze fragments.

Overall, therefore, there exists a tantalising body of evidence for Norse burial activity at

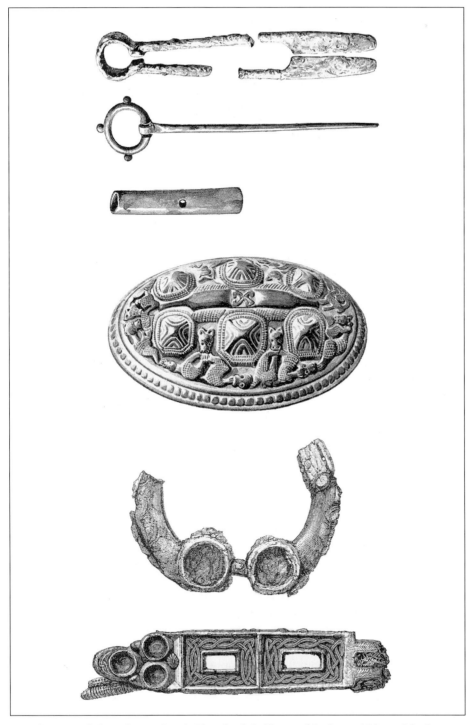

7.2 *Grave-goods from the two female Norse burials discovered in Càrn a' Bharraich, Oronsay, in 1891 and 1913 (after McNeill, 1891; Symington Grieve, 1914).*

Càrn a' Bharraich during the ninth century, including the inhumations of perhaps two successive generations of well-dressed women of some social standing. One of them was buried wearing what may well have been heirloom brooches – oval brooches which were most probably brought over from Scandinavia during the initial settlement period. However, it is only a matter of conjecture as to whether this was by the woman herself or, say, by her mother. On the other hand, she had acquired a fashionable Irish ringed-pin. Did her family go raiding/trading in Ireland from Oronsay? Or might they be numbered amongst those who had tried, and failed, to establish themselves along the northern coast of Ireland? A piratical Viking profile is, however, indicated by the jewellery of the other woman who was buried dressed in the Scandinavian mode, but with the normal oval brooches replaced by a pair made from Celtic Christian shrine-mounts.

The evidence suggestive of the burning of a boat is yet more tantalising, for this rite is otherwise unknown in Britain or Ireland, although used for a tenth-century Norse chieftain's burial on the Ile de Groix, off the Brittany coast. For an old find of an unburnt boat-burial, we can turn to the adjacent island of Colonsay and the burial at Kiloran Bay.

KILORAN BAY, COLONSAY

The sand-dunes backing the beautiful Kiloran Bay, on the north-west coast of Colonsay, provide an obvious location for a Viking boat-grave, even though no Norse settlement has yet been located in this vicinity. Such, indeed, was discovered and partly explored in June 1882 by Malcolm M'Neill, although the excavation was completed the following year by William Galloway, an architect working on Oronsay at the time, who was responsible for drawing the two plans which survive today (Figure 7.3). The initial exploration uncovered a male inhumation within a rectangular stone setting, accompanied by a rich variety of grave-goods, and numerous boat-rivets; in the second, the skeleton of a horse was found, with further boat-rivets. Finally, 'some time after the exploration was completed, as the sand within the enclosure dried and was blown away, there were found within its limits three Anglo-Saxon Stycas'.

Only two of these three Northumbrian coins were legible, one being of Æthelred II (841–4) and the other of Archbishop Wigmund of York (837–54). They are, however, both perforated and thus demonetarised, increasing the problem of guessing how old they might have been when they were buried.

Galloway's section (Figure 7.3) shows how the stone setting, which measured 15 ft by 10 ft (4.6 x 3.1 m), had been exposed through erosion, with a caption stating: 'The stones much displaced, undermined by rabbits, and probably disturbed by searchers for treasure; side-stones fallen inwards and outwards, covering stones also are fallen in'.

One suspects therefore that some 'tidying-up' was done in the representation of the neatly rectangular setting in his drawing (elsewhere described as 'irregularly rectangular') where the main slabs are all shown in vertical positions. In 1883 he discovered that two of them were incised with simple crosses, and this has given rise to the suggestion that the burial was of mixed pagan/Christian rite. It is of course possible that the man's wife, or some other member of his family, may have been Christian and thus have chosen to mark these two stones with the protective sign of the cross, but it must be emphasised that, in all other respects, this is a purely pagan burial. An alternative explanation could be that

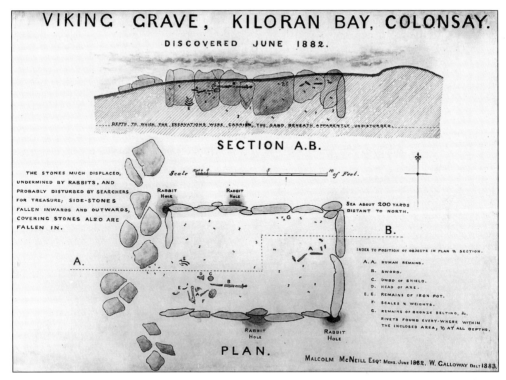

VIKING GRAVE, KILORAN BAY, COLONSAY.

DISCOVERED JUNE 1882.

SECTION A.B.

THE STONES MUCH DISPLACED,
UNDERMINED BY RABBITS, AND
PROBABLY DISTURBED BY SEARCHERS
FOR TREASURE; SIDE-STONES
FALLEN INWARDS AND OUTWARDS,
COVERING STONES ALSO ARE
FALLEN IN.

SEA ABOUT 200 YARDS
DISTANT TO NORTH.

A.

B.

INDEX TO POSITION OF OBJECTS IN PLAN & SECTION.

A.A. HUMAN REMAINS.
B. SWORD.
C. UMBO OF SHIELD.
D. HEAD OF AXE.
E.E. REMAINS OF IRON POT.
F. SCALES & WEIGHTS.
G. REMAINS OF BRONZE BELTING, &c.
RIVETS FOUND EVERY-WHERE WITHIN
THE INCLOSED AREA, & AT ALL DEPTHS.

RABBIT HOLE   RABBIT HOLE

PLAN.

MALCOLM McNEILL ESQ: MENS. JUNE 1882. W. GALLOWAY DELT 1883.

7.3 Plan and section of the Viking boat-grave at Kiloran Bay, Colonsay, drawn by William Galloway in 1883 (Crown copyright: RCAHMS).

some of the stones which had been brought to the site might first have served as grave-markers in an Early Christian cemetery.

The stone setting formed a simple grave-enclosure, as found at Ballinaby on Islay (described below), and elsewhere in Scandinavian Scotland. The man's body had been placed in one corner, lying on its side in a flexed position; the state of his teeth suggests that he was over forty years old when he died, of causes unknown. Behind him were laid his weapons: a sword (with a silver inlaid pommel), axe, spear, shield (with conical boss, covered with cloth) and a couple of arrows, as well as an iron handled pan. The find-spots were not recorded of a simple silver cloak-pin of Norwegian type, of an iron horse-bit and of some knives, including one now known from an X-ray to have a pivoting blade of Anglo-Saxon or Anglo-Scandinavian type. The recent re-examination of some miscellaneous pieces of badly corroded ironwork has also revealed a hinge from a chest or large casket. Some of the nails found, in addition to the many boat-rivets, might well have derived from some such object, rather than all having formed part of the boat itself.

In front of the body had been placed a pair of scales, together with a set of lead weights, all except one of which have decorative mounts (Figure 7.4). These include fragments of both Anglo-Saxon and Irish ornamental metalwork, including two with enamelled fragments which have patterns that have in the past been likened to Arabic script, but which can in fact be reconstructed into a recognisably Insular pattern. It is possible that

7.4 Scales and weights from the Kiloran Bay boat-grave, Colonsay (K. Gordon).

the perforated coins also formed part of this weight-set, unless they were being worn as pendants – or had some purely symbolic function in the grave. At the opposite end of the grave enclosure was found a set of bronze harness-mounts of Insular workmanship, with four ornamental studs, most closely paralleled by a bridle from the Viking boat-grave at Balladoole, in the Isle of Man, which also contained a conical shield-boss of the same Irish Sea type as from both Kiloran Bay and Ballinaby, on Islay.

The horse had been placed outside the east end of the stone setting, in or under what would have been the prow or stern of the vessel, with an iron girth-buckle beneath its belly. Recent re-examination of the skeleton shows it to have been a healthy animal, 6–8 years of age, with an estimated withers height of about 14.2 hands (c. 1.46m). It has been suggested that damage to its right metatarsal and tibia was inflicted in battle by cutting the hamstring to immobilise the animal. This cannot be proven, but the position of the cuts, angled down from above, is consistent with this interpretation.

If it is assumed that the body of the horse filled the prow/stern of the boat, and that the grave-enclosure was centrally placed, then it is possible to estimate the length of the vessel as having been about 11m. This is twice that of those recorded at Westness and longer than the Scar boat, but it is similar in size to that in the Balladoole boat-burial, mentioned above. There is a problem, however, as to how it was placed in the grave – above or below the burial?

According to the caption on Galloway's plan, during the 1882 excavation, the boat-rivets were found 'every-where within the inclosed area, & at all depths'. Another version of this statement is contained in his manuscript account of the burial prepared when his plan and the grave-goods were displayed at the International Fisheries Exhibition, held in London in 1883: 'They were found strewn indiscriminately and at all depths through the body of sand filling the grave'. There also survives, in manuscript, the text of a paper read by Galloway to the Society of Antiquaries of London, in June 1885, on his discovery of the horse in 1883, which accounts for the preservation there of his second plan. Unfortunately, no copy of his earlier paper on the 1882 discoveries is now known to exist. This he had read in London in May 1883, which was presumably when he presented the Society with three water-colours which illustrate the principal artefacts. In his 1885 paper, he stated:

> One of the most noteworthy features of the discovery was the large number of clinker nails or rivets and other iron objects, both in and around the remains [of the horse] as found. They seem to have permeated the skeleton in every way and with the undisturbed state of the remains found now, and previously, suggest the idea, that the ship may have been capsized over them, the clinker nails falling down as her timbers gradually decayed.

In considering this account, it is important to note that he makes no mention of having encountered any rivets on top of the undisturbed skeleton, as one would have expected if the boat had indeed collapsed onto it, but describes it as being 'permeated' with them. This description brings to mind that by Professor Gerhard Bersu of the human skeleton resting on the bottom of the Balladoole boat: 'clench-nails lay under the bones and were mixed with them'.

However, Galloway seems to have made his mind up previously on this point, on the basis of the evidence from the grave-enclosure. His paper continues:

> Had the Norseman, his horse, arms, and other grave-goods, been disposed *within* the ship, set upon an even keel, as in several recorded instances in Scandinavia it seems impossible for them, on the decay of the wooden structure by which they would in that case have been supported, to have subsided in the absolutely undisturbed manner in which they were found.

We must, however, remember the fact that the 'chamber' is elsewhere recorded as having been disturbed by rabbits and the plan seems to indicate that the human remains, at least, were in part redistributed, for there is no evidence amongst the surviving skeletal material for there having been more than one body in the grave. It is also probable that it contained riveted/nailed wooden artefacts, such as one or more chests (perhaps even a bier or coffin). Several features concerning the relative disposition of the body and the grave-goods, if accurately portrayed in the plan and section, require some such explanation to account for their varying levels in the sand filling. It is to be hoped that a new examination of the ironwork and wood remains may help to resolve some of these problems.

Finally, the considerable depth to which rivets appear to have been found seems hard to explain if they are supposed to have fallen from above, unless some were transported downwards by rabbit activity. On the other hand, if the body had been placed within the boat, in the conventional manner, then rivets would indeed have been encountered 'at all depths', as a result of the planking of the boat decaying *in situ*. Unfortunately, we know nothing about the care with which M'Neill conducted his excavation – nor even whether

Galloway was present himself. This, however, seems unlikely since his first plan is based on M'Neill's measurements and not his own.

Galloway's theory that the boat was 'capsized' over the burial convinced Joseph Anderson, Keeper of the National Museum, who published the first account of this boat-grave (in 1907), after Galloway's death, but using his notes. Most who have followed in his footsteps have accepted that a vessel had indeed been inverted over the rich burial at Kiloran Bay, even though such a practice is only doubtfully recorded elsewhere amongst Viking boat-graves. All the surviving evidence is currently undergoing re-evaluation from which new conclusions may be expected to emerge, although the incomplete nature of the original records means that it may never be possible to come to a definitive conclusion.

The warrior/trader who was buried in some style at Kiloran Bay possessed a combination of Scandinavian and Insular weapons and other belongings, including the set of scales and a silver pin. These combine to demonstrate his high status, which is emphasised by the presence of the horse and boat – and even by the inclusion of a saucepan with which to cater for his crew! Kiloran Bay is the prime location for a chieftain's burial on Colonsay, but even if that island was his to control, it would seem to have served him also as a base for forays beyond the Hebrides.

The coins in this grave establish that the earliest possible date for the occasion of the burial would have been the mid-ninth century, but the overall nature and range of the grave-goods suggests that this took place somewhat later, towards the end of the century – or even c. 900 – at a similar date therefore to that which now seems most probable for the closely comparable Manx boat-grave at Balladoole.

BALLINABY, ISLAY

When, in 1772, Thomas Pennant visited Ballinaby, on the north-west coast of Islay, he noted three standing stones of which only two now remain. In his book, *Voyage to the Hebrides*, there is an illustration of a Viking sword from Islay which may well have come from there, for as early as May 1788 two oval brooches were presented to the Society of Antiquaries of Scotland, which had been found 'under a large standing stone' at Ballinaby. These are not absolutely identical, but would certainly have passed as a matched pair and are thus presumably from a woman's grave. Next, a sand-hill near the largest of the standing stones is known to have attracted the attention of Captain Burgess and the crew of the *Savage*, a 'sloop of war', which visited Islay several times between July 1788 and July 1789. They are reported to have dug up 'one or two swords' and 'a pike-head', with 'many human bones', but 'the arms they carried away' and are unfortunately now lost. We can thus only conjecture that it was pagan Norse graves which they had discovered, but this is most probable given the nature and contents of the burials found subsequently at Ballinaby.

In 1877, erosion of the Ballinaby sand-dunes revealed two contiguous inhumations of a man and a woman, placed side by side within simple stone settings, with their heads to the east; they were both accompanied by rich grave-goods (Figures 7.5–6). The man was buried with his sword (in its scabbard), a small shield, one or possibly two spears and two axes, together with a fishing-spear, an adze, a blacksmith's hammer and tongs, his drinking-horn (represented mainly by its ornamental terminal) and a cauldron. The sword is one of

7.5 Grave-goods from the male Norse burial found at Ballinaby, Islay, in 1877 (NMS).

7.6 Grave-goods from the female Norse burial found at Ballinaby, Islay, in 1877 (NMS).

the most numerous of the Viking period types found in Norway, but the conical shield-boss belongs to the Irish Sea type, which was mentioned above in connection with that from the Kiloran Bay boat-burial. The Ballinaby example is, however, superior in that it has a decorated bronze grip which is paralleled by one in iron from the Balladoole boat-burial, in the Isle of Man, and by a plain bronze example from the River Bann in Northern Ireland. In discussing the latter example, Raghnall Ó Floinn has drawn attention to the similarity in metalworking technique required for its manufacture with that used to make Irish sheet bronze ladles of the type present amongst the adjacent woman's grave-goods at Ballinaby. An Irish origin might also be suggested for the man's drinking-horn, although a Scottish source is also possible. The man's social status is confirmed by the presence of a blacksmith's tools, for in the context of pagan Norse graves these are not necessarily to be interpreted as simply the workaday equipment of an artisan, but rather as belonging to a skilled weaponsmith. The possible social significance of the apparently lowly cooking-pot has already been noted in the context of the handled pan from Kiloran Bay, but in this case it takes the form of a true cauldron with a bow-handle for suspension.

Some 'fragments of corrugated iron' were originally interpreted as part of a helmet, but they have since been re-identified as forming part of a heckle (or even a pair) which thus belongs amongst the woman's textile-working equipment. This otherwise consists of a black glass linen smoother and a tinned bronze needle-case, with a bronze needle. She was buried in Scandinavian dress with a fine pair of double-shelled oval brooches, embell-ished with silver wire, although their ornamental bosses are now missing. She also had a necklace or festoon of twelve beads and a remarkable silver pin with a chain, which was presumably used for fastening her cape or cloak. This splendid object was made by mounting a filigree-ornamented bead of Scandinavian workmanship on to the looped top of a plain pin and holding it in place with a ring. To this was originally attached a length of so-called 'Trichinopoly' chainwork which terminates in a similar ring; this type of tubu-lar chain is most probably of Insular manufacture. Her Irish bronze ladle has already been mentioned, but it is worth noting that this is the only example known from Scotland, whereas at least fourteen have been found in Viking period graves in Norway. It is generally assumed that they were used for the ceremonial service of drink.

The woman's grave also contained some tinned bronze mounts of non-Scandinavian workmanship, in the form of five discs with repoussé ornament. These are now incom-plete and, although three of them have band-shaped extensions suggesting that some or all of them were linked together, their original arrangement and function is unknown. Three tinned bronze plaques which are very similar to those from Ballinaby have been found in Ireland, but they are lacking in context and so do not help with their interpreta-tion.

It is a matter of considerable regret that no plans were made of this exceptional pair of late ninth/early tenth-century graves of a wealthy couple who were both buried with a wide-ranging variety of artefacts, linking Norway with their new community on Islay – and onwards to Ireland.

A further male grave was discovered at Ballinaby in 1932, some 400 yards west of the double burial just described. This was a stone cist-grave, although the end slabs were missing; it contained an extended inhumation with the head to the south-west. Once again there is no plan, but a full description was made and some photographs were taken.

Although the skeletal remains were poorly preserved, the condition of the skull and the worn teeth were taken to indicate 'that the individual was advanced in years'.

A sword lay on the right side of the skeleton, with the hilt near the waist; the shield-boss was also on the right, 'opposite the breast', as also the fragmentary remains of what appears to have been a knife. An axe had been placed on his left side, with its head found 'just about the position of where the right elbow would have been'. 'In addition, a buckle and a free ring-headed pin of bronze were found near the centre of the body.' The central location of the pin (rather than being worn at the shoulder) may indicate that the man had been wrapped and fastened in his cloak to form a shroud. The D-shaped buckle-loop is gilt, with settings of red enamel, and a contrasting tongue apparently coated in white metal; the plate is plain. This fine object is clearly of Insular manufacture and quite possibly from Ireland, together with the pin. The Scandinavian weapons and Insular ornaments are not closely datable, but the burial could well have taken place before the end of the ninth century.

This lengthy saga of artefacts and burials from Ballinaby concludes, most recently, with an episode as enigmatic as those with which it began. A report published in 1960 states that 'a rusted *Shield Boss* (possibly Viking) was found in July 1958 on rock near the farm. The vicinity of the find was carefully investigated for further remains, but with no success.'

The Ballinaby burials and finds, discovered at intervals over a period of almost 200 years, are for the most part poorly recorded. They have, however, furnished us with a wide-ranging array of artefacts and thus of general archaeological information for the Norse presence on Islay during some part of the ninth and tenth centuries. A small amount has also been learnt of the burial rites in use by this community, but all too little is known of the organisation of what would seem to have been a somewhat dispersed cemetery, although an element of focus on the standing stones seems to be indicated.

This apparent lack of organisation at Ballinaby may be misleading, but it does appear to be reflected, for instance, at Bhaltos in Lewis and at Reay in Caithness, which will be considered next.

REAY, CAITHNESS

Viking period material has been eroding out of the sand-dunes at Reay, on the north coast of Caithness, since 1912, although there is a much earlier record of stonework, possibly representing a settlement, being revealed there in 1751 during storms. The artefacts, however, clearly derive from a pagan Norse cemetery of unknown size.

In 1912, a skeleton was revealed accompanied by a buckle and a 'horse-bridle' (bit?) and then, in the following year, a female burial was discovered. According to the original report:

> No signs of a cist were discovered, and the bones, which were few in number, were simply those of an unburnt body which appeared to have been laid in the sand possibly in a doubled-up position.
>
> Upon the body at the time of burial had been laid a pair of oval brooches, which were found at a depth of one foot below the skull, and appeared to have been placed together face to face.

Although this description of the position of the oval brooches is compatible with them being worn by the woman on burial, it raises the possibility that they had simply been placed in the grave, in the same manner as the equal-armed brooch in the Scar boat-grave (described below). Near these brooches lay a bronze ringed-pin and buckle, a steatite spindle-whorl and an iron horse-bit. Two additional objects, picked up shortly afterwards in the vicinity (a pair of iron tweezers and an iron buckle), were thought at the time to have been thrown out with the sand from this grave and so have been added to this assemblage, as had an astragalus bone from a small horse. The latter was one of 'quite a number of bones lying about' when the site was visited in September 1926, but this was after the discovery earlier that summer of a well-equipped male grave.

After the legs of a skeleton had been seen eroding out of a sand-dune, the grave was opened and its contents removed, without archaeological supervision, although a detailed sketch was made 'showing the disposition of the relics' (Figure 7.7). This was an extended inhumation, oriented north-west/south-east, although the right forearm was bent over the chest. The teeth were described as 'well worn down' and the man's height was estimated as 5 ft 6³/₄in from his thigh bones. The body had been laid out on a paved surface, on which an axe had first been placed because the axe-head (no. 1) was found beneath his left knee. The whole burial is described as having been 'surrounded and covered' by 'large stones and sand'.

The man had been buried in his clothes, as is indicated by an *in situ* iron belt-buckle (no. 6), whilst the position on the pelvis of a small perforated whetstone (no. 9) suggests that this was hanging from the belt. However, he had been wrapped in some covering as a shroud, no doubt his cloak, for the bronze ringed-pin (no. 8), which would have fastened it, was over his right thigh, instead of on the shoulder. A sickle (no. 4) and knife (no. 3)) were placed in line beside his left arm; there was a piece of flint by his right elbow (no. 10) and another between his legs (no. 11). Finally, the body had been covered with his shield, so that the boss (no. 2) was found over his chest; the iron clamp (no. 5), found above the left shoulder, and a nail or rivet (no. 7), by the right elbow, were presumably connected in some way with the construction or repair of the wooden shield-board.

After Arthur Edwards, who was the Assistant Keeper of the National Museum, visited Reay to record the find in August 1926, he commented that 'in the cleared spaces between the dunes [caused by wind-erosion], I saw numerous traces of what must be either graves or other regularly constructed works in stone', but his subsequent investigation, in 1928, 'of quite a number of small mounds and likely sites' produced no more pagan Norse burials. Instead, he found traces of circular structures, including one adjacent to the 1913 grave, which was still identifiable from 'the quantity of horses' bones lying in the sand', as well as some burials in long cists without grave-goods, and (as a surface-find) an eighth/ninth-century Anglo-Saxon strap-end of a type similar to those found in the hoard of Pictish brooches from Rogart, Sutherland, and in the richest of the pagan Norse female graves at Westness in Orkney. It has been suggested that the long-cist burials may belong to the Christian Norse period, but they might just as well date back to the pre-Viking period.

These additional observations suggest a complex sequence of occupation and burial at Reay, and, despite Edwards' failure to locate further Viking period graves in 1928, it still seems probable that the minimum number of pagan Norse burials will have been in excess

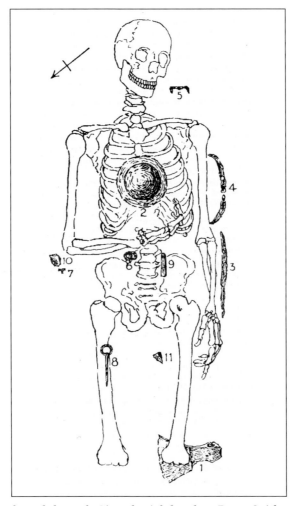

7.7 Sketch-plan of the male Norse burial found at Reay, Caithness, in 1926 (after A. J. H. Edwards, 1927).

of the three noted above. We are faced here with the particular problems of interpreting cemetery evidence from an eroding sand-dune site, recovered over a period of time and then only incompletely preserved – problems which will be encountered again, on an even larger scale, with the Pierowall cemetery on Westray, Orkney.

BROCH OF GURNESS, MAINLAND, ORKNEY

Recent re-assessment by John Hedges of the early excavation records for the Broch of Gurness, on the Mainland of Orkney, indicates that the single female grave of Viking period date, discovered in 1932, had formed part of a larger cemetery which had suffered subsequent disturbance. This particular corpse was interred as an extended (west–east) inhumation, in an oblong stone setting formed in the core of the northern part of the broch's rampart-wall, after which the grave was sealed with flagstones and, possibly, an earthen mound. The skull, which was placed at the west end, is the only surviving skeletal element because of water penetration, but even so it was badly damaged (Figure 8.2).

The woman was wearing a pair of double-shelled oval brooches, 'which were lying at breast level', and around her neck was an iron necklet. This was originally described incorrectly as being 'composed of sea-shells, or possibly fragments of lobster shell', but although badly corroded, it is evident that it carries some amulets, most clearly one in the shape of a Thor's hammer. This is a unique discovery in Scotland for, although such amulet-rings can be readily paralleled from Viking period Scandinavia, they are most characteristically found in central Sweden (see p. 149). In addition, a small sickle had been placed by the woman's right hand and a wooden-handled iron knife lay on her left side; a small bone pin was recorded at the shoulder. The excavator noted that the foot of the grave appeared to have 'been disturbed, as the cover-stone at this end had been removed at one time'.

When this pagan Norse burial was eventually published, in 1969, the use of a stone setting for such a Viking period grave in Scotland was considered to be 'not entirely characteristic'. However, subsequent excavations, particularly those at Westness in Rousay (discussed below), have shown that this particular aspect of the burial-rite was more widespread than was then supposed.

In his re-assessment of the original excavations at the Broch of Gurness, Hedges identified six further 'putative' graves of Viking period date, although few of the finds in question have recorded skeletal remains. However, a number of unassociated human bones could not be brought fully into the discussion and so the possibility remains that there were, indeed, more burials on the site, not all of which can be dated. The recovery of isolated Viking period finds during the excavations, which commenced in 1930, led early on to the suggestion that there might have been pagan Norse burials in and around the broch mound – or that it had, at least, been the focus for some kind of Norse presence. Two shield-bosses, for example (possibly suggesting two separate burials), were found high in the fill of the broch tower and one or other might have been associated with an unidentified (and now lost) find described as an 'iron sock for a hand plough'.

In 1935 the excavation of the upper layers in the broch's 'Great Ditch' led to the discovery of a glass linen smoother, a folding bronze balance, a large jet bead, a whetstone and some small pieces of 'iron ore' (possibly iron nails or other box fittings?), which do not now survive. These Viking period artefacts might well suggest the presence of one or more further pagan Norse graves at this site which had presumably been disturbed. The bronze ringed-pin found with an amber bead, to the south-west, associated with fragments of a human cranium, might well represent another disturbed burial; on the other hand, the recovery of a single amber bead, from the top of the broch-period furnishings to the south-west of the tower, is far too scanty evidence to support Hedges' suggestion of a further putative grave. What was probably a complete inhumation was found in a small chamber to the west of the broch tower, with five bronze finger-rings *in situ* on its hands, but this must also be rejected as a putative Norse burial because the rings are not of Viking period types.

This supposed evidence for a half-a-dozen or more pagan Norse graves within and around the mound at Gurness is admittedly somewhat limited, but it is important to note that what at first appeared in print as a single grave has in fact turned out to be part of a larger group, which is dated by Hedges to the period from the late ninth to the tenth century. Larger groups of definite pagan Norse burials are, however, known in Orkney from both Pierowall on Westray and Westness on Rousay.

PIEROWALL, WESTRAY, ORKNEY

On Westray, the sand-dunes that fringe the Bay of Pierowall have brought to light a number of Viking period finds over the years which indicate the presence there of numerous pagan Norse burials (Figure 7.8). However, it is clear that the overall area of the Norse cemetery in the general vicinity of Pierowall was much greater in extent, even if much of our information about it is scrappy and most of the material has been lost. As described in the *Inventory of Orkney*:

> A broad band of blown sand extends from the shore of Pierowall Bay, across a neck of land, barely half a mile wide, to the N.W. shore of the island. On the Pierowall side it extends round the bay to the neighbourhood of Gill, and on the hill behind the village the surface of the sand has, by a process well known to the botanist, become converted into links. The links stretch from Noltland Castle, which is not itself on the sand, in a N.E. direction to Rackwick Bay and Biggins, but do not reach the house of Trenabie.

This whole area is on the estate of Trenabie, and for this reason the Links of Pierowall have sometimes also been known as the Links of Trenabie.

From the seventeenth to the nineteenth century there were several reports of what, for the most part, must have been pagan Norse burials being found as a result of erosion taking place in various parts of this sandy area. The earliest such account is that written by James Wallace (who died in 1688) for his *Description of the Isles of Orkney*, which was first published in 1693:

> Likewise in the links of *Tranabie*, in *Westra*, have been found graves in the sand, (after the sand hath been blown away with the wind) in one of which was seen a man lying with his sword on the one hand, and a *Daneish* ax on the other, and others that have had dogs, and combs and knives buried with them, which seems to be an instance of the way how the *Danes* (when they were in this Country) buried their dead.

Rudimentary though this account may be, there can be no doubt that Wallace was describing the discovery of pagan Norse burials, even if he mistakenly attributed them, in the fashion of his time, to a Danish presence in Scotland. Another group of burials, exposed by a north-westerly gale, was described in 1788 by the Revd George Low who recorded the bones of horses and dogs, weapons of various sorts, knives, brooches, beads and combs, a metal spoon and 'a Gold ring encircling a thigh bone', as well as a glass vessel. This last happens to have survived and is in fact a Roman glass cup; another account of its discovery suggests that it was most probably deposited in a Late Iron Age burial and is thus not to be numbered among the pagan Norse grave-goods.

Low does not specify the location of these burials, but the *Inventory* concluded that 'the context suggests that it was somewhat near the shore on the other side of the Links from Pierowall'. On the other hand, Low did observe that there were

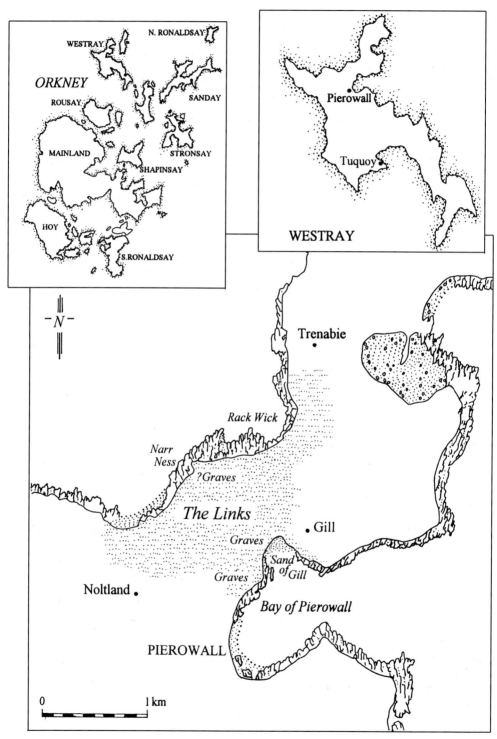

7.8 Location map of the Links of Pierowall on Westray, Orkney.

two sorts, the Tumulus, or grave, made up into a vast heap of stones and rubbish, or the second kind which has the grave simply set round with a tire [row] of small stones on end. The last are generally in clusters, and even within the sand.

Over several decades, during the mid-nineteenth century, the eroding sand-dunes brought further graves to light which were then subject to rudimentary archaeological investigation. The major worker was William Rendall, the local surgeon, whose first excavation took place in 1839, when five graves were identified. In 1841, George Petrie, a distinguished Orkney antiquarian, who lived in Kirkwall, visited Westray when he is known to have recovered some of the contents of a Viking period grave, containing boat-rivets, a man and a horse, found 'shortly before' in the sand at Gill, on the north side of Pierowall Bay. Rendall continued his work throughout the decade to 1849, finding an additional nine graves. In 1851, he donated some antiquities, both weapons and women's ornaments, to the National Museum in Edinburgh; the weapons most certainly came from an additional grave, presumably found between 1849 and 1851, as it does not match any of those in his earlier accounts. In 1855, and then in 1863, James Farrer discovered two further graves, one in each year, on the latter occasion working together with George Petrie (again in the Sand of Gill), in what was the last recorded excavation of a pagan Norse burial from the Links.

The nineteenth-century written sources provide far from adequate accounts of these various excavations, with the result that subsequent attempts to describe this Pierowall material became very confused, with items being wrongly ascribed to individual graves. However, in 1965 the Faroese archaeologist, Arne Thorsteinsson, undertook a detailed reassessment of all the available evidence for these particular finds, with the result that he established the existence of a minimum of seventeen burials, although a small number of objects remain which are not known to belong to any particular grave. The following account of the contents of sixteen graves follows closely Thorsteinsson's catalogue, although it omits a Grave 5, for it was entirely his research which brought order out of chaos. However, further work on the documentary sources is leading towards some minor modifications to his conclusions.

The first burial area to be investigated in 1839 contained three graves (Figure 7.9). Grave 1 was a male inhumation, with a large stone standing behind the head at the west end and the knees bent upwards. He was accompanied by a sword on his left side and a spear on the right (the spear-head described as a 'dagger'), with its point upwards towards the armpit, a shield on edge behind the skull (so that the boss was described as 'the top of a helmet'), and a comb. Grave 2, a few yards away, was excavated on the same day in April and contained a badly decomposed skeleton which appeared to have been buried face down, with the head to the north. A ringed-pin lay beneath the skull and so had presumable fastened a shroud, with a pair of oval brooches *in situ* below the head and an iron implement on the right side (a knife or weaving-sword?). Grave 3 was uncovered in the same location as Grave 2 and contained a second female inhumation, again badly decomposed, but with clearly flexed knees and arms crossed on the abdomen. A pair of oval brooches was *in situ* (one on each collar-bone) and a ringed-pin lay in the angle formed by the right elbow joint. A bone needle-case, containing an iron needle, was found beneath the chin and the presence of this small sewing-kit might suggest that a 'small circular perforated

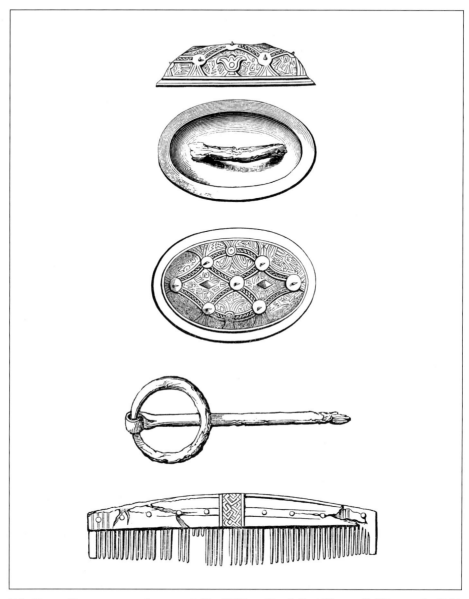

*7.9 Pagan Norse grave-goods excavated by William Rendall at Pierowall, Westray, in 1839
(after T. Crofton Croker, 1847).*

stone' on her breast should be interpreted as a spindle-whorl, rather than as a single bead,
with her spindle having been placed upon the corpse in the grave, with a sickle and a
comb by her left arm.

A second burial area, some thirty yards to the east of Graves 1–3, was the location of
Grave 4, which was both surrounded and covered by large flat stones. It contained a female

inhumation, this time lying on the left shoulder with head to the south. There was a pair of oval brooches *in situ* on each breast, with seven beads beside one, and a ringed-pin upon the abdomen, with another pin or brooch below the chin; two combs had been placed in line over the right elbow.

The next two groups of graves, nine in all, were excavated by Rendall 'at the burying-ground at the north of Pierowall'. Graves 6–9 were located 'near the Sea-shore on a line running north–south', and nos 10–14 were found 'round a Mound of Sand and Small Stones, at a considerable distance from the Sea, in a line running north-west from the former Sites of Graves'.

Graves 6–8 all seem to have been disturbed before Rendall's investigations, although in the case of Grave 6 (which had the head to the north), he suggested that the damaged skull may have been cleft before burial. The only grave-goods recovered were an axe and half a shield-boss, but there was also a scatter of small pieces of iron around the grave. It is obviously not possible to tell at this remove whether these were nails/rivets from a wooden coffin or part of a boat, or whether they simply represent the damaged remains of the shield-boss – or of some other disturbed item, such as sword. The occupant of Grave 7, who had been buried north–south with crossed legs, lacked a head, but was accompanied by a horse (complete), its bit between its teeth, and a dog (part missing). Apart from 'much remains of iron rust', Rendall recovered only a buckle, a piece of iron, thought to be either a spear-head or small sword, and an unidentified piece of bone with traces of corroded iron. Grave 8 contained parts of a human skeleton and of a horse, with the remains of bridle-bits and a small 'dagger'. This is once again most probably to be interpreted as a spear-head, as daggers were not in use during the Viking period. On the other hand, it is easy enough to understand the confusion of a nineteenth-century antiquary faced with a double-edged blade extending from what would have appeared (in a corroded state) to have been a hilt, but was in fact the socket for the spear-shaft. Grave 9 lay 'a considerable way towards the north' and appears to have been an unaccompanied flexed inhumation.

Grave 10, a male inhumation, was located on the south side of the 'Mound', mentioned above, contained within a rectangular setting of large stones (as at Kiloran Bay and Ballinaby). The head was to the north, the legs flexed and arms crossed. A shield-boss was found by the top of the head and a sword by the left side of the skeleton. There were also a large whetstone, a comb, several glass beads and some fragments of iron with wood attached (perhaps parts of the shield?). Graves 11–13 were found on the north side of the 'Mound', all three containing inhumations with their heads to the south. Graves 11 and 12 were both female, each containing a pair of oval brooches, the former having also a trefoil brooch over the stomach region, which Thorsteinsson was mistaken in supposing never to have existed. Grave 12 also contained a ringed-pin, as well as two decorated combs, in cases held together with copper or bronze nails, one placed above each shoulder. Grave 13 had been badly disturbed and only part of the skeleton was surviving; no grave-goods are recorded. Grave 14, on the north-east of the 'Mound', was another female inhumation, with head to the south, accompanied by a pair of oval brooches, a ringed-pin and two combs.

Grave 15 is that found by Rendall sometime between 1849 and 1851, which contained a large skeleton said to have been in the region of 6ft tall; the surviving grave-goods consist of part of a shield-boss, from beside the cranium, an axe of unusual form and a spear-head, but there was also a lost sword, as well as various fragments of iron. Grave 16 had clearly been a rich one, but Farrer recorded no details about the burial itself. The grave-goods donated to the National Museum consist of a knife, and part of a second, a sickle and an iron key, with a bronze drinking-horn mount of Insular manufacture, and a baked clay bead (Figure 7.10). In addition, there are iron rivets, with wood adhering, of the type to suggest the possibility of a boat-grave, but other explanations, such as a wooden coffin or chest, cannot be ruled out.

The remaining grave in Thorsteinsson's list, no. 17, was excavated by Rendall and Petrie in July 1863, in the lower part of the Links, probably to the north of Pierowall. It was apparently covered by a sand-hill, but this may have been a natural dune, as there were no stones or other features to suggest a burial construction. Parts of a human skeleton and of a horse were found, with two iron buckles, some miscellaneous iron fragments and what was described as 'half of a bone button', together with twenty-one typical iron boat-rivets, three of which have wood adhering. This is most likely to have been a boat-grave, but as with the other Westray burials containing these rivets, their recovery and/or survival in such small numbers (while probably the result of erosion, disturbance and the work of inexperienced excavators) means that it is not now possible to have any real confidence in this interpretation.

Another problem connected with the interpretation of the Pierowall graves is an uncertainty as to whether they were originally all under mounds, as has commonly been believed, although Low's account would indicate otherwise. However, Thorsteinsson's reassessment suggests that few had, in fact, been so covered. Instead, most seem to have been found between natural mounds – the sand-dunes of the Links – and, in some cases, as secondary burials within these mounds. The recovery of most of the graves between mounds would be consistent with their partial exposure through wind erosion and as such would have been easier to identify and excavate than graves concealed beneath mounds of any size.

Even without the pagan Norse graves from the Links of Pierowall mentioned in the earlier documentary sources, this nineteenth-century collection of burials catalogued by Thorsteinsson certainly represents the largest such concentration to have been identified in Scandinavian Scotland. In addition, there are also the various unassociated artefacts, known from other graves, which need to be taken into account. These include an eighth-century Irish-style brooch, with replacement pin in the Pictish tradition, which Rendall sent in to the Museum in 1851; this brooch is of particular interest because others like it have been found in Co. Louth in Ireland, at Llys Awel on the north coast of Wales, and at Eidfjord in western Norway.

Uncertainty as to the number of Pierowall graves, as also concerning much of their contents, inevitably hinders their overall interpretation. The continuing work of reassessment has, however, demonstrated that the cemetery covered a wide area in which there were several discrete groupings of burials, suggesting that it was most probably in use by a number of families, even if burial location may have shifted through time. On the other hand, the quantity and quality of the grave-goods is a direct reflection of the overall wealth of the Norse population on Westray, which was doubtless derived in part from the maritime traffic through Pierowall Bay.

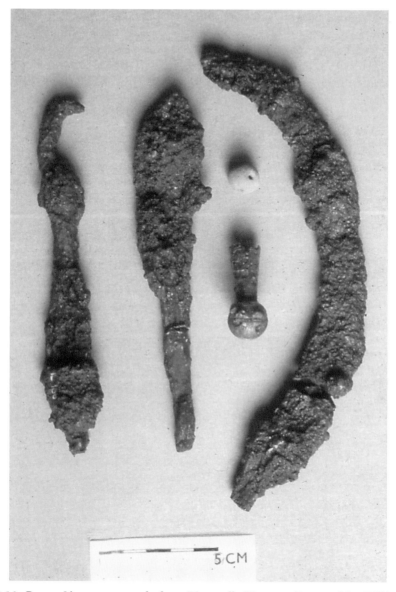

7.10 Pagan Norse grave-goods from Pierowall, Westray, discovered by William Rendall (K. Gordon).

WESTNESS, ROUSAY, ORKNEY

The pagan Norse cemetery at Westness, on Rousay, was excavated between 1968 and 1984, as part of a larger complex of archaeological sites, including a Norse settlement and noust, or boat-house. It is across the bay from the Knowe of Swandro, a stony mound where there was, when inspected by the Historical Monuments Commission in 1928, 'a series of large slabs set on edge' which suggested a group of disturbed cist-graves, 'possibly of Viking origin'. As the *Inventory* comments,

> This conjecture is to some extent supported by the fact that a typical Viking sword and a shield-boss, both now in the National Museum, were ploughed up separately close to the site; on the other hand, these Viking relics may have been intrusions in a previously existing structure.

The sword was ploughed up in 1826 and, following its discovery, it was noted that 'In this field there are many graves, in one of which the fragments of an iron helmet [shield-boss] were found several years ago'. Other sources suggest the discovery of a male inhumation from the mound itself. It is therefore obvious that there is a degree of uncertainty about the number of graves at this location. Although both sword and shield-boss might well be from the same grave, there remains the possibility that there were a number of graves in this vicinity, some of which may have had slab settings, if these are not in fact the disturbed remains of structural features, as in the nearby Westness cemetery.

The Westness cemetery itself was situated on a low-lying ness or peninsula, which was generally lacking in any surface features to suggest the presence of burials at the time of the accidental discovery of the first grave in 1963. This was disturbed by the farmer burying a dead cow, so that little is known about the actual form of this grave. However, subsequent investigation, following the disinterment of the cow, revealed that it had contained a woman with a full-term infant, who had presumably died in childbirth, buried with an exceptionally rich selection of ornaments and other objects, a selection of which is illustrated in Figure 7.11. In addition to a pair of ninth-century oval brooches, with forty assorted beads, there was a splendid eighth-century Irish brooch-pin of silver, with gold filigree decoration and settings of glass and amber, an unusual gilt-bronze mount with animal ornament (also of Insular manufacture), and two Anglo-Saxon strap-ends. As well as her comb, sickle and a bronze basin, there were several textile implements, including a weaving-sword, shears and a pair of heckles.

The Norwegian archaeologist, Sigrid Kaland, who undertook the excavation of the rest of the Westness cemetery (which contained thirty-two graves), has established, through radiocarbon dating, that it was in use from the seventh to the ninth century. The earliest burials were therefore pre-Viking in date. These Pictish graves, some of which were slab-lined, lacked grave-goods; most were marked with a head-stone which had resulted in them being respected during the Viking period. In contrast, a variety of demonstrably pagan Norse graves existed at the site, although all were inhumations (both extended and flexed). There were seven further burials containing grave-goods, including two well-equipped boat-graves (Figure 7.12), which were the first of the type to have been excavated under modern conditions in Scotland, before that at Scar in 1991.

Apart from the boat-graves proper, there were some oval-shaped graves lined with slabs, set on edge, which may have symbolised boats, for in some cases the stone behind the head was higher, forming a 'prow-stone', pointing towards the sea. These graves, which could have been slab-covered, were used for both men and women, with the normal range of weapons, tools and ornaments. For example, one young man was buried with his shield standing behind his head, together with arrows, a sickle, ringed-pin and

7.11 Grave-goods from the female Norse burial discovered at Westness on Rousay, Orkney, in 1963 (NMS).

comb, as well as a set of gaming-pieces; whereas the grave of a woman, which also contained a sickle and a comb, had a penannular brooch and two spindle-whorls.

The two boat-graves contained the remains of clinker-built oak vessels, measuring 5.5 m and 4.5 m long. As usual, the wood had rotted so that their plans have had to be reconstructed from the lines of rivets. These indicated that one had had three strakes and the other four and that they resembled the type of *færing* (or four-oared boat) found complete in the large ship-burial at Gokstad, in Norway. In both cases, a hole was dug to receive the boat, which was stabilised in place with stones and clay, after which a central burial-chamber was created by infilling each end of the vessel with flat stones. The man's body was then laid out, with his weapons and tools; both contained a sword, shield and arrows, but one had a spear and axe as well, together with farming implements, such as a sickle and a ploughshare; both had also a whetstone and a strike-a-light, whilst one had a fishing weight. Both men had seen fighting; the shield-boss of one had been slashed and the other is reported to have been shot by four arrows.

Other interesting aspects of the cemetery include an unfinished boat-shaped setting at the beach edge and the pathology of the skeletons which include trepanation, as well as signs of arthritis or tuberculosis. Further details of this important cemetery, the only one yet to have been completely excavated in Scandinavian Scotland (and to modern standards), are thus eagerly awaited.

7.12 Viking boat-grave in the pagan Norse cemetery at Westness, Orkney.

This is therefore to be considered as only a provisional account of what was but one part of the Westness excavations (see also p. 195), as are the following descriptions of two further recent finds of pagan Norse graves, which were still undergoing research at the time of writing.

SCAR, SANDAY, ORKNEY

The excavation of a boat-grave in 1991 at Scar, which is located on a north-west-facing bay on Sanday, has made a significant addition to the corpus of pagan Norse burials, not just for Orkney but also for the whole of Scandinavian Scotland. This discovery took place after human bones and iron rivets were found eroding out of a low sandy cliff, although the first object to be discovered at the site, picked up sometime previously by the local farmer on the beach below, was a small lump of lead which was subsequently identified as a Viking period scale-weight.

The excavation, which was undertaken in very arduous circumstances during November and December storms and high tides, revealed the sequence of events connected with the burial (Figure 8.1). First, a large pit had been dug in the sand, down to the boulder clay, on a roughly east–west alignment; the boat was then lowered into it and the gaps at either end filled with stones. Next, a simple grave-chamber was created by filling the east end of the boat with stones, behind a large upright slab placed across the boat. The remaining two-thirds of the boat, at the west end (probably the stern), was then utilised for the burial of three bodies, those of a man, a woman and a child, together with a rich variety of arte-facts. Finally, this chamber had been covered over, perhaps with planks, but there were no indications of there having been a mound; indeed, it is thought 'possible that the stem of the boat had stood proud of the ground surface as a grave-marker, before it rotted away'. About half of the boat, part of both the male and the child's skeleton, and an unknown quantity of grave-goods, had already been lost through erosion before the excavation began.

The man, who was about 5 ft 11 in tall and who had probably died in his thirties, was buried lying on his back, with his legs flexed, at the west end of the boat; his skull and much of his upper body had been lost to the sea. The skeleton of the woman, being in a more protected part of the boat, should have survived better, but an otter had made its nest in the chamber causing a great deal of disturbance to her and her immediate environment. Even so, it was possible to tell that she had been buried on her back and had reached her seventies – a remarkable age at this period. The child, who was aged about ten, had been placed next to the woman, lying on his or her back, but had again been badly disturbed by erosion.

These three individuals had all been buried at the same time, but it is not yet possible to confirm, as might be supposed, that they formed part of a family group. Advances in the new technique of DNA-analysis could well prove informative in this particular case.

The boat itself formed the largest of their grave-goods and is estimated to have been c. 7.15 m in length. It was constructed of oak with some pine fittings, fastened by iron rivets and nails, in the Nordic tradition of clinker-built vessels; it had five strakes on either side, with a probable sixth (or washrail). It is suggested that it was propelled by more than two pairs of oars – so it was perhaps a *sexæring* in comparison with the Westness *færings*. Laboratory examination of the remains of the caulking between the overlap of the two bottom strakes, amongst the few fragments of wood to survive through waterlogging, dis-covered grains of sand which had become trapped there during the construction of the vessel. These are not of types local to Orkney, or found elsewhere in northern Scotland; the boat must therefore have been built somewhere else altogether, perhaps in Scandinavia, as further study will hopefully reveal.

This is an exciting example of how modern techniques of laboratory analysis can be applied to the study of excavated material, acting at the same time as a reminder of the variety and quantity of information which will have been lost in early antiquarian, as well as many later, diggings into Viking period burials.

Despite the fact that some of the artefacts from the Scar boat-grave will have been lost to coastal erosion, the remaining grave-goods are certainly characteristic of those typically found in such burials in Norway. The man was, at least, accompanied by a sword (broken in its scabbard), with a silver and brass inlaid hilt, a quiver of arrows, a set of twenty-two whalebone gaming-pieces (presumably for playing the board-game of *hnefatafl*), which seem to have been in a bag, a comb, a couple of lead scale-weights (the early find, as well as a second), and possibly also a shield.

The woman was buried with, at least, two exceptionally fine objects, as well as a number of more ordinary items from everyday life. The most spectacular of her grave-goods is a complete whalebone plaque, most probably of north Norwegian manufacture (Figure 7.13); it is preserved in remarkably good condition and survives virtually complete, carved with a pair of stylised 'horse' heads. It is presumed, on the basis of ethnographic evidence, that these flat boards were used for polishing linen caps and smoothing pleats, but during the Viking period they were clearly artefacts that carried some degree of status, for they are found in well-equipped female burials, such as the enigmatic cremation grave on King's Cross Point, on Arran. Otherwise they have not often been found in Scandinavian Scotland, there being one from the settlement at Saevar Howe, Orkney, a chance find on Berneray, Harris, and another newly discovered in the excavations at Bornish, South Uist.

The Scar plaque had been positioned at the woman's feet, standing up against the drystone wall, so as to face her. Most of her other grave-goods had been placed on her right side, including a gilt-bronze equal-armed brooch, found upside down beneath the wooden handle of a sickle. This splendid specimen is exactly paralleled by several examples from northern Norway, although the type is otherwise known in Scandinavian Scotland by only a single fragment from Harris. In fact, she does not appear to have been buried wearing brooches – or even any beads. On the other hand, she had a comb, two stone spindle-whorls, an iron weaving-sword, shears, needle-case and a maplewood box, as well as the afore-mentioned sickle.

The combination of her brooch and plaque have suggested that the woman might have been of north Norwegian origin and, given her advanced age, that she might have been amongst the first generation of settlers. The dating of this important find must inevitably await the publication of the final report, but meanwhile it is proposed that the burial most probably took place towards the end of the ninth century.

Finally, it should be noted that additional work in the vicinity of the boat-grave, in the form of magnetometry, resistivity and contour surveys (followed by computer landscape modelling), has indicated that this is not necessarily an isolated burial. Likewise, it is probable that such a rich multiple burial indicates the existence of a nearby settlement which remains to be identified.

BALNAKEIL, DURNESS, SUTHERLAND

In May 1991, human bones were seen eroding out of a sand-dune on the beach at Balnakeil, on the north coast of Sutherland, about 4m above high-water mark. The skeleton was some 5–6m below the top of the dune, which created problems for the investigators, but the excavation that followed revealed this to be the pagan burial of a young Norse boy.

7.13 The whalebone plaque from the boat-grave excavated at Scar, Sanday, Orkney, in 1991 (Crown copyright: Historic Scotland).

The depth of the unstable overburden of sand militated against detailed examination of even the immediate vicinity of the grave, but it appeared to be that of an isolated individual. However, there could well be a Norse settlement awaiting discovery further round the wide sandy bay at Balnakeil (Figure 4.6).

Despite some damage from sand movement and erosion, it is clear that the body of the boy, who was between 8 and 13 years old, had been laid on his right side. He was about 4 ft 9 in to 5 ft tall, with a number of interesting pathological features (identified by Ywonne Hallén), such as an enlarged right clavicle, humerus and ulna – in addition to asymmetrical development of the skull (the left eye-orbit being set higher than the right one). A shield-boss was located at the rear of the head, together with a spear, and the body lay on a sword; there were also items of dress and further grave-goods, which have been examined in detail in the laboratory following their excavation.

The corrosion products on the dome of the shield-boss have preserved organic remains, such as straw and twigs, and both textile and feathers have been preserved on the sword, suggesting that a pillow was placed beneath the body at burial. The sword, which is full-sized and would thus have been too large for the boy to have used effectively, has a virtually complete blade contained within an organic scabbard. Its hilt has a domed pommel, with traces of a decorated cross-bar, and padding on the grip which was secured with wire.

Items which relate more to the boy's dress include a possible strap-end; this was located in the area of the lower body and thus suggests the presence of a belt. There were also three beads (amber and glass) and a simple bronze brooch-pin in an eighth/ninth-century Irish tradition.

Other pieces represent conventional grave-goods, whether favourite personal possessions buried with the deceased or gifts for use in the after-life. There was, for example, a bag of fourteen conical gaming-pieces, made of antler, each with a bone or metal peg for use with a wooden gaming-board, which may be represented by some small fragments of wood; this might perhaps have been something similar to the well-known example from Ballinderry in Ireland.

A fragmentary antler comb, a possible needle-case, with thread preserved in the corrosion products of the iron needles, and a fish hook make up the rest of this assemblage. Full details await the completion of the final report, but this single boy's grave makes a most valuable addition to the small number of young persons' burials known from this period in Scandinavian Scotland.

Chapter 8

PAGAN NORSE GRAVES PART II: INTERPRETATION

THE AFTER-LIFE

Norse ideas of an after-life in the pagan period can be traced in written sources from the tenth to the thirteenth century, but for the most part our knowledge of these beliefs is from the latter part of this period, after long transmission through Christian hands. It must therefore be treated with great caution, but this is not the only problem presented by these sources. As Ray Page has written:

> Norsemen were no more willing than most to meet their end, and they have many tales that tell of life after death: a shadowy life in a grave-mound; a life that allows the dead to walk again; a life of revelry within a holy mountain; and so on. These, though delightfully improbable, are hardly mythology. Their variety suggests there was no very clear-cut or coherent view of the dead that applied to the whole of pagan Scandinavia.

The mythological accounts of Valhalla make it clear that Odin's hall was reserved only for the bravest warriors slain in battle; other references are to Hel as being the abode of the dead, but this remains a shadowy place.

Despite this apparent variety of belief as to what happened after death, there existed the widespread practice in Scandinavia of burying the dead fully clothed, together maybe with a selection of grave-goods, whether the rite chosen was cremation or inhumation. Cremation might be seen as a means to prevent the dead from walking again and it is notable that weapons in cremation burials have often been deliberately damaged to render them useless, although this practice has also been encountered to a lesser extent in inhumations. On the other hand, was it imagined that Odin needed slain warriors to be buried with their weapon-kits, although not apparently with their helmets, for use by those who were taken to Valhalla?

BURIAL RITES

A passage in the early part of *Heimskringla*, Snorri Sturluson's history of the Norwegian kings, written about 1230, relates of Odin that:

> He decreed that all the dead should be burned, and put on the funeral pyre with all their possessions. He also said that everyone should come into Valhalla with all the

property that he had on the pyre, and he should also enjoy the use of what he had himself buried in the earth, and mounds should be raised in memory of men of rank.

It is somewhat ironic that Snorri as an Icelander should have put such emphasis on cremation as a pagan Norse burial-rite, for it has often been noted that there are no cremation graves among the more than 300 pagan burials known from Iceland. This practice does not seem to have been transplanted there from Norway, although the limitation in the availability of timber for pyre-construction might have been a constraining factor.

Evidence for pagan Norse cremation burial in Scotland is in fact slight, despite its popularity in much of Norway. In Orkney, for example, only a couple of possible cremations are on record (both found in the nineteenth century): a grave-mound at Lyking, Mainland, contained 'burnt bones' together with an iron spear-head, buckle and an unburnt comb; whilst 'a layer of burnt bones' in the middle of a mound, in the vicinity of Lamba Ness on Sanday, was associated with (also unburnt) a pair of oval brooches, a lignite arm-ring, a ringed-pin and an amber bead. The presence of unburnt objects in cremation graves is not in itself a problem because this practice can be readily paralleled in Norway.

The most notable example of a cremation grave from western Scotland is the ninth-century woman's grave at King's Cross Point on the Isle of Arran. The apparent absence of any skeletal remains with the Viking weapons found in the mound of Boiden, by Loch Lomond, which include a bent sword and a damaged shield-boss, suggests that this may have been another cremation grave. On the other hand there is no mention of any burnt bone either, so that the alternative of a cenotaph burial of weapons must also be considered, such as that found at Claghbane in the Isle of Man, which likewise consists of a sword, spear-head and shield-boss (together with a single bead). Other possible cremation graves, in the west, comprise both the elusive burnt boat at Càrn a' Bharraich on Oronsay, and the enigmatic contents of the Blackerne cairn, Kirkcudbrightshire, whereas the weapons from Millhill, on Arran, might represent either another cremation or another cenotaph (pp. 95–6).

Inhumation was thus the normal pagan Norse burial rite in Scandinavian Scotland, in line with that of its native Christian population, who made use of stone long-cists where suitable slabs were available for their construction. There are, however, no grave-goods with the native Christian burials, nor even any dress accessories which would suggest that the use of shrouds was standard practice. The pagan Norse settlers do not seem to have had any obvious desire to bury their dead in the existing Christian cemeteries, although this practice is well documented in the Isle of Man, Ireland and the north of England. The male burial, with a sword, in St Cuthbert's Churchyard, Kirkcudbright, and the axe from St Olaf's Churchyard, at Whiteness in Shetland, provide the clearest examples from Scandinavian Scotland, whereas the recent finds from Mail, also in Shetland, may represent another. On the other hand, the discovery of tenth/eleventh-century ringed-pins in Christian grave-yards does not necessarily indicate the presence of pagan burials, for the practice of using them as shroud-pins will have survived the Conversion.

However, not all pre-Viking burial took place at church or chapel sites and future excavations of pagan Norse graves might well reveal, as at Westness, evidence for continuity in cemetery use. In the same way, in recent years, it has become clear in both northern and western Scotland that graves which once appeared to be isolated do in fact belong to family groups or even larger cemeteries. The possibility therefore of examining family relationships through the study of DNA will obviously be of future significance.

Little or nothing can be said regarding the siting of individual burials or cemeteries in relation to settlement-sites, with the probable exception of Westness, as it is not known where the ninth/tenth-century occupants of the Brough of Birsay, Skaill, Jarlshof, the Udal, etc., were buried. Equally, it is not known where the farms and houses of those buried at Reay, Pierowall, Bhaltos, Ballinaby, etc., were sited. It is obviously tempting therefore to suggest that the dead were removed some distance from the living for burial – in some cases no doubt to prominent mounds and perhaps also to pre-existing burial places. However, most of the excavated settlement-sites are in zones of coastal erosion and so, if many of the burials had been located on or near the shore, for which there is good evidence elsewhere, they are likely to have become lost to the sea. On the other hand, the casual disposal of bodies, particularly of the young, has been noted in some settlements and their middens, indicating that no great need was felt in such cases to distance the living from the dead.

The situation at Westness is potentially most instructive in this respect, if only it were known whether or not the ninth-century settlement lay beneath (or even adjacent to) the partially excavated remains of the later Norse farmstead. The location of the pagan Norse cemetery on the low-lying headland meant that it would have been easily visible from both the site of this farm and the sea; indeed, it is passed by the path from the buildings to the noust. At the same time, it does not occupy any of the arable land. This is therefore an entirely logical choice of setting, but then the selection of the headland may equally have been influenced by its use for burial already when the Vikings took possession of Westness for themselves. The excavated buildings are, however, in the immediate vicinity of the Knowe of Swandro where at least one pagan Norse burial appears to have been found in the nineteenth century (p. 136), but the nature of the relationship between these two burial places is inevitably unknown.

Most pagan Norse inhumations seem to have been extended, although flexed burial was clearly not uncommon, as at Kiloran Bay (Figure 7.3); orientation was variable. There is no certain evidence for the use of biers or coffins, even if burials containing just a few rivets and/or nails may well have contained one, if these do not derive from a chest (although the re-use of chests as coffins is well documented during the Viking period both in Scandinavia and the West). Burials in boats, in cists, in slab-lined graves and within simple stone settings have all been noted, but not all graves had such features. In several instances there is clear evidence that the body was shrouded, most probably with the person's own cloak, but just how common this was as a practice is inevitably unknown, given that traces of textiles are normally preserved only in the corrosion products on any metalwork in the grave. It must also be remembered that various other funerary rites which may well have taken place, such as the pouring of libations or the scattering of plants, are most unlikely to have left any recoverable archaeological traces.

Many of the burials seem to have been flat graves, with no surviving surface indications of their presence, although low mounds were doubtless created at the time of burial. Such must have existed, for example, at Westness where several graves were in close proximity without any intercutting. In other cases, mounds were raised over the graves, as in Scandinavia and Iceland (and notably also in the Isle of Man), but there appears to have been a marked tendency in Scandinavian Scotland to utilise pre-existing mounds, thus ensuring the identification of the burial place in the landscape. As in Iceland, there is no evidence to indicate that any further marking had existed at most of these sites, although it was suggested by the excavator that a pair of stones had been erected on Càrn a'Bharraich on Oronsay and, in a small number of cases, prehistoric standing-stones appear to have been chosen to serve this function, as at Ballinaby on Islay, and possibly Ospisdale, Sutherland. On the other hand, it is worth remembering that Gerhard Bersu's skilful excavations in the Isle of Man demonstrated that both the Balladoole boat-burial and the Ballateare mound had been marked by the erection of a single wooden post.

A small number of boat-graves have been identified with certainty in both Orkney and Colonsay and there are hints of several more in antiquarian sources (Figure 8.1). The technical problems of excavating a wooden vessel, when all the wood has rotted away and only its impression survives in the ground, delineated by rows of iron rivets, have militated against identification in the past. The boats themselves, as grave-goods, will be considered further in the next section, but some mention is needed here of the three main ideas which have been advanced concerning the actual custom of boat-burial.

The simplest explanation for the boat-grave custom is the practical one: that the boats either provided fuel for the pyre or acted as superior 'coffins'. A second explanation is the symbolic one: that the presence of the boat symbolised the power and/or the seafaring life of the deceased. The third is religious: that the boat was required either for the deceased to undertake a sea-journey or for the worship of a particular god.

The practical explanation is obviously based on factual observation – boats were used for these purposes in pagan Norse burials – and does not rule out the possibility of them also having symbolic and/or religious content. Some consideration of the possible symbolic or other nature of grave-goods is given below, but here it is worth noting that boats are used for both male and female burials, some of which are by any standards 'richer' than others (the size of the boat/ship being important in this connection). The idea of the boat as a ferry to the realm of the dead is not substantiated in the written sources, and attempts to bolster it by reference to the occasional presence of coins in pagan Norse graves, as if payment for a ferryman in accord with the Greek Charon myth, have not rendered it any the more convincing. On the other hand, others are convinced that the tradition of boat-burial, which has prehistoric origins in Scandinavia, is related to the fertility cult of Freyja/Freyr who were associated with ships and the sea. The interpretation of boat-graves as those of this cult's priesthood may well be of importance for the consideration of the prehistoric origins and development of the boat-burial custom, but it is not so obviously relevant in the sea-faring days of the Viking period. There is, at any rate, nothing else obviously different about the boat-graves from Scotland, or from the Isle of Man, as to suggest that their occupants had particular priestly status. Their contents do indeed mark out their occupants as being of some social standing and, in the case of chieftains, this would have conferred a priestly role in pagan Norse society.

A burial rite of particular interest, although unique in Scandinavian Scotland, reveals a somewhat unexpected connection with central Sweden – in the form of the iron neck-ring with hammer-pendant, as associated with the worship of Thor, from the female grave at Gurness, Orkney (Figure 8.2), described above (p. 128). Its potential significance is best explained in the words of Anders Hultgård:

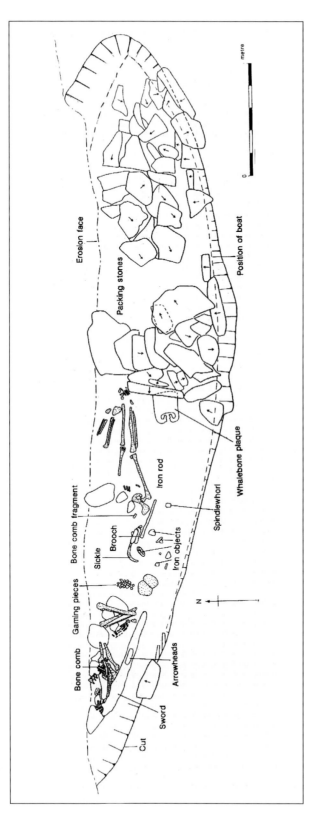

Labels within figure: Erosion face · Packing stones · Position of boat · Whalebone plaque · Iron rod · Spindlewhorl · Brooch · Iron objects · Bone comb fragment · Sickle · Gaming pieces · Bone comb · Arrowheads · Sword · Cut · N · metre

8.1 Plan of the pagan Norse boat-grave containing three inhumations, with grave-goods, excavated at Scar, Sanday, Orkney, in 1991, although partly destroyed by coastal erosion; the man was buried, in a flexed position, at the west end of the boat, and the woman and child were placed beside each other at the centre, with the east end being simply packed with stones (Crown copyright: Historic Scotland).

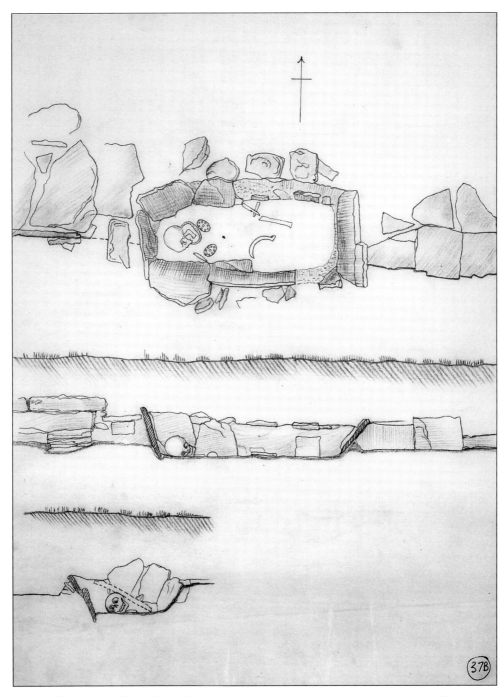

8.2 Sketch-plan of the Norse female inhumation, in a stone cist, excavated at Gurness, Orkney, in 1939; the woman was buried wearing a pair of oval brooches and an amuletic iron ring about her neck, together with her knife and sickle (Crown copyright: Historic Scotland).

Hammer-pendants of iron attached to rings of about 15 cm in diameter, mainly from the 9th and 10th centuries, have been found in many female graves in Birka and the Mälaren region, with a slight preponderance in female graves. The hammer-rings were most probably put around the neck of the dead and after cremation usually placed together with the bones in an urn. This mortuary practice was in all probability confined to the provinces of the Svear around Lake Mälaren and mostly in use in the early Viking period. We do not really know to what extent these hammer-rings were carried in life. Irrespective of their usage in lifetime, a ritual investment with the hammer or hammer-ring symbol during the burial procedure appears to be a plausible hypothesis. But what did the hammer mean to the people who deposited it in the grave? The answer is, I think, that it indicated the hope for a communion with the deity in and beyond death. Protection would be given to his worshippers not only in life but also in death, in the journey to the Other World.

These attempts by others to establish the significance of boat-graves and hammer-rings have served to introduce here the general problem of the interpretation of grave-goods, with the realisation that some may well have possessed a symbolic-cultic character.

GRAVE-GOODS

In any consideration of grave-goods, it is essential to bear in mind the distinction between those objects which form part of the everyday (or best) dress of a fully clothed individual, when prepared for burial or for the pyre, and any further objects which may be selected, for whatever reasons, to accompany the deceased into the ground. This distinction is not, however, by any means a clear-cut one, as it can be difficult to determine in some cases whether objects, such as a needle-case or comb, had been suspended on the person, from a brooch or belt, or had simply been placed on top of or beside the corpse. A man might be buried wearing his sword in its scabbard, but it might, alternatively, be placed beside him in the grave along with his other weapons.

Dressed burial, although a form of conspicuous consumption, is a rite which does not necessarily convey information other than that which may relate to social ranking, in the same manner as aspects of the burial rites reviewed above. It is the second category of 'selected' grave-goods which are most likely to carry symbolic-cultic significance, if not simply intended to be representative of the occupation(s) of the deceased. As already demonstrated, however, it is simply not possible to determine whether the pagan Norse actually believed that a slaughtered horse, for example, would have been of use to its owner in an after-life. On the other hand, it is clear that the artefacts selected for burial were normally taken from those in use in daily life and are thus not to be considered symbolic objects in the sense of having been made especially for burial purposes. However, in the case of at least some of the damaged or broken weapons, such as the sword in the Scar boat-burial, the burial rite may have involved them being deliberately rendered useless.

It is hard to point to any purely cultic objects in the pagan Norse graves of Scotland, other than the iron hammer-ring from Gurness, previously discussed, although it is possible that the wearing of an amber bead, as observed commonly enough amongst both men and women, may have been more than merely fashionable, given that amber has often been regarded as having amuletic properties.

The female graves, with their paired oval brooches, indicate the burial of women in Scandinavian dress (cf. Figures 5.3 and 8.2), and it seems reasonable to suppose that the majority of them, at least, were of Scandinavian blood, even if it cannot be ruled out that in a mixed marriage a native woman might have been persuaded to abandon her own costume for that worn by members of her new family. Insular influences are most clearly seen in cloak-fasteners, for the customary third brooch was often replaced by a ringed-pin in the native Irish tradition (and were also adopted by the men). An heirloom or treasured gift might likewise serve this purpose, as is most notably the case with the Westness brooch-pin (Figure 7.11). Combs are found in the graves of both sexes, as are sickles – the possession of a harvesting implement perhaps symbolising the status of a land-holding family in a settled community.

Further grave-goods selected for inclusion in female graves most often reflect the central role played by women in textile production, from carding and spinning to weaving and sewing. Indeed, the additional presence of a whalebone plaque and/or a weaving-sword in a woman's grave in Scotland marks it out as being of the highest rank, as at Scar (Figure 8.1). In contrast, high-status males have the addition of other tools of trade, such as scales (as at Kiloran Bay: Figure 7.4) or those of the smith (as at Ballinaby: Figure 7.5). In this division between the sexes as evidenced by grave-goods, it is of interest that cooking vessels have only been found in male boat-graves in Scotland, although the status of the so-called 'Pagan Lady' of Peel, in the Isle of Man, was in part manifested through the cooking-spit placed in her grave.

In Viking period Scandinavia, a man's ranking might be indicated at death by the completeness of the weapon-kit placed in his grave. Such would appear to have been no different in Scotland where the range is from the Kiloran Bay boat-grave, with sword, spear, axe, arrows and shield (Figure 7.3), to those graves which contain only a spear (e.g. Lyking, Orkney: Figure 4.3). The 'richest' male graves in Norway contain multiple weapons, but none such is known in Scotland. Sword-burial is, however, relatively common in Scotland when compared with Iceland.

During the Viking period in Scandinavia, boats, horses and dogs might accompany either sex to the grave, although the only dogs known from pagan Norse burials in Scotland are those recorded from Pierowall and that found in a female grave at Machrins on Colonsay. The number of boat-graves and horse-burials to have been found in Scotland is uncertain, given the imprecise nature of the antiquarian records, but there could be as many as eight or nine boats and several horses are recorded from Pierowall, as well as that found at Kiloran Bay. It is worth noting, by way of comparison, that five boats and seventy-one horses were known in Iceland out of a total of 308 pagan graves.

These Icelandic boats, like the Scottish and Manx vessels, are all small rowing boats. According to Michael Müller-Wille, who has surveyed boat-graves throughout north-western Europe, most of the boats placed in graves measure 5–15 m in length, in contrast to the few magnificent Scandinavian ship-graves which contain vessels from 15–27 m long. Boats 7–10 m in length, which would have had 3–7 pairs of oars, are commonly found, for such were well suited for use in inland and coastal waters. The Westness boats measured 4.5 m and 5.5 m in the ground (Figure 7.12) and the length of the Scar boat has been reconstructed at about 7.15m, whereas that of the Kiloran Bay vessel may have been as much as 11m; the mound over that at Machrins was reported to be 'about 30ft' long (c. 9 m).

Overall, the nature and range of the grave-goods may leave us uncertain with regard to pagan Norse views of the after-life, but instead these artefacts provide vivid glimpses of life in Scandinavian Scotland. A rowing-boat and a hammer or sickle, a spindle and sewing-kit, all relate to the humdrum existence of daily-life in island communities. Splendid brooches and rich ornaments illuminate festive occasions, whereas their varied origins demonstrate a network of external connections. Weapons are not to be found on abandoned house-sites, or discarded in middens, so that their recovery as grave-goods provides an important reminder of the more violent aspects of life, be it of Viking raids or the blood-feud.

REGIONAL COMPARISONS

In 1929 the Norwegian archaeologist, A. W. Brøgger, observed in his book, *Ancient Emigrants*, that there was a marked difference between the nature and range of the grave-goods from Orkney and those from the Hebrides. His explanation for this was that the settlers in the west were of 'an aristocratic class', whereas the Northern Isles had been populated by 'peasant families'.

Brøgger's hypothesis has become deeply rooted in the literature on Scandinavian Scotland. Barbara Crawford, for example, concluded (in 1987) that 'the archaeological material found in the graves of the Western and Northern Isles is a broad indicator of the rather different nature and status of the Gaelicized petty chieftains of the west as compared with the Norse farmers of Orkney'.

In the 1920s, Brøgger's data-base numbered a mere sixty graves, which might be considered rather few on which to base such far-reaching conclusions. The corpus has since doubled in size and it has now become possible to suggest, particularly in light of the reassessment of Pierowall and the excavations at Westness and Cnip, as well as the recent discovery of the Scar boat-grave, that this interpretation of the grave-material is no longer tenable. The pattern which is emerging in the 1990s is one of greater uniformity between north and west, with both areas displaying a similar mixture of graves and grave-goods.

In fact, already in the 1980s the Icelandic archaeologist, Kristján Eldjárn, considered the graves in the Northern Isles and the Outer Hebrides to be directly comparable. He considered them both as representing 'a real settlement of Norwegian farming people'. On the other hand, he thought that the people in the Inner Hebrides were 'more like real Vikings in the true sense of the word'. Eldjárn was struck by the fact that the majority of the pagan Norse graves in the west, which include some 'of the richest ones in the entire Scottish area', had been 'found in the small and, as it seems, not very important islands'. He thus concluded that:

> The small islands may have been an easy prey and at the same time convenient temporary bases where the newcomers could stay while taking their bearings in a foreign country and finding out what their possibilities were as raiders, or possibly as future settlers and rulers. Anyhow, it does not seem likely that the relatively rich graves such

as those on Colonsay and Oronsay can be attributed to people who intended to stay in these small unassuming islands.

The smaller islands were, indeed, most probably an easy prey to the well-equipped Vikings, but the interpretation of the grave-evidence for them having served only as 'temporary bases' is not entirely satisfactory.

There is no denying that the woman's brooches at Càrn a' Bharraich on Oronsay, made from shrine-mounts (Figure 7.2), represent the work 'of real Vikings in the true sense of the word', for Christians did not trade in sacred things or break them up for jewellery – such would have been an act of sacrilege.

At the same time, in the case of the Kiloran Bay boat-grave, we should avoid making a too facile equation of scales with peaceful trade. As Patrick Wormald has observed, 'scales were needed to assess the value of any precious metal, and would be as useful to the warrior-chief in distributing his loot as a trader'. On the other hand, piracy and trade can go hand in hand and the contents of the Kiloran Bay burial, with both weapons and scales, could well be said to reflect the life of a character like Bjørn in *Egils saga*, where he is described as 'a great traveller sometimes as Viking, sometimes as merchant'.

The accumulation of wealth on Colonsay and Oronsay does not necessarily imply that these islands were in use only as 'temporary bases', for such could as well be taken to be the product of permanent settlement and a diversified economy. It might also be argued that some degree of permanency is indicated by the very number and distribution of the burials. In particular, it was suggested above that more than one generation of graves was represented at Càrn a' Bharraich. Finally, the economic potential of these islands was perhaps under-rated by Eldjárn, for their machair and mild climate provides for a natural fertility, in addition to which they are well positioned for the exploitation of the western sailing-routes.

CHRONOLOGY

The dating of the pagan Norse graves in Scandinavian Scotland is a matter of continuing discussion and it is to be hoped that a clearer understanding of their chronology will be one outcome of the complete catalogue which is currently under preparation. Nevertheless, it is important that the matter be given some consideration here, particularly with respect to their overall date range.

In the first place, it should be remembered that there are only three graves which contain coins. In the case of the female cremation at King's Cross Point, on Arran, there is no reason why the burial should not have taken place as early as the mid-ninth century, on the basis of its one styca of Archbishop Wigmund (837–54). On the other hand, it might well have been somewhat later, as was argued above (p. 122) for the Kiloran Bay boat-grave, with its three perforated stycas, one of which is also a Wigmund; the only other legible one is of Æthelred II (841–4). The male grave at Buckquoy, Birsay, contained a cut halfpenny of Eadmund (939–46) showing little wear, so that a date for its burial in the mid-tenth century is entirely plausible.

There can be no doubt that the majority of the grave-goods in the form of brooches and weapons date, on typological and stylistic grounds, to what has been termed the

'Middle Viking Period' – that is the period from the late ninth to the second half of the tenth century. The rest of the material dates from the earlier part of the Viking period – that is the late eighth to the late ninth century, except for a few even earlier objects (such as the Westness brooch-pin). There is nothing attributable to the later Viking period, which is considered to begin in the second half of the tenth century. A major problem is, however, that an early object, particularly a piece of fine jewellery, may become an heirloom, handed down one or more generations until deposited in a 'Middle Viking Period' grave. It is therefore essential to consider only combinations of associated artefacts in order to establish a reasonable chronology, but this requirement inevitably limits the number of graves available for study.

The earliest dates attributed by Norwegian archaeologists to pagan Norse graves in Scotland have been c. 750 for the male grave/cenotaph at Millhill, on Arran (by Professor Shetelig) and c. 800 or earlier for that at Skaill, Orkney (by Professor Brøgger), although Shetelig himself rejected Brøgger's eighth-century date for the Skaill spear-head. Shetelig's date for Millhill has also been criticised for, although it contained the only single-edged sword then known from a Norse grave in Scotland, such were certainly still being used by Vikings in the West until well into the ninth century, as is demonstrated by their presence in the burials at Kilmainham/Islandbridge which can scarcely pre-date the foundation of the Dublin *longphort* in 841. Moreover, the distinctive form of the Millhill shield-boss is far more likely to represent a ninth-century Insular variant than to be of eighth-century Norwegian manufacture, as Brøgger believed.

8.3 *Pair of oval brooches and a trefoil brooch found together, in 1863, in a female grave at Clibberswick, Unst, Shetland, together with a silver arm-ring and two glass beads, which are now lost (K. Gordon).*

The majority of the women's oval brooches belong to the most popular of the standard 'Middle Viking Period' types, but earlier examples have been found at both Ardvonrig and Bhaltos in the Western Isles, as well as at Pierowall and from near Pool in Orkney (together with the unlocalised pair in the Perth Museum). Only two pairs of the earliest type of Viking period oval brooch, the so-called 'Berdal type', which has its origins in the eighth century, have been found in Scotland, at Càrn a' Bharraich, Oronsay (Figure 7.2), and at Clibberswick, Unst (Figure 8.3). In fact, variants of the Berdal type were manufactured well into the ninth century and it is to one of them that the Clibberswick pair belongs. Indeed, these brooches are worn and one has even been repaired; they were combined in the grave with a splendid Borre-style trefoil brooch – an association which suggests that this burial did not take place before the second half of the ninth century.

It is notable that the latest, and most baroque, of the standard 'Middle Viking Period' types of oval brooch, which went out of use in Scandinavia during the tenth century, is only represented in Scotland by a single pair – that from Castletown, Caithness. This and other factors, including the absence of any ornaments or other grave-goods with Jellinge-style decoration, suggest that pagan burial did not persist to any great extent into the tenth century, even in Orkney, and certainly not as late as 995 when, according to *Orkneyinga saga*, the last pagan earl was baptised, under duress from the King of Norway.

The general impression is thus that the period from about the mid-ninth to the mid-tenth century would appear to include the great majority, if not all, of the pagan Norse graves known from Scotland. However, the *floruit* of pagan burial with grave-goods was most probably of much shorter duration, falling within the second half of the ninth and the early part of tenth century.

Chapter 9

VIKING PERIOD SETTLEMENTS

Within the last twenty-five years the general picture of Viking and Late Norse period settlement and economy in Scotland has altered radically. On a limited number of sites –
Jarlshof in Shetland, the Brough of Birsay in Orkney and Freswick in Caithness – early
excavators concentrated on gaining a picture of the structural remains and associated artefacts, often at the expense of the rich middens in the immediate vicinity. Although, with
Jarlshof as the type-site, there was an awareness of building sequences in the settlements
examined, others, such as Underhoull on Unst, Shetland, were mistakenly ascribed to the
early phase of Viking settlement rather than, as can now be suggested, to the Late Norse
period. A far greater awareness of differences in constructional techniques and complexities,
in artefact types and in changes in economic activities exists as a result of the extensive
excavations which have been undertaken in recent years.

Continuing the broad period distinctions of Viking (c. 800–1050) and Late Norse
(c. 1050–1350 and beyond), this chapter will examine the information available from the
Viking period settlements at Jarlshof in Shetland; Brough of Birsay, Brough Road and
Buckquoy (Birsay), Saevar Howe (West Mainland), Skaill (Deerness), and Pool (on Sanday),
Orkney; the Udal on North Uist and Drimore Machair on South Uist.

These are the main settlement sites which can be ascribed to the earlier phases of
Scandinavian settlement in Scotland. Following an outline of the structural sequences and
dating evidence, aspects of the economic and subsistence activity will be considered in
relation to the Late Norse evidence in Chapter 11.

There is an obvious imbalance in the amount of information available for the earlier
settlements, since many were excavated prior to the standard use of large-scale environmental sampling. However, a number of general indications can be considered. The
explosion of information concerning the Late Norse activity is yet to be fully realised since
many of the sites are still in the process of reaching full publication – the corollary of
working in large multi-disciplinary teams on large, rich assemblages. However, clear
general trends are emerging enabling much greater inter-site comparability.

SHETLAND

Jarlshof

At the beginning of the publication of the work at Jarlshof, J. R. C. Hamilton records the
history of excavation at the site. He states that 'the excavation of the Jarlshof site covers a

period of over fifty years since its discovery in 1897'. The site is multi-period, spanning the Bronze Age to Medieval period, and has been subjected to several different campaigns of excavation (Figure 9.1). Hamilton's volume, written in 1953 and published in 1956, provides a summary of this work and attempts to collate the activity at the site prior to his own work there which commenced in 1949. It is important to be aware of this situation because in some cases the record of the stratigraphy, or indeed the method of excavation, may not have been of sufficient clarity to ensure that all relationships could be understood. The great complexity of the site of Jarlshof, where stone was reused throughout its occupation and where the dating of the structural sequence is intimately related to its association with midden banks, may have had to be either simplified or, in fact, over-complicated given the dearth of written observations from the earlier excavators. This is of crucial importance because the dating of the structural phases is largely dependent on the chronologically sensitive elements of the artefactual assemblages within the associated middens. There are few floor deposits which have yielded datable items. There is no doubt that the records for this site are in need of detailed re-examination, but this process is not yet completed so that the fully published (although problematic) sequence of Hamilton is used here.

Hamilton distinguished seven phases of settlement within the Viking and Late Norse period settlement, with the logical chronological break between Viking and Late Norse appearing at the end of Phase IV (eleventh century), before the point at which the settlement expanded.

In Phase I, dated AD 800–50 in Hamilton's chronology (although not necessarily beginning much before the mid-ninth century), the first Norse farmstead was built to the east of the enclosure of earlier settlers. The main structure was stone-built and sub-rectangular; it had an entrance in the narrow wall to the east end, and there were two opposing entrances in the long walls towards the west end. Three smaller buildings were erected in association and were interpreted as a bath-house or *hof* (a pagan cult building), a smithy and a byre (with servants' quarters). The main structure was some 70ft by 20ft (c. 21 x 6m), with one wall slightly bowed (probably due more to collapse and repair than an original intent), and a maximum interior width of 18ft (5.5m). The walls of drystone construction had an earthen core; the internal face was coursed, but externally the use of alternating stone and turf was noted. The original west gable was also built in the same manner, but subsequent remodelling of the building led to the removal of the east gable, the line of which was marked by a row of post-holes. During the lifetime of the building, the internal paving was replaced three times. Midden deposits associated with the occupation of this primary building were dumped to the south, adjacent to its southern entrance.

Within the building, which was of aisled construction, two rooms were created; the largest part was the living area, dominated by a central hearth, and a change in floor level (higher) marked the start of the kitchen area. The kitchen was dominated by a central fireplace and had an oven partially built into the wall.

The associated outbuildings of this initial phase were all considerably smaller than the main building. The bath-house (or supposed *hof*) was a small square structure, internally 13ft by 12ft (c. 4 x 3.5m), with a paved floor which was dominated by a central hearth. This had a short duration of use because it became covered by midden material, dated by Hamilton to the ninth century, discarded from the parent dwelling. To the north-west of

9.1 Aerial view of Jarlshof, Shetland (Crown copyright: Historic Scotland).

the bath-house, a smithy was located; despite the fragmentary remains, Hamilton identified an interior length of 21 ft and width of 10 ft (c. 6.5 x 3 m). Once more, a large central
hearth dominated the interior, revealing clinker debris on excavation, and a possible stone
anvil was identified. On the same orientation as the main dwelling, the third outbuilding
was located across the slope to the east. A rectangular structure 53 ft long by 16 ft wide
(c. 16 x 5 m), had been badly reduced by later stone robbing. The floor consisted 'of
stamped earth resting on stained sand' and lacked all internal features. This was identified
as a byre. A fourth outbuilding, which is not included on the published drawing, although
noted in the text, lay to the west of the byre. Hamilton recorded that 'though rectangular
in plan, the technique employed recalls the tradition of stonework common in pre-Viking
times' – upright slabs supporting horizontal masonry. It need not, however, have housed
'native serfs' as Hamilton suggested, but instead may have belonged to the period of
pre-Viking activity on this part of the site.

Several contemporary midden dumps were distinguished by Hamilton, but he noted
the problem of wind scouring the deposits in some areas and causing a conflation of
material onto a single blown-out surface. However, the 'Upper Slope Peat Ash Midden' is
clearly distinguished beneath the two subsequent farmsteads. In addition, a midden was
also located immediately over the cobbled surface to the south-west of the main structure.
For this phase, the bulk of the finds were recorded from the 'Upper Slope Midden'. Items
from the floor level of the main building structures were mixed during excavation 'owing
to the continued occupation of the house, the finds recovered by Dr Curle show an

admixture of late types'. This may be a problem which is not confined to this phase or this excavator.

Several loom-weights were recovered and over 270 sherds of steatite vessels of varying forms (small round flat-bottomed vessels and larger semi-spherical ones, as well as a handled type). The inclusion of this latter category in such an early midden is problematic. Other finds include stones with graffiti, several types of bone pins, including animal-headed forms, and a limited amount of slag.

The actual finds recovered from the floor level of the main structure should provide a more accurate dating of the occupation. However, the admixture causes uncertainty in this case. Several items are highlighted by Hamilton as being of ninth-century date, but it is clear that such precision needs to be treated with caution since some could be much older than the deposits in which they were found.

Phase II (c. AD 850–900) comprises buildings which are added to the initial farmstead, whereas the small bath-house structure falls out of use (Figure 9.2). Two new outhouses were built; one, with a cobbled floor, is interpreted as a stable. The main focus remains on the initial 'parent dwelling' of Phase I, although the major development is in the construction of a large farmstead building (House 2), located downslope and at right angles to the parent dwelling. Identification of this building was hampered by the almost constant redevelopment of that part of the site over the next two centuries. The house was 70 ft (c. 21 m) long and had straight sides, with opposing entrances in the short sides and one part way along the long west wall. Traces of central paving were located in the lower part of the building, interpreted as an integral byre which would have freely drained down-slope. It is, however, difficult to relate this information to the published plan. The foundations partially overlay the middens deposited from the first phase farmstead.

The outbuildings for Phase II comprise a stable range and a 'yard outhouse', the bath-house by this time being buried by a build-up of midden. The precise dimensions of the stable building are obscured by later building. Both floors of this two-roomed structure were paved with large slabs which were replaced once in the lifetime of the building. The other new outbuilding for this phase, although much robbed of its stonework, did have stalling surviving. It was identified as a latrine, but may have been for livestock.

The midden development in this phase was concentrated in the area of the original bath-house, with no apparent usage of the large midden on the upper slope. However, it is not likely that there was a complete cessation in the use of this large midden and, indeed, Hamilton noted later activity in that area. This certainly also has implications for the dating of material from within it.

The range of artefacts recovered from the Phase II middens is very similar to that from the preceding ones and the same problem of thin floor deposits, with admixing, was also noted by Hamilton. The few finds from the floor deposits within the houses result in dependence on the correct identification of the middens in use at the time. Given that, in some cases, dumping was apparently taking place away from the houses, such an indirect association can cause problems when the dating is transferred to the occupation of the nearby structures. This is a problem throughout all phases at the site.

Phase III (tenth century) is characterised by the building of a third large farmstead, parallel to that of Phase II. There was a clear stratigraphical relationship between this building and those nearby, and Hamilton suggested that this is the home of a third- or

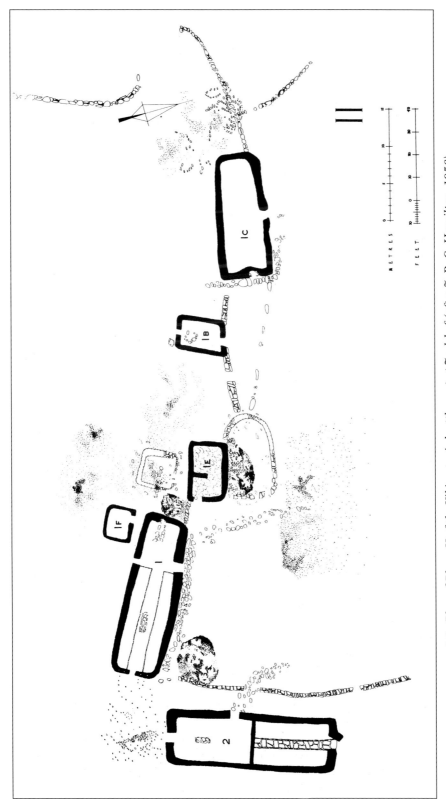

9.2 *Plan of Phase II of the Viking period settlement at Jarlshof (after J. R. C. Hamilton, 1956).*

fourth-generation member of the family. Two new outbuildings were required in this phase, one a barn and the other an extension to the Phase II farmstead.

The new farmstead (House 3) was sited in the angle between the two earlier farmsteads and, in common with all other buildings on the site, suffered severely from stone robbing and remodelling at a later stage. Approximately 73 ft (c. 22m) long, with at least three entrances, it partially overlay banks of midden from the earlier Viking period occupation. The larger portion of the house was probably dominated by a hearth, although little but ash survived, and a partition enabled one end of the house to be given over to a paved byre. In common with the earlier phases, this building had a yard-wall around it, which was later to become buried by developing midden deposits.

A new barn was built to the south of the smithy, although its precise dimensions have been lost through rebuilding on that part of the site. The other structural change was a paved extension to the south part of House 2.

A communal midden continued to develop, growing to a depth of over 1 metre. Distinctive items, such as a trefoil mount and a carved antler (which have been dated to the tenth century), were recovered from its upper layers. The steatite material in this phase is characterised by oval vessels. Amongst other items, most of which are of types common to all phases, there is a bronze strap-end, with Ringerike-style decoration, dating to the eleventh century, from the upper part of the midden. The House 3 midden was once more a mixed deposit, including square steatite vessels which are more distinctive of the Late Norse period and beyond.

The final phase at Jarlshof to fall within the Viking period is Phase IV (eleventh century), when there were minor alterations to the complex. A large paved outhouse, 45 ft (13.7m) long, was built parallel to House 3, with their doors opposite each other; it seems that they functioned closely together. This was built on top of the communal midden as well as the yard-wall. Despite the fragmentary nature of the remains, there were traces of an internal partition. The floor deposit was thin, but included chiselled fragments of steatite.

The excavated sequence at Jarlshof is long and complex. The problems presented by the superimposition of buildings and midden dumps have been compounded by excavation over several decades and by many archaeologists. The seminal work of Hamilton in bringing the material together remains a milestone for the discipline, but it is clear that there is more to be done with the surviving records. It is difficult enough to date structures which have well-sealed floor deposits and immediately adjacent middens. However, disturbed and conflated floor deposits, combined with rubbish disposal some distance from the buildings in use, suggest that the dating of the building sequence is in need of re-examination. The major elements of the buildings have stratigraphical relationships, so the problem may not lie there. However, minor structures and the apparently precise dating of general artefact types may combine to distort the perceived sequence. Given that the chronology of this site is so commonly referred to, the time for its re-appraisal is long overdue.

ORKNEY

Buckquoy

Three distinct phases of Norse settlement were distinguished by the excavator of this site,

Anna Ritchie. Built on top of, and adjacent to, the important complex of Pictish cellular dwellings described in Chapter 1, three fragmentary ninth-century Norse buildings were identified, labelled as 'early', 'middle' and 'late' Norse (Figure 9.3). Ritchie points out that 'Each of the three buildings represents a stratigraphically and chronologically separate phase of the farmstead, and each must originally have been accompanied by at least one other building which has vanished into the sea'.

The 'early Norse', or primary Viking period, farmstead is represented by the remains of a sub-rectangular structure (House 3), aligned roughly north-east to south-west, with traces of a byre in the part towards the sea, which has completely destroyed its gable end. The byre measured 4m across internally, and about 8m of the overall length of the building survived. Its landward part could simply have been a storage area, but it is possible, on the basis of the published plan, to interpret this structure as a small dwelling with integral byre – a true long-house. However, Ritchie suggested that a separate dwelling may have been lost to the sea.

House 3 was built with its south-east wall partially overlying one end of an abandoned Late Pictish farmstead (House 4), although this part of its walling had been destroyed by ploughing. Its surviving gable-end is curved in plan, in contrast to the rectangular gable-ends of both the subsequent Norse buildings (Houses 1 and 2), suggesting that it may have had a hipped gable. This feature raises the possibility that House 3 was a modified Pictish building, in a similar manner to native buildings at Pool on Sanday. A further possible indication that it was originally a Pictish construction is that it appears to have been partially dug into the ground, for Ritchie records that the internal face of the north-west wall stood up to five courses high, behind which she found only 'a basal compacted sandy layer, bordered by a line of small stones which indicated that the original wall had been about 1.5 m thick'. This she interpreted as being the remains of 'a turf backing' without an outer face because she felt that there was no reason why, if such had existed, it should not have survived. However, had the basal course of the outer face been that much higher than the inner face, at this point, it would most probably have been removed by ploughing. Indeed, the plan of House 3 seems to show the surviving part of the south-east wall as being constructed in the standard double-walling technique, as also a fragment of the (obviously damaged) gable-end.

The two interior zones of the building were divided by a stone partition, and high phosphate readings from the drain fill at its seaward edge support the presence of animals in the structure. Subsequent modification of the interior allowed for storage, and it was suggested that a defined oval area may have been to hold a water butt or milk churn. This feature is paralleled at Simy Folds in Teesdale, northern England, as well as at Stöng (and other sites) in Iceland. When the building fell out of use it was used as a midden dump.

The artefactual material from this phase, as also the succeeding phases of activity at Buckquoy, has assumed considerable significance with the benefit of hindsight. Unfortunately, House 3 had no clearly defined floor deposit and 'it was impossible to attribute finds from its interior to the period of its occupation'. Finds from the contemporary occupation were recovered from outwith the structure to the north-west, where they were stratified below later structures. Due to the undistinguished nature of this material, none of it was illustrated in the published report.

The 'middle Norse' farmstead (House 2) comprised a small rectangular building north

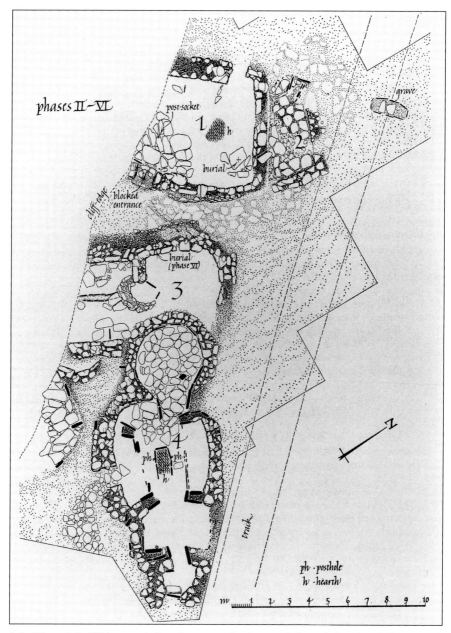

9.3 Plan of the Viking period settlement at Buckquoy, Orkney (after A. Ritchie, 1977).

of House 3. Also aligned north-west to south-east, it was securely stratified between the other two phases of Norse settlement activity. Although its remains were fragmentary, it is clear that it was of careful construction, having walls with straight wall-faces and angular internal corners and a well-paved interior. As with the preceding building, no trace of an entrance was located in the surviving structure. Substantial slabs paved the floor, and there were no traces of a hearth. A setting of upright slabs in one corner, rather similar to the post-settings of the Late Pictish structure, was suggested as a storage 'cupboard'. This building has been interpreted as a threshing barn on the basis of the carefully paved floor and its orientation at right angles to the prevailing wind. This is the only evidence at the site for arable activity. Following the deliberate dismantling of this intermediate structure, the 'late Norse' farmstead and its paving were built on the site.

The few artefacts from this second phase of Norse activity came predominantly from the midden infilling the earlier structure, and others were from deposits sealed between 'middle' and 'late Norse' paving. The assemblage is dominated by a range of ten well-crafted bone pins, several of which appear to be of native rather than specifically Norse manufacture. Other distinctive items in the assemblage also have pre-Norse antecedents, including one comb, and the fragment of another, and three sherds of pottery – some (or all) of which may well have been residual. A stone gaming-board for *hnefatafl*, or similar game, was stratified in this phase; two others were also recovered during the excavation.

The suggested cross-over nature of this assemblage – an admixture of Pictish and Norse – has provided a central element in the discussion about the nature of the takeover of Pictish settlement by the Norse. In view of the less clear-cut evidence for the primary phase (House 3), it would seem appropriate to be somewhat circumspect about the use of this small artefactual assemblage from Buckquoy in this connection.

The 'late Norse' farmstead (House 1) was identified as a dwelling-house, measuring internally c. 4.5–5 m wide, with a surviving length of six metres. Only the inner stone faces of the walls survived with sufficient 'turf backing', or wall-core, to show that they had been c. 1 m wide; the north-east corner was squared and the gable-end was constructed of more substantial stone blocks. Two entrances, one blocked, indicated remodelling of the structure and, as clearly shown in the published plan, there seems to have been some rebuilding of walling on the north-west side. In all, therefore, the surviving structural remains of this building are not only fragmentary, but have been subjected to remodelling. Paving by the original south entrance was not carried though the rest of the interior, which was of beaten earth. A single depression in one of the paving slabs was suggested as being for a roof support and was the only evidence for the superstructure. On the basis of its location, approximately one third of the way across the width, Ritchie suggested an aisled construction. An area of burning along the central axis suggested the position of a central hearth, and fugitive traces of possible side benches may have been identified. A potential foundation deposit, in the form of an infant burial under a slab, was also recorded in this building. The exterior was paved.

The artefactual assemblage from this phase had been widely scattered by ploughing activity. However, the admixture of Pictish material continues into this phase, most clearly seen in the one near-complete comb and two fragments recovered, and the eight pins of types which have been seen as combining aspects of both Norse and Pictish traditions. A small lead weight is one of the few specifically identifiable Norse items surviving. The degree of plough damage to this horizon, as well as to that of the pagan Norse burial over House 3 (together with coastal erosion to the seaward edge of the site itself), will have militated against the full survival of the later elements of this assemblage through the loss of the midden deposits.

To summarise, three phases of fragmentary structures were distinguished overlying the distinctive cellular Pictish dwellings. A possible long-house, identified as a byre, a barn and a dwelling were stratigraphically separated from each other. The form of the buildings, being more rectangular than cellular, has reinforced their identification as buildings of Norse occupation, whilst an assemblage with what appears to be a considerable degree of cultural admixture has reinforced the suggestion of social intercourse between the incoming Norse and native peoples. The overall chronology of these Norse phases is based on the assumption that the date of the ogam-inscribed whorl from the Late Pictish phase falls within the first part of the eighth century and the fact that the Norse structures have a *terminus ante quem* of the mid-tenth century, based on the dating of the pagan grave inserted into the settlement mound after the last structure (House 1) had gone out of use. Ritchie concluded that all three Norse phases fall within the ninth century, based on the belief that the 'early Norse' building is entirely Norse (discussed in relation to building types above), and thus most unlikely to predate AD 800 and on her dating of the burial to the third quarter of the tenth century.

It seems safest to suggest that the Norse phases are all developments of a single farmstead, occupied by one family group, and modified to suit its changing requirements. Without the missing structures and middens at the seaward edge, little further can be established. However, it is clear that this activity cannot be seen in isolation, given the proximity of other near-contemporary Norse settlements, particularly on the Brough Road and on the Brough of Birsay, discussed below.

The Brough of Birsay

Excavations on this tidal island off the north-west coast of the Orkney Mainland have been undertaken since the 1930s (Figure 9.4). With the exception of the detailed study of Pictish and Viking period artefacts recovered during the work prior to 1974, by Mrs Cecil Curle, little is available in published form for this earlier work. The excavations undertaken after 1974 by John Hunter and Christopher Morris concentrated on apparently previously undisturbed areas of the Brough, and revealed considerable structural complexity, spanning the Pictish and Viking periods. The initial work undertaken in the apparent structural heart of the settlement, so-called 'Room 5', yielded evidence of complex stratigraphy which, at most points, was not confined by the walls delimiting the 'Room'. These walls were thus later than many of the occupation layers and have perhaps given a spurious impression of this area. In other words, 'Room 5' is not a series of contexts lying within a single room, but a series of complex layers and structural fragments indicating the overall depth of the deposits in that part of the site. As elsewhere on the site, re-use of stone and levelling deposits were identified, the latter containing debris from metalworking, suggesting that it may have been introduced from elsewhere on the site, albeit nearby. The complexity and richness of these deposits was, however, the impetus for the following seasons' work and the subsequent re-examination of the site.

The most visible elements on the Brough of Birsay comprise a small stone church and enclosure which date to the Late Norse period and will be considered below. However, to the west and east of this complex lie the turf-covered remains of sub-rectangular buildings (at the west) and a tangle of such buildings to the east. In the eastern part, the area of so-called 'Thorfinn's Hall', several superimposed structures are visible, Viking period

9.4 General view of the Viking period and Late Norse settlement and church on the Brough of Birsay, Orkney (W. Vaughan).

buildings overlying Pictish ones. It is from this area of the site that much of the important Pictish metalworking evidence has been recovered, as described in Chapter 1. However, up the slope to the west, the sub-rectangular buildings which lie, with a single exception, across the contours appear to be more readily intelligible as single-phase, Viking period long-houses or hall-buildings. Recent re-examination of parts of this area proves that this view is in fact too simplistic – here too there were structural modifications.

Work undertaken between 1956 and 1961 concentrated on the Viking period buildings to the west of the church, Sites C and D in S. H. Cruden's nomenclature. Site C included three buildings, two lying side by side with a narrow passage-way between; these are thought to have been broadly contemporary and Cruden dated them to the ninth century. A subsequent modification of one of these structures to form the third building 'must be ascribed to the tenth or eleventh century'. The two earlier structures were about 15m long by 5m wide and the long walls appeared to be bowed. The turf walls were internally dry-stone clad and a combination of turf and flagstone formed the external face. This is a common combination on this site. Internal divisions were marked by upright flagstones and Cruden suggested an aisled roofing construction on the basis of the internal post-holes. The northern building was subdivided into a dwelling area and a byre.

Site D also produced three structures with the same date range; each structure in this part of the site replacing another, with the earliest lying along the contour (the only such one to be identified in this part of the site). The natural slope of the island and the naturally high level of precipitation would have necessitated a swift modification of this building to reduce flooding of the interior, but it is not possible to tell how long that building was in use. Many of the other structures in the western part of the site were equipped with an efficient external drainage system to reduce this problem. The second building on this part of the site had benches along the sides which ran the length of the interior. Rebuilding on both Sites C and D restricted the amount of information which could be salvaged about the earlier structures there.

Other buildings to the west of the churchyard (Sites L, N, E and S) have been examined by Morris in the renewed work at the site since 1974. It is clear that this whole area had been examined in the 1930s, but it was the interiors of the buildings that had then been of greatest interest and the walls were examined only with a view to enabling their coherent presentation to the public. The renewed activity concentrated on the areas between the obvious structures, as well as on a detailed examination of the remaining internal features. The western end of Site L was dominated by a drain to keep the structure dry and the internal features, which included a bench on one side, were clear. However, there had been structural modification, suggesting at least one rebuilding phase; the original structure (c. 10m long by 6m wide) was shortened by the insertion of a more flimsy wall. Lying to the east of Site L was Site N. Excavations between the buildings revealed traces of small stake-holes and a pit, possibly the remains of flimsy structures. The structure in Site N had largely been cleared internally by the earlier excavations, but it shared common construction features with the adjacent building, L.

Sites E and S were excavated through more extensive area excavation. Considerable structural complexity in these areas was superimposed, in the case of Site E, on top of massive post-holes and timber remains of the pre-Viking period. The area immediately to its north, Site S, had suffered greatly from earlier 'excavations' which had scoured the upper layers and truncated all the stratigraphy. This material is not yet fully published, but it will clearly provide crucial information for the understanding of the secular settlement on the Brough.

The area north of the church, Sites VII and VIII, was relatively undisturbed, although suffering from severe coastal erosion; excavations by John Hunter revealed a number of structures. Several stone and timber pre-Viking buildings, as described in Chapter 1, were superceded by stone, double-walled buildings of Viking period date. Sites P and R nearby also produced great structural complexity.

Site VII yielded three structures which could be dated to the earliest Viking period activity on the Brough. Dominated by drainage channels, two of the structures at this part of the site had been truncated by coastal erosion. The most northerly structure had walls of turf, with stone facings placed on clay foundations, and all lay with their main axis along the cliff edge. The precise function of these structures is not clear.

The next phase of Viking period building on this part of the site was characterised by buildings which were aligned at right angles to the earlier ones; gable-end on to the sea, they have consequently suffered badly from erosion. It was in this phase that Structure 6 was distinguished by traces of metalworking and it may have been a smithy; iron slag, fragments of burnt clay and a series of open hearths dominated the area. A similar situation was noted at Site IX nearby.

Most of these structures lay within the area distinguished as the focus of the settlement which is today delimited by fencing. However, several hundred metres to the south of this area, Morris has distinguished a number of additional structures from this period. Aligned along the cliff-edge, each has suffered through erosion. The most completely examined, and most impressive, lies on the Peedie Brough, a narrow neck of land today with sea on both sides. This was a sub-rectangular building with stone-faced walls, distinguished by the lack of any available space outside its walls – with cliffs to both sides – and by the presence in the artefact assemblage of many boat rivets. It is presumed that this indicates the re-use of ship's timbers in the construction rather than the building of actual boats in this unlikely location!

Brough Road, Birsay

In the course of excavations undertaken by Christopher Morris on the Brough Road sites, Birsay, a number of cultural phases were identified. The most significant results relate to pre-Viking activity – the cairn burials and a distinctive figure-of-eight building, described in Chapter 1, located a few hundred metres from Buckquoy. However, these were succeeded in Areas 1 and 2 by midden deposits and scattered areas of paving. Within the midden build-up there had been incorporated a Viking period burial (see p. 58). Although the actual structural remains are fugitive in the area excavated, it is likely that they are periph-eral to settlement activity which may have been centred around the mound still visible to the north of the Brough Road. Much of the material has been lost through aggressive marine erosion in this area, but Viking period settlement is identifiable. Limited archaeological investigation was possible, and the middens have at least been characterised (as discussed below). Unfortunately, a seemingly similar site at Skara Brae, a few miles to the south on the Bay of Skaill, where Viking period buildings and middens have been distinguished eroding from the section, has to date remained unexcavated due to problems in prioritising funding.

Saevar Howe, West Mainland

Excavations undertaken in 1977 by John Hedges demonstrated the importance of the eroding settlement mound of Saevar Howe which is located only a few hundred metres to the south of Birsay Village (Figure 9.5). Earlier excavations by James Farrer, in 1862 and 1867, had identified a long-cist cemetery, and some fragmentary structures, of uncertain date, but the 1977 work demonstrated that a Viking period settlement had overlain a Pictish one and that the cemetery was to be dated no earlier than the tenth century and was thus most likely of Christian Norse use.

Farrer described the structures he encountered as being made of both sea-worn and quarried stone and that they were in a ruinous state. Work in 1867 indicated a well-built wall and traces of paving with 'a sort of Orkney kitchen midden' of limpet and whelk shells. These remains were further examined in 1977 and three superimposed Viking period buildings were identified on top of either destroyed or abandoned pre-Viking buildings (Phase I). The Phase II (Viking) occupation comprised these three superimposed structures but the excavators had a difficult task investigating and interpreting the 'islands' of material remaining after the work undertaken by Farrer. However, it could be discerned that, although the earliest building was badly preserved, its successors were 'hall-houses',

9.5 The 1997 excavations at Saevar Howe, Orkney (Crown copyright: RCAHMS).

between 11 and 12 metres in length. The earliest structure (Phase IIa) was apparently aligned almost east–west with an uneven floor, distinguished by the presence of a series of thirteen unbaked clay loom-weights. Nearby a midden was located, but this had been largely removed during Farrer's excavations. This building fell into disrepair and was covered by blown sand, prior to the construction of the next Viking period building above it (Phase IIb).

Phase IIb was a 'hall-house' constructed with new walls and internal divisions; it has been calculated that the maximum width was 4.4m and minimum length 11–12 metres. The only walls identified in this phase were a short length of the north wall and a longer piece of the south wall, with central southern entrance. Within the building was a central paving of large flags, a burnt area representing the position of the hearth and suggestions of an internal partition. Twenty-eight loom-weights were recovered from the floor level. Outside the building was an area enclosed by walls, possibly a yard.

Following sand-blow onto the abandoned building, there was reoccupation of its upstanding fragments and the north wall was completely rebuilt. Internally a central path of flagstones led from a suggested entrance in the east wall to a burnt area (hearth); upright stones formed part of a bench. Following the abandonment of this structure, midden material spread over this part of the site.

Skaill, Deerness

Excavations at Skaill, in the East Mainland of Orkney, were undertaken by Peter Gelling over several seasons which spanned two decades, commencing in the 1960s. During this period, a large complex of buildings was excavated, indicating occupation in the area of Sandside Bay from the Early Iron Age to the present day (Figure 9.6).

On Gelling's Site 2, the earliest Norse building to be identified (House 2) was built from the fragmentary remains of an underlying, roughly rectangular, structure which was identified as Pictish (House 1) (although the recently published report by Simon Buteux points out that, on the available evidence, this could equally have been Viking). Rebuilding on this site provided a narrower structure, about 4.3 m in width (compared to 5.2 m in the preceding period), with a single entrance (instead of the previous two). A bench was identified along the west side of the new building, possibly matched on the east side, and traces of a hearth were found. This building was identified as a temporary structure by the excavator and it was replaced, after its dereliction, by another which he described as being 'more like a conventional long house' (House 3). It is clear that there were problems in distinguishing the assemblages associated with Houses 1 and 2 (i.e. in differentiating, on stratigraphical grounds, the Pictish from the Norse). However, these varied assemblages included steatite vessel fragments, a possible rough crucible, and bone pins of types paralleled in Viking period layers at Jarlshof.

House 3 overlay the northern part of House 2. Neither end of this structure had survived, but its extant length was 18.9 m and it had a maximum width of 4.6 metres. The walls were thick, up to c. 1.2 m in parts, and in places founded on earlier walling or sand. The doorway was located in the west wall; the east wall had been repaired and a wall projecting from it was interpreted as the remains of an additional room. Several such structural modifications indicate that this building was used over an extended period, which Gelling

9.6 The excavations at Skaill, Deerness, Orkney (Crown copyright: RCAHMS).

suggested lay within the bracket AD 850–1000. It is clear that the complexities of construction, which mirror those encountered by Hamilton at Jarlshof in Shetland, created
many problems for the archaeologists who worked at this site.

The main structure, with its possible adjacent room and enigmatic squared structure
incorporating upright stone slabs, was dominated at one end by a long hearth, 4.3 m long,
with fugitive traces of benches at the other end. Its floor deposits produced few finds:
spindle-whorls and a bone needle. Outside the building, associated midden deposits were
identified. Midden 2, which consisted mainly of burnt stones (pot-boilers), was thought
to be contemporary, although its precise relationship with the building had been lost
through the insertion of a pathway.

House 4, which replaced House 3, lay partially over one end of the earlier structure,
incorporating one of its walls. Fitted out with opposing benches and a drain, this short
rectangular structure was identified provisionally as a kitchen building and was itself
subsequently remodelled into a smaller structure (House 5), tentatively suggested as being
for livestock. The excavated middens associated with the period during which both
Houses 4 and 5 were in use were remarkably rich in artefacts; antler combs of Norse types,
bone and antler pins, including cruciform varieties, as well as needles, formed only part of
this assemblage.

Site 4 lay to the south of Site 2 and included substantial remains of Norse origin, with
a building which Gelling suggested was 'erected rather late in the Viking Age'. A further
building was examined on Site 1, immediately south of Site 4, 'in all probability . . . dated
not later than the eleventh century'. This period of the site is considered below in relation
to the Late Norse material from the rest of Scotland (Chapter 10).

The significance of the work at Skaill lies in the complexity of the structures recovered.
The discussion of the economic aspects of the assemblage, published by Buteux et al. in
1997, is a significant contribution to our knowledge of the economic and environmental
situation in this part of the Orkney Mainland in the Viking and Late Norse periods.

It is important to recall that pre-Viking rectilinear structures were identified at Skaill
in view of the common assumption that all pre-Viking buildings were cellular (discussed
in Chapter 1). The relationship suggested between the Picts and the incoming Vikings is
interesting, for Gelling proposed that the Norse settlement brought about a regression in
material culture rather than an enhancement. The evidence for this seems to be based
not only on the quality of the surviving structural remains, but most particularly on the
fact that whereas the Picts had produced pottery of reasonable quality, the Vikings only
used stone vessels. This is a simplification because good-quality steatite vessels would
certainly have obviated the need to produce pottery, so long as a supply of raw material
was available from Shetland or the Norwegian homelands; but he did note that

> The picture at Skaill may be distorted by a lack of ninth-century finds, but the evidence
> as it stands does not suggest much cultural continuity between the Pictish and the
> Viking periods. That there was considerable integration between the two peoples can
> hardly be doubted, but the sense of a clean break, and of a change for the worse in many
> material respects, is very strong at Skaill.

However, Buteux observes that 'it is very difficult to discern the basis for [the clean
break] in the evidence available'.

The lack of demonstrably ninth-century evidence from Skaill certainly needs to be highlighted in this connection. It is presumed that this interface material lies elsewhere in the immediate vicinity or, as Gelling believed, it has been lost to the sea, for it is unlikely that there was no primary phase of contact at this site. Meanwhile, our views on the inter-relationships between the Picts and incoming Vikings remain in need of further careful consideration.

Pool, Sanday

Excavations undertaken in the late 1980s by John Hunter of Bradford University centred on a large man-made mound which had been sectioned by the sea at Pool, on Sanday. To date, the published record of this site is only interim, and so conclusions may be subject to modification in the light of the final report (Figure 9.7).

The mass of the mound at Pool was made up of burnt peat, or turf-like material, and massive structural activity from the Neolithic period into the Iron Age. Immediately pre-Viking settlement at Pool centred around a circular or sub-circular building, with an internal diameter of c. 6m, which had been formed out of a remodelling of previous structures on the site. Many of the features of this structure survived the subsequent Viking period activity on the site. Further pre-Viking features included an extensive area of paving which allowed access to a series of cellular units. Large parts of the area which had been occupied in the Neolithic period were then paved over in the sixth century AD. As an integral part of this phase, Hunter notes 'a courtyard-type component of rectangular form more in keeping with Norse architectural styles than with expected native traditions'. This represented the maximum extent of the Pictish settlement, for there followed a slight contraction.

On the arrival of the Vikings at the site, which radiocarbon dating has suggested to Hunter could possibly have been as early as the late eighth to early ninth century, the site was partially levelled and a sub-rectangular building (10 x 5m) was created out of fragments of existing structures. Construction in turf and stone is suggested for the new walling. Internally, no sub-divisions were identified, but the hearth was placed roughly in the centre. The artefacts were not in general culturally specific, showing an admixture of both native and Norse types, and Hunter notes that this 'serves additionally to cast at least some shadow of doubt over the cultural pedigree of the building itself'. However, some changes in material culture, such as the introduction of steatite vessels, and also changes in the economy, such as the introduction of flax, do suggest a cultural change.

Other Viking period structures were then built to the north-east; one building, although badly damaged by ploughing, was not fully excavated but is likely to have been of c. 14.5m internal length, and approximately 5m wide (Structure 25). This building was of timber construction, and survived only in the plan of its post-holes and slots. Of particular interest in this structure are the remains of an inner timber framework, com-prising traces of sockets and slots. These were too small to have been load-bearing and thus integral to the actual building construction. Such evidence is often not recovered or would be impossible to identify on other sites where paved stone floors inhibit interpre-tation. The floor level comprised burnt deposits, but lacked paving or a hearth; Hunter has suggested an industrial purpose for this structure. Ten metres to its south, an Iron Age

9.7 The excavations at Pool, Sanday, Orkney (J. R. Hunter).

cellular structure had been modified in this phase by the insertion of a raised hearth, also suggested as being industrial in character.

Structure 27 falls within the later part of the 'interface period' distinguished by Hunter. Internally measuring only 9.5 x 3.5 m, it is about half the size of Structure 25. The walling is a 'combination of residual, collapsed and newly-built lengths of stone footings of varying thickness, quality and stature', based in part on the former Iron Age 'courtyard'. Hunter has suggested that this must have had a turf superstructure, probably of limited height. The interior was dominated by a rectangular stone-sided hearth, and the artefact assemblage dominated by iron items, mostly rivets. Other finds include hipped pins of pre-Norse types alongside Viking period items. Grass-tempered pottery is found throughout all these phases – from pre-Viking to Late Norse – and certainly emphasises that care is needed in ascribing this type of pottery exclusively to the Late Norse period, as this is now clearly not the case. Ecofactually the material is dominated by animal and fish bone, leading to the suggestion that this may have been an area for the processing of meat.

It is also of particular interest at this site that the Iron Age round-house survived relatively intact (at least at ground level) into the eleventh century, when it was levelled and partially incorporated into another longhouse.

WESTERN ISLES

The Udal, North Uist

The extensive remains of the Norse settlement at the Udal in North Uist have been completely excavated by Iain Crawford, although the site has still to be published so that detailed information is not yet available. The broad outline of events is, however, evident – from the ninth-century intrusion by the Vikings to the apparent expulsion of their descendants by the expanding Gaelic *revanche* at the end of the twelfth century.

The Aird a'Bhorrain peninsula, on which the Udal is a central feature, is an extension of the Uists' machair plain (Figure 9.8). There, the Vikings established themselves on the site of a flourishing native settlement, renaming the local landscape in the process, the Udal being the English form of An t-Udal which is the Gaelic version of an Old Norse settlement name. This was presumably *den Oðal*, indicating the homestead of some prominent Norseman (see p. 80). These two factors taken together suggest that, in this area of the Western Isles at least, the Norse takeover was a sudden event, doubtless violent in nature.

The native settlement, consisting of characteristic figure-of-eight buildings, was obliterated with parts of some of them being incorporated into the Norse sub-rectangular structures. The former were well built of drystone construction, whereas the Norse buildings were of turf and stone, or even of turf alone in the case of one open-ended outbuilding. The native wooden enclosures, curtilages or pounds, were also replaced in turf and stone. However, these Viking period buildings were poorly preserved as a result of the continuing occupation of the site, including the effects of medieval ploughing and subsequent erosion.

One of the earliest Viking period constructions seems to have been a fortlet in the form of a polygonal enclosure, only 7 m across, built on the highest point of the site. Its construction technique was completely novel at the Udal, involving the digging of a trench which was then filled with upright stones, packed with turf, in order to form a foundation for horizontal courses of massive stones – the largest readily available in the immediate locality. However, as Crawford has observed: 'This fort soon went out of use and the indications are that it was downgraded to a cabbage patch enclosure'. The threat, real or

9.8   The location of the multi-period settlement site on the machair at the Udal, North Uist (J. Graham-Campbell).

imaginary, from the displaced native community or other Viking would-be settlers, was clearly not such as to require its maintenance.

The domestic buildings lay to the west of the fortlet in two sectors, on either side of a ploughed field over the, by then, midden-filled bunker around which the native settlement had curved. During the tenth/eleventh-century phase, there were some six building units in use, including a cluster of agricultural and industrial function adjacent to the abandoned fortlet, for corn-drying, threshing and metalworking.

Preliminary indications are that, as at Barvas on Lewis, dairy production played a central role in the agricultural economy, with cattle and sheep also providing meat (as well as hides and fleeces), and barley and oats forming the staple crops – the latter seemingly a Norse introduction to the Western Isles. Fishing was also important, both offshore and inshore, and fowling to a lesser extent.

The Viking period buildings were associated with characteristic Norse artefacts of metal and bone, but also somewhat surprisingly with pottery – given its lack of use in Viking period Norway and absence from contemporary settlements in the Northern Isles, with the apparent exception of Pool in Orkney. This pottery differs in both form and construction from that in use at the Udal on the arrival of the Vikings. It consists of sagging and flat-based bowls and cups, together with platter-like flat discs which were presumably used as baking-plates; much of this has grass-marked bases, but decoration is minimal. There are possible affinities to the so-called 'Souterrain Ware' of the north-east of Ireland where the Vikings apparently failed to establish themselves permanently during the ninth century, despite the evidence of the Rathlin and Larne burials (p. 93). As noted above (Figure 3.5), Alan Lane has identified this Udal-style pottery from some forty sites in the Western Isles, extending from Lewis to Tiree.

No precise date can be put upon the Viking incursion at the Udal on archaeological evidence alone – and no pagan Norse burials have been located on the peninsula. The one radiocarbon date for the initial phase of Norse occupation, taken from a whalebone, gives only a probable (calibrated) range of 880–1020. This does, however, remain consistent with Crawford's suggestion that the Viking takeover 'seems likely to be later 9th century', even if there is 'no reason why it could not be a little earlier'.

Drimore Machair, South Uist

Excavation of a Norse settlement on Drimore Machair, South Uist, was undertaken in two weeks in July 1956, by Alistair MacLaren, in advance of construction work for a guided-missile range. The site was located by the presence above ground of a group of stones, the rest of the site being sealed by blown sand up to 1.5m in depth, which had accumulated after a period of erosion. Beneath this sand, the remains of a structure, 14m long by 5m wide internally, was aligned east–west. Reduced by erosion and stone-robbing to foundation level, the north and west walls survived only as a single row of water-worn boulders; the other walls were a double row. The wall construction is interpreted as double-faced with a turf core, and possibly with an external face comprising turf and stone. Although largely surviving only at the lowest foundation course, parts of the north wall survived to four uneven courses.

The plan of this house (Figure 9.9) was roughly sub-rectangular with the long walls slightly bowing outwards. The western end was rounded; the east end was straight, and at an oblique angle to the side walls, suggesting possibly a partition between the examined part of the building or a phase of rebuilding. The entrance in the north wall had a whale-bone pivot for the door, and there was paving both inside and outside this doorway. A central hearth, some 8m in length, dominated the interior, and MacLaren identified lateral benches, without any obvious supporting evidence. Examination of other features contemporary with the use of the structure was restricted by a high water table.

The limited nature of this excavation and the obvious extensive stone-robbing which had taken place have clearly resulted in a most incomplete picture of activity there. Certainly, MacLaren's view that there was no evidence of structural alteration within the interior of the house cannot be sustained on the evidence of the plan presented. Several parts of the wall are irregular, most specifically the west wall (especially at the south-west corner) and the north wall. The apparent battering of the wall at the south-west corner could have been necessitated by collapse, or perhaps as battering against a low dune face. In construction, it is made up of a basal row of vertical slabs superimposed by horizontal ones, a typical pre-Viking method of construction, as seen at the Udal and elsewhere. It is possible that this part of the walling was originally an arc of a pre-Viking cellular structure, as suggested at Buckquoy. There was a lack of finds material in this area, and MacLaren recorded 'persistent dark stains' below the Norse floor level in the area marked 'e' on the published plan (Figure 9.9).

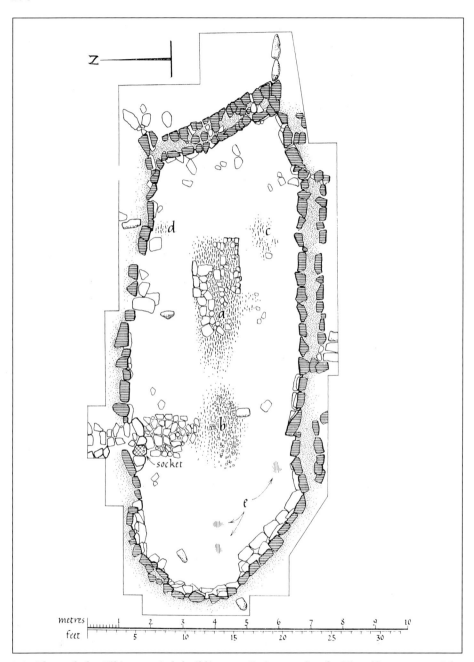

9.9 Plan of the Viking period building at Drimore, South Uist (Crown copyright: RCAHMS).

The north wall consistently lacks an outer face, according to the published plan. This could be because the area excavated was not large enough to include it, but it is possible that the wall was turf-backed, or recessed into the dune at that side. This cannot be resolved at this remove. The published photographic detail of the entrance on the north side clearly shows a butt joint; this could indicate a rebuilding phase, or possibly a blocking or remodelling of the entrance.

The south wall has a relatively straight stretch of double-sided walling, which deteriorates towards the east end. It may have been built at the same time as the east wall, which lies at an angle to it, and which is itself suggested as a rebuild. Adjacent to the east end of the building, two large upright slabs may represent the start of a yard area, as at Jarlshof Phase I (Building Ic) or at the Udal, North Uist.

MacLaren noted the presence of a 'layer of dirty sand, dark brown in colour and between 0.3 m and 0.6 m deep, representing the occupation debris that had accumulated within and around the building'. In other words, there was no distinction made between material overlying the abandoned structure (as clearly seen in the published photograph of the northern entrance) and the occupation level itself. The overlying deposit is clearly seen in the overall photograph of the site in the published report; although it is possible that this might have been part of the wall core, its obvious organic nature suggests a lost opportunity for detailed analysis. However, most of the finds were recovered from the area 'towards the outer edges of the floor-area and at the east end', with nothing being recovered from the smaller western section of the structure. Maclaren suggested that this may indicate a different function for this part of the dwelling and probably therefore the presence of a partition which was not identified on the ground.

The small range of artefacts recovered includes a few badly corroded iron finds, such as nails and pieces of knife-blades, five sherds of pottery, sixteen steatite vessel-sherds, several simple bone pins and one antler comb of distinctive Early Viking period type. Perhaps the most enigmatic artefact to be recovered from the site was a small thin silver plaque which is decorated with rows of ring and dot decoration. This has been suggested as being of 'post-Norse medieval date'. In the light of more recent work, it is possible to propose that this piece may have been of pre-Viking origin. Such a piece may well have decorated a Pictish comb, of the type we now know to have originally formed part of the (lost) Burgar hoard or as found on the Brough of Birsay in Orkney (in antler). If this is credible, it could support the suggestion of the origins of the western part of the building in the pre-Viking period.

That the occupation of the dwelling was apparently of short duration was suggested by the lack of stratigraphic differentiation in the small assemblage. It is important to underline that no associated middens were excavated at this site. However, it seems that there was some modification of the structure, seen in the nature and position of the east wall and also by the presence of a possible blocked entrance in the middle of the south wall of the published plan (irregular double walling with adjacent paving). It is unfortunate that time did not allow for any additional work in the immediate vicinity, since it is possible that this was only a phase of activity on a more complex site, with adjacent structures possibly using the building as a dump. Consideration of the overlying and floor deposits was of necessity limited, although aspects of the ecofactual assemblage were collected for analysis, and are discussed below.

The excavated evidence from the sites dated to the Viking period in Scotland is considerably less than that for the Late Norse period. There are, however, constant additions to the material from this exciting phase. As part of a major area survey, new excavations are currently being undertaken on Unst, Shetland, where a number of superimposed structures of Viking and Late Norse date are indicated (personal communication, A.-C. Larssen). In the Western Isles, projects on Barra, at Bornish on South Uist and Bosta on Lewis have all indicated the presence of Norse material, the precise dating of which is eagerly awaited.

Chapter 10

LATE NORSE SETTLEMENTS

In recent decades many new settlement sites have been excavated from the Late Norse period, and previously identified ones have been re-examined in the light of these new studies. It is evident that considerably more Late Norse sites are known than from the earlier Viking period. There are several reasons why this may be the case. It is possible that some of the Viking period buildings may not have been all that distinct in appearance from their native predecessors and that more substantial timber elements in the buildings may have been introduced from Scandinavia. The re-use of building material has certainly militated against the survival of the earlier structures during the continuing use of sites.

In the Late Norse period, buildings appear to have been more substantial than before, often made with coursed stonework. The use of flagstone in the north, in place of the previous predominance of beach pebbles, has enabled the better survival of building plans. The structures tend to have corners which are more squared, possibly indicating a change in the roofing construction.

A change in settlement layout, with the use of byres, separate annexes, etc., has been shown at sites such as Jarlshof in Shetland. More recently, G. F. Bigelow has argued that the inclusion of an internal byre – to create a true 'longhouse' – may also be a feature of the Late Norse period, at least in Shetland. This point is certainly open for discussion because, in the extended farm units of the period, a variety of out-buildings is also common, including external byres. It could be the case that internal byres were for smaller ventures, where fewer livestock were present on the farm.

The extent of individual settlements in the Late Norse period, with their rich associated midden dumps, has also aided location and identification of sites. However, the explosion of information about Late Norse settlement, particularly in the north of Scotland, which has taken place within the last two decades or so, could not have been predicted. Before the 1970s, later Viking period settlement had been published from Jarlshof, Underhoull, Birsay and Freswick. However, since then, Sandwick and the Biggings (in Shetland), Birsay, Beachview, Orphir, Pool, Tuquoy, Westness and Skaill, Deerness (in Orkney); Robert's Haven and Freswick (in Caithness), as well as Whithorn (in the south-west of Scotland), have all been the subject of detailed work. Most of these sites have been presented in interim reports, and some have reached final publication. The picture has changed beyond recognition, and in most cases this new evidence has been not only structural or artefactual, but also ecofactual. This aspect is examined in Chapter 11.

It is an interesting but sobering fact that *Orkneyinga saga* does not mention a single settlement in Shetland, although several are referred to in some detail from Orkney. This does not mean that there was a lack of settlement in Shetland, but rather that the author(s) of the saga were less familiar with that most northerly group of islands. However, it is obviously neither wise nor possible to equate definitively the individuals brought to life in the sagas with the sites excavated in Orkney, tempting as this may be in the reports of 'tabloid archaeology'.

Although there must have been close cultural links between Orkney, Shetland and Caithness, which all formed part of the same northern earldom for several hundreds of years, there is considerably more evidence available from Orkney. Could this simply be a function of the concentration of archaeological work in those islands? Or does it result from the better agricultural prospects there? Ongoing major projects in Caithness, and also now in Shetland, are redressing this apparent imbalance.

The evidence will be reviewed for Orkney, the heart of the northern earldom, from whose islands the greatest variety of evidence has been recovered. As for all areas with Late Norse archaeological evidence, the richness of the extensive middens from most of the recently excavated sites has resulted in delayed publication, and many projects are so far known only through interim reports. Full publication of Jarlshof appeared in 1956, and other site-reports are also available, but the earlier excavators were generally unencumbered by the detailed study of middens associated with the buildings examined.

SHETLAND

Jarlshof

The final phase of Jarlshof to fall within the Viking period was Phase IV, and it is of particular interest that with Phase V, dated to the late eleventh/twelfth centuries – and thus to the Late Norse period – there are major changes in the settlement morphology (Figure 10.1). The parent dwelling was enlarged by the attachment of a byre to the east gable, and to replace lost living space the west gable was itself extended. Access paths to this area of the site were also repaved and extended. The secondary farmsteads of the subsequent phases were abandoned, with House 2 being demolished to be replaced by cattle enclosures. House 3 was converted to a byre. These changes suggest that there were no longer several farmsteads in the same area but one main farm with its associated structures – outhouses, byres and enclosures.

In the area west of the parent dwelling two new houses were built (6 and 7), one overlying the original smithy. The new buildings, shorter in length than earlier ones (15 m), were set at right angles down the slope and appear to have been unpartitioned dwellings with large central fireplaces. Considerable midden deposits developed downslope from the new buildings and it is in this phase that pottery, often with grass 'backing' (marking and/or tempering), is first identified at the site.

Phase VI, dated to the twelfth/thirteenth centuries, was characterised by the building of a small number of outhouses adjacent to the parent dwelling. House 6 was extended downslope by the addition of a possible byre and House 7 extended in the opposite direction to incorporate an earlier structure, necessitating a massive reconstruction of the building as a whole.

Phase VII, the final phase of the Norse settlement, has been dated to the thirteenth

10.1   View of a Late Norse building (House 3) at Jarlshof, Shetland (C. E. Batey).

century. Although various structural changes could be distinguished, the settlement was on the decline, most noticeably by the abandonment of the parent dwelling. A new building (5) was established at right angles to the former parent dwelling and parallel to both Houses 6 and 7. House 6 was itself modified, with the original south gable abandoned and the interior shortened, changing in function perhaps to a store. House 7 had earlier masonry walls demolished and a number of small hearths were placed by the partition walls. A small building was placed at the west side, measuring 28 ft long (c. 8.5 m) and overlying the earlier structural remains in that part of the site. With the addition of a small porch at its north end, this structure was transformed from a plain rectangular building to a more complex and squat structure, similar in form to that excavated at Sandwick by G. F. Bigelow, described below.

Underhoull, Unst

The apparently simple nature of the structure excavated in 1962 by Alan Small at Underhoull on Unst, lacking in both associated contemporary buildings and structural complexity, was perhaps partly behind the original identification of the site as of Viking period date (Figure 10.2). The full artefact assemblage is currently being re-examined by Steffen Stumann Hansen and the structural remains studied in relation to the recent evidence from Sandwick, Unst (Bigelow), and Freswick, Caithness (Batey). There are certainly indications that Underhoull may have continued in use into the Late Norse period, if not actually originating during this later period.

The settlement is located on the eastern shore of Burga Sand, on an area of gently rising land above the cliff edge and below the Iron Age broch of Underhoull. Several episodes of rough ploughing may have brought artefacts to the surface before excavation, and Small noted the concentration of artefacts within the upper topsoil. Small also noted that additional structures in the vicinity seem to have been identified (although not excavated): one near the broch was mentioned by Irvine in 1865, as well as another south of the broch, near Newhouse. Small did, however, note in his (1966) publication that there was an eroding midden on the western shore of Burga Sand, several hundred metres from the longhouse at Underhoull, which was producing Viking period material in the form of steatite vessel sherds and an iron axe. This midden was clearly not related to the excavated building, and this suggests the presence of further buildings nearby.

The excavated site was in fact multi-period; an early Iron Age souterrain and broch-period occupation was followed by a 'Viking farmstead' which, it was suggested, began in the ninth century and continued with modifications for 'some considerable time'.

The site had been abandoned prior to its occupation by the Norse, and it is clear that stone was recycled from the broch and other structures. Considerable effort was expended to produce a near-level terrace over the earlier structures, and the size of the area available was increased both by quarrying into the bedrock and, on the south side, by building up the ground.

The structure which occupied this newly formed terrace was 56ft in internal length (c. 17m) and, at its maximum, had an internal width of 15ft (c. 5m). The long walls tapered slightly to produce a rounded west gable, with a more markedly squared east

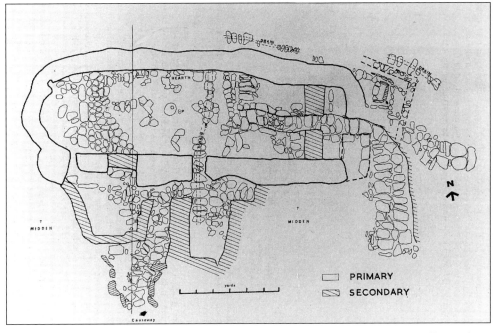

10.2 Plan of the Late Norse building at Underhoull, Unst, Shetland (after A. Small, 1966).

gable; the walls were of drystone construction, roughly 1–1.5 m thick, probably with alternating turf and stone exterior faces. Traces of reinforcement and rebuilding of the outer faces were identified on the west and north sides, and fragments of broken soapstone vessels had been used as packing within the rebuilt sections. Only two post-holes were distinguished, both along the mid-axis; unusually, the hearth was located adjacent to the north wall. Drainage problems were elaborately dealt with by drains, with the underlying souterrain acting as a most effective sump.

The east and central parts of the house provided the living accommodation, with access by a doorway in the south wall. A further door in the east wall was postulated, but the massive reconstruction of the walls in that area did not allow the matter to be resolved. Small also identified possible sleeping benches in the east part of the building, and also in the living area west of the central doorway.

The west part of the building was different. It had a paved floor and was entered, in its first phase, by a broad doorway from the yard; it is suggested that this was an area for livestock. The paved courtyard to the house on the south side had been relaid and reinforced a number of times. Modifications certainly took place as part of a phase of structural alterations to the building when the broad doorway in the south wall was blocked, the length of the overall building was reduced by about 6 ft (c. 2 m) by the insertion of a cross-wall with medial access, and a number of secondary walls were built to the south of the single building. One of these annexes measured 7 ft by 16 ft 6 in (c. 2 x 5 m). Of further interest was a much reduced building at the north-east corner of the structure which Small identified as a possible 'drying chamber probably for grain'. It was a squared building, with large central fireplace littered with fire-cracked stones and supplied with flues. Unfortunately, it had been too badly damaged for there to be any more certainty as to its function, but it may have had a seasonal usage.

The varied artefactual assemblage is of particular interest, showing exploitation of local materials. The steatite vessels were probably from the local Shetland quarries and, from nearer to hand, beach pebbles were fashioned into line-sinkers for fishing. Broken stone points could have been used in cultivation, supporting the evidence from field clearance cairns in the vicinity of the site, as well as possible bases for hay-drying ricks. Haunched hones and sharpening stones could have been for honing knives and fish hooks – and more besides – but the enigmatic fragments of two 'vessels used for rendering down fish livers' are probably the most frequently cited artefact from Underhoull because of its unique identification. It is clear from the published report that the surrounding middens were rich in material, although in the early 1960s it was not common to lavish on them the expenditure of effort and finance which such demand.

There is clearly more structural complexity at this site than was first appreciated, and a number of issues need to be resolved by detailed re-examination of the available data. Is it, for example, possible that the rounded west gable may in fact have been part of an earlier Iron Age structure, as postulated in Chapter 9 for Drimore and Buckquoy? This would indicate that the first phase of Norse activity may indeed date to the Viking period. However, subsequent modifications, possibly including the irregular south wall with its randomly placed entrances, the inbuilt soapstone vessel fragments and problematic east wall, may well belong to the later Viking, if not the Late Norse period.

The fragmentary building remains on the south side of the longhouse could be of even later date, potentially representing a re-use of the old building as an animal shelter. If indeed the building was latterly used as a storage area or for stock, that would presuppose additional contemporary buildings in the vicinity. Could these be the buildings noted before excavation? Or might they be the fragmentary buildings identified in a recent survey? A possible mill structure has been noted on a nearby stream. There are many unanswered questions at this stage, but new research will certainly bring this, as yet somewhat under-studied, site to greater prominence in its contemporary context.

Sandwick, Unst

Excavations at Sandwick were undertaken by Gerald Bigelow, in the late 1970s/early 1980s, on a site which was located on the present-day beach and within immediate danger of being lost completely to the sea. Its location has clearly been considerably modified since the Late Norse period; living memory records the presence of large dunes at this part of the bay, whereas today the site is a flat beach. Archaeological remains had been recorded from 1904 onwards in this bay, and in 1936 three specific concentrations of ruins and artefacts were highlighted. The most northerly site is now lost, but there are several finds in the museum collections at Lerwick from there. The middle site survives, although it is badly battered by the elements. The most southerly site to be identified in 1936 (South Sandwick) was the focus of Bigelow's work. This was a rectilinear stone ruin, with an enclosure, and an eroded sub-rectangular feature nearby, in addition to the Pictish burial cairn described above (p. 11).

In 1978 and 1979 the main dwelling was examined and the associated middens were extensively sampled (Figure 10.3); the environmental results will be considered in more detail in Chapter 11. This rectangular stone building had at least two building phases and its walls were of drystone construction with smooth internal finish. In the first phase, the house measured approximately 17.5 x 4m internally and was subdivided into four main zones through the incorporation of raised floor platforms. The distribution of artefact types indicated that Area 1 was a cow byre, Area 2 a kitchen area, Area 3 a cross-passage and Area 4 the main living area with central long hearth. Several post-holes were found along the central axis, although some of these were covered over by stone slabs in the succeeding phase. It is also possible that two smaller annexes built onto the west side of the main structure may belong to this initial phase of construction which has been dated to the twelfth century. Doorways were identified in the middle of the east and west walls, in the south end of the west wall and also in the north gable, where there was a 'cow-shaped' doorway, narrow at floor level but expanding upwards to accommodate the middle of the cow! The north gable was of less strong construction than the other walls and it has been suggested that this was to enable it to be dismantled at the end of winter to facilitate cleaning out the byre. This feature has also been identified at Jarlshof House 6 (Phase VI) and at Underhoull. The two exterior rooms which were built to one side of the main structure are considered to be integral to the form of a 'typical' Late Norse building in Shetland. The paved flooring with drainage channel at one side suggests a specialised function, in this case possibly for small livestock, or even as an indoor lavatory.

This first main phase of activity at the site is dated by radiocarbon to the period from about 1200–1400 when the living room was remodelled. There were major changes to the internal layout, and a new gable was inserted to shorten the interior by 2m, blocking the south-west doorway. In the living area, the hearth was moved away from the central focus of the room to one corner. Increased bench space was created in the gable areas and a concentration of domestic artefacts was recovered from this area. Similarities with evidence from both Jarlshof and Underhoull in Shetland and Freswick in Caithness have been noted by the excavator for these latter details.

The Biggings, Papa Stour

Excavations at the Biggings, Papa Stour, have demonstrated the degree to which it is possible to integrate information supplied by written texts with archaeological data, for Barbara Crawford has used a document dated to 1299 to locate and identify the high-status building mentioned in the source. This is a detective story of a different sort, for here there is the potential to identify actions recorded both as history and as archaeology.

In 1299 a document was drawn up by the lawthingmen of Shetland to inform Duke Hakon of Norway of a dispute between his bailiff Thorvald Thoresson of Shetland and a woman, Ragnhild Simunsdatter, who lived on the island of Papa Stour. The matter concerned deception in the assessment and collection of ducal rents from the island, where the altercation took place in the main room of the duke's house, or 'stofa'.

There has been much discussion concerning the nature of such a stofa, but it is clear that it was part of a major structure, perhaps a farm complex located on the island. Such a building would have served as the dwelling of the duke during visits to the island and was perhaps more permanently occupied as the official residence of the duke's sysselman (ombudsman). It is feasible to suggest that it would have had within it a fine living-room, with timber walling and flooring, as the name stofa should imply.

The study of this document was the beginning of the search on Papa Stour for the farmstead associated with the events described. The potential areas were limited; only the eastern third of the island is cultivable (in fact the soils are very rich in comparison to elsewhere in Shetland) and in the central area of settlement the Biggings lies on a rise between two bays. This prime location would certainly meet the criteria suggested by Clouston for an Orkney bu (as discussed below). Following examination of the place-name record in this area of the island, excavations were undertaken at the Görl, east of Uphouse, which yielded evidence of a substantial structure.

The building itself had a width of 5m with walling surviving to a width of 1.2 metres. The walls, reduced almost to foundation level by the later building on the site, were carefully made of an outer skin of well-laid stones and a core of compacted earth and small stones. Possible traces of a cross-wall or partition were also noted. A line of stones running along the interior face has been tentatively suggested as a sill for supporting a timber lining. This is complemented by the rare discovery of a fine timber-planked floor with cross-beams or joists (Figure 10.4). This has been radiocarbon dated to 960±55 bp (calibrated to AD 1013–1156). Fragments of panelling may have also been identified at part of one side of the structure, possibly from a bench construction. This wooden flooring is unique in the Northern Isles and represents physical evidence for the Late Norse timber trade which encompassed the Norwegian homelands and the treeless colonies of Shetland and the Faroe Islands.

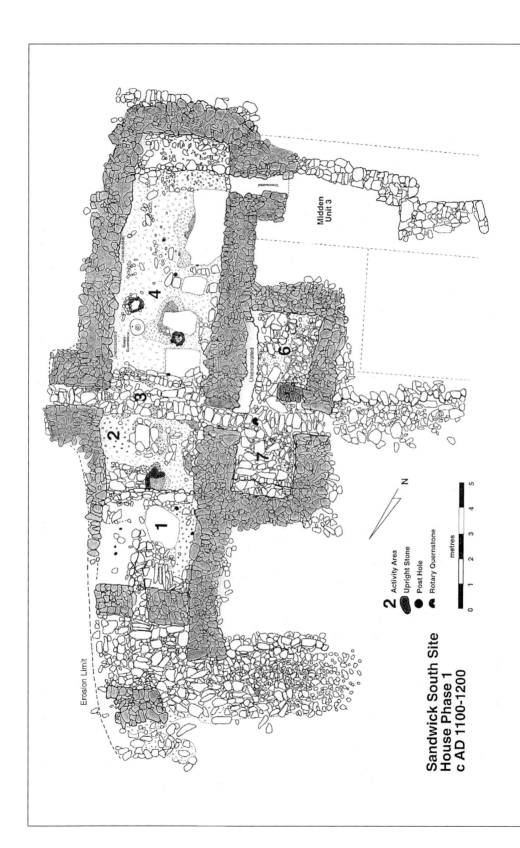

Sandwick South Site
House Phase 1
c AD 1100–1200

2 Activity Area
   Upright Stone
● Post Hole
◖ Rotary Quernstone

metres

0   1   2   3   4   5

N

Erosion Limit

Midden
Unit 3

Unexcavated

Unexcavated

Unexcavated

Rotary
Quernstone

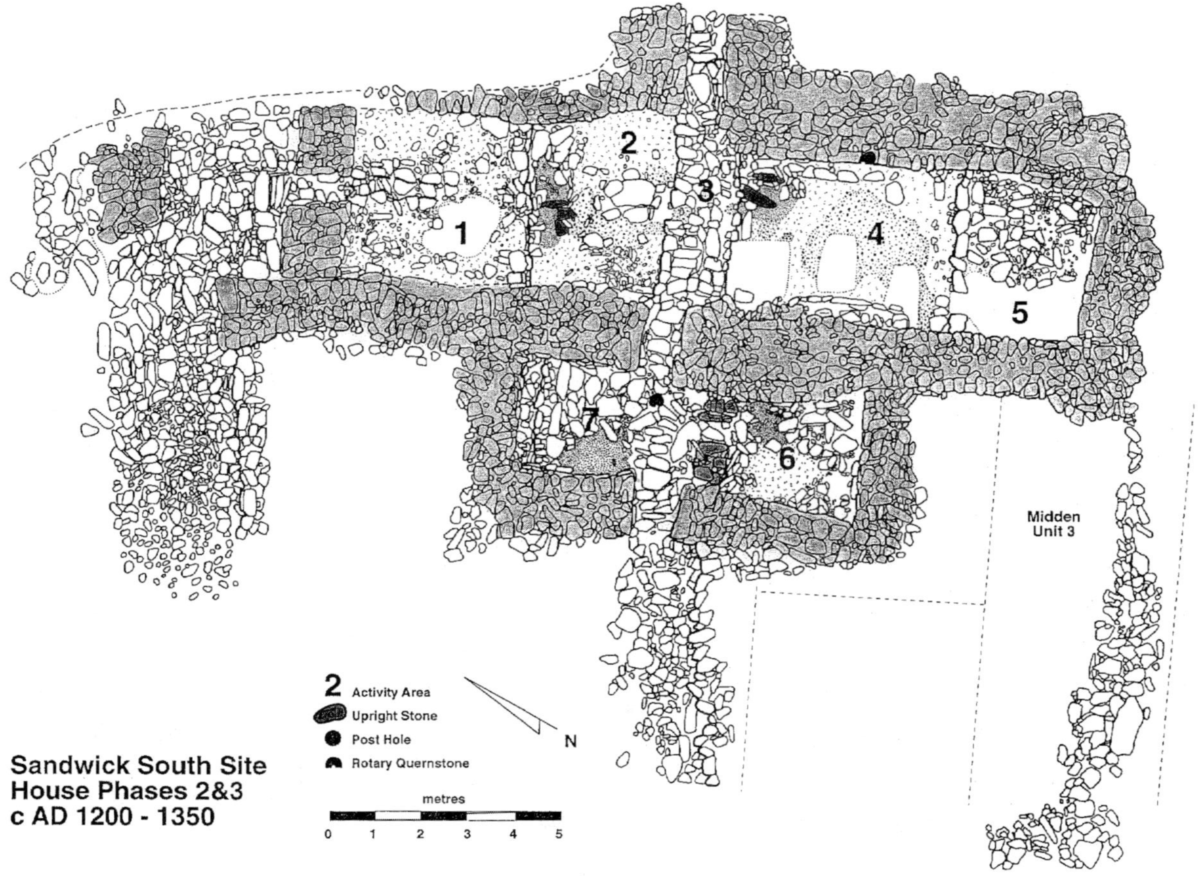
Sandwick South Site
House Phases 2&3
c AD 1200 - 1350
2 Activity Area
Upright Stone
Post Hole
Rotary Quernstone
N
metres
0 1 2 3 4 5
1
2
3
4
5
6
7
Midden
Unit 3

10.3 *Plan of the Late Norse building at Sandwick, Unst, Shetland (G. F. Bigelow).*

10.4 Wooden flooring in the Late Norse house excavated at the Biggings, Papa Stour, Shetland (B. Crawford).

The rest of the Late Norse structure is very fragmentary – pieces of birch bark are likely to be from the roof or wall insulation – although there was a substantial hearth, with scored steatite and schist baking plates nearby. A series of pits filled with burnt seaweed are of great interest and will be discussed in the light of similar findings at other sites of the period in Chapter 11. Other Norse artefacts include steatite vessels (square-sided and round) and spindle whorls, and lamps of sandstone and pottery. Small items of wood, such as spoons and spatulas, have survived, as well as examples of woven cloth and possibly knitting. There is no doubt that Scandinavian influence continued long after the traditional view of the end of the Late Norse period here (usually the pledging of the islands in 1469), for Papa Stour was held by Norwegian interests until the seventeenth century.

ORKNEY

The Brough of Birsay

Amongst the most obvious group of buildings which are visible on the Brough of Birsay today, the small twelfth-century church, dedicated to St Peter, and its associated buildings are perhaps the most evocative. It is clear that the initial foundation on the Brough of Birsay was religious, at least in part, and the Pictish symbol stone and early enclosure support this, although the recent excavations published in 1982 and 1986 have shown categorically that there was also a secular element at the site. The phase of secular Viking period activity described in the previous chapter then followed on the island, becoming a major focus of the earls of Orkney in the mid-eleventh century. The building of the church in the twelfth century, together with its associated structures located mainly on its north side, brought the focus back to a religious one – but not exclusively so.

Late Norse secular activity on the Brough of Birsay has been distinguished by Mrs Curle (defined as the Upper Norse horizon) and by John Hunter (the Later Norse phases of Sites VII and VIII at the northern cliff-edge). Although several other Viking period structures have been examined by Christopher Morris, as discussed in Chapter 9, at present it does not seem likely that their use continued into this later period.

In the area located to the east of the ecclesiastical buildings, Curle reported limited occupation in the Upper Norse horizon. The buildings (13–19) were positioned periph-erally to those of the previous phase, and those fragments of walling which could be distinguished were badly made, with elusive internal features. Of the limited artefact assemblage, there are few finds of the Late Norse period; a coin of Olaf Kyrre (c. 1080) from the graveyard, a single-sided comb with copper-alloy rivets which can be paralleled at Freswick Links, and, most importantly, at sites in Scandinavia, such as Lund and Oslo, in contexts dated to the twelfth and thirteenth centuries, as well as two sherds of grass-tempered pottery of the type recovered at Freswick Links.

The structural remains in this part of the site are on the whole insignificant, with Buildings 15 and 18 being little more than secondary modifications of previous struc-tures. Of perhaps greater interest, in the light of Hunter's subsequent work, are Buildings 16 and 17 which are isolated to the north of the rest of the group. Building 17 appears to have been virtually square, but Building 16, lacking its northern wall, could have been either square or more likely similar in form to Hunter's rectangular Structure 2 nearby.

10.5 View of Late Norse Structure 4 (Site VII) on the Brough of Birsay, Orkney (J. R. Hunter).

Hunter recorded seven structures of the Later Norse period on Sites VII and VIII (Figure 10.5). Site VII comprised a number of structural modifications of earlier buildings, such as the shortening of Structure 1 (to become Structure 4), but most specifically there was a deliberate reorientation of the buildings, potentially as one simultaneous building programme. In each case, it appears that there had been a deliberate pairing of a major building with an outhouse; this multiplicity of structures echoes the evidence from other sites of the period. One of the buildings, Structure 7, produced extensive quantities of metalworking debris, but others may have served as storehouses, whereas Structure 5 with its large kerbed hearth served a domestic function.

Buildings on Site VIII showed similar orientation and modifications; three individual structures were noted, each probably domestic. This area had suffered more severely from coastal erosion, but sufficient remained to identify the presence of side benches in Structure 10, although the central hearth had been lost to erosion.

Hunter notes that the Later Norse settlement was characterised by little more than substantial alterations to existing structures, usually with the retention of part of the original floor area and wall footings. Clearly this mirrors Curle's observations, and both areas therefore contrast markedly to the high-quality structural remains in the area of the church. Is it possible that these poorer structural remains were indeed contemporary with the building of the church complex, serving as dwellings for the workmen?

Beachview, Birsay

Excavations in the mainland area of Birsay, in the heart of the modern village, revealed the remains of a substantial stone structure infilled with midden (Figure 10.6). This formed the final phase of activity on a mound, some 10m high, which proved to be totally man-made – a farm mound. The detail of the environmental indicators are dealt with below, but the highly fragmented nature of the artefacts – steatite sherds, whalebone, industrial material and distinctive types of antler comb – suggests dumping activity from a building in the immediate vicinity in the Late Norse period, as has been confirmed by radiocarbon dating. Such a phenomenon is not out of place in modern island life, where unwanted materials may be dumped in abandoned structures elsewhere on the farmstead.

However, the form of the structure, which was ruinous by the time this material was deposited within its walls, is of some considerable interest. It has many similarities in constructional details to other Late Norse structures. The main structure had five major building phases: the construction of a sub-rectangular building approximately 8m in length (although the west wall was not actually located) and 4m internal width; the south wall of this was subsequently re-built; there followed the addition of a circular corn-drying kiln at the north-east corner; the building was subsequently narrowed; and then the final stage was the building of two successive new structures overlying the west end. The earlier of these was only partially excavated; it had a central drain indicating a byre function. The later structure, which had survived better, may also have made use of this earlier feature. Although occupation deposits were identified, the majority of the infill was subsequent midden dumping, as noted above. It is considered that virtually all stages of building, and indeed dumping, fell within the Late Viking/Late Norse periods.

There are two particularly interesting points to consider in relation to this structural

10.6   View of the Late Norse building excavated at Beachview, Birsay, Orkney (C. D. Morris).

evidence. The first relates to the building of the possible byre at the west end of the site. Although excavation of this part of the site was not completed, it is possible that the byre may in fact have been a separate structure, sloping away from the main part of the settlement (to facilitate drainage). This would have resulted in a pair of structures in a row, gable-end on to the sea, although not necessarily under a single roof. The other aspect of note is the early dating of the corn-drying kiln at Beachview. It is of the type commonly found on traditional farmsteads in Orkney today, but the oldest comparable example is in the final phase building at Jarlshof (the medieval farmstead) which is dated to the thirteenth/fourteenth centuries. The Beachview example would seem to predate this, perhaps by almost a hundred years (Figure 11.1).

Earl's Bu, Orphir

The site of the Earl's Bu at Orphir lies on the north side of Scapa Flow, and encompasses the remains of the Round Church and the adjacent Norse 'Hall', which has often been equated with references in the *Orkneyinga saga*, for the year 1135, to the drinking hall of Earls Paul and Harald. The *bu* element in the site's name has a great significance; it indicates that this was *bordland*, i.e. earldom property. The term *bu* was a generic term for a large farm, which shared a number of characteristics, as defined by Clouston in 1927: they consisted of large units of land, with the farmhouse usually built on a slope looking down to the sea and often a church or chapel on the estate. There are thirty such farms mentioned in *Orkneyinga saga*, of which twenty are on Orkney, such as Swein's *bu* on Gairsay, the *bu* at Paplay, the Bu of Cairston and, probably the best known, the Bu of Orphir.

Today, the visible structural remains, which were largely uncovered in the 1930s, are difficult to interpret. They are an amalgam of different structural phases, probably all or mostly dating from within the Late Norse period. It is, however, clear that these fragmentary buildings are not the drinking hall of the saga, but parts of several other structures, only some of which are partially exposed (Figure 10.7). Geophysical survey in this area has clearly shown that several other buildings lie in this area.

The first recorded investigation at the site took place as early as 1758, and other archaeological activities are recorded in 1899–1901; excavations were undertaken in the 1930s when the site was taken into Guardianship. Nothing further happened until 1978, when excavation began on a drystone linear construction which had slab lintels. This had been revealed by the farmer while trying to find a site without archaeological features on which to build a barn! Initial investigations indicated that this was most likely to be part of a souterrain, an underground passage and chamber, of a form found elsewhere in Orkney, such as at Grain or Rennibister. However, after considerable debate and further work, this feature was radically re-identified in 1988 as the remains of a horizontal water-mill – chamber, leat and lade – infilled with Late Norse midden debris (Figure 10.8). These excavated deposits are the first to have been recovered from stratified contexts at the Earl's Bu site, comprising the debris thrown away from the 'Earl's Hall' and its associated

10.7 General view of Late Norse structures at Earl's Bu, Orphir, Orkney (C. D. Morris).

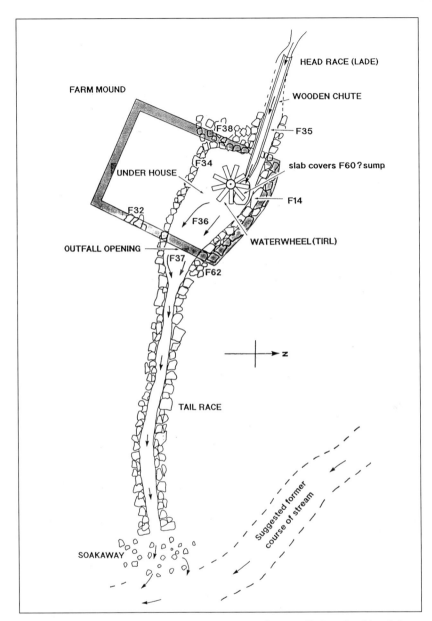

10.8 Plan of the horizontal water-mill excavated at Earl's Bu, Orphir, Orkney (L. McEwan).

buildings to the south, which had been noted only in a cursory manner in the earlier excavations. Their contents will be considered in Chapter 11.

The mill's underhouse survived to over 1m in height, but there were few traces of the upper house above it. This upper room would have contained the workings of the mill – the millstones and working floor. The lade, or head race, was distinguished as a narrow chute-like feature with substantial slabs standing on end, which gradually sloped eastwards towards the underhouse, where later examples of this mill-type often have a wooden chute. The existence of a small pond to allow a build-up of water pressure was suggested by features at the west end. The lintel-covered leat or tail race (the original feature to be found in 1978) allowed water to flow away to the east towards the burn.

Within the underhouse itself, traces of a small clay-lined depression were located on the line of the lade. It was thought that this must have been the position of the driveshaft for the wheel itself. This is unusual because the driveshaft would not normally make contact with the ground, but would be supported instead on a cross-piece or sole-tree. It is, however, interesting to note that this depression had been protected by the careful positioning of a large slab after it went out of use. Within the overlying deposits, a number of stones were found with incomplete perforations which could originally have been the pivot stones for the driveshaft, but only one possible piece of millstone has been recovered. It seems that the age-old tradition of the removal of millstones from such sites in Orkney applied even in the Norse period!

The underlying deposits suggest that the feature may have been built in the Late Viking period, and it had certainly fallen out of use within the Late Norse period. The mill seems therefore to have had only a brief spell in use. Although it could be argued that the horizontal water-mill was not the most efficient way of milling on Orkney's shallow gradients, the type continued to be used into the present century in the Northern Isles, as can be seen from the well-preserved Orkney example known as the Click Mill, near Dounby.

This is the first horizontal water-mill in the north to have been dated to the period of Norse presence, although the technology certainly existed in the preceding centuries in Ireland, where several timber mills have been examined. In contrast, only one horizontal mill of Viking period date has so far been excavated in Scandinavia – at Omgård in Denmark. It is clear from this that its introduction to Orkney was not from Norway, and this common term for the type – the Norse mill – should be abandoned.

The mill is a significant addition to the Earl's Bu complex at Orphir, but its discovery is just part of its ongoing re-appraisal. Extensive geophysical work in adjacent areas suggests the existence of several further structures. Beyond the immediate vicinity, traces of the waterway for a mill dam have also been located and, although several later mills were in action at this location, it is possible that the route may have had earlier use. The additional identification of a probable Late Norse industrial complex at Lavacroon, nearby, indicates that the Bu complex is much more extensive than anticipated. It is also one of the few large-scale Norse sites which remain to be examined in Orkney, with the potential for enabling a wide range of aspects of the Late Norse economy to be understood more fully.

Skaill, Deerness

The structural remains identified by Peter Gelling at the site of Skaill, Deerness, cover a long time-span (as noted in Chapter 9), although their fragmentary nature means that in some cases positive identification by phase was difficult. However, the *Orkneyinga saga* places Thorkell, foster-father to Earl Thorfinn (who had taken over from his own father, Amundi) at Skaill in the eleventh century. There are several structural elements which may belong to the Late Norse period, including the substantial remains of a rectangular building, 11.6 x 4m, with walls having a turf core and 'relatively well-built facing on the inside'. Both long walls had an entrance and there are patches of paving and clay within the building; at the east side, a heating duct was identified. The structure could have been a large bath-house, or more likely a heated building for grain storage.

A further structure, probably dating to the Late Norse period, is on Site 1, immediately to the south of Site 4. Although the walling was badly reduced, it was associated with middens in which a fine Late Norse antler comb was recovered. The excavation of this site was complicated by the shallow deposits in some areas having been susceptible to blow-out so that it did not prove an easy task to disentangle the stratigraphical relationships between all the fragmentary buildings recovered. It is clear, however, that this formed the settlement focus, and a first-floor hall has been suggested by Buteux in the 1997 publication.

Westness, Rousay

Excavations by Sigrid Kaland at Westness have revealed the pagan Norse cemetery on Moaness, which was described in Chapter 7, and a pair of rectangular stone buildings representing a Late Norse farmstead, with a boat-house nearby. Described in *Orkneyinga saga* as the home of Sigurd of Westness in the early twelfth century, this was indeed a favoured location. The farm buildings, which are located with their gable-ends almost on the present-day beach, were linked by a paved area.

Building I, 35m long and 6.5–7m wide, was a dwelling, with the interior subdivided into two large rooms separated by a third; it had been rebuilt during its lifetime. Side-benches beside the large central hearth were found in the north room which had an eastern entrance, whilst the southern room, some 10m long, had a protected western entrance leading into a paved interior.

The adjacent Buildings II and III were conjoined; Building II was 15m long and 5–5.5m wide, with curving outer walls; the doorway at the north corner was approached by a sunken paved area supporting its identification as a byre, with room for eighteen cows. Building III was a possible sheep byre, being much smaller in area, measuring only 5 x 5m, with a paved floor enabling good run-off for the waste products.

The boat-house, or noust, had been built at the best location, the most sheltered from the winds and fierce currents of Eynhallow Sound. It has been truncated by the sea, but some 8m survived of the length and it was 4.5m wide, so that it could have housed either a single large vessel or two small *færings* (rowing boats), like those excavated in the cemetery.

No further Late Norse structures have been identified in the immediate vicinity, although this part of Rousay's coastal fringe is the richest on the island. However, the presence of several stone walls upslope from the site may help to explain why no structures of the Viking period, contemporary with the pagan graves, have yet been identified – unless they have been claimed by the sea.

Tuquoy, Westray

A different type of site has been excavated at the badly eroded cliff edge near Crosskirk Church, at Tuquoy on Westray. The impressive stone remains, which are falling from the cliff, have been assessed and partially excavated by Olwyn Owen. They may potentially be associated with Thorkell Flettir and his heir Haflidi, although not specifically mentioned in *Orkneyinga saga*. The well-preserved, massive, structural fragments, covered with lime plaster, comprise only one edge of a large settlement. The exposed remains cover 150m at the cliff edge and have been traced up to 50m inland; other isolated buildings and field remains cover a larger area. Owen has suggested that 40m of land could have been lost to the sea within the past century.

A substantial structure of minimum dimensions 3.75m wide and 6.65m in length, with walls 1–1.4m thick, had a well-paved floor. It underwent several phases of modification, suggesting varying functions at different times. The recovery of a runic inscription (translated as: 'Thorstein Einarsson carved these runes') and a distinctive kidney-ringed pin indicate a date range of the late eleventh to early twelfth century. Initially, it was suggested that this structure might have been of similar type to Cubbie Roo's Castle, i.e. defensive in nature (as discussed below, in Chapter 13), but the preferred identification is that of a well-built dwelling of some high status, conceivably more similar to the hall-type structure at the Wirk, near Westness, Rousay. The Wirk has a small square tower with an attached hall (26m long and c. 7m wide) where the main accommodation was on the first floor. This is similar in scale to that surviving from the twelfth-century Bishop's Palace in Kirkwall (see also Chapter 13).

A further building had been appended at right angles to the main structure, and it has been suggested that this was a smithy, on the basis of a series of quenching boxes and associated metalworking debris.

These structures were the main elements recovered at the site, although a number of Viking period features were also distinguished, most notably a substantial pit containing waterlogged wooden debris and artefacts (see p. 221), as well as an enigmatic feature which may have been pre-Viking in date. The wealth of the artefactual and ecofactual material from Tuquoy, in conjunction with the substantial stonework remains, has secured its central position in any future study of the northern earldom.

CAITHNESS

Caithness was an integral part of the Orkney earldom, sharing the same earl as ruler for several hundred years. It is indeed only seven miles by sea from the southern tip of Orkney, but the archaeological remains of the Norse earls have proved elusive to locate. Two *bus* are noted in the *Orkneyinga saga* as being located in Caithness – one at Freswick and the other at Duncansby, the general area of Robert's Haven in the northern part of the county. It is therefore not surprising that both these locations have produced evidence of occupation in the Late Norse period. It is of greater moment, however, that to date these are virtually the only such sites on the mainland to have been located. Further detailed fieldwork is required to redress this lack of knowledge, but it is most likely that the Late Norse sites on the mainland are beneath existing crofting settlements.

Freswick Links

Although excavations have been undertaken on Freswick Links since the 1890s, it was not until the work of Alexander Curle in 1937 and 1938, followed by V. Gordon Childe in

1941, that the site was identified as Norse in origin. Several complete and incomplete structures were excavated and ascribed in the first report to 'a considerable settlement of the Early Norse or Viking period' and in the second to the Late Viking period. Little attention was paid in these excavations to the extensive midden banks which were associated with the buildings, although a simple species list was appended to Curle's report published in 1939. Instead, work was concentrated on the buildings themselves, in line with common archaeological preoccupations of the time. The more recent excavations, undertaken from 1978 onwards, were able to concentrate on the exposed midden deposits, although structural traces were few.

Curle recorded seven structures in the central part of Freswick Links (Figure 10.9). These are published as Groups A, B and C, with A being the first found and possibly therefore the latest in the sequence. Extensive reconsideration has been undertaken of these groups and the structural sequences. As a result, it is clear that Curle's published phasing, and indeed his structural understanding, was in error in many cases. These elements are dealt with exhaustively in the recent publications on the site, and only the major modifications will be indicated here.

Group A formed the largest part of the complex and consisted of four buildings (I–IV) and a suggested boat noust (V). Building I had walls of stone with an earth core and measured internally 9.2 x 4.3 metres. No clearly defined floor level could be detected which might suggest a beaten-earth floor. Differences in the methods of construction of the east and west walls of the building indicate rebuilding activity. The central axis was dominated by a long hearth, screened by large upright slabs on the doorway side. A drain was sealed with heavy slabs and led from a small, asymmetrical interior chamber in the east of the

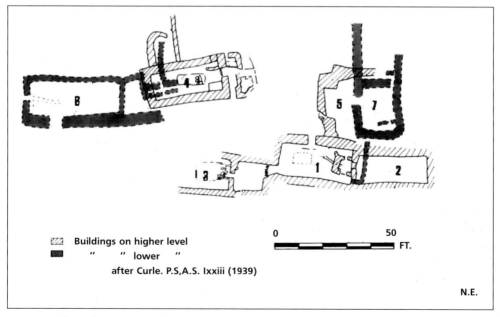

Buildings on higher level

" " lower "

after Curle. P.S,A.S. lxxiii (1939)

0   50
FT.

N.E.

10.9 Plan of Late Norse buildings on Freswick Links, Caithness (N. Emery, after A. O. Curle, 1939).

building which had its own fireplace. A sump towards the north wall would have facilitated good drainage and Curle suggested therefore that this was a bath-house. It had been inserted into an existing building, necessitating the blocking of a former east entrance to Building I. The floor of the small structure was covered with midden and a pile of levigated clay, for pottery production, lay in one corner.

As part of the re-examination of this building through the surviving records, several problems became clear, the most significant being the complete stratigraphical separation between the secondary structure and the underlying drain. These could never have been associated and thus the secondary building is unlikely to have been a bath-house. It is also clear that the four walls of Building I may represent two or even three separate building phases, or at the least this part of the complex saw considerable remodelling during its use.

Building II lay on the same alignment as Building I, and measured 9.2 x 3.35–3.66m internally. Its initial interconnecting doorway with Building I had been blocked off when the 'bath-house' had been inserted. No internal features were identified in this structure, and it was interpreted as a storehouse. A stretch of walling which ran at right-angles (N–S) beneath this building was drawn on the published plan as a 'building on a lower level'; it is in fact at a substantially lower level than Building II, also underlying the east end of Building I.

Building III was a range of two badly damaged rooms at the south-west corner of Building I. It is possible that the common entrance between both I and II had been closed by a wooden partition and that there was a narrow entrance to the eastern area in the south wall. This area had a flat paved surface which had been repeatedly resurfaced; in the final phase this paving had been placed over a hearth. In the western compartment of the building, only the east was paved and the whole was dominated by a large hearth (3 x 2.44m). The rest of the building was not located. Reworking of this evidence has clearly indicated that the west and east compartments represent different building phases and were in fact probably different structures.

Building IV, 8.8 x 3.8m internally, was located to the north of these structures. The walls were badly damaged, only surviving at foundation level, and, despite its different alignment, Curle included this in the same general phase of the site as Buildings I–III and V. The walls of Building IV were considered to be of a single build, gradually widening towards the east end. In the north wall were two blocked entrances, with a number of possible annexes. The gable at the north end had subsided due to the compression of underlying midden deposits, and it had been necessary to level up the floor within the building. A slightly raised area in the south of the building was suggested as a sleeping area or bench. Beneath the west wall were traces of earlier channels and/or vents. It is clear that this area of the settlement is also most complex and that the fragments of walling identified by Curle certainly represent several modifications to the initial structure, including walling north and east of the building.

Building V, the so-called noust, is the last of the structures in Group A. This is a palimpsest of structural fragments and even Curle doubted its identification as a boathouse. It apparently abutted the north wall of Building I and clearly post-dated Building VII.

Curle dated Group A to the thirteenth century on the basis of a single sherd of medieval pottery and a surface find of a coin of Henry III (1251–72). However, given the inevitable complexity of deposits associated with the excavated structures, and the fact that several artefacts – grass-tempered pottery, steatite sherds, femur-head spindle-whorls, etc. – were also recovered, it is quite possible that only a few of these deposits may be dated to that period.

Group B was a single building (VI) which partially underlay Building IV of Group A. According to Curle's publication, the structure had been created by building on the north side of a very substantial wall which ran for some 17 m in an east-west direction. The building thus formed had an internal length of about 12 m and width of 4 metres. The entrance was in the south wall and a vent led through the west wall. Internal details included a number of post-holes indicating an 'aisled' construction and a substantial hearth along the central axis. Details of an apparently secondary cross-wall were omitted from the final plan as published, although Curle recorded the information in his site notebook. To the north-east corner had been added various disparate stretches of walling, the function and form of which remain obscure.

This building has been re-examined by excavation (Figure 10.10), and a number of discrepancies were discovered between the earlier and more recent results. The most significant is that the substantial south wall of the building was in fact later than the rest of the walling of the building, and clearly overlay the original south wall. Additionally, another section of wall of this nature which was identified further west, suggested by Curle as being part of the same long wall (extending it by several metres), is obviously on a different alignment. It may well therefore indicate a further structure of some considerable size nearby. The internal deposits of Building VI, examined by Curle, at least in part pre-date the west, east and north walls of the building which appeared to delimit them. His supposed 'dais' at the east end of the building is most likely to have been part of an earlier wall underlying Building VI, rather than a contemporary internal fitting. There was probably an entrance in the narrow east wall which possibly led into another structure. This was blocked up so efficiently that its location is suggested only by the presence of paving at either side of the walling at this point.

The final 'group', Group C, also consisted of a single structure, Building VII. Unlike the rest of the complex, this building was aligned north–south and underlay the structural fragments of Building V. Only the southern part of this structure was excavated due to sand burden over the northern part, and the western wall was examined only by deep-trenching the overlying fish-rich middens. The single doorway identified was in the southern part of the west wall. There were no traces of a central hearth, leading Curle to suggest that it was used as a storehouse. A round kiln had been built into the south-east corner and a possible second one may have been located on the north side of a secondary partition wall. The large deposits of pot sherds invited the identification by Curle of this structure as possibly a potter's workshop. Reworking of the evidence from this part of the site supports the presence in the vicinity of a later structure which was using Building VII as a midden dump.

The excavations by Childe in 1942 were undertaken at the coastal margin in response to the actions of both war-time sand removal and coastal erosion. The area he examined was limited and there was great structural complexity. However, he managed to distinguish three main phases of activity. Phase I was a 'longhouse' approximately 8.5 m in length; its east end had been lost through erosion and the west had been remodelled in a subsequent phase. It had a central hearth with an oval fire pit at one end and a partially paved floor.

10.10 View of Freswick Links Building VI under excavation (C. E. Batey).

Phase II was a phase of considerable remodelling and it is hard to distinguish any specific structures, although traces of walling, paving, hearths and entrances do relate to this phase. Phase III had a new construction built over the east part of earlier buildings and in the main this was separated by a sand accumulation from earlier activity. No hearth or floor level could be distinguished in this phase.

Detailed re-assessments of the records of this excavation have shed little light on the structural complexities. Childe noted a Phase O, pre-dating Phase I, which is likely to have been a timber phase. Lack of identified midden deposits from this phase could support a short-lived occupation. However, despite this study of the site documents, the combination of war-time excavation, sand removal, depth of deposits and truncation by erosion severely limit the extent to which Childe's evidence can be integrated into an understanding of the site as a whole.

Renewed excavation in 1978 by Colleen Batey and Christopher Morris concentrated on the eroding coastal margin and to a lesser extent on the site of Curle's Building VI. The results of the re-examination of Building VI are dealt with above, but the structural and artefactual remains at the coastal margin were considerably more fragmentary. Traces of a probable rectangular structure, with central drain at its east end, were discovered in the central zone, close to the site of Childe's excavations (and due east of those of Curle), and nearby trenches also indicated some very incomplete stretches of walling. It is clear from this that, as the evidence survives today, the central part of the Links at Freswick was the main occupation focus. To the north and south, traces of cultivated horizons and vast midden dumps have been the subject of a detailed programme of study. This evidence is reviewed in Chapter 11.

The excavations by Curle produced the most coherent structural evidence at Freswick, probably lying at the heart of the settlement, in an area where the deposits had not been subject to erosion. However, it is still possible that some conflation of midden material may have taken place and resulted in the admixture of material from different periods in this inland area. It remains clear, however, that there have been several phases of rebuilding activity throughout the site, which makes it hard to assess the overall scale of the settlement at any one phase; this situation is most pronounced in the central area on which Curle concentrated. It is not possible to assess the time-span of all the Norse activity at this stage. A few artefacts from the site can with confidence be dated exclusively to the Viking period, but all subsequent dating evidence, and the re-working of the assemblages recovered by Curle and Childe, indicates a concentration of activity in the Late Norse period. The almost complete lack of deposits which can be dated to the Viking period might be explained by the extent of the coastal erosion.

Robert's Haven

Preliminary survey of the coastal margin of the north coast of Caithness, between 1980 and 1982, revealed two sites which had been previously unrecorded. One, at Huna to the west of John o' Groats, seemed to comprise a complex structural sequence of buildings placed gable-end on to the sea, associated with coarse pottery of a type noted both at Freswick and, more recently, at Robert's Haven. Unfortunately, before work could be undertaken to characterise the eroding site, it was virtually flattened by the construction of modern farm buildings. However, Robert's Haven, to the east of John o' Groats, has been examined in some detail, although more especially for its midden material rather than for structural traces; however, its significance in the limited corpus of mainland sites is clear.

Robert's Haven was a settlement site which had long been abandoned. Sand quarrying and wind-blow have revealed traces of rich midden deposits and fragmentary buildings amongst deep banks of shell sand. The site itself is bisected by a seasonal stream which has revealed extensive traces of midden material. The preliminary indications are that this is a site of similar character to Freswick, only some two miles to the south on the east coast.

The site clearly extended over several hundred metres, both along the coast and well inland. James Barrett has recently characterised and plotted this material in some detail, although the structural remains at the cliff edge were not specifically examined by him because much had been taken by erosion, although the single identified building at the cliff edge, whose walls had been partially held together by lime-mortar, was clearly associated with midden debris. The structural remains were too fragmentary to discern their precise character. The remains of an upstanding stone structure, 150 m inland, have been revealed through sand removal in the recent past. Although local informants have suggested that this may be of Norse date (and, indeed, a fine Viking period bone pin was recovered from deposits nearby a number of years ago), the building need not be contemporary with the middens in the area. It might, however, be located on top of an earlier structure which could be contemporary with those at the coast. The bulk of the midden material from the site consisted of fish, and Barrett has discussed the precise economic base for this in some detail, as will be considered in Chapter 11.

WESTERN ISLES

The Udal, North Uist

The accumulation of the tenth/twelfth-century deposits at the Udal is interrupted by a dense burnt layer, dated archaeologically to the late eleventh century, in part because it seals a coin of the Norwegian king, Harald Hardrada, which was minted c. 1055–65. There is obviously no certain explanation for this episode, but the excavator's guess is that 'the well-attested raid of Magnus Barefoot from Norway in 1098 might be in question'.

The Late Norse phase at the Udal was terminated, in Iain Crawford's words, by 'clearance and redevelopment of the whole site on an unprecedented scale. Drystone walling of excellent technique is employed and turf and enclosures have gone.' Also gone is the distinctive 'platter' pottery. This event, which seems to have taken place towards AD 1170, is attributed by Crawford to a takeover by the Gaelic lords expanding their control northwards.

SOUTH-WEST SCOTLAND

Whithorn

Whithorn remains the only other settlement of the Late Norse period to be considered here – one of the small number of sites so far identified on the Scottish mainland. In a detailed discussion of the contemporary situation in south-west Scotland, Dorothy Brooks has suggested that during the takeover of estates by incoming Norse settlers 'part of the bargain struck may have included the Vikings' acceptance of Christian baptism'. This may well explain why some of the Norse chose to settle away from the coastal waters, at Whithorn – the ecclesiastical centre of the area. Indeed, the key to a new understanding of the history of this area lies in Whithorn and the recent work which has been undertaken there.

A major excavation programme, initially undertaken by Peter Hill (and more recently by the York Archaeological Trust), began at Whithorn in 1984, and much information has been recovered about this important religious centre. Although deposits associated with the Northumbrian phase of occupation (seventh/eighth centuries) have been revealed, including the fragmentary remains of a timber church which may have replaced an earlier chapel, the structures which date to the period of Norse presence have caused much discussion (Figure 10.11).

There can be no doubt that there were links with Scandinavian colonies across the Irish Sea, the most convenient means of access to the area. Although Whithorn lies 5 km inland, its port at the Isle of Whithorn provided good harbourage. This must have been the route for the Norse material found at the site. The problem remains, however: what was the nature of the settlement at Whithorn and when did it flourish?

In preliminary reports on the excavations, Peter Hill refers to there being a 'thriving commercial settlement at Whithorn by 1000 AD', with a Hiberno-Norse population. Several timber structures of squared rather than rectangular form were uncovered, similar to examples from both Dublin and York. The term 'sub-square' is introduced in the final report. These consisted of a single 'room' with a central hearth, and, in the case of the first two encountered (in 1986), both had doorways to the west. The early reports refer to 'a settlement of small houses lying either side of a road running N/S across the slope of the hill'. The nature of this apparent proto-urban community has been re-assessed in the final report by Peter Hill, published in 1997.

Building 1 was separated from Building 2 by a 6m gap which included drainage gullies, midden and paving. House 1 was built on a level platform and had a patchy clay floor (c. 4 x 4m). The walling was of wattles and in parts these were placed on a low clay bank. A small square stone hearth in the middle of the floor was surrounded by flagging. A stone-lined drain outside the door carried away the run-off. Building 2 was slightly larger (4.5 x 4m) and had good preservation of the structural timbers of the wall due to the underlying waterlogged deposits. The outer wall comprised a double line of stakes and the outer skin was surrounded on three sides by shallow drainage gullies. To the south-east of this building, a waterlogged ditch was located, which was filled with organic deposits.

When these buildings had fallen into decay, two further houses were built (Buildings 4 and 5) on new sites. Although these were poorly preserved, with interior detail being restricted to the presence of a large hearth in each, they seem to have been positioned at right angles to the road and had their doors opening onto it. The next phase of buildings included the construction of a rectangular timber building (Building 9) orientated N–S on the east side of the road. In all there were five main phases of activity, with a complex history of rebuilding.

Building 9 was constructed over Building 4 and the intervening deposits included comb-working debris. The walling of the structure was ill-defined and the interior plotted by central ash spreads and a drain. Its width was in the order of 3.2m and it was at least 6m long, although the north end of the building was not located. It is likely that the building was sub-divided into three rooms, the central one with a hearth and another with a paved floor. Following a further phase of modification, when the building may have been

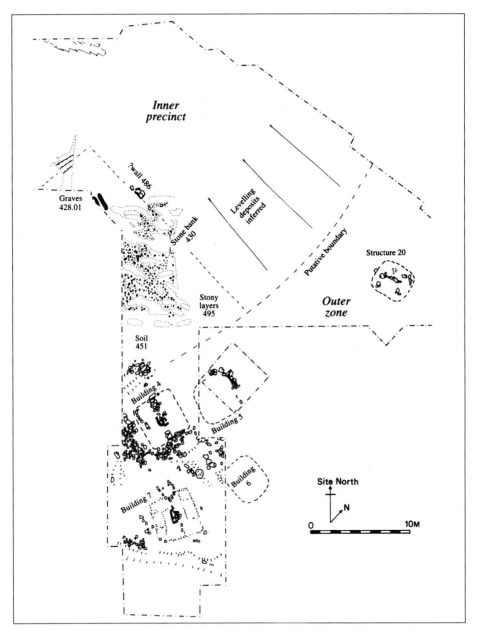

10.11 *Plan of one phase of the excavated Late Norse buildings at Whithorn, Wigtownshire (after P. Hill, 1997).*

used as a metalworking area, the area fell out of use and there was a build-up of rubbish over this part of the site.

Further structures were identified – Buildings 3, 8 and 7 – each with great structural complexity. Building 3 was defined by a square patch of paving with large central hearth, and Building 7 produced further evidence of comb-making.

This settlement was clearly part of a maritime network and may well have processed raw materials from the Galloway hinterland into products which were exchanged for luxuries or imported commodities. There is evidence for the manufacture of antler combs, with fragments of worked antler and unfinished blank plates being identified. From the animal bone assemblage it is clear that cat skins were also being prepared, for there are several cat skulls showing incisions where the pelt was removed. In the damp conditions, offcuts of leather survived in some of the middens. Elsewhere, iron working is suggested, with the possible existence of a smithy, in addition to suggestions of lead and copper alloy working. Imported goods included bronze stick-pins and a ringed-pin from Ireland, glass beads, soapstone vessel sherds and whetstones, as well as a coin of Cnut (minted in Chester) and a Hiberno-Norse coin from Dublin.

It appears most likely that the excavated settlement at Whithorn dates to the Late Viking/Late Norse period. Of those objects which can be most readily dated, there would seem to be a group which dates to the tenth century (with a few items of the eleventh century) and another which is later, coinciding with the radiocarbon determinations which have been received for the structures, and which span the period from the late tenth to the early twelfth century.

Chapter 11

THE NORSE ECONOMY

All excavated sites dating from the Viking and Late Norse periods have produced evidence of both economic and environmental indicators. Where recovery methods have allowed, material ranges from fragmentary animal and fish bone to carbonised seeds. Intra-site comparability can take place with some degree of confidence where similar methods of recovery have been undertaken, such as on-site wet-sieving and sampling. However, several major assemblages were recovered prior to the widespread use of wet sieving, such as Jarlshof, Underhoull, Buckquoy, Drimore Machair and the earlier work at Freswick Links. The species lists for these sites therefore, although informative, are necessarily limited in scope. Although there are, for example, numerous references to midden deposits at Jarlshof, there is little detail in the published record to enable the ecofactual elements to be considered. Elsewhere, for Drimore and the early Freswick work, simple listings of the species identified are provided, usually with animal bone the most dominant element. From Buckquoy there is a detailed report which provides data for comparative purposes, but the lack of sieving negates detailed comparison with other sites for, in particular, carbonised elements, such as seed and chaff, and small fish bones.

Detailed sampling programmes became a feature of excavation from the late 1970s onwards, enabling a more in-depth consideration. However, even with this data it is important to underline the potential problems of comparison resulting from differing mesh sizes. Large-gauge mesh, perhaps up to 1 cm, has been commonly replaced by finer meshes of 1 mm, with the floating carbonised material (flot) being collected on 500 micron meshes. This refinement has enabled fuller recovery of smaller material, such as fish-bone fragments and, most particularly, carbonised cereals and weed seeds. This material is by its very nature small, friable and seldom readily visible to the excavator. Its preservation by carbonisation ensures that this part of the assemblage usually floats to the surface during the wet-sieving procedures. The combination of evidence recovered from Norse excavations in Scotland is, however, of great importance to an overall understanding of the nature of their everyday livelihood in northern Britain, and enables a view of farming and subsistence which is more broadly based than a simple consideration of such obvious economic activities as trade and object exchange.

In this chapter, the major aspects of the natural economy will be discussed by commodity. Since the bulk of the evidence which is available relates to the Late Norse period, this will clearly predominate, but there is evidence to be considered for the Viking period also, and this will be discussed with a particular view to distinguishing it from the pre-Viking material as well as the Late Norse.

AGRICULTURE

Livestock

The few Viking period sites which have produced published evidence for the presence of livestock are Saevar Howe, Drimore, Buckquoy, the Brough of Birsay, the Brough Road, Birsay, Jarlshof, and Whithorn in the south-west. This category of evidence is not so obviously affected by the lack of a sieving and sampling strategy as the carbonised or fish assemblages, although the smaller elements will still be under-represented. The extensive work undertaken at Jarlshof produced evidence of several structures with byre elements, also barns probably for the storage of fodder, while the report on the animal-bone assemblage indicates that cattle were consistently represented throughout most Viking period layers, as were sheep; frequently these were the bones of young animals.

Through an examination of the place-names, it is also sometimes possible to gain insights into the keeping of livestock: Old Norse *kví*, for example, indicating a 'cattle-fold', as in Buckquoy, Orkney, or Quinish, Harris. The grazing of sheep is suggested by the island name Soay, and Haversay means 'he-goat-island'; Calva, 'calf-island', could indicate similar livestock practices. The presence of horses is also indicated by the names Rossal ('horse-field') or Hestaval ('horse-hill').

The commonly identified names in -ary, derived from Gaelic *airigh*, denote summer shieling sites in the west (such as Kernsary in Wester Ross), in the north, -*sætr* appears in Shetland (as in Swinister, Dunrossness), but not so often in Orkney where there was less need for this practice amongst the low-lying fertile lands.

Turning to the archaeological record, the tight topographical grouping of the Birsay sites – Saevar Howe, Brough, Brough Road and Buckquoy – should enable a good comparative assemblage to be established, with marked differences due to economic or micro-climatic variants being clearly visible. At Saevar Howe, no major changes could be detected in the main domestic species between the Pictish and Viking phases, although the proportion of sheep declined from 66 to 48 per cent and the cattle increased from 18 to 32 per cent. However, these changes have been suggested as resulting only from the small sample size. Of the overall assemblage of sheep, cattle and pigs, most of the animals died young (as at Buckquoy) and in the case of cattle some died 'within the first few weeks of life'. This could suggest a need for dairy produce, when young calves did not take the milk from their mothers, rather than the need to preserve winter fodder, given that there was no concentration of mortality in the autumn. In the case of pigs, they too were killed young, probably for meat. Most of the sheep were killed well before full maturity, probably for meat, and it is possible that some degree of milking may have taken place with the sheep, as with the cattle.

At Buckquoy there are more cattle in the assemblage throughout all phases than sheep and it has been suggested that this difference may have related to the need to supply also the people living on the Brough of Birsay at that time. The assemblage from Buckquoy is fully published and it is clear that there is a gradual increase at the site in the number of cattle. This is not particularly noticeable between the pre-Norse phase IIii (minimum of five individual animals) and the first Norse phase III (minimum of six animals). The marked increase occurs between phases III and IV (a minimum of sixteen individuals).

For sheep the variation is less pronounced between these phases (10:10:8 minimum animal numbers), as it is for pigs (8:5:5 minimum animal numbers). At all stages the animal-bone assemblage is highly fragmented.

On the Brough of Birsay few animal bones were recorded from the earlier excavations, but in the assemblages from 1973–4 the kitchen refuse included cattle, sheep, pig, rabbit, otter, rat and vole. With the exception of the vermin, this was likely to be food debris, and the presence of small phalangeal bones supports the view of local slaughter. Cattle were dominant through most of the Viking period phases, always providing in excess of 95 per cent of the meat eaten. In the case of sheep, in the earlier Viking period phases they were used for wool and possibly milk production, but were then increasingly used for both wool and meat until, in the final Norse phase, they were almost exclusively used for meat. The slaughter of young animals could indicate the cropping of the flock in this case.

At Pool, on Sanday, the proportions of cattle do not vary from the Neolithic period onwards, although evidence of stress in the skeletons suggests that the beasts were additionally used for traction. The presence of both sheep and horses has been noted, and red deer bones from the whole skeleton, and of varying ages, suggest that this too was a locally exploited resource (mostly at the 'interface' between the Picts and the Vikings).

At Drimore the bulk of the faunal remains came from domesticated animals, and these are listed as ox, sheep, pig, horse and dog, in addition to red deer (which were presumably hunted). At Whithorn the layers of organic Norse debris were sieved and the evidence produced indicates the exploitation of both red deer and cattle, as well as cats which had been skinned.

The evidence from the Late Norse sites is variable, ranging from the small list by species in the Jarlshof report to the detailed evidence available from sites where more emphasis has been placed on full recovery of the ecofacts. At Freswick Links, for example, despite a large and impressive assemblage of fish bones, the animal-bone assemblage was highly fragmented and generally smaller in number. This high degree of fragmentation, combined with the absence of teeth, suggests that these midden dumps were not the primary place of deposition for the animal bone. The greater part of the bones are from juvenile animals – mostly cattle, sheep and pig – suggesting a high infant-mortality rate as a result of meat- rather than wool-oriented husbandry.

This situation is matched at Beachview. However, the preponderance of species at this site is consistently sheep, then cattle and then pigs. All elements of the cattle skeleton have been found in the middens, which suggests local butchering, and there is also evidence of substantial calf mortality. Rackham has suggested that this may in part be due to winter deaths, a situation mirrored at Buckquoy.

There are numerically more sheep bones at Beachview than cattle, and 60 per cent of the sheep had died under 24 months of age. This may in part have been natural. Three distinct groups have been discerned: first-year lambs and neonates; a large group of second-year animals; and adults over five years old which would have been exploited for breeding, wool and milk. This pattern would support the over-wintering of animals indoors and is similar to that from the earlier assemblages at Buckquoy and Saevar Howe. It may be that this was a response to local environmental conditions. A small but significant assemblage of pig bones was noted at Beachview, again indicating early slaughtering but with the presence of a few mature beasts. This age range would suggest that pigs were being bred there. Other creatures distinguished include horses, domestic cats and dogs, with occasional seal and red deer. Elsewhere in Orkney (at Orphir and Westness for example), where details are available, the same species range is indicated.

In Shetland, Bigelow has suggested that the Sandwick assemblage indicated a rise in dairy production with an increase in cattle bones from the twelfth century onwards. The majority of the bones are from young calves, suggesting a slaughter pattern which would have maximised milk rather than meat production. Bigelow has also suggested a similar situation at Jarlshof on the basis of his review of the faunal assemblage there. He has suggested additionally that this increase could have been the result of the introduction of formal taxation relying on payment in butter. The sheep bones indicate a concentration on wool and food production, possibly also in part a response to the payment of taxes in woollen cloth. Bigelow, following Hamilton, has also drawn attention to the worked bone pieces or *kevl* in the Shetland assemblages which are identified as bits for lambs, to prevent suckling. Few pig bones have been recovered from the assemblage at Sandwick; possibly its scavenging was too costly in such a marginal environment. However, the lack of pigs in the assemblage from Orphir cannot be so easily explained.

Structural elements which relate to the livestock economy have been noted from a number of sites, ranging from byres and barns to stock enclosures. The presence of an integral byre, as demonstrated for example at Jarlshof in several phases, as well as at Sandwick, Beachview and Freswick, implies the need for overwintering of livestock indoors. Other settlements have phases where separate byres and also barns were built, although this can be most clearly seen at Jarlshof. Bringing stock indoors for the winter implies above all a climatic imperative, but it has a major implication for the provision (and also storage) of fodder. A settlement which has byres must have access to hay fields; the possible hayrick stands from Jarlshof and Underhoull play their part here. These elements lie at the heart of a mixed farming economy, which will be demonstrated by the presence of arable weeds in the nearby pollen record, as at Freswick Links, and other evidence for cereal cultivation, to be discussed next.

Cereals

Agricultural implements have rarely been found, other than occasional sickles for harvesting which have been identified in both male and female grave assemblages. A single iron ploughshare has been recovered from one of the boat-burials at Westness (grave 11). In other cases, 'plough shares' are more commonly stone points, as found at Underhoull.

Place-names also play a part in identifying cultivation: for example, Cornabus would suggest 'corn farm', and as will be seen below flax can also be so identified in the naming record. However, increasing use of large-scale sampling and sieving procedures on Norse sites has produced the main evidence of cereal and legume cultivation and associated weeds. Without doubt this is a most significant addition to our knowledge and is a direct result of the changes in recovery methods. Identification and, where possible, correlation with nearby pollen records yields information about aspects of both cultivation and processing and consumption practices.

Assemblages recovered from Viking period settlements, such as Saevar Howe and Pool, have produced a preponderance of six-rowed barley (bere) and cultivated oats (Figure

11.4), in addition to species such as crowberry, as well as seaweed which may have been used as a fertiliser. The recovery of carbonised six-rowed barley, from Viking period levels at Pool, with whole heads and stalks preserved is exceptional, but such is likely to be the result of local production. When the larger body of evidence from the Late Norse settlements is taken into account, it is possible to see variations in the relative percentages of these two main crops throughout the area. For example, at Tuquoy, the common oat dominated the assemblage, as at Beachview and Orphir. However, this contrasts with the evidence from the Brough Road sites in Birsay, where bere barley (*Hordeum vulgare*) was numerically dominant. It is not possible to be sure whether oats and barley were grown together or as separate crops; indeed, oats could have been a weed crop in fields of barley. However, both crops would have had great significance in the subsistence economy. Bere meal can be used for bread and makes a denser food than wheat flour; the grain could also be used in soups or stews, as well as an animal food, or even in the production of ale. Oats, both cultivated and wild varieties, could have been used as oatmeal or for porridge. The rare identification of rye (*Secale sp.*) has been noted only at Westness.

The presence of locally produced rotary querns on a number of sites, Jarlshof and Freswick amongst others, additionally supports the presence of grain and the small-scale production of flour. The water-mill at Orphir suggests similar activity on a larger scale. Querns of garnetiferous schist, found at Jarlshof as well as Freswick, may suggest a wider network of exchange, since such material would have been more readily available in Shetland than Caithness.

At three sites, Tuquoy, Freswick Links and the Udal, the actual cultivation plots or fields have been identified. At Tuquoy, Owen defined the cultivated field soils and suggested the presence of an infield and outfield system of land management, while at Freswick the striations indicating areas of cultivation were defined in the coastal midden banks (Figure 11.2). Both of these activities have been dated to the Late Norse period, although the Udal evidence exists from the Viking period. At Underhoull in Shetland, Small drew attention to the presence in the midden of the broken stone points of ploughshares (in addition to rotary querns) to indicate the existence nearby of cultivation areas, although no seeds were recovered due to the lack of sieving (in common with other sites excavated at that time).

Without the presence of actual cereal grains and the debris associated with its processing (chaff and stubble), it cannot be concluded with certainty which were the fields where barley and oats were grown, and there are certainly traces in the record of other crops. At Freswick there is a general lack of chaff debris in the assemblage and the nearby pollen record, from the Hill of Harley, had led Jacqueline Huntley to suggest that the barley consumed at this site was most likely to have been grown locally. From this it could be assumed that the cultivation traces were for this and other crops, discussed below.

This degree of resolution is hard to find at other sites on the evidence so far available. At Beachview, in the Late Norse phase, chaff was recovered in quantities consistent with on-site cereal processing, whereas the circular corn-drying kiln, which forms an integral part of the excavated building, is the earliest yet to be distinguished of the type which was to predominate in Orkney in more recent centuries (Figure 11.1). In considering the actual processing of the cereal crops, the discovery of the Norse horizontal water-mill at Orphir is of significance. Although the surviving botanical evidence relates to phases of either the infill of the mill structure, or the underlying deposits which predate the mill building, the

11.1   Corn-drying kiln at Beachview, Birsay, Orkney (C. D. Morris).

mill itself must have been related to the grinding of cereals brought to the earl's *bu* from the surrounding lands. Whether this was a form of taxation, or perhaps a centralised service, cannot be judged on the present evidence.

Other crops

As described above, it is clear from the botanical assemblages that oats and barley were the predominant crops. However, in a Late Norse context at Freswick a small amount of wheat grain and chaff (*Triticum aestivum*) was recovered from Area 7. It is not clear how this had arrived at the site, or whether there had in fact been an attempt to cultivate wheat in what was then, as it remains, a marginal area for the species.

Several other plant species have been identified in the assemblages examined, possibly

11.2 Freswick middens and cultivation marks, Caithness (C. E. Batey).

cultivated in the ubiquitous enclosed plot or *planticrue*. These crops include fat hen (*Chenopodium album*), crowberry (*Empetrum nigrum*), sheep's sorrel (*Rumex acetosella*) and Celtic bean (*Vicia faba*), which are the more common of those represented at Freswick Links. Of these the Celtic bean would probably have been a common local product, being a forerunner of the modern broad bean. The recovery of hazel nuts may also indicate a food crop. Crowberry has also been noted at Beachview and Saevar Howe, as well as henbane for medicinal purposes at Beachview. The Pool assemblage produced a similar weed flora to that found elsewhere. The mixture of cereals and weeds recovered from the large pit at Tuquoy could have been the result of reaping the cereal stalks for straw and so this could have been a deposit of animal bedding (or roofing material) rather than of food-processing debris.

Other possible crops which have survived less well include legumes and root crops, such as cabbage. Unfortunately, these distort badly on carbonisation and hence become difficult to identify. However, possible examples have been recovered from Freswick and Orphir. Corn spurry (*Spergula arvensis*) was noted in the carbonised material from Saevar Howe.

The deliberate collection of other plants may have taken place for medicinal purposes, as in ribwort plantain (*Plantago lanceolata*) to act as an astringent, meadowsweet (*Filipendula ulnaria*) to help control bleeding and common henbane (*Hyoscyamus niger*) as a sedative, for all have been detected in excavated assemblages. Some may also have been helpful in the prevention of scurvy, and/or in the provision of dye colorants.

Flax

The place-names of Lionel ('flax-field') and Linshader ('flax-farm') in the west are important reminders of the presence of an important crop, now more commonly identified in the archaeological record. A few sites have produced flax seeds, preserved by carbonisation, of a type which is slightly smaller than present-day examples. These have been recorded from Norse contexts at Barvas on Lewis, at Saevar Howe and Pool, in Orkney, as well as at sites in Birsay and at Orphir, at Westness on Rousay, and at Freswick and Robert's Haven in Caithness. These seeds are usually found in association with cultivated barley and oats and, although they may have been an accidental inclusion, the amount of evidence would suggest deliberate cultivation. Both seed and fibre could be produced from one crop and its use for linseed oil and linen is possible. It has been suggested that this would have been a luxury crop, with linen being a prestigious product, but there are several other uses for this potential subsistence crop. Linseed oil would have been used for food or as a preservative, having domestic and/or medicinal use, while linseed cake could have been for cattle feed. These various uses may have needed some form of drying which could have resulted in carbonisation. Apart from linen for clothing, another product would have been ropes or sail-cloth and the chaffstems could even have been used for cattle feed or fuel. The uses were clearly varied and thus suggest that flax may have been a subsistence commodity rather than just a luxury product.

At Pool, in Sanday, Hunter noted that flax was not recovered from immediately pre-Viking period contexts and so this could have been a major crop introduction with the Norse arrival. At Saevar Howe, it is also confined to Viking period levels, with the recovery of hundreds of seeds of cultivated flax (*Linum usitatissimum*) supporting the view that this crop was being cultivated locally. Nearby, flax has also been recorded from the sites on the Brough Road and at Beachview, Birsay. Preliminary results from the settlement at Westness, on Rousay, have also demonstrated the presence of flax amongst the carbonised grain assemblage, as at both Freswick Links and Orphir where a few seeds have been recorded from Late Norse contexts.

In summary, it appears most probable that flax was being cultivated, perhaps for both fibres and linseed oil, in conjunction with other crops. On present evidence it seems that this was likely to be an introduction by the Norse to Scotland.

Textile production

The identification of a large and varied artefactual assemblage related to the production of textiles demonstrates its significance in the Norse economy. Woollen cloth would have been used for both clothing and ships' sails, and rarer finds of linen suggest that variety in clothing would have been the norm, as in Scandinavia at this period.

Badly corroded iron heckles or wool-combs have been noted from graves, such as Westness, Ballinaby and Ardvonrig (Barra); possible handles of bone have been noted from Jarlshof as well as Drimore. Spindle-whorls of stone, steatite and bone are common finds, but the spindles rarely survive. Pebble and steatite loom-weights are known, but the clay examples from Saevar Howe, clearly in their original line, remain unique. Weaving battens or swords are known from Westness, Scar, Cruach Mhor (Islay) and Ardvonrig

(Barra), all of iron, and antiquarian reports of finds from Pierowall record the presence of bone swords, presumably weaving battens.

Pin-beaters of bone, iron shears, sewing kits (usually a perforated hollow bird bone with fabric and needles housed within) and bone tablet-weaving plaques have all been identified with varying frequency. Rarer finds include glass linen-smoothers and also whalebone plaques, commonly found in northern Norway, but rarer in the British Isles. The fine complete plaque from Scar in Orkney is a welcome addition to this sparse element of the textile assemblage.

Discoveries of actual cloth are rare, and the evidence more commonly survives in the corrosion products of metal objects, usually brooches or belt-buckles. Detailed examination of these traces, from both new finds and older finds which have been little conserved, suggests that a tabby-weave was common (identified at Cnip for example, although linen was noted there on the belt-buckle). In excess of twenty groups of impressions have been studied to date, and new finds add greatly to this data-base. The full reports on both Scar in Orkney and Balnakeil in Sutherland will be of significance here.

EXPLOITATION OF MARINE RESOURCES

Fish

The artefactual debris associated with fishing activity is relatively widespread, although always in considerably smaller quantities than the ecofactual assemblages would lead one to expect. The ubiquitous line-sinkers, commonly little more than a perforated pebble, are complemented by more highly worked weights of stone and other line weights of lead. These would suggest both the activities of net-fishing and line-fishing. Few fish hooks have been identified, amongst assemblages at Freswick Links, Jarlshof and in the grave at Balnakeil for example. An antler chafing-piece for fishing line from Jarlshof can also be matched at Westness. Possible pumice floats have also been noted from the Brough of Birsay amongst other sites. The vessel fragments from Underhoull, uniquely categorised as having been used for 'rendering down fish livers', are amongst the more enigmatic pieces from the fishing assemblage. The identification of a fishing spear from one of the graves at Ballinaby, Islay, recalls perhaps the hunting of salmon (Old Norse *lax*), complementing the place-name evidence on Lewis (Laxey) and Harris (Laxadale) amongst others.

It is, however, the ecofactual assemblage which provides the majority of the evidence for fish exploitation in the Norse economy. Fish bone forms a major component of the faunal assemblage of Norse sites. Where conditions of preservation and recovery have allowed, it is clear that for some sites marine exploitation was just as significant as agriculture. Fish bone is exceptionally difficult to excavate without damage by conventional methods and does not survive well on damp or clay sites, although it tends to be well preserved on machair (sand) sites. The friable nature of fish bone has therefore resulted in there being an under-representation from sites which were not routinely wet-sieved.

It is important to be aware of this imbalance in the record because, although it is clear that there was a great increase in the exploitation of fish during the Late Norse period, it is also the case that the Viking period settlers fished extensively. The major change in economic activity in the Late Norse period is due to the commercial scale of the operation, which can now be more fully understood because of the recent large-scale excavation projects.

The excavated assemblage from Buckquoy produced

a considerable quantity of [fish] bones. These were in most cases in broken condition, some even fragmentary, and many were not identified even to family . . . recovery was by hand-picking of excavated material and no sieving was attempted. The interpretation . . . is therefore dependent on the supposition that they represent only the larger species of fishes caught and consumed at the site.

Even with these provisos it is clear that there were more fish recovered from the Norse phases IV and V at Buckquoy than from all the preceding phases together, including Norse phase III. Cod, ling and saithe predominate over conger eel, haddock, red seabream and ballan wrasse, for example. The Viking period fish assemblages include species which would have been caught by long lines set in deep water, although Wheeler has suggested that larger fish may have been available closer to the shore at this period than today. The situation at Saevar Howe is very similar, with gadids dominant (cod family: cod, saithe and ling). On the Brough of Birsay, where conditions of preservation are particularly difficult, Seller has identified cod, mackerel and ray from the middens, with cod predominating.

Despite the problems of recovery bias, it is clear that there was an expansion of fish exploitation in the Late Norse period. In Shetland, Bigelow's work at Sandwick has revealed an expansion of fishing in the Late Norse period, marked not only by the fish bone, but also by an increase in the number of line-sinkers. He suggests that there may have been a Shetlandic element in the dried fish trade between Lofoten and south-west Norway, given that Shetland is three times nearer to Bergen than the Lofoten Islands. In his study of the fish bone from Robert's Haven, in Caithness, Barrett has also considered the wider context for this element of the assemblage; such work emphasises the need to view the total assemblage rather than isolated elements.

At Beachview, although a few small, inshore, fishes were noted, the major focus of activity was on catching cod and saithe, with some ling. It is possible that there was seasonal exploitation of saithe, with large numbers being caught in the late autumn and early winter when they would have been shoaling nearer the shore. The cod sizes recorded are between 0.35m and c. 1m, with the ling being slightly larger. At Beachview, saithe predominates numerically, which contrasts with the evidence from the earlier deposits on the Brough Road where cod predominates over saithe. This difference is likely to be a reflection of sampling procedures, with a percentage having been hand-collected and some wet-sieved on the Brough Road. This does not therefore seem to reflect a change in fishing practices between the Viking and Late Norse periods. Detailed examination of the bones from Beachview has revealed some trace of cut-marks related to the preparation of the catch, although this was not a common feature. The scale of fishing indicated at Beachview does not necessarily suggest anything other than the provision of fish for the immediate household.

Elsewhere in Orkney, several other sites have produced fish-bone material, although few of them are fully published. At Westness, Kaland has noted the presence of both cod and ling in the settlement middens; however, there was no large-scale sampling or sieving of that material. At the Earl's Bu site, Orphir, which is also awaiting full publication, large-scale sampling and sieving will eventually allow comparison with similar assemblages from elsewhere, particularly in Caithness. Preliminary indications show a concentration on gadid species, with the notable exception of ling, but also on pollack and haddock. These fish are of substantial lengths, often in the region of 1–1.5 m for the gadids; detailed analysis shows the presence of cut-marks and the preferential retention of skeletal elements. This site is of great interest because, unlike all the others discussed, it is not coastal and was thus presumably supplied by another site nearby, perhaps as part of the earldom network.

Major developments in the understanding and interpretation of the Late Norse fishing economy have taken place in Caithness. Two sites, Freswick Links and Robert's Haven, are distinguished by the dominance of fish-bone remains in their overall ecofactual assemblages. Through extensive detailed sampling strategies, first at Freswick and then Robert's Haven, it has been possible to identify clearly their reliance on marine resources in the Late Norse economy.

The excavation strategy of the Freswick Links middens was defined by the identification of particularly rich fish-bone remains in the deposits which were eroding at the cliff edge. In some cases, these deposits were incredibly dense in fish bone. Extensive sampling and wet-sieving on site enabled this material to be set first of all in its immediate stratigraphical context and then in its local context. It soon became clear that there were differences in the types of bone recovered on different parts of the site. For example, the middens from one area located 30 m inland, Area 2, produced twice as much mammal bone as cliff-side areas and had no deposits of comparable fish density to those at the cliff edge. The dense coastal middens included articulated fish bones which would suggest the 'processing of a reasonably large number of fish at approximately the same time'. Some of the samples taken included between 0.3 and 0.5 kg of fish bone, and a particularly remarkable deposit from Area 7, Phase S, included the otoliths of at least forty-eight large cod, saithe and haddock. This has been interpreted as representing part of a single large catch, with possibly more than 100 fish being processed at one time. The concentration of size ranges of the fish in each layer has been taken to indicate that single catches are represented.

The identification of the cleithrum, dentary, premaxilla and otoliths, from the head end of the fish, in these middens suggests that deheading, and possibly filleting (Figure 11.3), was taking place in the vicinity of the midden deposits at the present-day cliff edge. The inclusion of large groups of limpet shells in the middens could indicate the bait used. Clear differences in fishing strategy could also be discerned; concentrations of small saithe (less than 0.2 m long) could be distinguished from those of larger fish (saithe over 0.4 m and cod over 0.8 m in length), which could be indicative of seasonal fishing.

Although the Late Norse economy at Freswick was mixed, with some evidence of animal husbandry and possible cultivation, the dominance of fish material is clear. Activities such as cooking, fish-drying and smoking, bait-preparation and fish-filleting were probably taking place on or near the excavated middens. In some cases, it is remarkable that the weight of fish bone in a sample or area exceeded that of the much heavier shell component, and is clearly indicative of the enormous original weight of fish meat.

The extensive analysis of the fish-bone material from Freswick has been undertaken with the particular aim of identifying the precise nature of the activities represented. It is

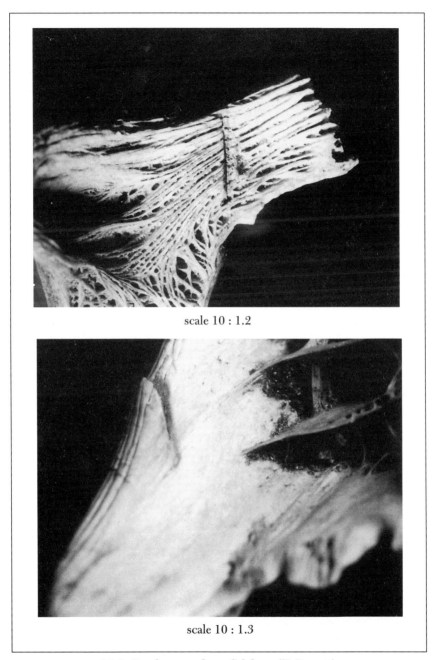

scale 10 : 1.2

scale 10 : 1.3

11.3 Butchery marks on fish bone (J. Barrett).

important to determine whether the density of bone is sufficient to be interpreted as the result of activity on a commercial scale. Many thousands of fish are represented, deriving from innumerable fishing trips. Although catches in excess of 100 fish may be represented, none of the excavated deposits can be seen in terms of the large-scale processing of many hundreds of gadids typical of the Norwegian stockfish trade for example. A single context excavated at Freswick would seem to be on this scale, but if this had been the common pattern at this site, there should have been many more such deposits. It would seem therefore that it is more appropriate to explain the fishing activity at Freswick in terms of possible seasonal inshore and offshore activity, perhaps for exchange in an area with limited potential for cereal cultivation and pastoral farming. This interpretation may not be the whole story, but it is clear that the rest of the subsistence economy at Freswick is certainly not as developed as, for example, on contemporary sites in Orkney. The bias towards fish meat at Freswick is clear, but large-scale exchange cannot be readily detected by the presence of imported goods such as imported pottery, although cereals such as barley and perhaps wheat would seem to represent likely exchange commodities.

Building on the work at Freswick, James Barrett has undertaken work on the middens at Robert's Haven, just a few kilometres to the north, where comparable middens have been exposed. Twenty-eight metres of fish-rich midden, with a maximum thickness of 1.3 m, were selectively sampled. It is suggested that the deposits built up within a century and date to the period of the thirteenth/fourteenth centuries, slightly later than the date range suggested for Freswick. Extensive sieving and collection of articulated skeletal elements was undertaken and cod proved to be the most abundant, followed by saithe and ling. Analysis of the surviving elements of the fish skeletons indicates an underrepresentation of appendicular elements which would be consistent with the curing of fish. Extensive processing traces on bones support the suggestion of decapitation of the fish at Robert's Haven, the removal of the anterior vertebrae whilst retaining the cleithrum; these are all elements consistent with the evidence from stockfish centres elsewhere in the North Atlantic region.

This analysis is ongoing, but at this stage one possible explanation is that there may have been an increase in the need for fish meat in the region following the adoption of the Christian ideology of eating fish as lenten fare. Exports of dried cod (stockfish) are recorded from Arctic Norway in the twelfth century, and as early as 1103–23 King Eystein Magnusson imposed a tax on fishing. It is recorded that, in 1329, 15,000 dried fish were purchased from Caithness by the Royal Exchequer of Scotland. The large-scale preservation of fish by drying and/or salting would have enabled this commodity to be more widely dispersed. The remaining problem lies in the identification of the return cargoes to Caithness.

The rocky foreshore

All excavated Norse sites have produced marine shell in great quantities, predominantly limpets (*Patella vulgata*) and edible winkles (*Littorina littorea* (L)). In most cases these may have been collected as bait for fishing, in some others they could have been introduced during the application of seaweed as manure on the areas of cultivation. In all cases this represents the exploitation of the rocky foreshore. The presence in the faunal record of both seal and whalebone could also suggest the maximum use of animals flung onto the foreshore, rather than actual hunting activity. Although not as common as might be expected, the bones of seal and whale have been noted from the assemblages at several sites – such as Orphir, Westness and Sandwick (see also p. 220). At Buckquoy, Drimore and Freswick, whalebone was actually used as a structural element in the buildings.

Seaweed

Recovered as a by-product of the examination of the carbonised assemblage, a large number of seaweed fragments have been identified from several sites. Although this could have been gathered and used as a source of iodine, it is most likely to have been applied as fertiliser to the fields – a practice which still takes place in parts of northern and western Scotland.

At Pool, the distribution of seaweed is spread through the 'interface' between the Pictish and Norse horizons, and Hunter has suggested that it may have been used as fodder, in addition to fuel and fertiliser. In Late Norse contexts, concentrations of seaweed in pits at the Biggings and Tuquoy have been tentatively identified as having served an industrial function, possibly even acting as a lye to clean wool. Bladderwrack has been found in the assemblages from the Brough of Birsay, Room 5, and Buckquoy, as well as from Beachview and Orphir. It is clear that this component of the record has been under-represented in the past, given that all major projects on Norse sites which have undertaken sampling procedures of any kind have produced evidence of this material.

Seabirds

The exploitation of wild fowl, for food, feathers and oil, has been common practice in Scotland into the twentieth century, and it is clear that this was also the case in the Norse period. Areas of cliff provided nesting grounds for several species, commonly guillemots, razorbills and kittiwakes, but other species such as gannet, puffin, shag, gulls and eider duck have also been identified in the faunal records of Norse sites. Buckquoy, for example, has an extensive listing of marine bird species, and the more recent work at Freswick Links has produced a listing of some nineteen species, including gannet, cormorant, fulmar and great skua, in addition to domestic varieties such as chicken and duck. Evidence from the Late Norse structures at Westness indicates the exploitation of different seabirds, probably from the nearby towering cliffs of Scabra Head. At Sandwick on Unst, which is a major bird centre today, the picture would seem to have been similar.

At Beachview, in the Late Norse period, the range of birds is similar, probably as a result of exploitation of the cliffs to the south of Birsay Bay, as is also to be seen to a lesser degree in the Viking period assemblage from Saevar Howe. It is interesting to note that few bird bones were recovered from the early work on the Brough of Birsay, but this must result from the poor recovery techniques, because the west part of the Brough of Birsay is high cliff, occupied today by puffin colonies.

Recent advances in the study of egg shell have provided valuable information concerning the exploitation of the marine species in the area of Freswick Links. The identification, by Elizabeth Jane Sidell, of egg-shell fragments (and in some cases egg membrane) to species indicates egg collection on nearby cliffs, along with other fowling activities in the form of catching birds for meat and the collection of feathers/down. The collection season for the species identified at Freswick was March to June, with fulmar and Manx shearwater probably available into September. Seabirds' eggs provide a high-energy food source and would certainly have been a welcome addition to the Norse diet.

OTHER NATURAL RESOURCES

Hunting

It is clear that whilst fowling took place on the cliffs, other birds were sought through hunting, and indeed this activity was the subject of a short poem in the *Orkneyinga saga*:

> *Out after eating-birds!*
> *Fine archers, the Earl's men:*
> *hard for the hen-bird,*
> *the head-shot on the hill.*
> *Excellent the aim*
> *of the elm-bowes, savage*
> *the grouse-hunt, grim*
> *the guardian of the land.*

These events took place in Orkney, but the saga also tells of the hunting of otter and hare in Orkney, as well as of deer in Caithness. The archaeological record reveals seal and whale bone at sites such as Orphir, Freswick and Birsay. These animals would have been exploited for oil, hides, furs and bone; most particularly whalebone was used for artefacts, as well as structural pieces (as at Freswick and Drimore). The choice of whalebone for artefacts such as whorls, snecks and plaques (such as that from Scar) complements the use of antler especially for comb production (see p. 222). Hunting would have been a popular occupation in Norway and it is clear that this interest, perhaps a necessity, took place in areas of Scotland too.

Wood

Several assemblages have produced fragments of carbonised wood; fragments of native trees and shrubs, such as willow, aspen and some birch are complemented by pine, hazel and occasionally oak, most commonly identified as driftwood. However, in a few notable cases, the quality of this wood seems to suggest that timber was being imported for building purposes. This is significant for it expands the horizons of the Norse economic contacts beyond the individual settlements. The source of the timber is, however, under discussion. Barbara Crawford has recently examined the evidence for the presence and exploitation of major timber sources in Ross. Lying immediately north of the lands of Moray, this area was a buffer zone between the Norse and the Celtic-speaking peoples. This was an area of excellent and prolific forest, of oaks in particular – a source to be exploited by the seafaring Norse of the treeless northern lands.

Traces of timber were recovered from the Viking period deposits on the Brough of Birsay and the nearby site of Saevar Howe. This would have supplemented the meagre supplies of fuel, from peat for example, and possibly seaweed and heather. The situation is mirrored on the Brough Road sites and in the Late Norse phases at Beachview and Orphir. Notable exceptions to the quality and quantity of wood represented are provided by Tuquoy and Papa Stour.

A remarkable deposit was recovered at Tuquoy infilling a substantial pit which, uniquely for the period in this region, was largely waterlogged. This resulted in the recovery of several wooden artefacts, round wood and woodworking debris. The contents of the pit included willow twigs and branches, probably from the local scrub and used to make small domestic articles, such as knife handles, as well as twine for securing thatching. However, large quantities of pine suggest imported wood rather than just driftwood, with offcuts indicating the trimming of radially split planks. Pieces of worked maple, larch and spruce, some trimmed for use in construction, were clearly imports to the area. This rare survival of such a commodity is most important for any assessment of the external contacts which Orkney must have had in the Late Norse period.

The situation was clearly the same in Shetland, as demonstrated by the remains of the wooden floor from the Biggings on Papa Stour (Figure 10.4). This formed part of the high-status *stofa* discussed by Barbara Crawford, a feature of mainstream life for the elite of Norway transferred to Shetland. Such activity must have been part of a series of Late Norse trading links in timber known from later records in Bergen and the Faroe Islands.

It is clear that timber would have played a major part in other aspects of the construction of buildings at this period, and this is often considered to be driftwood. However, at sites such as the horizontal mill at Orphir, major structural timbers and worked elements, such as the floor to the upperhouse, linings to the water chute, sole tree and even the tirls, must have been specifically prepared for this use and possibly even imported.

Other significant uses for timber by the Norse in Scotland will have included boat-building, although there is no direct evidence for the building of boats in Scotland by the Norse, the Eigg stem-posts of oak being not yet dated. The three examples revealed through excavation in recent years were buried as vessels for the dead at Westness (two examples) and Scar, both in Orkney. Each boat was clinker-built and made of oak, the washrail made of Scots pine at Scar. The Westness vessels, at 5.5 and 4.5m in length, are unlikely to have been rowed from Norway. However, the Scar boat, with its original length of c. 7.15m, may well have been made in Scandinavia, for the sand caught in the boat's caulking does not seem to be Scottish in origin.

Iron

This commodity is so ubiquitous as to have been found on all excavated sites. It is clear that during the Viking and Late Norse periods local sources of bog ore must have been exploited. The identification of a number of on-site smithies confirms the domestic nature of this production, although the identification of smithing tools in graves at Ballinaby and possibly Dunrobin may indicate that professional smiths were at work too.

The confirmation that a structure was built for smithing activity is usually aided by the presence of massive central hearths, as at Freswick Links Building III, or perhaps a series of open hearths within a structure, as in the Brough of Birsay Structure 6 excavated by Hunter. However, the recovery of iron slag, ferrous debris, burnt clay and perhaps tuyères is perhaps more conclusive. With the expansion of on-site wet-sieving, the tiny prills and hammer-scale fragments can also be recovered and provide final confirmation of the presence of metalworking activity.

Specific structures for smithing have been noted at Jarlshof (Phase I); the Udal; Skaill, Deerness; as well as on the Brough of Birsay and possibly also Pool in Orkney. Associated debris, suggesting nearby activity, has been distinguished from Beachview, as well as Earl's Bu, Orphir, and nearby Lavacroon, the latter particularly producing large quantities of both iron smithing and smelting debris. In some cases, the working of bronze is also indicated in association with this activity as at the Brough of Birsay and Orphir in Orkney, and at Whithorn in south-west Scotland.

The recovery of associated artefactual evidence is also important in relation to these assemblages of industrial debris including items such as tuyères for the protection of the bellows and wire-drawing tools as found on the Brough of Birsay. For casting finer metals, which would have needed to be sought more widely, small crucibles and bar moulds have been noted from Orphir, as well as Birsay and elsewhere.

From this apparently unpromising source of evidence derives the information for our understanding of the basic tools of everyday life; without such things as knives or nails and rivets for boats, life would have been impossible.

TRADE LINKS

In addition to the timber trade and the postulated trade in fish, there are several other aspects of the artefactual assemblage which indicate trade links, both local and international.

There are three main categories of material which can be considered under this heading, other than the silver and gold discussed in Chapter 12: antler, stone (most specifically steatite) and pottery. During the Viking period, two of the most obvious commodities which were hall-marks of the Scandinavian presence were antler combs, so distinctive from the preceding Pictish forms, and soapstone or steatite vessels. The case for distinctive pottery types is less clear and will be discussed below.

Antler combs

Many Viking period settlements and burials have produced comb-types which can be readily paralleled in the Scandinavian homelands in the ninth and tenth centuries. These are single-sided composite combs, most commonly with iron rivets and simple incised line decoration on the back. The finest example from Birsay was recovered from a pagan grave on the Brough Road, whereas other classic examples, such as those from Jarlshof and Drimore, are from settlement deposits. Two recent finds have been noted from Dunbar (Figure 6.7) and North Berwick in Lowland Scotland. It is clear that this type of comb was brought from Scandinavia in the first waves of contact, and examples were retained for a generation or so. However, only one site in the region – Whithorn – has so far produced published evidence for the actual manufacture of antler combs, but these were presumably copies and modifications of the earlier types. The Viking urban centre of York was also producing antler combs, as can be seen particularly in the evidence from the area of Clifford Street. However, despite detailed examination of deposits of Viking period date in northern Britain, no other centres of manufacture have so far been located, with the possible exception provided by the small number of antler fragments identified from the Brough Road sites at Birsay. The source of the antler is open to discussion, but it could have been either Scandinavia or, more likely, mainland Scotland.

It is clear that combs were being brought into Scotland from Scandinavian manufacturing centres, probably in south Norway, during the Late Norse period. Examples from Freswick Links, the Brough of Birsay, Beachview and Orphir were all clearly imported from such a source during the twelfth and thirteenth centuries. These composite combs are distinguished by the use of copper-alloy rivets and complex decoration on both single- and double-sided types. It seems most likely that these combs represent a commodity which formed part of the trading network developed in the Late Norse period by the earls. The Late Norse examples therefore represent something different to the earlier combs which may well have been brought in by the earliest Norse settlers.

Stone

In the Viking period, a further commodity which marks out the presence of the Norse is the use of hemispherical steatite bowls, although steatite had been used in the Bronze Age in Shetland and Orkney to produce vessels of different forms. This typical type of cooking vessel, as produced in Norway and then also in Shetland quarries, became increasingly common as the Viking period developed. Distinctive tooling patterns and types of repair can be used to identify such vessels, and virtually all sites from the Viking period in Scotland have examples of the type. These were clearly used instead of ceramic vessels in the early phases of settlement, and it was only in the Late Norse period that both ceramics and proficiently tooled steatite vessels were in use together. Unfortunately, it is not yet possible to distinguish steatite between quarries, but it would seem most likely that the quarries of Shetland would have supplied the neighbouring site of Jarlshof at least, where-as mainland Scotland and perhaps Orkney may have been additionally supplied direct from Norway. The richest assemblages of steatite are to be found on the Shetland sites, where proximity to the raw material enabled invention of forms rather than constant re-use of broken pieces. Line-sinkers, weights and loom-weights as well as handled vessels are common in the Viking period levels.

In the Late Norse period, there are distinctive forms of steatite vessels. At Jarlshof, rectangular vessels and some with elaborate handles, as well as hanging lamps, have been found. However, some unusual pieces as at the Biggings, Papa Stour (an hour-glass lamp), or Freswick (a straight-sided vessel form), are considered likely to be direct Scandinavian imports. The detailed study of 'baking plates', flat pieces of heavily tooled schist or steatite, suggests that this commodity at least was being introduced from Scandinavia during the Late Norse period, although examples could easily have been produced locally in Shetland. This trade may also be reflected in the distribution of fine-grained schist hones which were Norwegian in origin, as found at Beachview, for example.

Pottery

The types of ceramic evidence on Norse sites vary from crude locally made vessels to a small quantity of imported fine table wares from Yorkshire and the Low Countries.

Several northern sites have produced sherds of relatively crude, hand-made ceramics, their introduction seeming to be a Late Norse innovation (with the exception of Pool), with a date range between the eleventh and thirteenth/fourteenth centuries, as at Jarlshof, Kirkwall, Freswick Castle and Freswick Links, as well as at Robert's Haven where thermo-luminescence dating indicates manufacture into the fourteenth century. At the Biggings in Shetland, Crawford has recorded a large amount of coarse hand-made pottery, over 500 sherds in all, with dating into the fifteenth century. Hand-made squared vessels have been noted from Sandwick as well as Jarlshof. Detailed analysis of the material from Freswick has been undertaken by David Gaimster, who has confirmed that the ubiquitous vegetal tempering at this site represents the use of animal dung, with the possible addition of vegetal debris associated with crop processing (suggested by the impressions of oat and barley seeds within the fabric (Figure 11.4)). Simple vessel forms ranging from 'bucket-shaped' down to small globular bowls are represented, rarely decorated and usually with simple, slightly flattened rims.

11.4 Cereal impressions on pottery (T. Woods).

An examination of the ceramics from the Western Isles, undertaken by Alan Lane, has distinguished a 'new Viking Age pottery style' in the northern Hebrides (Figure 3.5). This is characterised by sagging and flat-based bowls, cups and flat pottery discs or platters, which are grass-marked. Despite a superficial fabric similarity, it is likely that the wares from the West and North are different; local variations in raw materials may account for this, but there are certainly differences in the forms represented and it seems that there is also a difference in the dating of these assemblages.

It is clear that the crude wares would have had only a local distribution because they would not have travelled well. However, they may have been made for local markets, but the extent of this remains unclear, unlike the trade in more exotic wares which is easier to identify.

This can be seen in sherds from Tuquoy in particular, where contacts with the Low Countries can be identified through the 'exceptional' recovery of red-wares. At Freswick, a few sherds of so-called 'East Coast Gritty Wares' and Aberdeen Local Wares suggest contact with the eastern Scottish coast in the twelfth and thirteenth centuries, although the quantities are small. The situation is the same at Orphir, with the addition of a number of sherds from, as yet, unidentified Yorkshire kilns, virtually all of thirteenth/fourteenth-century date. Of particular note from Orphir is the identification of a basal fragment of a jug type seen as a local Orcadian copy of a form commonly identified in Yorkshire; this has similarities with a contemporary group of pottery from excavations in Kirkwall (personal communication, Robert Will). From the early work on the Brough of Birsay, there are four pieces of a tall face-mask jug with lustrous green glaze, identified as Scarborough ware (dated to the thirteenth/fourteenth centuries), as was also found at Freswick Castle. At Sandwick, Bigelow has recorded both Scarborough and Grimston wares in conjunction with North German proto-stonewares, and Yorkshire pottery types have also been noted on Papa Stour. This apparent preponderance of Yorkshire wares could be a reflection of links with that area, although kilns elsewhere (as yet unidentified) may provide more widespread sourcing. These finds do, however, all indicate wider contacts, the extent and nature of which remain conjectural, but they are clearly part of a larger network which encompassed several commodities ranging from fish to antler combs.

Chapter 12

SILVER AND GOLD

Norse settlements cannot by themselves provide more than a partial picture of their occupants' wealth. Valuable objects, such as a sword, brooch or ring, are not discarded about the house or dumped on a midden; they would naturally have been searched for if lost by chance. The materials from which fine artefacts were manufactured were recycled when the objects themselves became damaged or worn out, or even when just old-fashioned. These factors mean that such prestige items are recoverable today only if they had been deliberately deposited in the ground – whether for religious reasons or simply for safe-keeping. Some of the portable wealth which belonged to the first Norse settlers of Scotland has been recovered archaeologically through their grave-goods – and the same applies to the wealth inherited, or otherwise acquired, by their heirs and immediate successors. With the abandonment of pagan burial practices, however, this source of economic information is replaced during the tenth and eleventh centuries, at least in part, by treasure hoards of precious metal.

The production of basic weapons, tools and ornaments was rooted in the natural wealth of Scandinavian Scotland, exploited through arable and pastoral farming, through fishing, fowling and hunting, as well as through such resources as timber, iron and soap-stone. Much of this production was for internal consumption, but the grave-goods and treasure hoards demonstrate that surpluses were achieved during the Viking period with which to equip boats for piracy and external trade – the source of luxury goods, such as silver. The wealth of the Earldom of Orkney during the Late Norse period is still manifest today in the form of stone buildings, such as Kirkwall Cathedral and Cubbie Roo's Castle, which will have been raised in part at least on the proceeds of tolls and taxation. These will be considered in Chapter 13, but first the portable treasure of Scandinavian Scotland is presented here – the gold and silver ornaments, coins and hoards which together constitute the most tangible forms of wealth to have survived from the Viking/Late Norse period.

NATIVE SILVER

Although there are some silver sources in Scotland, there is no evidence that they were being worked either before or during the Viking period. Indeed, it would appear that David I turned to northern England for a supply of silver in order to strike Scotland's first native coinage during the mid-eleventh century, with his principal mint being situated at Carlisle. Neither were any silver sources then being worked in Scandinavia. Even so, some of the treasure which reached Scotland during the Viking period had travelled across the North Sea, being ultimately of oriental origin.

There was, however, silver in circulation in native hands throughout Scotland at the time of the Viking raids, as is demonstrated most notably by the Pictish hoards from St Ninian's Isle, Shetland, the Broch of Burgar, Orkney, Rogart, Sutherland, and Croy, Inverness. The silverware in these hoards, which contain no gold objects, consists for the most part of vessels and brooches. This contrasts markedly with the main Scandinavian manner of displaying silver – in the form of rings.

The important Broch of Burgar hoard is unfortunately known only from nineteenth-century accounts of its discovery, for it has since gone missing and has presumably been melted down. The St Ninian's Isle hoard was, however, found during excavation in 1958 and it was thus possible to have its silver scientifically analysed. The results are of interest because the silver content of the twelve Pictish brooches which form part of this hoard was found to vary from 82 per cent to as little as 30 per cent, with three-quarters of them containing less than 50 per cent silver. This poor standard differs markedly from the fine quality of earlier Pictish silverwork, when Late Roman treasures, such as that found on Traprain Law, would have provided a ready source of precious metal. These and other results suggest that the Picts had had no regular access to further supplies of silver, even though some Anglo-Saxon coins and silverwork, such as one of the bowls in the St Ninian's Isle hoard, are known to have reached Pictish hands during the eighth and ninth centuries (Figure 1.3).

It has been plausibly suggested that the St Ninian's Isle hoard was concealed beneath the floor of St Ninian's chapel in order to hide it from Viking raiders. Other Pictish silver did, however, fall into Viking hands for Pictish brooches have been found in Viking period graves in Norway – and some were even copied there. Excavations of Norse levels on the Brough of Birsay produced a couple of pieces of scrap silver, from a Pictish brooch and a pin, presumably lost on the way to the crucible. Such must have been the fate of the great majority of the native treasures acquired by the Vikings – to be recycled into the standard types of Norse arm- and neck-rings.

No native hoards from this period have yet been found in Dalriada, although the Scots certainly possessed ornaments of precious metal. There are, however, three hoards from south-west Scotland which contain the ninth-century copper-alloy coinage of the Anglo-Saxon kingdom of Northumbria, known as 'stycas'. Two of these are poorly recorded eighteenth-century finds: that from Paisley, Renfrewshire, is known only to have contained stycas, whereas 'a silver crucifix' is reported to have been found with 'Saxon' coins in Lochar Moss, Dumfriesshire, although this is now lost. The most interesting of these three hoards is that described above (p. 109) from Talnotrie in Kirkcudbrightshire which was deposited c. 875. Its varied contents, ranging from Anglo-Saxon silver coins and ornaments to a scale-weight and a lump of wax, suggest that it was the property of a Northumbrian metalworker. Amongst its scrap silver are two fragments of Arabic coins and one of a Frankish denier. These would have been much more at home in a 'Viking' hoard, given that foreign coin was not then permitted to circulate in Anglo-Saxon England – and that both these types of coin are known from hoards found in the north and west of Scotland.

Although the native treasures were clearly attractive to the Vikings, they sought their portable wealth more widely than just in Scotland. This is revealed by the contents of their own hoards, as well as by those ornaments of precious metal which were occasionally included amongst their grave-goods.

PAGAN NORSE GRAVE-GOODS

Treasure, in the form of silver and gold, was not habitually buried as part of the normal range of grave-goods during the Viking period, even in Scandinavia, although some individuals were provided with a coin or two, or maybe a single ornament of gold or silver. We cannot tell whether this was because treasure was buried separately in the form of offerings, although this matter will be considered further below – or because it was normal for it to be passed on as family wealth. On the other hand, its absence from graves might have resulted simply from a desire to discourage grave-robbing – of the kind witnessed, for example, at the royal ship-burial at Oseberg, in Norway, from which almost all the woman's jewellery had been looted. Small quantities of silver did, however, form part of the embellishment of ordinary grave-goods, such as oval brooches and sword-hilts, in the form of decorative wirework and of inlays (as also did gilding).

It is not surprising therefore that little in the way of precious metal has been found in the Viking period graves of Scotland, with the most obvious exception being the magnificent eighth-century brooch-pin of Irish manufacture from the richest of the female burials in the cemetery at Westness, Rousay (Figure 7.11). The next most notable find is the elaborate silver pin, with its head fashioned from a filigree-ornamented bead of Baltic origin, combined with a silver chain of Insular manufacture, which marks out a wealthy woman's grave at Ballinaby on Islay (Figure 7.6). In contrast, the well-equipped male boat-grave at Kiloran Bay, Colonsay, contained only a much simpler silver cloak-pin of Norwegian type.

A gold ring was reported amongst the lost finds from the Westray graves, whereas another lost gold ring from Orkney, found at Colli Ness, on Sanday, was said to have been found in a grave which might well have been of Late Norse date. The woman buried at Clibberswick, Unst, was wearing a silver arm-ring formed from a plain penannular band – and a fragment of another arm-ring was part of the enigmatic (1756) find from a cairn at Blackerne, Kirkcudbrightshire.

Finally, there is just the one excavated grave which contains a silver coin, that found at Buckquoy, Orkney – in the form of a cut halfpenny of the Anglo-Saxon king Eadmund (939–46). On the other hand, however, the burials at King's Cross Point, Arran, and at Kiloran Bay, Colonsay, both contained ninth-century copper stycas from Northumbria.

VIKING PERIOD HOARDS

Some important pieces of Viking period treasure from Scotland are single-finds, mostly in the form of rings, but such are readily identifiable from their more common occurrence in hoards. Several of these also contain coins, thus allowing their deposition to be more or less precisely dated. Over thirty Viking/Late Norse period hoards are known from Scotland, most of which can be associated directly with Norse activity (Figures 12.1–2).

The largest Viking period treasure found in Scandinavian Scotland, that from Skaill in Orkney (to be discussed further below), provides a classic example of what has been

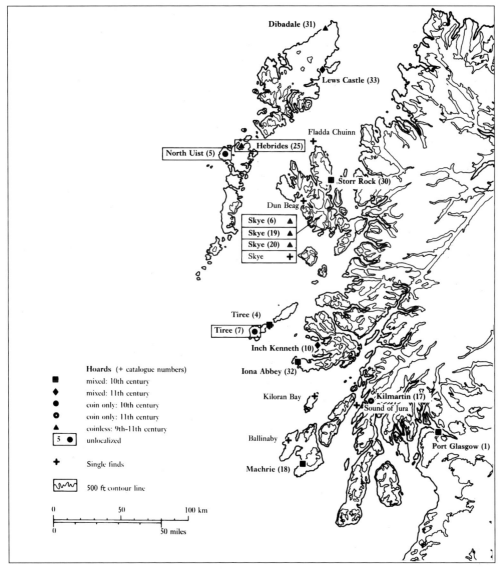

12.1 Map of hoards and single finds of gold and silver from the West Highlands and Islands (after J. Graham-Campbell/NMS, 1995).

termed a 'mixed hoard', consisting of coins combined with bullion, in the form of ingots, ornaments and/or hack-silver (Figure 12.3). Hack-silver comprises the cut-up fragments of ingots and ornaments which were used as 'small change', while silver was being used for payment by weight rather than in the form of counted money (Figure 12.7). In fact, although imported coins would have been weighed out in Scandinavian Scotland, using a balance of the type present in the Kiloran Bay boat-grave (Figure 7.4), and found on Gigha, it was more usual for them to be melted down during the Viking period in order to convert them into ornaments or ingots. Ingots formed a convenient method of silver storage and

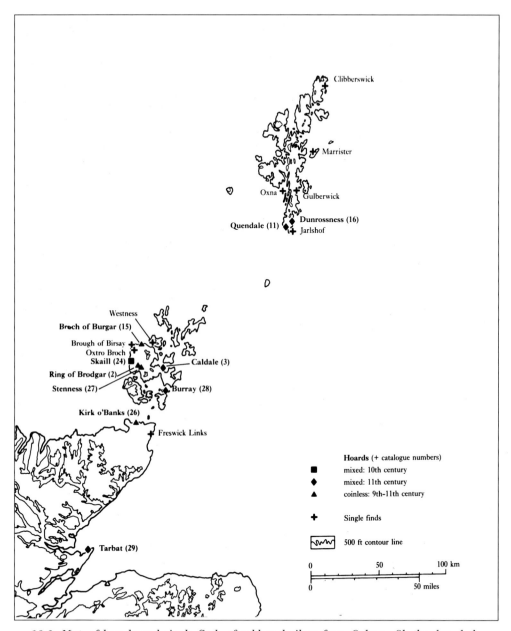

12.2 Map of hoards and single finds of gold and silver from Orkney, Shetland and the north-east mainland (after J. Graham-Campbell/NMS, 1995).

could readily be cut up into whatever size pieces were required to complete a transaction. On the other hand, to turn silver into ornaments meant that one's wealth could be displayed, with the added advantage that rings and brooches made suitable gifts with which to reward retainers – or whenever a prestigious present might be required. The hoards

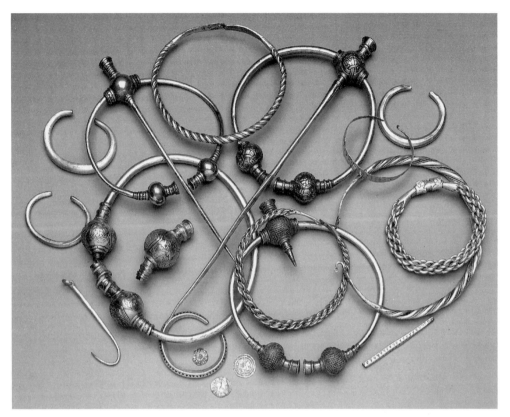

12.3 Selection of brooches, rings, etc., from the Skaill hoard, Orkney, deposited c.950–70 (NMS).

demonstrate, however, that such ornaments were themselves regularly rendered into hack-silver. One consequence of this commercial use of whatever silver came to hand was the necessity for those involved in such transactions to check its quality. It is thus a characteristic of Viking period hoards that the contents have been subjected to nicking and pecking – the cutting of their surfaces as a simple form of hardness test; likewise, coins were sometimes subjected to bending.

Some hoards consist exclusively of manufactured bullion and these have been termed 'coinless hoards', in contrast to those which consist exclusively of coin. With one exception (from Iona) the mixed hoards from Scandinavian Scotland consist entirely of silver and the coinless hoards consist of either silver or gold, although that from Gordon, in Berwickshire, contained a gold finger-ring along with four pieces of silver, comprising two ingots and two fragments of hack-silver (Figure 12.4). Two gold finger-rings form part of a mixed hoard from Bute, although this treasure is somewhat anomalous given its Viking period character but Late Norse date, having been deposited in the mid-twelfth century.

About two-thirds of the Viking period silver hoards from Scotland are known to have contained coin, but there are only half a dozen of them with a large enough number of coins surviving for the purpose of detailed numismatic analysis.

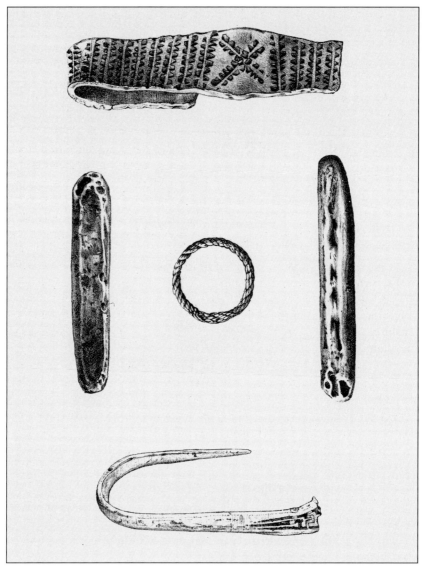

12.4 *The lost silver hoard from Gordon, Berwickshire, which included a gold finger-ring (after W. Stobbs, 1885).*

Coins

The sources of the coins, whether Arabic, English, French, Hiberno-Norse or Norwegian, indicate something of the various ways in which silver reached Scotland during this period. Arabic coins, or dirhams, carry inscriptions in Kufic script which are mostly quotations from the Koran in praise of Allah, but which also identify exactly where and when they were struck. They have been found in three hoards from Scandinavian Scotland, but only survive from two (Storr Rock and Skaill). Storr Rock is the earliest coin-dated hoard of Norse type known from Scotland, having been buried c. 935–40 on the shore of the Sound of Raasay, below the great rock known as the Old Man of Storr, on Skye. Its nineteen dirhams are remarkable in being mostly complete, if worn, which is scarcely surprising given that they were minted in Tashkent and Samarkand. The same mints are represented amongst the nineteen fragments which survive from the later Skaill hoard, Orkney (deposited c. 950–70), but with the addition of Baghdad. There is, finally, a lost fragment on record from the Machrie hoard, Islay, which was deposited c. 970–80.

These Arabic coins, which are of the highest-quality silver, streamed into Scandinavia from the beginning of the ninth century, with their import peaking in the mid-tenth, after which it seems to have declined rapidly, ceasing altogether in the early eleventh. It is probable that the dirhams which reached Scotland did so by way of Denmark and the Danelaw area of England (whether by way of York or through the Irish Sea area), given that over 5,000 such coins are known from Viking period Denmark, as against only about 400 from Norway. In this connection, it is worth recalling that dirhams have also been found in south-west Scotland: a couple of dirham fragments are present as scrap silver in the earlier Talnotrie hoard (c. 875), and there is a stray-find of an early tenth-century coin from the sands at Ardeer in Ayrshire. By way of a postscript to this Viking period import of Kufic coin, there is an exceptional single-find known from Monymusk, in Aberdeenshire, of an Arabic gold coin (or dinar) which was minted in Morocco in 1097.

The most numerous coins in the Storr Rock hoard are silver pennies from Anglo-Saxon England, reflecting the pattern for Viking period Scotland as a whole. As Michael Metcalf has commented: 'The proportions of coins from different English mints emphasize the very close link with north-eastern England (York and Lincoln) and, to a much lesser extent, north-western England.' However, the Scottish hoards 'reflect coins that have mingled after leaving England' and, in some cases, this process might well have taken place in Ireland, before the silver was carried north.

This seems most probable in the case of the ninety Anglo-Saxon coins in the Storr Rock hoard, for about half of them are from the south of England. The Storr Rock coins are completed by two which have been attributed to a Danelaw mint at Lincoln, when it was under the rule of Sihtric (921–7). On the other hand, the Skaill hoard is known to have contained only one Anglo-Saxon penny in addition to its Kufic coins, together with one from Viking York.

One of the most interesting of the tenth-century mixed hoards is that found at Iona Abbey in 1950, containing over 360 coins, which is the largest number in any of the Viking period hoards on record from Scotland, with the possible exception of Tiree, as discussed above (p. 87). These include 345 Anglo-Saxon coins, from the latest of which it has been concluded that this treasure may well have been buried on the occasion of a known raid on Iona at Christmas 986. In fact, a third of the coins are considerably older, dating back from before the reign of Eadgar, who ascended the English throne in 959. The Iona coins also include five from Viking York, with another eight which may perhaps be from Danish Northumbria, as well as three deniers (continental pennies) from the Duchy of Normandy.

The French deniers which reached Scandinavian Scotland are likely to have done so direct (given that they were not allowed to circulate in Anglo-Saxon England); however, their number is not large. The Iona deniers were minted in Rouen under Richard I (943–6), as was a group of four from an unknown location in Scotland. Two mixed hoards, from the opposite ends of the Great Glen, include late tenth-century deniers minted in Quentovic (Pas de Calais): that from Tarbat churchyard, Ross-shire, contained five (with a further six French coins which have not survived) and that from Inch Kenneth, off Mull, at least five (together with one each from Paris and Strasbourg). Two tenth-century coins from Cologne are also known: one in the Machrie, Islay, hoard and the other in that from Burray, Orkney. Finally, there were small fragments of two more Rouen deniers in the hoard found at Stornoway, Lewis, but of these it can only be said that they were struck sometime between about 990 and 1030/40.

The Inch Kenneth hoard, which was found about 1830, is reported to have contained 'nearly a hundred' coins; although only a few are known to have survived, sufficient were recorded to establish that it was deposited c. 1000. The survivors include three Hiberno-Norse coins, from amongst the earliest to have been struck for the Viking kings of Dublin, where minting only commenced at the end of the tenth century. A small hoard of later Hiberno-Norse coins was found in 1989 at Dull, Perthshire, and another has been reported from Fife; a couple of single-finds are known, less surprisingly, from Whithorn in the south-west. It is a matter of speculation, however, as to whether some additional, but unlocalised, Hiberno-Norse coins in the Edinburgh collection (including one group of four) may or may not also represent Scottish finds.

The latest of the Viking period hoards from Scandinavian Scotland, for which much information survives, was found in 1774 at Caldale in Orkney. This contained more than 300 coins of the Anglo-Danish king Cnut (deposited c. 1032–40), many of which had been minted in York (Figure 4.4). As Metcalf has observed in this connection: 'The north-eastern or northern Danelaw connection with Norse Scotland thus survived well into the eleventh century'.

The only later mixed hoard is from Dunrossness, Shetland, and was first recorded in 1844. Its existence is sufficiently shadowy for it to have been suggested that its one surviving coin is in fact derived from the only other such hoard known from Shetland, that found in 1830 at Quendale, in the same parish. The Quendale coins, however, suggest that this hoard was most probably deposited c. 991–1000, whereas the only known Dunrossness coin was minted much later, c. 1055–65, for Harald Hardrada, king of Norway.

This is one of only three Norwegian coins which are so far known from Scotland, but then there was no truly national coinage in Norway, where most of the minting took place in Trondheim, before Harald's reign. A second example of his coinage has been excavated at the Udal in North Uist. The latest Viking/Late Norse period coin on record from Scotland is one that was struck c. 1080, for Olaf Kyrre; it is a stray-find from the Brough of Birsay, Orkney.

Rings

Rings – for neck, arm and finger – form the most numerous category of personal ornaments during the Viking period in Scandinavia, made from both silver and gold. The standard type of neck-ring was manufactured from twisted or plaited rods, fitted with hooked terminals for ease of use (Figure 12.3). There are several fine examples of these in silver from the Skaill hoard (c. 950–70), and a couple also form part of the later Orkney hoard from Burray (c. 997–1010). On the other hand, a lost gold neck-ring from Braidwood Fort, Midlothian, was completely annular in form, but then it must have been of sufficient size to be placed directly over the head, given that on its discovery, at the end of the eighteenth century, it was described as 'a Roman girdle'! Such large gold neck-rings are something of a rarity even in the Scandinavian homelands, but this is all the more an exceptional find for Scotland because the other surviving gold rings consist of Viking/Late Norse period finger-rings, with the exception of two fine arm-rings. The latter were both discovered on their own: one in the small island of Oxna, Shetland, and the other on the sea-bed in the Sound of Jura. In addition, two gold arm-rings are reported to have been found together in the Broch of Burgar, Orkney, during the nineteenth century, but these are now lost; they were presumably melted down for their precious metal, as was the fate of the Braidwood ring, which was sold to a jeweller for twenty-eight guineas.

Twisted-rod arm-rings are known from only two Scottish finds, although there are three examples in the Skaill hoard. These include the most magnificent specimen of all from Scandinavian Scotland, which is exceptional in having prominent animal-head terminals (Figure 12.3). The only other twisted-rod arm-ring from Scotland forms part of the tenth-century hoard found near Port Glasgow. This is unusual in having knobbed terminals, although there is a similar arm-ring of this period in a hoard from the Isle of Man.

Two further types of arm-ring are represented in the Skaill hoard by single examples: one made from a single rod, with its ends twisted together, and the other from a narrow band with punched ornament and hooked terminals. On the other hand, the most numerous type of arm-ring in the hoard (with a total of twenty-seven complete examples and several fragments) is the simplest of all, consisting of just a single penannular rod. This type, which has become known as 'ring-money', is the commonest form of silver ornament known from Scandinavian Scotland. It is present in over a third of all the hoards, with a total of more than ninety complete examples and a couple of hundred fragments. Its importance is therefore such as to require separate discussion below.

Another distinctive variety of penannular arm-ring is the one most closely associated with the Scandinavian settlement of Ireland. This so-called 'Hiberno-Viking' type consists of a broad thick band of silver, hammered out of an ingot; it is characteristically decorated with rows of massive punched ornament, most often with a diagonal cross at the centre, repeated towards both ends, although some rings were left plain (cf. the rings in the Raphoe hoard: Figure 6.2). This particular form of ring, which had its main period of manufacture between about 880 and 930/40, was developed from a ninth-century Danish prototype which was both narrower and less ornate. It is thus conceivable that the simple ring fragment of this type from the probable grave at Blackerne, Kirkcudbright, is of Danish origin, although it could well be a Hiberno-Norse copy.

An example of the plain variety of the Hiberno-Viking type was found in the female grave at Clibberswick, Unst, where the ring (now lost) was said to have been on the left wrist. Fragments of two decorated rings are known from south-east Scotland, one of which seems to have become mixed up in the nineteenth century with a find of much earlier Pictish silver from Norrie's Law, in Fife, whereas the other formed part of the (lost) hoard from Gordon, Berwickshire (Figure 12.4). Two complete rings said to have been 'found in Scotland' are now in the British Museum (bought in Edinburgh in 1851) where they are now associated with a third ring, of unknown origin, which has punched decoration executed with the same stamps as one of the others. To further complicate this matter, the National Museum of Ireland possesses nineteenth-century copies of these three rings as part of a group of five, of which the other two are no longer known to exist! Are we to suppose therefore that a hoard of five complete Hiberno-Viking rings had originally been discovered in Scotland? Or did a couple of rings from an Irish hoard find their way into a private collection in Scotland, acquiring a false Scottish provenance in the process? We may never know the answer, but there is nothing improbable about such a hoard having been found in Scotland, given that a number of Hiberno-Viking rings did in fact reach Norway. In addition, there are other Scottish hoards of this period which appear to be Irish in origin, notably those from Gordon and Storr Rock, as probably also a (lost) hoard of linked rings found elsewhere on Skye.

Although the hack-silver in the Storr Rock hoard does not include any of these Hiberno-Viking ring fragments, there is part of a so-called 'ribbon bracelet' which may well be of Hiberno-Norse manufacture (Figure 12.7). The most exotic arm-ring fragment from Storr Rock consists of a bent rod with a corded appearance, for this originally formed part of a so-called 'Permian' spiral-ring of east European or south Scandinavian origin. This is the only such ring fragment known from Scotland, although there are fragments in three other Viking period hoards from England and Ireland. These ring fragments presumably crossed the North Sea in the company of the Arabic dirhams, such as those already noted from Storr Rock itself.

Most finger-rings are miniaturised versions of the plaited and twisted neck/arm-rings and are annular in form. Others were, however, fashioned from single rods or bands, both decorated and plain, with some being left open for ease of adjustment. As mentioned above, the commonest form of gold ornament during the Viking period was the finger-ring, simply because gold was in shorter supply and thus the more precious metal. Indeed, silver finger-rings are less usually found than gold, presumably because most of those who possessed silver would have had enough for at least an arm-ring. A silver finger-ring, with stamped decoration, excavated from the Norse settlement at Westness, Rousay, is the most notable example to have been found in Scandinavian Scotland, although a couple of plain bands form part of a coinless hoard from Dibadale on Lewis.

There are two notable hoards of Late Viking period gold finger-rings from Scandinavian Scotland, both of which were found in the nineteenth century. The Stenness, Orkney, hoard (Figure 12.5) consists of four such rings (one of plaited and one of twisted rods, with two fashioned from plain bands), but the larger and more important find is from the Hebrides – most probably from North Uist and the small island of Oronsay, close by the Norse settlement at the Udal. This treasure consists of five and a half plaited finger-rings, as well as a plain rod ring, together with the cut ends of two ingots and a small rod fragment. One of the five complete plaited rings appears to be unfinished and, as all the other pieces are in fresh condition, it could well be that the contents of this hoard represent the stock-in-trade of a goldsmith.

There is a fine example of a plaited-rod ring from Fladda-chùain, off Skye (Figure 5.4) – and Skye itself has produced two further single-finds of gold finger-rings (one of

12.5 Hoard of four gold finger-rings from Stenness, Orkney (NMS).

twisted rods and the other a plain band). A very different type of gold finger-ring is represented by a stray-find from Tundergarth, Dumfriesshire. This chunky specimen, with its elaborate stamped decoration, is a miniaturised version of another well-known type of Viking period arm-ring, although one of which no example has yet been found in Scotland.

It does not appear that the Scandinavian fashion for wearing elaborate neck- and arm-rings continued into the eleventh century in Scotland, for the surviving hoard evidence from this period consists only of plain 'ring-money'. Nevertheless, the traditional types of plaited, twisted and plain gold finger-rings continued to be worn well into the twelfth century, as is demonstrated by the two rings which formed part of the St Blane's, Bute, hoard (deposited in the 1150s) and that in a late, but coinless, hoard from St Ronan's Church on Iona.

An exceptional object in the earlier Iona Abbey hoard (c. 986) consists of a lozenge-shaped finger-ring bezel of silver, with gold filigree decoration around a green glass setting. This appears to be of tenth-century Anglo-Saxon manufacture, although the fact that its hoop was missing suggests that it had become no more than an exotic piece of treasure by the time that it was buried. This is the only item of Anglo-Saxon ornamental metalwork known from a Viking period hoard in Scotland, despite the presence of so many English coins. It has been suggested, however, that the ninth-century silver horn-mount, decorated in the Anglo-Saxon 'Trewhiddle style', which is known from the Pictish promontory fort of Burghead, on the Moray coast, reached there as the result of some Viking intervention (as perhaps also its stray-find of a coin of Alfred), but there is no evidence for this either way. On the other hand, swords and copper-alloy ornaments of Anglo-Saxon workmanship have been found in Viking period graves in both Scotland and Norway. One of the most remarkable finds in this connection is that of the remains of an eighth-century ornamental disc excavated on the Brough of Birsay, Orkney, which is the pair to one buried (as a brooch) in a woman's grave in north-western Norway, at Hillesøy, Tromsø.

'Ring-money'

As noted above, 'ring-money' is the name which has been given to the simplest type of silver arm-ring known from Viking period Scotland, defined as being 'penannular in form, made from a single rod and most often entirely plain'. The rod is normally four-sided and of lozenge-shaped section, although the angles may be flattened or rounded; however, there are some that are circular (cf. the rings illustrated from the Caldale hoard: Figure 4.4). The terminals are generally blunt-ended or hammered flat, with some that taper to points.

'Ring-money' is present in hoards ranging in date from Skaill (c. 950–70) to Caldale (c. 1032–40), but it is most probable that the 'several cut-up silver arm-rings' lost from the later Dunrossness hoard (c. 1065?) will also have been fragments of 'ring-money', given that this is the type which dominates the later Scottish hoards. The basic form seems to have come into being during the first half of the tenth century in the Irish Sea area, where some of the rings have stamped decoration around the hoop, as do four of those in the Skaill hoard (one of which is illustrated in Figure 12.3). Later examples are entirely plain, with just two exceptions, both of which have some stamping on their flattened terminals: one forms part of a coinless 'ring-money' hoard from Skye, and the other has been lost from the Burray hoard.

Over ninety complete examples of 'ring-money' are known from over a third of the Viking period hoards of Scotland, together with some two hundred fragments. It is somewhat surprising therefore that there is only one single-find, a complete ring from a drain associated with the 'parent' farm building at Jarlshof. This frequency of occurrence, combined with their simplicity of form, has suggested a payment function for these rings (hence their modern name) and thus their metrology has also been studied. Some clustering is evident in the weights of the complete examples in the low 20 grams, but more notably around 50 grams. From this it emerges that there was probably a unit of weight in use in Scandinavian Scotland of 24.0 ± 0.8g; this accords with other evidence for there having been an ounce weight of c. 24g in Viking period Scandinavia. The analysis by Richard Warner also revealed, however, that the standard deviation from the supposed target weights (of one and two ounces) is as much as 5 grams. This lack of precision with which the rings were made presents a real problem in accepting suggestions that 'ring-money' constituted a standardised form of earldom currency. On the other hand, it clearly provided a convenient means of payment, as witnessed by the quantity of hack-silver in the hoards, even if it still had to be weighed out for the purpose.

Despite the suggested Irish Sea origins for 'ring-money', there are no indications of its popularity continuing in that region, in part no doubt because of the shift towards a coin-using economy which culminated in the establishment of a mint in Dublin at the end of the tenth century. It is probable therefore that the 'ring-money' in two eleventh-century Manx hoards – West Nappin (deposited c. 1045) and Kirk Michael (c. 1065) – can be taken as evidence for the continuation of the contacts between Scandinavian Scotland and the Irish Sea region, despite the scarcity of Hiberno-Norse coins in the Scottish hoards. On the other hand, the prevalence of 'ring-money' demonstrates the extent to which the silver reaching Scandinavian Scotland continued to be recycled during this period.

Brooches and pins

The most striking element in the Skaill hoard consists of its large penannular brooches (Figure 12.3), ten in all, but with as many more represented by fragments. Seventeen of these Skaill brooches belong to the so-called 'ball-type', named after their bulbous terminals and pin-head, although those with a characteristic form of criss-cross decoration (or 'brambling') are more often known as 'thistle-brooches'. This originated as a native Irish brooch-type during the latter part of the ninth century, but it was soon copied and developed by Norse silversmiths.

Four of the Skaill brooches are so closely related in form, ornament and silver content that it has been suggested that they represent a single workshop group; indeed, they are most probably the work of an individual craftsman. Three of these large brooches are incised with high-quality ornament in the Mammen style of Viking art (which developed from the Jellinge style; cf. Figure 2.5), comprising stylised animals and birds, together with an enigmatic scene of a man-animal grappling with a snake (Figure 12.6). Some of the closest parallels for this ornament can be found on the tenth-century stone sculpture of the Isle of Man. One of the Manx hoards, from Ballaquale (c. 970), contains the pin-head from a 'thistle-brooch' which is so close in form and ornament to one in this Skaill group as to suggest that it represents another product of the same craftsman/workshop. Wherever these magnificent brooches were actually made, it seems likely that the silver-smith in question had learnt his craft in the Irish Sea region. In fact, only one other silver 'thistle-brooch' is known from Scotland – a stray-find from Gulberwick in Shetland.

It is an interesting phenomenon that when ball-type brooches were introduced into Norway they were copied not only in silver, but also in both copper alloy and iron, at a reduced size. The two small copper-alloy copies found in Scotland may well have been imported from Norway; one is from a male grave at Kildonnan on Eigg, the other a stray-find from near Kinlochleven, in Argyll. Indeed, only one further example of such a copy is known from Britain and Ireland – from a cave on the coast of Glamorgan in Wales.

Another of the penannular brooches in the Skaill hoard provides a fine example of a less elaborate type, with faceted rectangular terminals and stamped ornament, of West Norse manufacture. A terminal fragment in the Storr Rock hoard provides the only other example known from outside Scandinavia (Figure 12.7). It contrasts therefore in its origin with a second Storr Rock terminal fragment which is cut and broken from a so-called 'bossed' penannular brooch of Irish manufacture (Figure 12.7) – a unique example amongst the Scottish hoard material, although a fragment from another reached Iceland.

The most spectacular silver pin from Scandinavian Scotland is not from a hoard, but is

12.6 The Mammen-style ornament engraved on brooches in the Skaill hoard, as illustrated in Figure 12.3 (after J. Graham-Campbell/NMS, 1995).

that noted above from the richly equipped female grave at Ballinaby, Islay (p. 124). It consists of a filigree-ornamented bead mounted on a plain shaft which has a looped head containing a ring; this is matched by a ring on the end of a fine chain, the other end of which had presumably been attached to the pin-head so that the two will have functioned together (Figure 7.6). The Ballinaby pin is therefore a composite object, combining the only example known from Scotland of this elaborate type of Scandinavian bead with a chain of Insular origin, manufactured in the Trichinopoly technique of circular plaiting with a single wire. Trichinopoly chain fragments are also present in both the Skaill and Inch Kenneth hoards.

The simpler and smaller silver pin from the Kiloran Bay boat-burial, Colonsay, is clearly a Scandinavian import, belonging to a type named after the Vestfold region of south-east Norway. Only one other example has been found in Scotland (on the Brough of Birsay), but this is of copper alloy as is more usually the case. Both pins are now missing the small terminal ring which is a characteristic of the Vestfold type.

Copper-alloy ringed-pins of Insular type which originated in Ireland are commonly enough found in both male and female Viking period graves, as also on Norse settlement sites and as stray-finds, but silver examples are rare. Only two such pins are known from

Ireland, with a further two in the Skaill hoard, although one of the latter is now missing the ring from its head. The shaft of the complete Skaill example is so bent at the end that it was once identified as a silver fish-hook (Figure 12.3)! Finally, from Jarlshof, there is a large silver 'stick-pin', with straight shaft and polyhedral ring-stamped head, of tenth- or eleventh-century date. Its material and remarkable size make it unique in Scotland, although a similar example in copper alloy has been found in the Viking period levels of Dublin.

Ingots

Open moulds of steatite for the production of bar-shaped ingots have been excavated on the Brough of Birsay and at Earl's Bu, Orphir, although it is not known whether they were used for casting precious metal. However, even though ingots provide an obviously convenient method of storing silver for use in a bullion economy, as researched by Susan Kruse, it does not appear that they were much utilised for this purpose in Scandinavian Scotland. It is, however, difficult to document this in detail because many of the early records of old finds are particularly vague in this respect and ingot fragments would always have been the first to end up back in the melting pot for their silver.

The use of silver ingots during the Viking period in the West was most popular in Ireland, and it is notable that the two Scottish hoards in which they form a major component are those with the strongest Irish connection (Gordon and Storr Rock). Two of the four (lost) silver objects in the coinless Gordon hoard were complete ingots (Figure 12.4), whereas sixteen of the twenty-three pieces of bullion in the Storr Rock hoard (c. 935–40) are ingot fragments, but then its non-numismatic contents consist entirely of hack-silver (Figure 12.7).

In the later hoards from Scandinavian Scotland, ingots appear to have been of lesser significance. The Skaill hoard (c. 950–70) does contain four complete ingots and eight fragments, but then there are over 100 other pieces, in addition to the twenty-one coins, so that even their combined contribution to the total weight of the silver (over 8 kg) is negligible. The Burray hoard (c. 997–1010) comprised some 2 kg of silver in the form of about a dozen coins and 140 pieces of bullion, but of these only one is a complete ingot, together with one certain and two possible fragments.

The Iona Abbey hoard (c. 986) contains a complete silver ingot of standard form, but bent into a loop, together with the Anglo-Saxon finger-ring bezel and a small fragment of gold rod. A smaller complete ingot, with hammered upper and lower faces, survives from the Tiree hoard(s), although not mentioned in either of the original accounts. Some 'masses of silver' (now lost) found with the Machrie coins on Islay, which were deposited about 970–80, might have been ingot fragments. So too might have been some of the lost 'bits' in the eleventh-century Orkney hoard from Caldale (c. 1032–40), although there were none amongst the forty-two pieces of bullion in the broadly contemporary hoard found at Stornoway on Lewis. An ingot fragment excavated on the Brough of Birsay is also thought to date from this period. In addition, the Brough of Birsay has produced a tiny piece of a gold ingot, but this recalls the presence of the two larger fragments in the Hebridean finger-ring hoard, mentioned above. Finally, a single silver ingot forms part of the curious mixed hoard from St Blane's, Bute (deposited during the 1150s), already

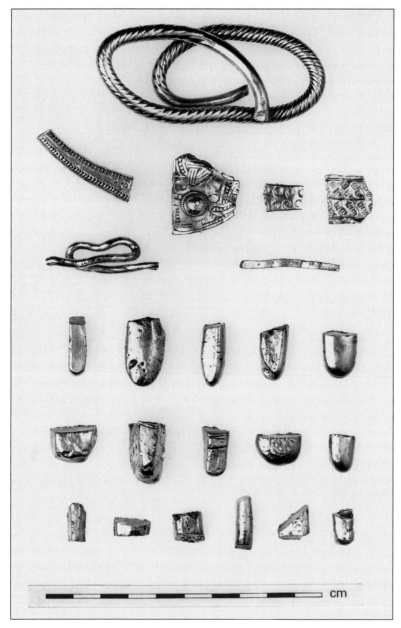

*12.7 The twenty-three pieces of hack-silver in the Storr Rock hoard, Skye,
deposited c. 935–40 (NMS).*

noted for its two gold finger-rings.

It appears therefore that the Norse in Scotland, after melting down coins and hack-silver,
deliberately chose not to leave their silver in ingot form. Instead, the ingots were hammered out into rods from which rings were then fashioned. Silver storage in the form of

ornaments, even those as simple as 'ring-money', seems to have been preferred therefore over storage and circulation in the form of coins or ingots.

Hack-silver

As we have seen, all the categories of object discussed above were cut up for use as small lumps of bullion in the prevailing metal-weight economy, as and when required to top up the scale-pan. It has been suggested that the relative quantity of hack-silver and complete ornaments in hoards, as well as the degree of its fragmentation, provides an indicator of the changing role of silver in the economy, as it ceased to be used primarily for display, and for prestigious gifts, and became needed increasingly for use in commercial transactions. This aspect of hoard analysis needs to be combined with a study of the extent of the nicking to which the individual pieces have been subjected. In this connection, it is instructive to compare and contrast the Storr Rock, Skaill, Burray and Stornoway hoards, which together span the period from the first half of the tenth to the first half of the eleventh century.

The Storr Rock hoard (c. 935–40) contains 111 coins which are almost all complete, together with twenty-three pieces of hack-silver, to a total weight of about 423 g, with the hack-silver weighing only some 40 g more than the coins. The hack-silver fragments are nicked from once to over thirty times, with an average of nine nicks per item (Figure 12.7).

The Skaill hoard (c. 950–70) contains twenty-one coins which are mostly fragmentary and have been subjected to bending, together with a large quantity of prestige ornaments and complete 'ring-money', and a small amount of hack-silver, to a total weight of over 8 kilograms. The average number of nicks on the ornaments and hack-silver is only four per item, but this figure disguises a considerable degree of variation indicative of the fact that such a quantity of silver (some 115 pieces in all) will have been assembled from several different sources. However, only some fifteen of the objects are without nicks, including two of the finest ball-type brooches. At the opposite end of the scale, there are fourteen objects with over ten nicks each, the highest incidence being thirty-four on an ingot fragment.

The Burray hoard (c. 997–1010) contains 140 pieces of bullion, with about a dozen coins, to a total weight of some 2 kilograms. There were twenty-six complete pieces of 'ring-money' (one now missing), with two small neck-rings, both of which were probably complete on burial, and one complete ingot. Otherwise, all the remaining 111 items consist of large and small hack-silver fragments. The contents must have been subjected to some severe cleaning on discovery, for the surfaces of all the objects are heavily abraded, making it difficult to determine the extent of the nicking with accuracy. However, the majority of the pieces appear to be without any nicks and the remainder averages about two, with a maximum of six to eight.

The Stornoway hoard (c. 990–1040) consists of thirty-seven small pieces of hack-silver and just two fragmentary coins, with a total weight of 263 grams. These had been wrapped up together in a linen cloth before being buried in a cattle horn. As the hoard has not been cleaned, with cloth still adhering to some of the pieces, it is not possible to determine the full extent of any nicking, but this appears to have been minimal, for only three items each have a single visible nick.

The Burray and Stornoway hoards therefore share a high degree of fragmentation, consistent with growing commercial activity, but with a low level of nicking, which seems somewhat contradictory. It is possible that nicking was not routinely practised in Scandinavian Scotland into the eleventh century, but a more likely explanation of this phenomenon might be that the 'ring-money' which provided most of this hack-silver was, in both cases, of recent manufacture and had not seen much in the way of circulation after it had been cut up.

The difference in degree of fragmentation is particularly marked between these two hoards and that from Skaill. In fact, although Burray is only one quarter by weight the size of Skaill, it actually contains more individual pieces of silver. The economic activities represented by the accumulation of the Skaill treasure, during the mid-tenth century, do therefore seem to have been somewhat different in nature to those represented by Burray and Stornoway.

There could not be more of a contrast than between the contents of the Skaill and Storr Rock hoards, even allowing for their difference in size. The total fragmentation of the bullion, combined with the frequency of nicking, together with the large number of coins and their high proportion by weight, removes Storr Rock once again from the Scottish zone of economic activity back to the Irish Sea where such a hoard would not have looked out of place alongside those from the beginning of the tenth century, such as the vast treasure from Cuerdale, in Lancashire (deposited c. 905), and the much smaller hoard from Dysart Island, Co. Westmeath (from c. 907).

It is interesting to note how the increased fragmentation of the hack-silver during the latter part of the Viking period seems to have led to the use of cattle horns as storage containers, as was the case with the smaller pieces of three late tenth/early eleventh-century hoards (Quendale, Stornoway and Caldale), whereas those of the Burray hoard were deposited in an alderwood vessel.

METALLURGICAL ANALYSIS

Recent analysis of the silver content of a selection of objects from five Scottish hoards has produced some interesting results. For the most part the silver is of high quality, generally over 90 per cent metallic silver, although 'silver' as it would have been perceived by a Viking period craftsman would have been the combination of silver, gold and lead resulting from the cupellation process. It is, in fact, the varying gold-in-silver ratio which theoretically allows for some distinction to be made between different silver sources. In practice, however, most of the silver objects analysed have been made from a mixed stock of silver, seemingly drawn from a wide area. There are nevertheless some interesting comparisons and contrasts to be made between Storr Rock, Skaill and Burray, the three hoards on which most work has been carried out, with the results having been expertly reviewed by Susan Kruse and James Tate.

The largest number of objects analysed are from the Skaill hoard which turned out to be distinctively pure, with almost all being over 90 per cent metallic silver. Kruse and Tate discerned evidence of the use of Arabic silver in some objects, which of course accords with the presence of Arabic coins in the hoard itself, whereas a distinctive alloy suggests a common source for the group of 'thistle-brooches' which are themselves stylistically related. In contrast, the silver alloy used for the Burray 'ring-money' is quite base, with two-thirds of the analysed rings being below 70 per cent, as is also its complete ingot. Kruse and Tate commented that:

> The gold-in-silver ratios are also quite low, noticeably lower than silver from earlier Scottish hoards. The new alloy may represent usage of contemporary Anglo-Saxon coins, which, especially from the reign of Æthelred II, employed a low-gold source of silver. However, the Anglo-Saxon coins are much purer, suggesting that if they were the basis of the Burray 'ring-money', the silver had been deliberately debased.

In view of the distinctive 'Irish Sea' characteristics displayed by the Storr Rock hoard, it is of particular interest that Kruse and Tate found that in five of the fifteen ingots (unlike the other Scottish material analysed):

> tin was present in measurable quantities, suggesting scrap bronze was in the alloy. In other respects, the alloy resembled that found in objects from two other contemporary hoards from Scotby, Cumbria, and from Co. Dublin. One of the Storr Rock ingots may have used Arabic silver as the main source. The use of zinc in the alloy of some of the ingots is closer, however, to that found in Anglo-Saxon coins, although these do not seem to have provided the sole silver source of the ingots.

The analyses have shown therefore that the situation was, not surprisingly, one of considerable complexity. In fact, it was not possible to identify a single source of silver for any of the objects analysed from the Scottish hoards.

CIRCULATION AND DEPOSITION

The hoard evidence suggests that there was less silver in circulation in Scandinavian Scotland during the early part of the Viking period than during the latter part – and virtually none at all in the twelfth century. The evidence of stray-finds and single-finds from excavated sites, of both coins and other objects of precious metal, lends support to this picture of events. However, it must be emphasised that we do not know the pattern behind the practice of burying treasure at this period, nor whether it changed during the course of the Viking period – or even between the Viking and Late Norse periods.

Some of the hoards buried during the pagan period in Scandinavia were deposited for ritual reasons, with no intention of recovery, such as those consigned to watery places. These might have been thank-offerings to the gods, or propitiatory gifts, although an alternative explanation for ritual deposition is to be found in the so-called 'Odin's law', mentioned by the Icelandic historian, Snorri Sturluson (who died in 1241). Snorri states that Odin had 'said that everyone should come into Valhalla with all the property that he had on the pyre, and he should also enjoy the use of what he himself had buried in the earth'.

This does not seem to have been the case in Scandinavian Scotland, if only because we know of so few hoards deposited during the period of pagan Norse burial (c. 850–950), although some objects of precious metal were included amongst the grave-goods. In the case of the fine gold arm-ring recovered from the Sound of Jura, it is reasonable to speculate that it may have been deliberately consigned to the deep, unless it derives from a lost shipwreck.

Even if we accept that the great majority of the hoards from Scandinavian Scotland were deposited in the ground by their owners with the intention of recovering them, we still do not know to what extent it may have been standard practice to keep such treasures buried – or whether they were concealed only during periods of warfare or local unrest. This may also have been a practice that changed through time, as the silver was needed increasingly for commercial use – rather than to be kept for display or distribution only on special occasions.

It is pure speculation, although entirely consistent with the evidence, to suggest that the treasure from beside the Bay of Skaill may represent the capital of the local chieftain who lived in this prime settlement location, buried by him in the side of a prominent landmark (now known as the Castle of Snusgar), before setting out to increase his wealth on an expedition from which he never returned. Likewise, one might speculate that the owner of the Burray hoard, in some sudden (and justifiable) fear for his safety, carried it up into the peat bog where a green mound, identifiable from landmarks, provided a remote and secret place for its concealment.

On the other hand, most single-finds from settlement sites are likely to have been casual losses (often as scrap on the way to the crucible), although the silver pin from the ruined broch at Jarlshof had presumably been deliberately secreted, as also the piece of 'ring-money' found there in a house-drain. Stray-finds, such as the Gulberwick 'thistle-brooch' and Oxna arm-ring, are inevitably enigmatic in terms of our being able to understand their loss or deposition.

Having recognised the growth in the supply and circulation of silver between the ninth and eleventh centuries in Scandinavian Scotland, it is necessary to consider possible explanations for the apparent reversal of this trend during the eleventh. A standard reason given for the cessation of 'Viking' type hoarding elsewhere is that this was the result of the economic changes which followed on from the full adoption of monetary instead of weight-based transactions. In the case of Scotland, however, the end of hoarding does not coincide with the monetisation of the economy. Indeed, the reverse is the situation given that hoards reappear anywhere in Scotland in the mid-twelfth century only after King David I had initiated the minting of the first national coinage; but even then a monetary economy was confined essentially to the Central Lowlands and southern Scotland for the duration of the twelfth and thirteenth centuries – a period from which there is no known hoard from the Northern Isles.

This stark contrast between the situation in the tenth/eleventh and the twelfth/thirteenth centuries, in Orkney in particular, suggests an outflow of silver followed by its substitution by other commodities, such as grain, fish and butter, for use in taxation and commercial purposes. However, Susan Kruse has argued that 'the role of silver in local exchanges was slight even in the Viking Age', with the consequence that 'the diminishing supplies would not have been a major economic issue'.

The suggestion of a developing silver shortage in the north emerges from the Burray analyses, with their evidence for debasement in the 'ring-money' (to as low as 40 per cent silver). It is unfortunate that we cannot verify this apparent trend, given that none of the bullion survives from the Caldale and Dunrossness hoards, although it may well be relevant that, in the 1050s, the Norwegian king, Harald Hardrada, undertook a massive debasement of his national coinage (to a median value of 33 per cent silver), while the half-dozen contemporary arm-rings to have been analysed in Norway contain only between 25 and 45 per cent silver.

As will be described in the final chapter, much of the surplus wealth of the Earldom of Orkney during the twelfth century was drained off into major building projects. At the same time, skaldic verses attributed to Earl Rognvald (1137–58/9) contain kennings or poetic images, in the old tradition of Norse court poetry, which hark back to the wearing of twisted neck- and arm-rings, although such would by then appear not to have been in fashion in Orkney for a century or more.

Chapter 13

EARLS AND BISHOPS

The beginning of the end of the Viking period in the Earldom of Orkney was the enforced conversion to Christianity of Earl Sigurd by Olaf Tryggvason (in about 995), after which 'all Orkney embraced the faith', according to *Orkneyinga saga*. During the eleventh and twelfth centuries the earls of Orkney were as likely to have gone on pilgrimage or crusade as on a traditional Viking expedition in the West. For instance, in about 1050, Earl Thorfinn made an epic journey to Rome by way of Norway, Denmark and the court of the Emperor Henry III. This is the Earl Thorfinn who has been described as 'a trail-blazer' in the history of the Church in Orkney, being responsible for the establishment of its first bishopric, in connection with which *Orkneyinga saga* records him as having built 'a magnificent church' at Birsay. According to Adam of Bremen, this first bishop, Thorolf, was consecrated 'by order of the Pope' – an event which can therefore be assumed to have taken place in about 1050, as a result of Thorfinn's visit to Rome.

In earlier chapters, evidence for the survival of Christianity in Scandinavian Scotland has been considered in passing, together with that for the abandonment of pagan Norse burial practices – a process which was seemingly completed well before Sigurd's personal conversion at the end of the tenth century. Chapels, churches and cathedrals will be treated in later sections because those which survive appear to be of Late Norse date. In fact, the greater part of the archaeological evidence for Christianity during the Viking to Late Norse period, such as it is, consists of stone sculpture.

STONE SCULPTURE

The evidence for continuity in Shetland of the native tradition of Christian stone memorials has been outlined above (p. 65), with particular reference to the cross-slab from the island of Bressay (Figure 4.5). The eventual adoption of stone memorials by the Christian Norse in the Earldom of Orkney has also been referred to, in the form of both rune-stones and hogbacks. Rune-stones are known from Orkney (p. 42), Shetland (p. 65) and Caithness (p. 69), but hogbacks have been found only in Orkney, where four are recorded (p. 61), and in Shetland which has just the one (p. 65). The distribution of hogback stones in Scotland (Figure 13.1) reveals that the few eleventh/twelfth-century examples from the Northern Isles represent a fashion in funerary sculpture most probably introduced from south-eastern Scotland (pp. 100 and 105).

The five hogbacks at Govan, on the Clyde, constitute a further outlying group in the overall distribution of this type of monument, but these are of earlier date, being contemporary

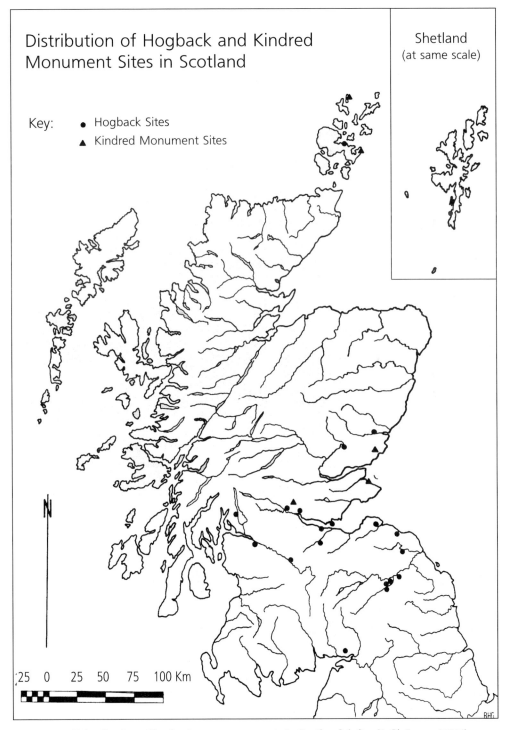

Distribution of Hogback and Kindred
Monument Sites in Scotland

Shetland
(at same scale)

Key: ● Hogback Sites
       ▲ Kindred Monument Sites

:25 0   25 50 75 100 Km

13.1 Distribution of hogback stone monuments in Scotland (after J. T. Lang, 1974).

with at least some of those carved in Cumbria when hogbacks were first in fashion. They merit further discussion here because the Govan hogbacks form the largest and most distinctive group of such stones in Scotland, with even the nearest examples, those from Luss to the north and Dalserf to the south, being of different types. In particular, it is the massive dimensions of four of the Govan group which are not matched elsewhere in either Scotland or England. However, the other stone is noticeably slimmer than the rest and in this, as well as other respects, it fits most closely into the Cumbrian group of hogbacks from the middle of the tenth century (Figure 6.5). So well, in fact, that James Lang once suggested that this particular monument might even have been transported by sea from Cumbria to the Clyde. A preliminary assessment of the geology of the Govan hogbacks has not, however, provided any support for this hypothesis.

These five hogbacks stand out amongst the great mass of other sculpture at Govan, which mostly takes the form of recumbent cross-slabs of ninth- to eleventh-century date. The hogbacks do therefore suggest an aristocratic Anglo-Scandinavian presence in the neighbourhood, but given that their similarities are such that they are all to be dated to within a generation of each other, 'it would be [as Lang concluded] unsafe to use them as indicators of protracted Viking colonial presence. As stone, the Govan hogbacks are indeed substantial; as evidence for settlement and communications, they will always be flimsy.'

The island monastery of Iona seems to have remained in use despite the impact of the Viking raids and the withdrawal of the main Columban community to Kells in Ireland (p. 88). There was continuity in the carving of gravestones and crosses, and thus it is not surprising that some converted Norsemen buried on Iona had stone monuments erected for them which display Scandinavian influence. There is even the intriguing possibility that one cross-slab amongst them might have been imported from the Isle of Man, where its shaly sandstone can be matched. This is today reduced to a fragment displaying part of a ringed cross-head on one side and an interlace pattern on the other, both of which can be matched on some of the tenth-century Manx slabs. Possible Manx influence on the design of the Kilbar cross-slab, on Barra (Figure 3.4), was noted above, together with its runic inscription, and that from Inchmarnock (p. 43).

A second cross of Scandinavian character on Iona is now represented only by the lower part of its shaft with clumsy interlace on one side, together with an animal, and a unique ship scene on the other, together with the figure of a smith, identified by his tongs and other tools (Figure 13.2). The significance of all this is uncertain.

The most evident of the Scandinavian memorial stones on Iona is a recumbent slab, decorated with an expansional cross, which has a Norse runic inscription contained in the border of the longer side (Figure 13.3). The distinctive design of the double-ribbon cross, interlaced with a central square, appears to have been copied from that on another recumbent slab at Iona which is of Irish type. The text is to be translated as: 'Kali Olivsson laid this stone over [his] brother Fugl', with the runes presumed missing from the end of the inscription, where the border is damaged, for the pronoun *sin* (meaning 'his').

The influence of Scandinavian art on the development of sculpture in Scotland was minimal in comparison with northern England and the Isle of Man. The Dóid Mhàiri cross-slab, on Islay (Figure 5.8), was singled out above for its exceptional use of foliate patterns derived from the eleventh-century Ringerike style of Viking art (p. 89). Other

13.2   The Iona ship-stone (Crown copyright: RCAHMS).

sculpture from the West Highlands and Islands attributed to between the tenth and twelfth centuries either shows no Norse influence or is essentially plain, such as the large cross which was removed from the island of Vallay, North Uist (where there remains the fragment of another) to Lochgilphead, in Argyll, during the nineteenth century. A tenth/ eleventh-century date has been tentatively advanced for the Vallay stones on the basis of comparisons with the disc-headed crosses of the 'Whithorn School' in south-west Scotland.

It was suggested above that the 'Whithorn School' of sculpture – and the other carved stones from the area – showed little or nothing in the way of Scandinavian influence (p. 107). However, the Kilmorie cross-slab, on the north coast of Stranraer, seems to be exceptional in this respect in displaying a scene from Norse mythology (Figure 6.8). One side of the slab has a cross above a panel of snake-headed interlace, but the other has a simple Crucifixion above a figure flanked by tongs (and an anvil?) on one side and a pair of birds on the other. The presence of the birds suggests that this is intended to be a depiction of Sigurd who, in Norse mythology, was warned by birds that he was about to be killed by his treasure-hunting companion, Regin, the smith. The treasure had been acquired by virtue of Sigurd having killed the dragon, Fafnir, who guarded over it – and then, licking his finger, scalded while roasting its heart, Sigurd accidentally consumed some of the dragon's blood, which gave him the power to understand the language of the birds. That this really is Sigurd is not improbable given that there are four tenth-century

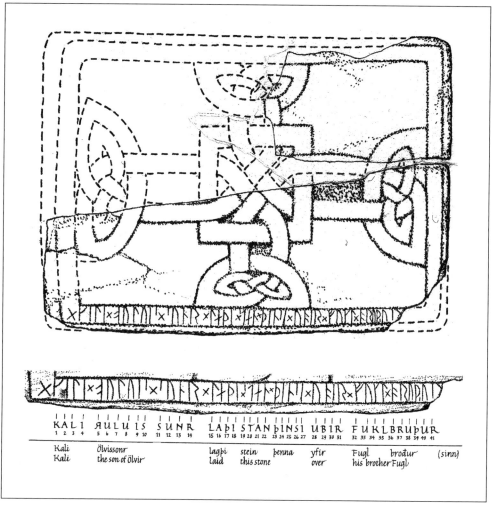

13.3 The Iona rune-stone (Crown copyright: RCAHMS).

slabs on the Isle of Man which are decorated with Sigurd iconography, including scenes of both dragon-slaying and heart-roasting, even if this does make the Kilmorie stone unique in Scotland.

CHAPELS AND CHURCHES

The overall lack of interest in Scandinavian Scotland in the carving of decorated stone monuments is matched by an even greater lack of interest in architectural ornament, with the result that considerable difficulty is encountered in trying to date the simple stone chapels and churches which belong to the period of Late Norse Christianity.

The chapel excavated by Christopher Morris on the Brough of Deerness, Orkney, was shown to have first been constructed in timber, with stone cladding. This may have been in the pre-Norse period because there was an intermediate phase of activity, associated with an Anglo-Saxon coin of Eadgar (959–75), before it was replaced in stone in the eleventh century or later. This Late Norse chapel consisted of a single cell (measuring 5.2m by 3m internally) and was surrounded by a rectangular enclosure which was probably a graveyard (Figure 13.4). The chapel remains stand amongst the earthwork traces of at least thirty rectangular buildings, none of which has been excavated. Their varying orientations suggest several building periods, but there is an overall appearance of organisation. It has been argued by Raymond Lamb that these constituted a Late Norse monastery, but others have suggested that they may just as well be secular and domestic. Indeed, Morris himself prefers an interpretation of Deerness, by analogy with the Brough of Birsay, as being a Viking/Late Norse period settlement with associated private chapel, which could also account for the apparent lack of a large cemetery. Only further excavation of this site can hope to resolve this problem – to reveal its origins.

Lamb has likened the plan of the Brough of Deerness to sites in Shetland at Strandibrough, Birrier of West Sandwick and especially Kame of Isbister. The proposal that these too are Late Norse monasteries likewise remains unchecked by excavation.

The official adoption of Christianity in the Earldom of Orkney in 995 will doubtless have stimulated the construction or renovation of chapels. These chapels would commonly have been built at the initiative of local chieftains, as Morris has postulated for Deerness. More substantial Orcadian examples, from the twelfth century, are provided by the churches associated with the high-status sites of Tuquoy on Westray (p. 195) and of Cubbie Roo's Castle, with the adjacent Bu of Wyre (p. 258); some others, such as Orphir, are described below.

The developing pattern of places of worship and burial in the Northern Isles, some going back to the pre-Norse period, was brought into ecclesiastical order, under parish priests, only in the period following the effective establishment of the Bishopric of Orkney in the mid-eleventh century, as described above (p. 248). As in Norway, priests were assigned to groups of parishes, each of which would have had a 'head-church', with some at least of the local chapels and their graveyards continuing in use. The evidence for Norse church organisation in the Western Isles is more scanty, but seems to have been along similar lines.

The early bishops will have been to some extent peripatetic, with seats on certain farms near the more prominent churches of Orkney, such as Egilsay. However, since the nineteenth century the church ruins on the Brough of Birsay have been identified as Earl Thorfinn's Christchurch built for Bishop Thorolf (Figure 13.5). Although some accept an eleventh-century date for the standing remains (and thus the saga identification), many today prefer to date them to the twelfth century. It has even been suggested that the church and its associated ranges of domestic buildings were monastic, although there is no documentary evidence to confirm or refute this idea. It may well be that Christchurch and the seat of the bishopric were not situated on the Brough itself, but on the mainland opposite, for there is archaeological evidence for an earlier building phase of some sophistication beneath the medieval foundations of the parish church, dedicated to St Magnus, in the modern village of Birsay. The village has itself produced evidence for both Late Norse burial (p. 57) and occupation (p. 190). However, there is also an earlier structural phase beneath the Romanesque church on the Brough which has generally

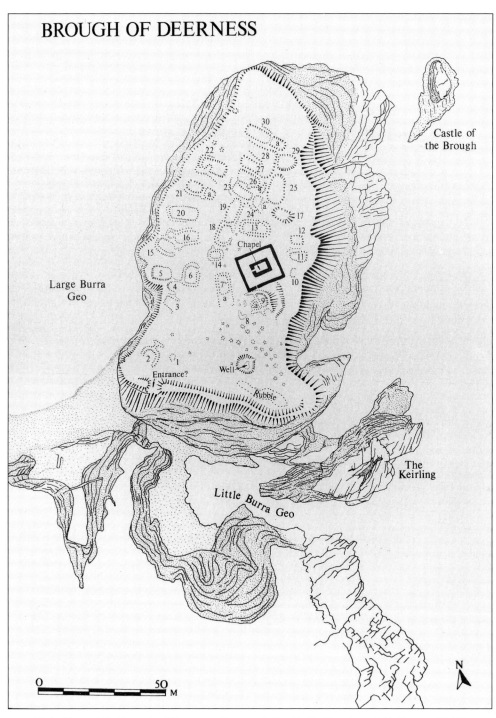

13.4 Plan of the Brough of Deerness, Orkney (after C. D. Morris and N. Emery, 1986).

13.5 The church on the Brough of Birsay, Orkney (Crown copyright: Historic Scotland).

been considered to be of pre-Norse date, although it has recently been suggested that this is not necessarily the case – with the result that the location of Earl Thorfinn's 'minster' remains an open question. Its successor, St Magnus Cathedral in Kirkwall, stands alone in Scandinavian Scotland, in the grandeur of its architecture, so that the history of its construction will be given separate consideration below.

The Brough church is small, with its nave measuring only 8.5m by 5.8m internally, with a square chancel and a semi-circular apse at the east end. The nave has recesses for altars on either side of the chancel arch (in the Norwegian manner), and stone benches along the walls. At the west end, there are traces of a probable square tower, as also seems to have been the case with another twelfth-century Orcadian church, that on Eynhallow, although this has been reduced to a porch. The domestic buildings associated with the church on Eynhallow may well have been those of a monastery.

Several demolished churches in both Orkney and Shetland are known to have had round towers, including that at Skaill, Deerness (p. 194), which was especially grand in having twin towers. The only surviving example of this group is St Magnus Church on Egilsay, the island on which Earl Magnus was martyred in 1116 or 1117. It was once thought that this was the very church in which Magnus prayed before his death, but it more probably dates to the second quarter of the twelfth century and is thus likely to have been built in commemoration of this event when his sanctity was acknowledged, twenty years later. Although now roofless, it is a fine building with its elegant, bottle-shaped tower surviving to a height of 14.9 metres. This is attached to the west end of the rectangular nave which has a square-ended chancel at its east end. The chancel had a barrel-vaulted roof supporting an upper floor, thus providing a chamber perhaps for the use of a visiting bishop or priest.

The architectural inspiration for these round-towered churches of the Northern Isles has often been sought in the contemporary round towers of Ireland, but these are normally free-standing. Round-towered churches are, however, widespread in East Anglia and are also well known in North Germany, where the design appears to have originated, extending into the South Scandinavian area. A North Sea origin thus seems more probable than an Irish connection, in this instance.

An even more distant source provided the ultimate inspiration for the round church associated with the Earl's Bu at Orphir (Figure 13.6). This is unique in Scotland, but belongs to the period after the first crusade in 1099, when there developed an interest in Western Europe in building churches with circular plans inspired by that of the church of the Holy Sepulchre in Jerusalem. In the early twelfth century, Orphir was the seat of the Earl Hakon who had been responsible for the murder of Earl Magnus, shortly after which, according to the saga, he went on pilgrimage to Rome and Jerusalem. If this visit actually took place, it is not improbable that it led to his commissioning the construction of such a round church on his estate in about 1120, although it has recently been suggested that its immediate source may have been Scandinavian.

Only a third of this small church survives, having been largely demolished in 1757, but there is enough to establish that its nave was 5.8m in internal diameter, with a semicircular, barrel-vaulted apse. The 'fine church' at Orphir receives several mentions in *Orkneyinga saga* and also has the remarkable distinction of featuring in one of the runic inscriptions from this site (p. 42).

In contrast to this wealth of twelfth-century ecclesiastical architecture still evident in the landscape of the Earldom of Orkney, there is little to compare it with from the west of Scotland, although there is a similar pattern of small unicameral chapels of uncertain date, as can also be paralleled on the Isle of Man. These drystone or clay-mortared buildings, which may be surrounded by small graveyards, are particularly common on Islay, and many of them are likely to date to the Viking/Late Norse period, from the tenth century onwards. However, as noted by Ian Fisher, these are the lesser ecclesiastical sites which fell out of use and thus a study of the main medieval church sites is also needed in order to build up a full picture of secular worship before the late twelfth century.

The continuity of Iona was considered above from the sculptural evidence, although a chapel which may well date from the Viking/Late Norse period has been excavated beneath St Ronan's Church, itself of late twelfth- or thirteenth-century date. This consists of a small unicameral building of stone, with clay bonded and whitewashed walls. It is unfortunate that we do not know its relationship to a small hoard of gold found during repair work to the church in 1923. This consists of a large part of a fine gold fillet, from a woman's head-dress, and a small part of another which was folded up and wedged, with a scrap of gold wire, inside an elegant finger-ring of Late Norse type. The fillets and ring are well matched by those in the coin-dated hoard from near St Blane's Monastery on the island of Bute which was deposited in the 1150s. St Oran's Chapel on Iona is a mid-twelfth-century building with an ornamented doorway in the Romanesque style, displaying Irish influence.

Another pre-Norse monastic site with evidence for some continuity of use is that on

13.6 View of the round church remains at Earl's Bu, Orphir, Orkney (C. E. Batey).

Eileach an Naoimh in the Garvellach group of islands. Such is indicated by the construction in the inner enclosure of this eremitic settlement of a chapel of clay-mortared stone, similar in size to that on the Brough of Deerness, Orkney, with which it is probably contemporary.

The recent suggestion, by Andrew Fleming and Alex Woolf (from field-survey), that the remains of buildings at Cille Donnain, and on the nearby island of Eilean Mór, together formed an important Late Norse religious and political centre on South Uist has been greeted with some scepticism, even to the identification of the supposed church remains. The attribution of a twelfth-century date to these various structures, which may well belong to more than one period – and thus their identification – can only remain matters of speculation in the absence of any excavation.

The structure identified as a church at Cille Donnain, by Fleming and Woolf, is considered by them to be bicameral in plan, with a square-ended chancel. It might therefore be analogous to a number of churches in the Northern Isles, as well as to that of Teampull Mhuir on Vallay, North Uist – with its probable Late Norse crosses (p. 251) – as well as to a couple of churches on Lewis, all of which have variously been assigned a twelfth-century date.

CASTLES AND STRONGHOLDS

There is evidence from both archaeology and the sagas that defended structures were in use during the Viking period in Scandinavian Scotland, although such are more commonly known from the Late Norse period. According to *Orkneyinga saga*, Earl Sigurd built a *borg*, or fort, at the end of the ninth century, in the south of Moray, presumably locating it there in order to create a power base on the southern frontier of his lands, so far from Orkney. In Taylor's translation:

> He [Sigurd] made an alliance with Thorstein the Red, the son of Olaf the White and Aud the Deep-minded, and they conquered all Caithness and much more of Scotland, and Moray and Ross. And he had a fort built there in the south of Moray.

In the Western Isles, the small defensive structure of early Viking period date excavated at the Udal, North Uist, has already been described (p. 173). Reference has also been made to a small number of native strongholds (both forts and brochs) which have produced a little Norse material. Some will doubtless have served as temporary Viking bases, others as occasional refuges. In the spring of 1153, according to *Orkneyinga saga*:

> Earl Harald made ready to leave Caithness, and sailed north to Shetland. He meant to take the life of Erlend the Younger; for he had sought to marry [his] mother Margaret, but [the Earl] had refused him. After that he got himself a band of men and carried her off from the Orkneys, and conveyed her north to Shetland; and he took up quarters in the Broch of Mousa, where he laid in a large store of provisions.
>
> Now when Earl Harald came to Shetland he took up his position round the Broch and cut off all supplies. But it [was] an awkward place on which to make an assault. Men now came forward and tried to bring them to terms.

A reconciliation was then agreed, allowing Erlend and Margaret to marry. This was, however, not the only time that the Broch (or *borg*) is said to have been used as a Norse love-nest, for it appears in *Egils saga* as a winter-refuge for tenth-century lovers fleeing from Norway, following their shipwreck on Mousa!

A few Norse fortified sites have been identified on the ground through references in the sagas combined with fieldwork. In addition, it is a matter of current debate whether the so-called 'hall-house' structures, as identified at Tuquoy, Westray (p. 196), and at The Wirk, Rousay, may fall into this category. These structures are not referred to specifically in *Orkneyinga saga*, although it has been deduced that Tuquoy, in the twelfth century (with also its church), was the home of the prominent Thorkell Flettir, his heir Haflidi and their family, whereas the home of Sigurd of Westness was situated on Rousay (p. 195). It may well be therefore that both these major buildings formed part of larger complexes rather than having had a specifically defensive function. As they have both been described above, this section will concentrate on those buildings given the name *kastali*, or castle, in *Orkneyinga saga*.

A *kastali* was clearly defensive in nature, consisting of a solid stone tower, which might be surrounded by banks and ditches. The best surviving example is undoubtedly that known as Cubbie Roo's Castle on the island of Wyre, in Orkney, identified as the mid-twelfth-century work of Kolbein Hruga, lying adjacent to the Bu of Wyre: 'At that time there lived [in Wyre in the Orkneys a Norwegian] called Kolbein Hruga, and he was the most outstanding of men. He had a fine stone castle built there; it was a safe stronghold.'

A further reference to this castle on Wyre is contained in *Hákonar saga* (or *Hacon's Saga*, in Dasent's translation), under the year 1231, when the murderers of Earl John of Caithness fled there and 'gathered to them stores enough . . . and kept them in the outworks of the castle. But . . . the friends of the Earl of Orkney . . . gathered a great force . . . and beleaguered the castle. But it was a very unhandy place to attack.'

Today, the imposing ruins on the highest point of Wyre comprise two semicircular ditches, some 2m in depth, surrounding a small mortar-built stone tower, approximately 8.5m square, standing up to a height of 2–3 metres (Figure 13.7). The site underwent a number of phases of development, but the defensive core is thought to be primary, even if the ditches may have been a subsequent addition. Nevertheless, Cubbie Roo's Castle remains the yardstick for the fortified sites of the Late Norse period in northern Scotland.

Three other such structures are given the name *kastali* in *Orkneyinga saga*. One of them was situated in Orkney at a place called *Kjarrekstaðir*, where Earl Harald fled in 1152 during a power dispute; this has been identified with Cairston in the parish of Stromness. In Taylor's translation of the saga:

> Earl Erlend and Sweyn [Swein Asleifsson] and their men leapt ashore after Earl Harald and his men in the castle, and attacked the whole day with both fire and missiles. They made a stout defence and nightfall broke off their encounter. There were many men wounded on either side; and Earl Harald and his men were on the point of surrender, had the attack lasted any longer.

The attribution of this event to Cairston has been studied in detail by Storer Clouston, who even undertook an excavation at the site. Although his arguments seem plausible enough for the square tower there being contemporary with the twelfth-century siege, they have not met with universal acceptance.

A third *kastali* to be mentioned in *Orkneyinga saga* was situated on the little island of

13.7 Aerial view of the remains of Cubbie Roo's Castle on Wyre, Orkney (C. D. Morris).

Damsay, in Orkney, where Swein Asleifsson stayed overnight on Christmas Eve in 1135: 'There was a castle on the island and the keeper of it was a man named Blan . . .'. The saga also contains a reference to 'a large hall' on Damsay, in 1154, but detailed fieldwork is required to identify these structures.

The site of Castle Howe, near the parish church of Holm, in Orkney, was considered by Storer Clouston to be a likely candidate for a Norse defensive structure, possibly related to the Bu of Paplay, although it is not referred to in the sagas. Excavations at this site revealed a substantial rectangular structure overlying a prehistoric chambered cairn. It remains unclear whether this could have been a Late Norse *kastali*, but on balance it seems unlikely. Several other sites in Orkney have also been proposed as the locations for Norse defensive structures, including Stenness church-tower and some excavated foundations on the peninsula of Gernaness in Stenness Loch, but none has met with universal agreement.

Outwith the Orkney islands, there are a small number of defensive sites which may potentially date to the Late Norse period. In Caithness, Eric Talbot has suggested the possibility that the Ring of Castlehill, Bower, may have been an earthwork enclosure of the type recognised at Cubbie Roo's Castle, on Wyre, but lacking the central stone tower. This has an internal diameter of c. 28.5 m, with its bank upstanding to a height of only one metre. It is certainly an unusual feature and could perhaps belong to an Anglo-Norman defensive tradition rather than being a Late Norse construction. Further work is clearly required at this site.

The remaining *kastali* referred to in *Orkneyinga saga* was located at Thurso, in the mid-twelfth century, which makes good political sense. The original Thurso Castle was destroyed in 1198, by King William the Lion, and no trace of it has yet been located.

Elsewhere in Caithness, the location of the defended site of *Lambaborg* has been much discussed. In *Orkneyinga saga* this is called a *borg* (as was Earl Sigurd's fort, noted above), rather than a *kastali*:

> Then Sweyn [Swein Asleifsson] gathers men, and marches to *Lambaborg*, and fortified himself there. This was a fine natural stronghold. And he took up his quarters in it with sixty men, and got in provisions and other necessary stores. The fortress stood on some sea-girt crags, and there was a stoutly built wall before it on the landward side. The crags stretched well out to sea on the other side.

Lambaborg was within marching distance of Duncansby to which Earl Rognvald and his supporters had sailed from Orkney, before laying siege to Swein. Otherwise its precise location on the Caithness coast is debated, but both the Broch of Ness, on the south side of the Bay of Freswick, and Bucholly Castle have been suggested. The evidence for the location and identification of *Lambaborg* is, however, more circumstantial than factual in nature.

A further candidate for a Late Norse defended site in Caithness is the Castle of Old Wick. This consists of a simple keep tower, dominating a rocky promontory, with traces of several other structures. It has no diagnostic dating features, but its simplicity of form provides the strongest argument for placing its construction in the late twelfth or the thirteenth century.

BISHOPS AND CATHEDRALS

After the body of the murdered Earl Magnus was buried at Christchurch in Birsay, it became a focus for pilgrimage and a source of miraculous cures. Thus, in time, Magnus was accepted as a saint, and as a result of instructions supposedly given by him in a dream to a man from Westray, 'Bishop William went east to Kirkwall with a worthy retinue, and carried thither the holy relics of Earl Magnus, and they set the shrine over the high altar in the church'.

As already mentioned, Orkney's first cathedral of Christchurch at Birsay would have been little grander than a palace chapel. It would thus have borne no relation to the architectural grandeur of the Cathedral of St Magnus, its successor in Kirkwall, which drew on the achievements of the Romanesque builders in Norman England. It was, however, only with the construction of this new cathedral that the bishop, in becoming the earthly guardian of a local saint, was settled in one location which thus allowed the organisation of the Church to become more centralised. The bishop's residence at Kirkwall is likely to have been established about 1137, when the building of the new cathedral seems to have got under way, in fulfilment of a vow made by Earl Rognvald – to build a church in Kirkwall to be 'more magnificent' than any in Orkney (in order to house the relics of St Magnus, his uncle, and to become the episcopal seat) – if and when he succeeded in obtaining total personal control over the whole of the earldom.

The choice of Kirkwall for the site of the new cathedral is of interest, but as noted above the relics of St Magnus had already been transferred there by Bishop William, presumably to St Olaf's Church. 'At that time', according to *Orkneyinga saga*, 'the market town in Kirkwall had few houses.' However, there seems to have been an earl's residence there as early as the eleventh century, given that the first mention of Kirkwall in *Orkneyinga saga* (for 1046) states that 'Earl Rognvald took up house in Kirkwall, and there laid in all the stores which he needed for the winter. He had a large following and kept open house.'

Archaeological evidence for the early development of Kirkwall is unfortunately slight. Of St Olaf's, where the relics of St Magnus were doubtless first brought, only one re-positioned Romanesque doorway survives, although an eleventh-century hogback monument was found in the 1970s when a trench was being dug across the old churchyard. The new cathedral seems to have been positioned on a virgin site, although another hogback (also dated by James Lang to the eleventh century) was found amongst debris under the chancel floor during restoration work in 1913.

The initial construction of St Magnus appears to have been undertaken by masters and masons from Durham Cathedral, who seem to have travelled north by way of work on Dunfermline Abbey. The initial speed with which the building was undertaken led to a financial crisis which was only rectified by the earl's outright sale of all the odal lands to their occupants (these had previously reverted to the earl on the death of their owners whose heirs had then had to redeem them each time), with the simultaneous introduction of a tax of one mark for each ploughland payable to the earl. 'And from that time on', according to *Orkneyinga saga*, 'there was no lack of money for the building of the church.' The result of the earl's lavish expenditure was, in the words of Stewart Cruden, that 'the choir, which is the earliest part, is the finest Romanesque work north of Durham which inspired it' (Figure 13.8). As the work progressed it became more elaborate, and Richard

13.8 St Magnus Cathedral, Kirkwall, Orkney: the choir as built about 1140 (Crown copyright: RCAHMS).

Fawcett has concluded that 'both the detailing and scale may be taken as pointers to the likelihood of continuing reliance on masons who reached Orkney through Lowland Scotland'.

The building was originally designed to be a cruciform Romanesque church with an aisled choir and nave, projecting transepts and an apse at the east end. It was, however, under construction for such a long time that this plan came to be modified and enlarged, as architectural styles and liturgical requirements changed. The alterations have included the removal of the original apse in the thirteenth century, for the purpose of extending the aisled choir.

It has been suggested that by about 1150 the work would have been sufficiently far advanced for the church to have been consecrated and for the relics of St Magnus to have been installed in an enriched shrine set in splendour over the high altar. At any rate, in 1151 Earl Rognvald and his bishop departed Orkney on a two-year crusade to the Holy Land.

In 1152/3 a new metropolitan see was established at Nidaros (Trondheim) which covered not just Norway, but also the six Norse dioceses in the West, from Orkney to Greenland, including the Hebrides with the Isle of Man. This binding of Scandinavian Scotland to the homeland within a new Norse archbishopric provides a fitting event with which to conclude this brief survey of Scandinavian Scotland during the Late Norse period, in the midst of what has been characterised as 'Orkney's twelfth-century renaissance'. It provides us also with a possible context for one of the most remarkable and enigmatic archaeological discoveries from the Late Norse period in Scandinavian Scotland – the Lewis chessmen.

THE LEWIS CHESSMEN: A CODA

There are contradictory descriptions of the discovery of the Lewis hoard of chessmen in 1831 and folklore tales of shipwreck and murdered seamen to account for their presence on the island. The pieces seem to have been found in a drystone chamber in the sand-dunes on the south side of Uig Bay. A total of ninety-three pieces are known today, but there may have been more (pawns, in particular), given that they comprise the greater part of four chess-sets, together with fourteen plain counters (for a board-game which was the predecessor of modern draughts) and an ornate belt-buckle (Figure 13.9). They are all carved from walrus ivory, with a few just possibly being from whale's teeth; some were reported to have been stained red on discovery. One can only presume that they represent a merchant's stock, abandoned in unknown circumstances.

13.9 A selection of the walrus-ivory chessmen found on Lewis (NMS).

The kings and queens are seated figures, as are some of the bishops, on thrones which are variously embellished with Romanesque foliate and other designs. The knights and warders are heavily armed. Details of ornament, weapons and dress all point to their having been carved during the second half of the twelfth century. The most recent assessment of the probable artistic milieu for their production, by Neil Stratford for the British Museum, assigns them to Scandinavia – and more particularly to Norway. Stratford's suggestion of Trondheim as a likely place for the workshop in question is much strengthened by the discovery there, in the nineteenth century, of part of a (now lost) queen who would certainly not have looked out of place amongst the Lewis hoard.

If this is indeed so, then the Lewis hoard of walrus-ivory gaming-pieces presents us with tangible archaeological evidence for the reality of the continuing links between Norway and Scandinavian Scotland at this period – links which were indeed to continue well beyond the chronological range of this survey.

SOURCES AND FURTHER READING

The general works listed here fall into two categories: those that deal with the Viking Age as a whole, and those that provide general historical and/or archaeological surveys of Viking/Late Norse period Scotland. Although many of them contain important material relating to topics covered in this book, they are not normally repeated in the further reading listed by chapter.

Full publication details of edited collections of papers are only given on the occasion that the volume is first listed.

THE VIKING AGE

Foote, P. and D. M. Wilson, *The Viking Achievement* (1970; 2nd edn, 1980), London: Sidgwick & Jackson.

Graham-Campbell, J., *Viking Artefacts: A Select Catalogue* (1980), London: British Museum Publications.

Graham-Campbell, J., *The Viking World* (1980; 2nd edn, 1989), London: Frances Lincoln.

Graham-Campbell, J. (ed.), *Cultural Atlas of the Viking World* (1994), Oxford/New York: Facts on File.

Jesch, J., *Women in the Viking Age* (1991), Woodbridge: The Boydell Press.

Jones, G., *A History of the Vikings* (1968; 2nd edn, 1984), Oxford: Oxford University Press.

Haywood, J., *The Penguin Historical Atlas of the Vikings* (1995), Harmondsworth: Penguin Group.

Pulsiano, P. and K. Wolf (eds), *Medieval Scandinavia: An Encyclopedia* (1992), New York: Garland.

Roesdahl, E., *The Vikings* (1991; 2nd edn, 1992), Harmondsworth: Penguin Group.

Roesdahl, E. and D. M. Wilson (eds), *From Viking to Crusader: The Scandinavians and Europe 800–1200* (1992), Copenhagen: Nordic Council of Ministers (The 22nd Council of Europe Exhibition).

Sawyer, B. and P., *Medieval Scandinavia: From Conversion to Reformation, circa 800–1500* (1993), Minneapolis: University of Minnesota Press (The Nordic Series, Vol. 17).

Sawyer, P. H., *Kings and Vikings: Scandinavia and Europe AD 700–1100* (1982), London: Methuen.

Sawyer, P. (ed.), *The Oxford Illustrated History of the Vikings* (1997), Oxford: Oxford University Press.

VIKING/LATE NORSE PERIOD SCOTLAND

Barrow, G. W. S., *Kingship and Unity: Scotland 1000–1306* (1981), London: Edward Arnold (The New History of Scotland, Vol. 2); and (2nd edn, 1989), Edinburgh: Edinburgh University Press.

Batey, C. E., J. Jesch and C. D. Morris (eds), *The Viking Age in Caithness, Orkney and the North*

Atlantic (1993; 1995), Edinburgh: Edinburgh University Press (Select papers from the proceedings of the Eleventh Viking Congress, Thurso and Kirkwall, 1989).

Crawford, B. E., *Scandinavian Scotland* (1987), Leicester: Leicester University Press (Studies in the Early History of Britain: Scotland in the Early Middle Ages, Vol. 2).

Crawford, I. A., 'War or peace – Viking colonisation in the Northern and Western Isles of Scotland reviewed', in H. Bekker-Nielsen, P. Foote and O. Olsen, *Proceedings of the Eighth Viking Congress, Århus, 1977* (1981), Odense: Odense University Press (Medieval Scandinavia Supplements, Vol. 2), pp. 259–69.

Duncan, A. A. M., *Scotland: The Making of the Kingdom* (1975), Edinburgh: Oliver & Boyd (The Edinburgh History of Scotland, Vol. I).

Fenton, A. and H. Pálsson (eds), *The Northern and Western Isles in the Viking World: Survival, Continuity and Change* (1984), Edinburgh: John Donald.

Graham-Campbell, J., *The Viking-Age Gold and Silver of Scotland (AD 850–1100)* (1995), Edinburgh: National Museums of Scotland.

Grieg, S., 'Viking Antiquities in Scotland', in H. Shetelig (ed.), *Viking Antiquities in Great Britain and Ireland*, Part II (1940), Oslo: H. Aschehoug & Co.

McNeill, P. G. B. and H. L. MacQueen (eds), *Atlas of Scottish History to 1707* (1996), Edinburgh: The Scottish Medievalists and Department of Geography, University of Edinburgh.

Ritchie, A., *Viking Scotland* (1993), London: B. T. Batsford/ Historic Scotland.

Smyth, A. P., *Warlords and Holy Men: Scotland AD 80–1000* (1984), London: Edward Arnold (The New History of Scotland, Vol. 1); and (2nd edn, 1989) Edinburgh: Edinburgh University Press.

CHAPTER 1: SCOTLAND BEFORE THE VIKINGS

Alcock, L. and E. A. Alcock, 'Reconnaissance excavations on Early Historic fortifications and other royal sites in Scotland, 1974–84: 4, Excavations at Alt Clut, Clyde Rock, Strathclyde, 1974–5', *Proc. Soc. Antiq. Scot.*, 120 (1990), pp. 95–149.

Alcock, L., *The Neighbours of the Picts: Angles, Britons and Scots at war and at home* (1993), Dornoch: Groam House Lecture.

Armit, I., *The Archaeology of Skye and the Western Isles* (1996), Edinburgh: Edinburgh University Press; see 'Picts and Scots', pp. 159–85.

Ashmore, P. J., 'Low cairns, long cists and symbol stones', *Proc. Soc. Antiq. Scot.*, 110 (1978–80), pp. 346–55.

Ballin-Smith, B. (ed.), *Howe: Four Millennia of Orkney Prehistory* (1994), Edinburgh: Society of Antiquaries of Scotland Monograph Series No. 9.

Clancy, T. O. and G. Markus, *Iona. The Earliest Poetry of a Celtic Monastery* (1995), Edinburgh: Edinburgh University Press; see Part One.

Close-Brooks, J. and R. B. K. Stevenson, *Dark Age Sculpture* (1982), Edinburgh: National Museum of Antiquities Scotland/HMSO.

Cramp, R. (J.), *Whithorn and the Northumbrian Expansion Westwards* (1995), Whithorn: Third Whithorn Lecture, 1994.

Curle, C. L., *Pictish and Norse Finds from the Brough of Birsay 1934–74* (1982), Edinburgh: Society of Antiquaries of Scotland Monograph Series No. 1.

Fisher, I., 'Early Christian archaeology in Argyll', in G. Ritchie (ed.), *The Archaeology of Argyll* (1997), Edinburgh: Edinburgh University Press, pp. 181–204.

Foote, P., 'Pre-Viking contacts between Orkney and Scandinavia', in R. J. Berry and H. N. Firth (eds), *The People of Orkney* (1986), Kirkwall: The Orkney Press (Aspects of Orkney, Vol. 4), pp. 175–86.

Foster, S. M., *Picts, Gaels and Scots* (1996), London: B. T. Batsford/Historic Scotland; see also the references cited therein.

Friell, J. P. and W. G. Watson (eds), *Pictish Studies. Settlement, Burial and Art in Dark Age Northern Britain* (1984), Oxford: BAR Brit. Ser., 125.

Morris, C. D., 'Birsay – a Pictish centre of political and ecclesiastical power', *Studia Celtica*, XXIX (1995), pp. 1–28.

Nicholl, E. (ed.), *A Pictish Panorama* (1995), Balgavies: The Pinkfoot Press.

Ritchie, A., 'Excavation of Pictish and Viking-age farmsteads at Buckquoy, Orkney', *Proc. Soc. Antiq. Scot.*, 108 (1976–7), pp. 174–227.

Ritchie, A., *Perceptions of the Picts: from Eumenius to John Buchan* (1994), Inverness: Groam House Lecture, 1993.

Ritchie, A., *Iona* (1997), London: B. T. Batsford/Historic Scotland.

Small, A. (ed.), *The Picts: A New Look at Old Problems* (1987), Dundee.

Spearman, R. M. and J. Higgitt (eds), *The Age of Migrating Ideas* (1993), Edinburgh: National Museums of Scotland /Alan Sutton Publishing.

Sutherland, E., *In Search of the Picts. A Celtic Dark Age Nation* (1994), London: Constable.

Thomas, C., *Whithorn's Christian Beginnings* (1992), Whithorn: First Whithorn Lecture, 1992.

Wainwright, F. T. (ed.), *The Problem of the Picts* (1955), Edinburgh and London: Nelson.

Weber, B., 'Norwegian reindeer antler export to Orkney. An analysis of combs from Pictish/early Norse sites', *Universitetets Oldsaksamlings Arbok 1991/1992* (1993), Oslo, pp. 161–74.

Youngs, S. (ed.), *'The Work of Angels': Masterpieces of Celtic Metalwork, 6th–9th Centuries* AD (1989), London: British Museum Publications.

CHAPTER 2: THE NORWEGIAN BACKGROUND

See 'The Viking Age' section (above) which includes much material on Norway, and also the following works (in English):

Clarke, H. and B. Ambrosiani, *Towns in the Viking Age* (1991; 2nd edn, 1995), London: Leicester University Press.

Helle, K., 'Norway, 800–1200', in A. Faulkes and R. Perkins (eds), *Viking Revaluations: Viking Society Centenary Symposium, 14–15 May 1992* (1993), London: Viking Society for Northern Research (University College London), pp. 1–14.

Hårdh, B., *Silver in the Viking Age: A Regional-Economic Study* (1996), Stockholm: Almquist & Wiksell International (= *Acta Archaeologica Lundensia*, Series in 8°, No. 25).

Lund, N. (ed.), *Two Voyagers at the Court of King Alfred* (1984), York: William Sessions.

Page, R. I., *Runes* (1987), London: British Museum Press.

Page, R. I., *Norse Myths* (1990), London: British Museum Press.

Sjøvold, T., *The Iron Age Settlement of Arctic Norway*, Vol. 2 (1974), Tromsø: Universitetsforlaget.

Skaare, K., *Coins and Coinage in Viking-Age Norway* (1976), Oslo: Universitetsforlaget.

Wilson, D. and O. Klindt-Jensen, *Viking Art* (1966), London: George Allen & Unwin; and (2nd edn, 1980), Minneapolis: University of Minnesota Press (The Nordic Series, Vol. 6).

CHAPTER 3: SOURCES FOR SCANDINAVIAN SCOTLAND

The following references are, for the most part, to general studies relating to Scandinavian Scotland published since Crawford, *Scandinavian Scotland* (1987), with those of a more specific nature being cited in connection with the relevant chapters below.

Language, personal and place-names

Barnes, M., 'Norse in the British Isles', in Faulkes and Perkins (eds), *Viking Revaluations* (1993), pp. 65–84.

Crawford, B. E. (ed.), *Scandinavian Settlement in North Britain: Thirteen Studies of Place-Names in their Historical Context* (1995), London: Leicester University Press (Studies in the Early History of Britain Series).

Fellows-Jensen, G., 'Viking settlement in the Northern and Western Isles – the place-name evidence as seen from Denmark and the Danelaw', in Fenton and Pálsson (eds), *The Northern and Western Isles in the Viking World* (1984), pp. 148–68.

Fellows-Jensen, G., *The Vikings and their Victims: the Verdict of the Names* (1995), London: The Viking Society for Northern Research (University College London: The Dorothea Coke Memorial Lecture in Northern Studies).

MacDonald, A., 'On "papar" names in N. and W. Scotland', *Northern Studies*, 9 (1977), pp. 25–30.

Nicolaisen, W. F. H., *Scottish Place-Names: their Study and Significance* (1976), London: B. T. Batsford.

Nicolaisen, W. F. H., 'The Viking Settlement of Scotland: evidence of place-names', in R. T. Farrell (ed.), *The Vikings* (1982), Chichester: Phillimore & Co, pp. 95–115.

Waugh, D. J., 'Place-name evidence for Scandinavian settlement in Shetland', *ROSC: Review of Scottish Culture*, 7 (1991), pp. 15–23.

Runic inscriptions

Barnes, M. P., 'Towards an edition of the Scandinavian runic inscriptions of the British Isles: some thoughts', *Northern Studies*, 29 (1992), pp. 32–42.

Barnes, M. P., 'The interpretation of the runic inscriptions of Maeshowe', in Batey et al. (eds), *The Viking Age in Caithness, Orkney and the North Atlantic* (1993), pp. 349–69.

Barnes, M. P., *The Runic Inscriptions of Maeshowe, Orkney* (1994), Uppsala: Institutionen för nordiska språk, Uppsala universitet (= Runrön, 8).

Hagland, J. R., 'Two runic inscriptions from Orphir, Orkney', in Batey et al. (eds), *The Viking Age in Caithness, Orkney and the North Atlantic* (1993), pp. 370–4.

Liestøl, A., 'Runes', in Fenton and Pálsson (eds), *The Northern and Western Isles in the Viking World* (1984), pp. 224–38.

Olsen, M., 'Runic inscriptions in Great Britain, Ireland and the Isle of Man', in H. Shetelig (ed.), *Viking Antiquities in Great Britain and Ireland*, Part VI (1954), Oslo: H. Aschehoug & Co., pp. 151–233.

Documentary sources

In addition to Crawford, *Scandinavian Scotland* (1987), with references therein, see especially:

Anderson, A. O. (trans.), *Early Sources of Scottish History, A.D. 500 to 1286*, 2 vols (1922), Edinburgh: Oliver and Boyd; and (2nd edn, 1990), Stamford: Paul Watkins.

Pálsson, H. and P. Edwards (trans.), *Orkneyinga Saga: The History of the Earls of Orkney* (1981), Harmondsworth: Penguin Group.

Taylor, A. B. (trans.), *The Orkneyinga Saga* (1938), Edinburgh: Oliver and Boyd.

Oral tradition

MacDonald, D. A., 'The Vikings in Gaelic oral tradition', in Fenton and Pálsson (eds), *The Northern and Western Isles in the Viking World* (1984), pp. 265–79.
Almqvist, B., 'Scandinavian and Celtic folklore contact in the Earldom of Orkney', in Berry and Firth (eds), *The People of Orkney* (1986), pp. 187–208.

Archaeology, environment and physical anthropology

In addition to the general works listed above, see also those cited below with reference to Chapters 4–13, as well as:

Berry, R., 'The saga of the field mouse', *New Scientist*, 65 (1975), pp. 624–6.
Brothwell, D., D. Tills and V. Muir, 'Biological characteristics', in Berry and Firth (eds), *The People of Orkney* (1986), pp. 54–88.
Grieg, S., 'Viking Antiquities in Scotland' = H. Shetelig (ed.), *Viking Antiquities in Great Britain and Ireland*, Part II (1940).
Morris, C. D., 'The Vikings in the British Isles: some aspects of their settlement and economy', in Farrell (ed.), *The Vikings* (1982), pp. 70–94.
Reid, R. W., 'Remains of Saint Magnus and Saint Rognvald, entombed in St Magnus Cathedral, Kirkwall, Orkney', *Biometrika*, 18 (1926), pp. 118–50.
Roberts, D. F., 'Genetic affinities', in Berry and Firth (eds), *The People of Orkney* (1986), pp. 89–106.

CHAPTERS 4–6: REGIONAL SURVEYS, PARTS I–III

The references for Chapters 4–6 are, for the most part, to regional studies published since Crawford, *Scandinavian Scotland* (1987), but they include some earlier works of continuing significance. In addition, specific references for settlement-sites and pagan Norse graves of particular importance are listed under Chapters 7–10, whereas the main references for the hoards and single finds of gold and silver are to be found under Chapter 12.

Chapter 4: Northern Scotland

Batey, C. E., 'Viking and Late Norse Caithness: the archaeological evidence', in J. Knirk (ed.), *Proceedings of the Tenth Viking Congress, Larkollen, Norway, 1985* (1987), Oslo: Universitetets Oldsaksamlings Skrifter, Ny rekke, Nr. 9, pp. 131–48.
Batey, C. E., 'Picts and Vikings in Caithness and Sutherland: a resumé', in C. Karkov and R. T. Farrell (eds), *Studies in Insular Art and Archaeology* (1991), Miami, Ohio: American Early Medieval Studies, Vol. 1, pp. 49–60.
Batey, C. E., J. Jesch and C. D. Morris (eds), *The Viking Age in Caithness, Orkney and the North Atlantic* (1993), as cited above.
Crawford, B. E., *Earl and Mormaer: Norse-Pictish Relationships in Northern Scotland* (1995), Rosemarkie: Groam House Lecture, 1994.
Crawford, B. E. (ed.), *Scandinavian Settlement in North Britain* (1995), contains four papers on aspects of the place-names of Shetland, Orkney, Caithness and Sutherland.
Hunter, R. J. and S. J. Dockrill, 'Some Norse sites on Sanday, Orkney', *Proc. Soc. Antiq. Scot.*, 112 (1982), pp. 570–6; this includes the Lamba Ness and Ness of Brough burials.
Morris, C. D., 'Viking Orkney: a survey', in C. Renfrew (ed.), *The Prehistory of Orkney, BC*

4000–1000 AD (1985; 2nd edn, 1990), Edinburgh: Edinburgh University Press, pp. 210–42.

Morris, C. D., 'Native and Norse in Orkney and Shetland', in Karkov and Farrell (eds), *Studies in Insular Art and Archaeology* (1991), pp. 61–80.

Morris, C. D. and D. J. Rackham (eds), *Norse and Later Settlement and Subsistence in the North Atlantic* (1992), Glasgow: University of Glasgow (Dept of Archaeology Occasional Paper Series, No. 1).

Thomson, W. P. L., *History of Orkney* (1987), Edinburgh: The Mercat Press.

Wainwright, F. T. (ed.), *The Northern Isles* (1962), Edinburgh: Thomas Nelson and Sons; see especially F. T. Wainwright, 'The Scandinavian settlement', pp. 117–62.

Waugh, D. J. (ed.), *Shetland's Northern Links: Language and History* (1996), Edinburgh: Scottish Society for Northern Studies.

Chapter 5: The West Highlands and Islands

Andersen, P. S., 'Norse settlement in the Hebrides: what happened to the natives and what happened to the Norse immigrants?', in I. Wood and N. Lund (eds), *People and Places in Northern Europe 500–1600: Essays in Honour of Peter Hayes Sawyer* (1991), Woodbridge: The Boydell Press, pp. 131–47.

Armit, I., *The Archaeology of Skye and the Western Isles* (1996), Chapter 10, 'The Vikings', pp. 186–204.

Beveridge, E. and J. G. Callander, 'Earth-houses at Garry Iochdrach and Bac Mhic Connain, in North Uist', *Proc. Soc. Antiq. Scot.*, 66 (1931–2), pp. 32–66.

Brown, M. M., 'The Norse in Argyll', in G. Ritchie (ed.), *The Archaeology of Argyll* (1977), pp. 205–35.

Cowie, T. et al., 'Excavations at Barvas, Lewis', forthcoming.

Crawford, I. A., 'Scot (?), Norseman and Gael', *Scottish Archaeological Forum*, 6 (1974), pp. 1–16.

Dunwell, A. J., T. G. Cowie, M. F. Bruce, T. Neighbour and A. R. Rees, 'A Viking Age cemetery at Cnip, Uig, Isle of Lewis', *Proc. Soc. Antiq. Scot.*, 125 (1995), pp. 719–52.

Fraser, I., 'The place-names of Lewis – the Norse evidence', *Northern Studies*, 14 (1974), pp. 11–21.

Fraser, I., 'Norse settlement on the north-west seaboard', in Crawford (ed.), *Scandinavian Settlement in North Britain* (1995), pp. 92–105.

Gordon, K., 'A Norse Viking-age grave from Cruach Mhor, Islay', *Proc. Soc. Antiq. Scot.*, 120 (1990), pp. 151–60.

Lane, A., 'Dark Age and Viking Age pottery from the Hebrides, with special reference to the Udal, North Uist' (unpublished Ph.D. thesis, University College London, 1983).

Lane, A., 'Hebridean pottery: problems of definition, chronology, presence and absence', in I. Armit (ed.), *Beyond the Brochs* (1990), Edinburgh: Edinburgh University Press, pp. 108–30.

McDonald, R. A., *The Kingdom of the Isles: Scotland's Western Seaboard c.1100–c.1336* (1997), East Linton: Tuckwell Press (Scottish Historical Review Monograph Series, No. 4).

MacLeod, D. J., W. J. Gibson and J. Curle, 'An account of a find of ornaments of the Viking time from Valtos, Uig, in the Island of Lewis', *Proc. Soc. Antiq. Scot.*, 50 (1915–16), pp. 181–9.

MacPherson, N., 'Notes on antiquities from the island of Eigg', *Proc. Soc. Antiq. Scot.*, 12 (1876–8), pp. 577–97.

Olson, D. K., 'Norse settlement in the Hebrides, an interdisciplinary study' (unpublished graduate thesis, University of Oslo, 1983); as cited in Andersen, 'Norse settlement in the Hebrides . . .', in Wood and Lund (eds), *People and Places in Northern Europe 500–1600* (1991), pp. 131–47.

RCAHMS, *Argyll: an Inventory of the Ancient Monuments*; Vol. 3: *Mull, Tiree, Coll and Northern Argyll* (1980); Vol. 4: *Iona* (1982); Vol. 5: *Islay, Jura, Colonsay and Oronsay* (1984), Edinburgh: HMSO.

RCAHMS, *Inventory of Monuments and Constructions in the Outer Hebrides, Skye and the Small Isles* (1928), Edinburgh: HMSO.

Taylor, A. B., 'The Norsemen in St Kilda', *Saga-Book*, 17 (1967–8), pp. 116–44.

Welander, R. D. E., C. Batey and T. G. Cowie, 'A Viking burial from Kneep, Uig, Isle of Lewis', *Proc. Soc. Antiq. Scot.*, 117 (1987), pp. 149–74.

Chapter 6: South-west, central, eastern and southern Scotland

Alcock, L. and E. A., 'Excavations at Alt Clut, Clyde Rock, Strathclyde, 1974–5', *Proc. Soc. Antiq. Scot.*, 120 (1990), pp. 95–149; see especially p. 117.

Crawford, B. E. (ed.), *Scandinavian Settlement in North Britain* (1995), contains several relevant papers, including S. Taylor, 'The Scandinavians in Fife and Kinross: the onomastic evidence', pp. 141–67.

Dumville, D. N., *The Churches of North Britain in the First Viking-Age* (1997), Whithorn: Fifth Whithorn Lecture, 1996.

Lang, J. T., 'Hogback monuments in Scotland', *Proc. Soc. Antiq. Scot.*, 105 (1972–4), pp. 206–35.

Nicolaisen, W. F. H., 'Arran place names. A fresh look', *Northern Studies*, 28 (1992), pp. 1–13.

Oram, R. D. and G. P. Stell (eds), *Galloway: Land and Lordship* (1991), Edinburgh: Scottish Society for Northern Studies; contains several important papers on Scandinavian settlement in the south-west, including D. J. Craig on 'Pre-Norman sculpture in Galloway: some territorial implications', pp. 45–62, E. J. Cowan on 'The Vikings in Galloway: a review of the evidence', pp. 63–75, and G. Fellows-Jensen on 'Scandinavians in Dumfriesshire and Galloway: the place-name evidence', pp. 77–95.

Ritchie, A. (ed.), *Govan and its Early Medieval Sculpture* (1994), Stroud: Alan Sutton Publishing; see especially B. E. Crawford, 'The "Norse background" to the Govan hogbacks', pp. 103–12.

Ireland

Almqvist, B. and D. Greene (eds), *Proceedings of the Seventh Viking Congress, Dublin, August 1973* (1976), Dublin: Royal Irish Academy.

Bøe, J., 'Norse Antiquities in Ireland', in H. Shetelig (ed.), *Viking Antiquities in Great Britain and Ireland*, Part III (1940), Oslo: H. Aschehoug & Co.

Clarke, H. B., M. Ní Mhaonaigh and R. Ó Floinn (eds), *Ireland and Scandinavia in the Early Viking Age* (1998), Dublin: Four Courts Press.

Graham-Campbell, J., 'A Viking-age silver hoard from near Raphoe, Co. Donegal', in P. Wallace and G. MacNiocaill (eds), *Keimelia: Studies in Medieval Archaeology and History in Memory of Tom Delaney* (1988), Galway: Galway University Press, pp. 102–11.

Isle of Man

Bersu, G. and D. M. Wilson, *Three Viking Graves in the Isle of Man* (1966), London: Society of Medieval Archaeology Monograph Series, No. 1.

Fell, C., P. Foote, J. Graham-Campbell and R. Thomson (eds), *The Viking Age in the Isle of Man* (1983), London: Viking Society for Northern Research (Select papers from The Ninth Viking Congress, Isle of Man, July 1981).

Freke, D., *The Peel Castle Dig* (1995), Douglas: The Friends of Peel Castle.

Graham-Campbell, J., 'The Irish Sea vikings: raiders and settlers', in T. Scott and P. Starkey (eds), *The Middle Ages in the North-West* (1995), Oxford: Leopard's Head Press/Liverpool Centre for Medieval Studies, pp. 59–83.

Wilson, D. M., *The Viking Age in the Isle of Man. The Archaeological Evidence* (1974), Odense: Odense University Press (C.C. Rafn Lecture, No. 3).

CHAPTERS 7 AND 8: PAGAN NORSE GRAVES

The pagan Norse graves of Scotland are in the course of being fully catalogued, for the first time since 1925, by James Graham-Campbell and Caroline Paterson for publication by the National Museums of Scotland. In the meantime, the main source remains:

Grieg, S., 'Viking Antiquities in Scotland', in H. Shetelig (ed.), *Viking Antiquities in Great Britain and Ireland*, Part II (1940), Oslo; with discussion by H. Shetelig, 'The Viking graves', in H. Shetelig (ed.), *Viking Antiquities in Great Britain and Ireland*, Part VI (1954), Oslo, pp. 65–111; following that by A.W. Brøgger:

Brøgger, A. W., *Ancient Emigrants. A History of the Norse Settlements of Scotland* (1929), Oxford: The Clarendon Press, in Chapter 5, 'Archaeological remarks', pp. 95–134; but see now:

Eldjárn, K., 'Graves and grave goods: survey and evaluation', in Fenton and Pálsson (eds), *The Northern and Western Isles in the Viking World* (1984), pp. 2–11; and for a recent map:

Crawford, B. E., 'Viking graves', in McNeill and MacQueen (eds), *Atlas of Scottish History to 1707* (1996), p. 71.

Recent regional reviews include:

Armit, I., *The Archaeology of Skye and the Western Isles* (1996); see the section on 'Burials' in Chapter 10, 'The Vikings', pp. 186–204, at pp. 195-202.

Batey, C. E., 'The Viking and Late Norse graves of Caithness and Sutherland', in Batey et al. (eds), *The Viking Age in Caithness, Orkney and the North Atlantic* (1993), pp. 148–64.

Brown, M. M., 'The Norse in Argyll', in Ritchie (ed.), *The Archaeology of Argyll* (1977), pp. 205–35; for burials, see pp. 208–30.

The following are the principal additional references for the graves considered in Chapter 7, in the order of their discussion:

Càrn a' Bharraich, Oronsay

McNeill, M., 'Notice of excavations in a burial-mound of the Viking time in Oronsay', *Proc. Soc. Antiq. Scot.*, 25 (1890–1), pp. 432–5.

Anderson, J., 'Notice of bronze brooches and personal ornaments from a ship-burial of the Viking time in Oronsay . . .', *Proc. Soc. Antiq. Scot.*, 41 (1906–7), pp. 437–50, at pp. 437–41.

Grieve, S., 'Note upon Carn nan Bharraich, or Cairn of the Men of Barra, a burial mound of the Viking time on the island of Oronsay, Argyllshire . . .', *Proc. Soc. Antiq. Scot.*, 48 (1913–14), pp. 272–91, at pp. 272–9.

Curle, J., 'On recent Scandinavian grave finds from the island of Oronsay . . .', *Proc. Soc. Antiq. Scot.*, 48 (1913–14), pp. 292–315, at pp. 292–5.

Kiloran Bay, Colonsay

Anderson, J., 'Notice of bronze brooches . . . with a description . . . of a ship-burial of the Viking time at Kiloran Bay, Colonsay', *Proc. Soc. Antiq. Scot.*, 41 (1906–7), pp. 437–50, at pp. 443–9.

Ballinaby, Islay

Anderson, J., 'Notes on the contents of two Viking graves in Islay...', *Proc. Soc. Antiq. Scot.*, 14 (1879–80), pp. 51–69.

Edwards, A. J. H., 'A Viking cist-grave at Ballinaby, Islay', *Proc. Soc. Antiq. Scot.*, 68 (1933–4), pp. 74–8.

Reay, Caithness

Curle, J., 'On recent Scandinavian grave finds from the island of Oronsay and from Reay, Caithness...', *Proc. Soc. Antiq. Scot.*, 48 (1913–14), pp. 292–315, at pp. 295–9.

Edwards, A. J. H., 'Excavations of graves at Ackergill and of an earth-house at Freswick Links, Caithness, and a description of the discovery of a Viking grave at Reay, Caithness', *Proc. Soc. Antiq. Scot.*, 61 (1926–7), pp. 196–209, at pp. 202–7 and 208–9.

Edwards, A. J. H., 'Excavations at Reay Links and at a horned cairn at Lower Dounreay, Caithness', *Proc. Soc. Antiq. Scot.*, 63 (1926–7), pp. 138–50, at pp. 138–40.

Gurness, Orkney

Robertson, W. N., 'A Viking grave found at the Broch of Gurness, Aikerness, Orkney', *Proc. Soc. Antiq. Scot.*, 101 (1968–9), pp. 289–90.

Hedges, J. W., *Bu, Gurness and the Brochs of Orkney. Part II: Gurness* (1987), Oxford: BAR Brit. Ser., 164; see especially pp. 72–3 and 86–7.

Pierowall, Westray

RCAHMS, *Inventory of the Ancient Monuments of Orkney and Shetland*, Vol. II: *Inventory of Orkney* (1946), Edinburgh: HMSO, pp. 353–5 (nos 1045–6).

Thorsteinsson, A., 'The Viking burial place at Pierowall, Westray, Orkney', in B. Niclasen (ed.), *The Fifth Viking Congress: Tórshavn, July 1965* (1968), Tórshavn, pp. 150–73.

Westness, Rousay

RCAHMS, *Inventory of Orkney* (1946), p. 580 (no. 579).

Kaland, S. H. H., 'The settlement of Westness, Rousay', in Batey *et al.* (eds), *The Viking Age in Caithness, Orkney and the North Atlantic* (1993), pp. 308–17, at pp. 312–17.

Scar, Sanday

Owen, O. and M. Dalland, 'Scar, Sanday: a Viking boat-burial from Orkney. An interim report', in Ambrosiani and Clarke (eds), *The Twelfth Viking Congress* (1994), pp. 159–72.

Balnakeil, Sutherland

Gourlay, R., D. Low and C. E. Batey, 'The Viking grave at Balnakeil, Durness, Sutherland', in J. Baldwin (ed.), *Strathnaver and the Northlands of Sutherland*, forthcoming.

Additional quotations in Chapter 8 are from:

Page, R. I., *Norse Myths* (1990), p. 61.

Wormald, C. P., 'Viking studies: whence and whither?', in Farrell (ed.), *The Vikings* (1982), pp. 128–53, at p. 132.

Hultgård, A., 'Ragnarok and Valhalla: eschatological beliefs among the Scandinavians of the Viking Period', in Ambrosiani and Clarke (eds), *The Twelfth Viking Congress* (1994), pp. 288–93, at p. 292.

CHAPTERS 9 AND 10: VIKING/LATE NORSE PERIOD SETTLEMENTS

Shetland

Jarlshof

Bigelow, G. F., 'Sandwick, Unst and late Norse Shetland economy', in B. Smith (ed.), *Shetland Archaeology: New Work in Shetland in the 1970s* (1985), Lerwick: Shetland Times, pp. 95–127.

Hamilton, J. R. C., *Excavations at Jarlshof, Shetland* (1956), Edinburgh: Ministry of Works Archaeological Report No. 1.

Small, A., 'The historical geography of the Norse colonization of the Scottish Highlands', *Norsk geografisk tidskrift*, 22 (1968), pp. 1–16.

Underhoull, Unst

Small, A., 'Excavations at Underhoull, Unst, Shetland', *Proc. Soc. Antiq. Scot.*, 98 (1964–6), pp. 225–45.

The Biggings, Papa Stour

Crawford, B. E., 'The Biggings, Papa Stour – a multi-disciplinary investigation', in Smith (ed.), *Shetland Archaeology* (1985), pp. 128–58.

Crawford, B. E., 'Papa Stour: survival, continuity and change in one Shetland island', in Fenton and Pálsson (eds), *The Northern and Western Isles in the Viking World* (1994), pp. 40–58.

Crawford, B. E., 'Excavations at the Biggings, Papa Stour, Shetland', in G. F. Bigelow (ed.), *The Norse of the North Atlantic* (= *Acta Archaeologica*, 61, 1990) (1991), pp. 36–43.

Crawford, B. E. and B. Ballin-Smith, *The Biggings: Excavation of a Royal Norwegian Farm, Papa Stour, Shetland* (1998, forthcoming).

Sandwick, Unst

Bigelow, G. F., 'Sandwick, Unst and late Norse Shetland economy', in Smith (ed.), *Shetland Archaeology* (1985), pp. 95–127.

Bigelow, G. F., 'Domestic architecture in Medieval Shetland', *ROSC: Review of Scottish Culture*, 3 (1987), pp. 23–38.

Bigelow, G. F., 'Life in Medieval Shetland: an archaeological perspective', *Hikuin*, 15 (1989), pp. 193–206.

Orkney

Buckquoy, Birsay

Ritchie, A., 'Excavation of Pictish and Viking-age farmsteads at Buckquoy, Orkney', *Proc. Soc. Antiq. Scot.*, 108 (1976–7), pp. 174–227.

Birsay (including Beachview)

Cruden, S. H., 'Earl Thorfinn the Mighty and the Brough of Birsay', in K. Eldjárn (ed.), *Third Viking Congress, Reykjavík 1956* (1958), Reykjavík, pp. 156–62.

Curle, C. L., *The Pictish and Norse Finds from the Brough of Birsay 1934–74* (1982), Edinburgh: Society of Antiquaries of Scotland Monograph Series No. 1.

Donaldson, A. M., C. D. Morris and D. J. Rackham, 'The Birsay Bay Project: preliminary investigations into the past exploitation of the coastal environment of Birsay, Mainland Orkney', in D. Brothwell and G. W. Dimbleby (eds) *Environmental Aspects of Coasts and Islands* (1981), Oxford: BAR Int. Ser., 94, pp. 65–85.

Hunter, J. R., *Rescue Excavations on the Brough of Birsay 1974–82* (1986), Edinburgh: Society of Antiquaries of Scotland Monograph Series No. 4.

Hunter, J. R. and C. D. Morris, 'Recent Excavations at the Brough of Birsay, Orkney', in Bekker-Nielsen *et al.* (eds), *Proceedings of the Eighth Viking Congress* (1981), pp. 254–8.

Lamb, R. G., 'The Cathedral of Christchurch and the Monastery of Birsay', *Proc. Soc. Antiq. Scot.*, 105 (1972–4), pp. 200–5.

Morris, C. D., *Church and Monastery in the Far North: An Archaeological Evaluation* (1990), Jarrow: Jarrow Lecture 1989.

Morris, C. D. and D. J. Rackham, 'Birsay Bay, Orkney: human exploitation of natural and agricultural resources', *Hikuin*, 15 (1989), pp. 207–22.

Morris, C. D., *The Birsay Bay Project. Volume 1. Brough Road Excavations 1976–1982* (1989), Durham: University of Durham, Department of Archaeology Monograph Series No. 1.

Morris, C. D., *The Birsay Bay Project. Volume 2. Sites in Birsay Village [Beachview] and on the Brough of Birsay, Orkney* (1996), Durham: University of Durham, Department of Archaeology Monograph Series No. 2.

Orkney Heritage, 2 (1983), on 'Birsay: a centre of political and ecclesiastical power'; see articles by R. G. Cant; C. A. R. Radford; R. G. Lamb; A. Ritchie; C. L. Curle; P. D. Anderson; B. E. Crawford; C. D. Morris; and J. R. Hunter.

Saevar Howe

Hedges, J. W., 'Trial excavations on Pictish and Viking settlements at Saevar Howe, Birsay, Orkney', *Glasgow Archaeological Journal*, 10 (1983), pp. 73–124 and Microfiche 40–102.

Skaill, Deerness

Gelling, P. S., 'The Norse buildings at Skaill, Deerness, Orkney, and their immediate predecessor', in Fenton and Pálsson (eds), *The Northern and Western Isles in the Viking World* (1984), pp. 12–39.

Gelling, P. S., 'Excavations at Skaill, Deerness', in Renfrew (ed.), *The Prehistory of Orkney BC 4000–1000 AD* (1985/1990), pp. 176–82.

Buteux, S., *Settlements at Skaill, Deerness, Orkney. Excavations by Peter Gelling of the Prehistoric, Pictish, Viking and Later Periods, 1963–1981* (1997), Oxford: BAR. Brit. Ser., 260.

Pool, Sanday

Hunter, J. R., 'Pool, Sanday, a case study for the Late Iron Age and Viking periods', in Armit (ed.), *Beyond the Brochs* (1990), pp. 175–93.

Hunter, J. R., J. M. Bond and A. N. Smith, 'Some aspects of early Viking settlement in Orkney', in Batey et al. (eds), *The Viking Age in Caithness, Orkney and the North Atlantic* (1993), pp. 272–84.

Hunter, J. R., 'The Early Norse Period', in K. J. Edwards and I. B. M. Ralston (eds), *Scotland, Environment and Archaeology 8000 BC – AD 1000* (1997), Chichester, pp. 241–54.

Orphir

Batey, C. E. with C. E. Freeman, 'Lavacroon, Orphir, Orkney', *Proc. Soc. Antiq. Scot.*, 116 (1986), pp. 285–300 and Microfiche 5, A3–D9.

Batey, C. E. with C. D. Morris, 'Earl's Bu, Orphir, Orkney: excavation of a Norse horizontal mill', in Morris and Rackham (eds), *Norse and Later Settlement* (1992), pp. 33–41.

Batey, C. E., 'A Norse horizontal mill in Orkney', *ROSC: Review of Scottish Culture*, 8 (1993), pp. 20–8.

Johnston, A. W., 'Notes on the Earls' Bu at Orphir, Orkney, called Orfjara in the sagas, and on the remains of the round church there', *Proc. Soc. Antiq. Scot.*, 37 (1902–3), pp. 16–31.

Westness, Rousay

Kaland, S. H. H., 'The settlement of Westness, Rousay', in Batey et al. (eds), *The Viking Age in Caithness, Orkney and the North Atlantic* (1993), pp. 308–17.

Tuquoy, Westray

Owen, O. A., *Tuquoy, Orkney: A Large Norse and Medieval Farm-Settlement* (forthcoming).

Owen, O. A. and J. McKinnell, 'A runic inscription from Tuquoy, Westray, Orkney', *Medieval Archaeology*, xxxiii (1989), pp. 53–9.

Owen, O. A., 'Tuquoy, Westray, Orkney: a challenge for the future', in Batey et al. (eds), *The Viking Age in Caithness, Orkney and the North Atlantic* (1993), pp. 318–39.

Caithness

Freswick Links

Batey, C. E., *Freswick Links, Caithness. A Re-appraisal of the Late Norse Site in its Context* (1987), Oxford: BAR, Brit. Ser., 179, 2 vols.

Batey, C. E., 'Recent work at Freswick Links, Caithness, northern Scotland', *Hikuin*, 15 (1989), pp. 223–30.

Batey, C. E., C. D. Morris and D. J. Rackham, 'Freswick Castle, Caithness, report on rescue excavations carried out in 1979', *Glasgow Archaeological Journal*, 11 (1984), pp. 83–118 and Microfiche 114–235.

Childe, V. G., 'Another late Viking house at Freswick, Caithness', *Proc. Soc. Antiq. Scot.*, 77 (1942–3), pp. 5–17.

Curle, A. O., 'A Viking settlement at Freswick, Caithness. Report on excavations carried out in 1937 and 1938', *Proc. Soc. Antiq. Scot.*, 73 (1938–9), pp. 71–110.

Morris, C. D., C. E. Batey and D. J. Rackham, *Freswick Links, Caithness. Excavation and Survey of a Norse Settlement* (1995), Inverness and New York: Highland Libraries in association with the North Atlantic Biocultural Organisation.

Robert's Haven

Barrett, J. H., 'Robert's Haven', *Discovery and Excavation in Scotland 1992* (1993), Edinburgh: Council for Scottish Archaeology, pp. 40–1.

Barrett, J. H., 'Robert's Haven', *Discovery and Excavation in Scotland 1993* (1994), Edinburgh: Council for Scottish Archaeology, pp. 42–3.

Morris, C. D., C. E. Batey and J. H. Barrett, 'The Viking and Early Settlement Archaeological Research Project: past, present and future', in Ambrosiani and Clarke (eds), *The Twelfth Viking Congress* (1994), pp. 144–58.

Western Isles

The Udal, North Uist

Crawford, I. A., 'Scot(?), Norseman and Gael', *Scottish Archaeological Forum*, 6 (1974), pp. 1–16.

Graham-Campbell, J. A., 'A preliminary note on certain finds of Viking Age date from the Udal excavations, North Uist', *Scottish Archaeological Forum*, 6 (1974), pp. 17–22.

Crawford, I. A. and V. R. Switsur, 'Sandscaping and C14: the Udal, North Uist', *Antiquity*, 51 (1977), pp. 124–36.

Crawford, I. A., *The West Highlands and Islands: A View of 50 Centuries. The Udal (N. Uist) Evidence* (1986), Cambridge: The Great Auk Press.

Crawford, I. A., 'Structural discontinuity and associable evidence for settlement disruption: five crucial episodes in a continuous occupation 250–1689 (the Udal evidence)', in R. Mason (ed.), *Settlement and Society in Scotland: Migration, Colonisation and Integration* (1988), Glasgow: Association of Scottish Historical Studies (ASHS, 2), pp. 1–34.

Selkirk, A. (with I. Crawford), 'The Udal', *Current Archaeology*, XIII:3, no. 147 (1996), pp. 84–94.

Drimore Machair, South Uist

Maclaren, A., 'A Norse house on Drimore Machair, South Uist', *Glasgow Archaeological Journal*, 3 (1974), pp. 9–18.

South-West

Brooke, D., *Wild Men and Holy Places: The Ancient Realm of Galloway AD 82–1513* (1995), Edinburgh.

Hill, P., 'Whithorn: the missing years', in Oram and Stell (eds), *Galloway: Land and Lordship* (1991), pp. 27–44.

Hill, P., *Whithorn and St Ninian. The Excavation of a Monastic Town, 1984–91* (1997), Stroud: Sutton Publishing for The Whithorn Trust.

CHAPTER 11: THE NORSE ECONOMY

This chapter should be used together with the settlement chapters above for reference to all sites. In particular, the full reports by C. D. Morris et al. and by J. R. Hunter on Birsay, Orkney, and by C. D. Morris et al. on Freswick Links, Caithness, contain detailed considerations of the results of the environmental analyses from the sites examined. Each has a full bibliography, and so only a small selection of sources is listed below.

General

Bigelow, G. F., 'Issues and prospects in Shetland Norse Archaeology', in Morris and Rackham (eds), *Norse and Later Settlement* (1992), pp. 9–32.

Kaland, S. H. H., 'Some economic aspects of the Orkneys in the Viking period', *Norwegian Archaeological Review*, 15: 1–2 (1982), pp. 85–95.

Methodology

Jones, A. K. G., 'A comparison of two on-site methods of wet-sieving large archaeological soil samples', *Science and Archaeology*, 25 (1983), pp. 9–12.

Rackham, D. J., C. E. Batey, A. K. G. Jones and C. D. Morris, 'Freswick Links, Caithness. Report on Environmental Survey 1979', *Circaea*, 2:1(1984), pp. 29–55.

Ecofactual aspects

Barrett, J. H., 'Fish trade in Norse Orkney and Caithness: a zooarchaeological approach', *Antiquity*, 71 (1997), pp. 611–38.

Batey, C. E. and C. D. Morris, 'Earl's Bu, Orphir, Orkney: excavations of a Norse horizontal mill', in Morris and Rackham (eds), *Norse and Later Settlement* (1992), pp. 33–41.

Bigelow, G. F., 'Sandwick, Unst and late Norse Shetland economy', in Smith (ed.), *Shetland*

Archaeology (1985), pp. 95–127.

Bond, J. M. and J. R. Hunter, 'Flax-growing in Orkney from the Norse period to the 18th century', *Proc. Soc. Antiq. Scot.*, 117 (1987), pp.175–81.

Hunter, J. R., J. M. Bond and A. S. Smith, 'Some aspects of early Viking settlement in Orkney', in Batey et al. (eds), *The Viking Age in Caithness, Orkney and the North Atlantic* (1993), pp. 272–84.

Huntley, J. P., 'Some botanical aspects of a Norse economy in northern Scotland', *Botanical Journal of Scotland*, 46 (1994), pp. 538–41.

Serjeantsson, D., 'Archaeological and ethnographic evidence for seabird exploitation in Scotland', *Archaeozoologia*, II:1–2 (1988), pp. 209–24.

Artefactual

Batey, C. E., 'Viking and Late Norse Combs of Scotland', in I. Riddler (ed.), *Combs and Comb-Making*, London: CBA Research Monograph, forthcoming; see references therein.

Bigelow, G. F., 'Archaeological and ethnohistoric evidence of a Norse island food custom', in Batey et al. (eds), *The Viking Age in Caithness, Orkney and the North Atlantic* (1993), pp. 441–53.

Buttler, S., 'Steatite in Norse Shetland', *Hikuin*, 15 (1989), pp. 193–206.

Buttler, S., 'Steatite in the Norse North Atlantic', in Bigelow (ed.), *The Norse of the North Atlantic* (1991), pp. 228–32.

Gaimster, D. R. M. and C. E. Batey, 'The pottery', in Morris et al. (eds), *Freswick Links, Caithness: Excavation and Survey of a Norse Settlement* (1995), pp. 136–48.

Lane, A., *Dark-age and Viking-age Pottery in the Hebrides, with Special Reference to the Udal, North Uist* (1983), unpublished Ph.D. thesis, University College London.

Lane, A., 'Hebridean pottery: problems of definition, chronology, presence and absence', in Armit (ed.), *Beyond the Brochs* (1990), pp.108–30.

McGavin, N. A., 'Excavations in Kirkwall, 1978', *Proc. Soc. Antiq. Scot.*, 112 (1982), pp. 392–436: see pottery report by N. MacAskill, pp. 405–13.

Weber, B., 'The baking plates', in B. E. Crawford and B. Ballin-Smith, *The Biggings: Excavation of a Royal Norwegian Farm, Papa Stour, Shetland* (1998, forthcoming).

CHAPTER 12: SILVER AND GOLD

The Viking–age hoards and single finds of gold and silver are listed and described, with a comprehensive bibliography, in J. Graham-Campbell, *The Viking-Age Gold and Silver of Scotland (AD 850–1100)* (1995), Edinburgh: National Museums of Scotland; but see also:

Graham-Campbell, J. and J. Sheehan, 'A hoard of Hiberno-Viking arm-rings, probably from Scotland', *Proc. Soc. Antiq. Scot.*, 125 (1995), pp. 771–8.

Hårdh, B., *Silver in the Viking Age: a Regional-Economic Study* (1996), Stockholm: Almquist & Wiksell (= *Acta Archaeologica Lundensia*, Series in 8°, No. 25).

Kruse, S. E., 'Silver storage and circulation in Viking-age Scotland: the evidence of silver ingots', in Batey et al. (eds), *The Viking Age in Caithness, Orkney and the North Atlantic* (1993), pp. 187–203.

Kruse, S. E. and J. Tate, 'XRF analysis of Viking Age silver ingots', *Proc. Soc. Antiq. Scot.*, 122 (1992), pp. 295–328.

Metcalf, D. M. (ed.), *Coinage in Medieval Scotland* (1977), Oxford: BAR Brit. Ser., 45.

Skaare, K., *Coins and Coinage in Viking-Age Norway* (1976), Oslo: Universitetsforlaget.

Small, A., C. Thomas and D. M. Wilson, *St. Ninian's Isle and its Treasure*, 2 vols (1973), London: Oxford University Press for the University of Aberdeen.

Stevenson, R. B. K., *Sylloge of Coins of the British Isles, 6: National Museum of Antiquities of*

Scotland, Edinburgh. Part I, Anglo-Saxon Coins (with Associated Foreign Coins) (1966), London: The British Academy.

Warner, R., 'Scottish silver arm-rings: an analysis of weights', *Proc. Soc. Antiq. Scot.*, 107 (1975–6), pp. 136–43.

CHAPTER 13: EARLS AND BISHOPS

For the main documentary and runic sources for the Late Norse period, see above under both General Sources and Chapter 3, with additional references for the Earldom of Orkney and the Kingdom of Man and the Isles to be found under Chapters 4 and 5.

Sculpture

Close-Brooks, J. and R. B. K. Stevenson, *Dark Age Sculpture* (1982), Edinburgh: National Museum of Antiquities of Scotland/HMSO.

Craig, D. J., 'Pre-Norman sculpture in Galloway: some territorial implications', in Oram and Stell (eds), *Galloway: Land and Lordship* (1991), pp. 45–62.

RCAHMS, *Argyll: an Inventory of the Monuments*, Vol. 4: *Iona* (1982), nos 6,69 6,94 and 6,95.

Lang, J. T., 'Hogback monuments in Scotland', *Proc. Soc. Antiq. Scot.*, 105 (1972–4), pp. 206–35.

Ritchie, A. (ed.), *Govan and its Early Medieval Sculpture* (1994); see especially R. N. Bailey, 'Govan and Irish Sea sculpture', pp. 113–21, and J. Lang, 'The Govan hogbacks: a reappraisal', pp. 123–31.

Stevenson, R. B. K., 'Christian sculpture in Norse Shetland', *Fróðskaparrit (Annal. societ. scient. Færoensis)*, 28/29 (1981), pp. 283–92.

Chapels, churches and cathedrals

Batey, C. E. et al. (eds), *The Viking Age in Caithness, Orkney and the North Atlantic* (1993); see especially I. Fisher, 'Orphir Church in its South Scandiavian context', pp. 375–80.

Cant, R. G., 'Settlement, society and church organisation in the Northern Isles', in Fenton and Pálsson (eds), *The Northern and Western Isles in the Viking World* (1984), pp. 169–79.

Cant, R. G., 'Norse influence in the organisation of the Medieval Church in the Western Isles', *Northern Studies*, 21 (1984), pp. 1–14.

Cant, R. G., 'The medieval church in Shetland: organisation and buildings', in Waugh (ed.), *Shetland's Northern Links: Language and History* (1996), pp. 159–73.

Crawford, B. E. (ed.), *St Magnus Cathedral and Orkney's Twelfth-Century Renaissance* (1988), Aberdeen: Aberdeen University Press; see especially the three papers on St Magnus Cathedral by S. Cruden, pp. 78–87, R. Fawcett, pp. 88–110, and E. Cambridge, pp. 111–26; and also, E. Fernie, 'The Church of St Magnus, Egilsay', pp. 140–61.

Fawcett, R., 'The excavation of the church on the Brough by Sir Henry Dryden in 1866', in Morris, *The Birsay Bay Project. Volume 2* (1996), pp. 210–26.

Fleming, A. and A. Woolf, 'Cille Donnain: a late Norse church in South Uist', *Proc. Soc. Antiq. Scot.*, 122 (1992), pp. 329–50.

Lamb, R. G., 'Coastal settlements of the North', *Scottish Archaeological Forum*, 5 (1973), pp. 76–98.

Lamb, R. G., 'The Cathedral of Christchurch and the monastery of Birsay', *Proc. Soc. Antiq. Scot.*, 105 (1972–4), pp. 200–5.

Morris, C. D., *Church and Monastery in the far North: an Archaeological Evaluation* (1990), Jarrow: Jarrow Lecture, 1989.

Morris, C. D. with N. Emery, 'The chapel and enclosure on the Brough of Deerness, Orkney: survey and excavations, 1975–1977', *Proc. Soc. Antiq. Scot.*, 116 (1986), pp. 301–74 and Microfiche 2 (A2–G14), 3 (A2–G14) and 4 (A2–G6).

Orkney Heritage, 2 (1983), on 'Birsay: a centre of political and ecclesiastical power'; see R. G. Cant, 'Introduction', pp. 7–11, C. A. R. Radford, 'Birsay and the spread of Christianity to the North', pp. 13–35, R. G. Lamb, 'Cathedral and monastery', pp. 36–45, and B. E. Crawford, 'Birsay and the early earls and bishops of Orkney', pp. 97–118.

O'Sullivan, J., 'Excavation of an early church and a woman's cemetery at St Ronan's medieval parish church, Iona', *Proc. Soc. Antiq. Scot.*, 124 (1994), pp. 327–65.

Radford, C. A. R., 'Art and architecture: Celtic and Norse', in Wainwright (ed.), *The Northern Isles* (1962), pp. 163–87.

RCAHMS, *Argyll: an Inventory of the Monuments*, Vol. 4: *Iona* (1982).

RCAHMS, *Inventory of the Ancient Monuments of Orkney & Shetland*, Vol. II: *Inventory of Orkney* (1946).

Castles and strongholds

Batey, C. E., *Freswick Links. A Re-appraisal of the Late Norse Site in its Context* (1987), for discussion of Lambaborg and Bucholly, pp. 21–3.

Clouston, J. S., 'An early Orkney castle', *Proc. Soc. Antiq. Scot.*, 60 (1925–6), pp. 281–300.

Clouston, J. S., 'Three Norse strongholds in Orkney', *Proc. Orkney Antiq. Soc.*, 7 (1928–9), pp. 57–74.

Clouston, J. S., *Early Norse Castles* (1931), Kirkwall.

Marwick, H. M., 'Kolbein Hruga's Castle, Wyre', *Proc. Orkney Antiq. Soc.*, 6 (1927–8), pp. 9–11.

RCAHMS, *Inventory of the Ancient Monuments of Orkney and Shetland*, Vol. II: *Inventory of Orkney* (1946).

Talbot, E., 'Scandinavian fortification in the British Isles', *Scottish Archaeological Forum*, 6 (1974), pp. 37–45.

The Lewis chessmen

Stratford, N., *The Lewis Chessmen and the Enigma of the Hoard* (1997), London: British Museum Press.

Taylor, M., *The Lewis Chessmen* (1978), London: British Museum Press.

INDEX

Page numbers in *italics* refer to illustrations and maps; page numbers in **bold** indicate a main reference to the subject. Subjects may occur more than once on a page.